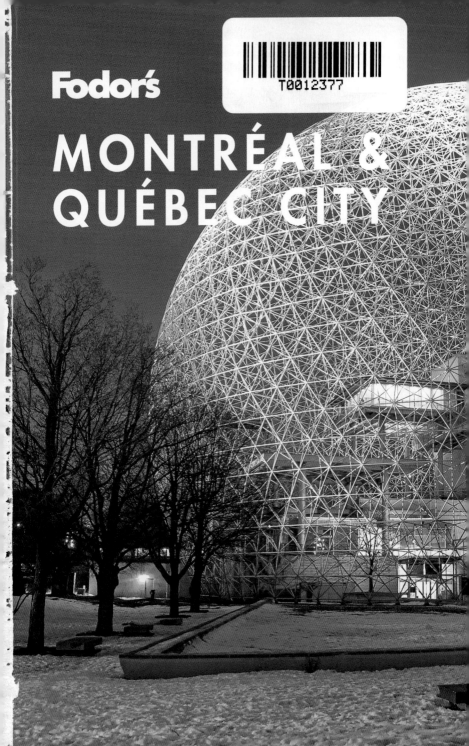

Fodor's

MONTRÉAL &
QUÉBEC CITY

Welcome to Montréal and Québec City

France's old-world charm lives on in Montréal and Québec City, two enchanting Canadian cities with rich pasts. Their French heritage is ever-present, from the language and wonderful food to pockets of cobblestoned streets. Cosmopolitan Montréal rocks with lively cultural and shopping scenes; smaller Québec City is jam-packed with history. Visits are lovely year-round: summer brings festivals galore; spring and fall are perfect for city strolls and countryside jaunts; and winter, despite the cold, heats up with Winter Carnival, hot chocolate, and snow sports.

TOP REASONS TO GO

★ **French food:** Cuisine ranges from haute to hearty—including poutine, fries with cheese curds and gravy.

★ **Shopping:** Fashion-forward local designers, top-notch cold-weather wear, and Inuit art is for sale.

★ **Festivals:** From Winter Carnival to Jazz Fest, Quebecers throw great parties all year.

★ **History:** Museums, monuments, and ancient fortifications bring the past to life.

★ **Hockey:** Tickets for Habs games are hard to get, but catch a game on TV at a local bar.

★ **Fun in the snow:** Winter brings ice-skating, tobogganing, skiing, and snowshoeing.

Contents

MAPS

EXPERIENCE MONTRÉAL AND QUÉBEC CITY

22 ULTIMATE EXPERIENCES

Montréal & Québec City offer terrific experiences that should be on every traveler's list. Here are Fodor's top picks for a memorable trip.

1 Exploring the Old Port

One of the city's most popular parks, Montréal's Old Port is the place to gallery-hop, cycle, stroll, take a jet boat ride on the Lachine Rapids, or just explore the waterfront at your leisure. *(Ch. 3)*

2 Strolling Rue du Petit-Champlain

Take the funicular down to explore lamp-lit Rue du Petit-Champlain, North America's oldest commercial street. *(Ch. 5)*

3 Carnaval de Québec

One of the world's biggest winter celebrations, this midwinter fête encompasses scores of activities that are bound to make you forget it's well below zero. *(Ch. 5)*

4 Saluting the Citadel

La Citadelle is home to Canada's Royal 22nd Regiment, who still turn out in bearskin caps and scarlet tunics for the daily changing of the guard. *(Ch. 5)*

5 Crossing Montmorency Falls

Ride an aerial cable car to admire the chute from above, or—if you're really daring—cross the suspension bridge above the breathtaking falls. *(Ch. 6)*

6 Visiting Île d'Orléans

This so-called Garden of Québec is a bucolic wonderland of centuries-old summer cottages, ancient churches, wineries, cider mills, culinary artisans, and produce stands. *(Ch. 6)*

7 Cheering for the Habs

Nothing is more Canadian than hockey, and the fans' energy and enthusiasm at a Canadiens (aka "Habs") game provide sport for even the most reluctant sports fan. *(Ch. 3)*

8 Bowing to the Basilique Notre Dame de Montréal

Everything about this magnificent Roman Catholic basilica is grand, from the 228-foot twin steeples to the 7,000-pipe organ to the 24-carat gold stars on the ceiling. *(Ch. 3)*

9 Posing on Dufferin Terrace

The long boardwalk in front of the Château Frontenac is one of Québec City's most romantic—and photogenic—spots. *(Ch. 5)*

10 Partying in the Village

Once a tiny nook carved out of Downtown, the Village can be great for shopping, strolling, people-watching, and partying. *(Ch. 3)*

11 Ferrying to Lévis

Treat yourself to lovely views by taking the quick (and inexpensive) 20-minute trip aboard the commuter ferry to the town of Lévis. *(Ch. 5)*

12 Enjoying Parc du Mont Royal

Snowshoe, ski, or hike a network of trails leading through the dense wooded areas of this hill overlooking the city. *(Ch. 3)*

13 Eating Poutine

Québec City has some of the best spots to sample poutine (fries drenched in gravy and cheese curds) including the Chez Ashton chain. *(Ch. 5)*

14 Musée des Beaux-Arts de Montréal

One of Canada's oldest museums has an exceptional collection of art including works by Rembrandt, Renoir, and Picasso. *(Ch. 3)*

15 Shopping at Marché du Vieux Port

At this foodie haven, you'll be tempted by maple syrup products, chocolates, iced cider, and other local specialties. *(Ch. 5)*

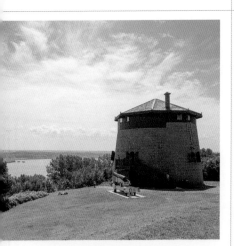

16 Reflecting at the Plains of Abraham

Filled with runners, picnickers, and cyclists, it's hard to imagine the fierce battles between empires that unfolded on this very spot in the 18th century. *(Ch. 5)*

17 Taking in Old Montréal

Many shops and restaurants are touristy in this part of town, so your time is best spent winding through the old lamp-lit streets and marveling at the architecture. *(Ch. 3)*

18 Eating Your Way up Jean Talon Market

As well as flowers, fruits, and vegetables, this European-style open market has food stands with crepes, samosas, Turkish pastries, and more. *(Ch. 3)*

19 Skiing Mont-Tremblant

With 662 acres of skiable terrain, this peak of the Laurentian Mountains, northwest of Montréal, is one of North America's top ski resorts. *(Ch. 4)*

20 Grooving at Jazz Fest

Montréal's annual International Jazz Festival is the largest in the world, attracting millions of fans for more than 400 (mostly free!) concerts every summer. *(Ch. 3)*

21 Marveling at the Oratoire Saint-Joseph

The oratory, gardens, and copper dome of the world's largest and most popular shrine to St. Joseph are a sight to behold. *(Ch. 3)*

22 Wandering Old Québec

A UNESCO World Heritage site, the enchanting Old City (Vieux-Québec) features cobblestoned streets lined with cafés, shops, galleries, and cathedrals. *(Ch. 5)*

WHAT'S WHERE

1 Montréal. This is a bustling, multiethnic city of neighborhoods, from the historic Old City to the hip Plateau.

2 The Laurentians. The Laurentians (les Laurentides) encompass thousands of miles of forests, mountains, and lakes, but for many people the draw is Mont-Tremblant and its world-class ski slopes.

3 The Eastern Townships. Called Les Cantons de l'Est in French, the Eastern Townships region has quaint architecture and rolling hills that recall New England. Atop imposing Mont-Mégantic, you're 3,150 feet closer to the heavens. Far from city lights, the sky here is ideal for stargazing. Indeed, the park received its certification as an International Dark Sky Reserve in 2007.

4 The Outaouais. Bordering the Ottawa River, the Outaouais is known for its many lakes, majestic views, hiking trails, and interesting wildlife, as well as the imposing Château Montebello, often called the world's largest log cabin.

5 Québec City. The capital of the province of Québec is the most French-influenced city in North America. Québec's Old City (Vieux-Québec) is split into two tiers, separated by steep rock against which are more than 25 *escaliers* (staircases) and a funicular. The surrounding cluster of small, low-rise neighborhoods all have their own charm and flavor.

6 Île d'Orléans. Famed for its wine and cider as well as its strawberry crop and other local produce, the Île d'Orléans is often called the "Garden of Québec." Made up of six small villages, this charming island has several bed-and-breakfasts and fabulous farm stands.

7 Côte-de-Beaupré. The coast hugged by the St. Lawrence River embraces the thundering Montmorency Falls and the impressive Ste-Anne-de-Beaupré shrine. It leads to Mont-Ste-Anne, famous for its skiing, golfing, and mountain biking.

8 Charlevoix. The big bang of an ancient meteor created picturesque valleys, cliffs, and mountains that brush the St. Lawrence River. This Québec region has inspired painters, poets, and musicians for generations.

What to Eat and Drink

POUTINE

Canada's national dish, poutine (from Québécois slang meaning "mess"), is a mushy mess of fries covered in melty cheese curds and dark gravy. The take-out mishmash was traditionally a bumpkin's meal until it was named Canada's national dish in 2010.

JULIETTE & CHOCOLAT

Chocolate is celebrated in all its chocolatey forms at this beloved dessert shop in Montréal, where highlights include crepes soufflés, candy, milkshakes, vegan brownies, and rich hot chocolate, all made from cocoa beans sourced in Peru, Madagascar, and Uganda.

TOURTIÈRE

This rib-sticking meat pie is a tabletop staple during the cold Québec winters. Named after the old-fashioned cooking vessel that was once used to bake it, tourtière is a dish recognized across the province and is often featured on Christmas Eve menus.

MONTRÉAL BAGELS

It's the ultimate rivalry among Montrealers: who makes the better bagel, St-Viateur or Fairmont? Both shops famously sell Montréal bagels, made by hand with sourdough and malt, boiled in honey-sweetened water, wood-fired, and sprinkled with sesame seeds. The result is a firmer, denser bagel than what European Jewish immigrants also brought over to the Big Apple.

SMOKED-MEAT SANDWICH

Smoked-meat sandwiches, like bagels, are another much-loved and much-argued-over classic Montréal eat. Sliced by hand and served over deli countertops, these juicy beef brisket sandwiches feature cured, spiced meat that is hot-smoked, stacked onto rye bread, and completed with a squirt of yellow mustard. Montréal smoked meat is pretty similar to New York pastrami, except for extra seasoning and less sweetness.

BOULANGERIE BREAD

The boulangerie (bakery) is an integral part of Québec's everyday meals and communities. In Québec City, there's no better morning start than Le Paingrüel, a long-standing artisanal bakery with daily specials including bread with dark chocolate and dried pear and cranberry-chocolate buns. In Montréal, the Plateau Mont-Royal is known for its croissant shops, and the La Petite-Patrie neighborhood has several, like the popular Le Pain dans les Voiles.

Treats from the boulangerie

ÎLE D'ORLÉANS
An island just a 15-minute drive from Downtown Québec City, Île d'Orléans is home to the Chocolaterie de l'Île d'Orléans, known for its deliriously delicious chocolate-dipped soft ice cream cones that have a cult following throughout the province.

ICE CIDER
A Québec specialty, ice cider is a sweet, delicate liqueur that is produced through the alcoholic fermentation of juice from slowly pressed frozen apples. It's a must-try in Québec, if only because it is so complex and complicated to produce.

ARTISANAL CHEESES
Québec is home to more than half of Canada's artisanal cheese makers. As such, there's a wealth of craft *fromage* to feast on here. Stock up at farmers' markets. The province boasts at least 700 varieties of cheese made of cow, goat, and sheep milk, although there are also a couple of funky varieties made from water buffalo milk. Rarer varieties can be found at farmers' markets, such as the Atwater and Jean-Talon Markets in Montréal and Marché du Vieux-Port in Québec City.

MAPLE SYRUP
Québec produces more than three-quarters of the world's maple syrup, and you'll find it right next to the salt and pepper on many table setups for breakfast, lunch, and dinner. Its origins date to the 1800s when the French learned how to tap trees from Indigenous peoples.

CRAFT BREWS
Québec takes microbrewing very seriously, specializing in strong beers that'll knock you over faster than you can say "Santé!" Montréal's first craft brewpub, Le Cheval Blanc, opened in the mid-'80s, well before the global craft beer revolution, and these days there are several more to choose.

Cool Things to Do in Winter in Montréal and Québec City

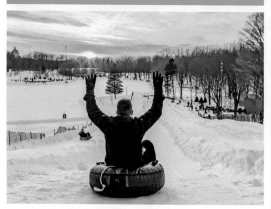

CROSS-COUNTRY SKIING, SNOWSHOEING, AND SLEDDING ON MONT-ROYAL

Take a guided nighttime snowshoe climb through the snow-covered forest of Mount Royal. By day, make for the summit to Beaver Lake, where a skating rink, tubing lanes, and ski trails facilitate the snow sport of your choice.

DANCING UP A STORM AT IGLOOFEST

Why should below-freezing temperatures stop anyone from having an outdoor dance party? Just as the glitter from New Year's parties and resolutions begins to dull, Igloofest takes over the Old Port for nine days and heats things up with electronic sets spun by the hottest local and international DJs. Thousands bundle up and head to Igloo Village to shake off their hats and scarves on the dance floor under the snow and stars.

COZYING UP AT CRAFT BEER BARS

Montrealers have long been spoiled for choice when it comes to finding warm watering holes with quality brews on tap. Like a hot chocolate but better, Dieu du Ciel's dark Aphrodisiaque stout is brewed with cocoa and vanilla beans, creating bourbon and toasty malt notes that will chase the winter blues away. Vices & Versa, L'Amère à Boire, Broue Pub Brouhaha, and MaBrasserie lead a long list of local craft breweries to hunker down in when the forecast reads hyperborean degrees.

PACKING ON THE POUNDS WITH POUTINE

When it comes to winter comfort foods, poutine reigns supreme in La Belle Province. Served with crispy fries, homemade gravy, and requisite squeaky cheese, the carb-heavy medley never fails to grease the arteries and warm the belly. Numerous establishments are dedicated to the dish—including La Banquise, Chez Claudette, Poutineville, and Paul Patates—but it can also be found on the menu at nearly every *casse-croûte* (greasy spoon). For a more gourmet—and gourmand—take, there's Au Pied de Cochon's foie gras poutine and Garde Manger's lobster-heaped frites. Also, look out for La Poutine Week, an annual fry fest that takes place every February in restaurants across the city.

LIGHTING UP WITH MONTRÉAL EN LUMIÈRE AND LUMINOTHÉRAPIE

A little light therapy goes a long way to combat the season's shorter days and longer nights. Every February, the Quartier des Spectacles is illuminated with Montréal en Lumière's light projects and installations, such as a bright, revolving Ferris wheel and a flood-lit toboggan run, and the bundled-up masses, crowding in for the winter fair. Beginning earlier and lasting longer, Luminothérapie illuminates the square with light art exhibitions from late November to early March.

Igloofest

SKATING IN WINTER WONDERLANDS

Whether for an improvised game of shinny (pickup hockey) or attempts at the quad, there's ample ice space in the city for every skill level. Outdoor ice rinks can be found in the parks of every neighborhood, like the Plateau's Parc La Fontaine pond or the Old Port's Natrel Rink. If you don't have your own blades to cut the ice with, many places have them for rent. For those who prefer to skate indoors, Atrium Le 1000 brings the best of both worlds together with its large inside rink and centerpiece skylight.

GOING FOR A DIP IN THERMAL SPAS

A warm bath is one of the best antidotes for the chill that settles into your bones midwinter, and a little massage therapy doesn't hurt either. Visit Bota Bota, a riverside boat spa located in the Old Port, for a steamy thermotherapy session to relieve aches and pains and release toxins in the body.

PARTYING WITH THE FAMILY AT FÊTE DES NEIGES

Pack the kids into snowsuits and hop across the river to Parc Jean-Drapeau for Fête des Neiges' outdoor snow festival. Among the many attractions are a 50-foot-high zip line, ice sculptures, a scenic skating path, giant foosball, and a 10-lane tube slide that includes two super-slides and one fitted for a four-seat tube. Plus, a packed program of games and performances for children is sure to keep *les enfants terribles* off thin ice and out of snowball fights during the cold weather season.

SWEETENING UP AT SUGAR SHACKS— CABANES À SUCRE

Before the season melts into spring, head to the sugar bush to tap Canadian maples for their syrupy gold. To enjoy the late winter harvest, Montrealers congregate in a *cabane à sucre* (sugar shack), a log cabin with a long communal table made for plate passing and syrup swapping. More than just a breakfast garnish, maple is drizzled into courses of the meal, which typically begins with yellow pea soup and is followed with savory traditional dishes such as tourtière meat pies, baked beans, and plenty of pork. The featured ingredient is the star of dessert, too, used generously in super-sweet treats like maple pies, taffy, and donuts.

Best Spa Experiences in Montréal and Québec City

SPA WILLIAM GRAY

This luxury spa (in an old graystone colonial home in Old Montréal) is a local favorite. Highlights include warm quartz massages, a Spa Wave sound therapy system, an herbal sauna, and a Himalayan salt room with walls of Himalayan salt bricks.

BOTA BOTA, SPA SUR L'EAU

A unique concept in this northern city, this spa is set on a repurposed ferryboat in Old Montréal. The floating spa features a garden, pool, terraces, and hammocks. Other facilities include a sauna, steam room, a water circuit (cold bath, exterior cold shower, lukewarm bath, jet bath). Silence and/or whispering is required everywhere on the boat.

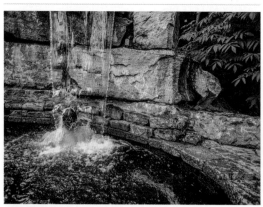

SIBÉRIA SPA

Located in a peaceful woodsy setting a 20-minute drive from Vieux-Québec, Sibéria Spa offers the opportunity to escape the daily urban grind. Guests can enjoy the hot and cold baths (or for the more daring, there's the invigorating river), choose between 12 massages, and reenergize with a snack or light meal at the spa's adorable café housed in an A-frame chapel.

SPA BOLTON

This spa in the Eastern Townships, set amid natural waterfalls from the Missisquoi River, allows for polar plunging in winter. Guests lie on beds in yurts for massages, while in summer only tent flaps stand between you and the sound of the river. A highlight is the Finnish wood-burning smoke sauna, or Savusauna, the only one of its kind in Canada.

BALNÉA SPA ET RÉSERVE THERMALE

This contemporary spa in the Bromont ski resort is surrounded by trees and overlooks a lake. In addition to treatments and wraps, guests can float outdoors on air beds among the lily pads, soak up the sun on tiers of sun decks, bliss out in one of the hot or cold pools, or practice yoga by the lake.

STRØM SPA—NUNS' ISLAND

This peaceful respite located minutes from Downtown Montréal boasts outdoor whirlpools, hot and cold baths, Finnish saunas, a eucalyptus-scented steam bath, thermal and Nordic waterfalls.

STRØM SPA—VIEUX-QUÉBEC

Overlooking the St. Lawrence River, this spa in Old Québec offers a thermal experience that takes you through outdoor whirlpools, thermal and Nordic baths, Finnish saunas, a eucalyptus steam bath, and indoor and outdoor relaxation areas with fireplaces.

The Nordik Spa-Nature

SCANDINAVE SPA

Located in Old Montréal, Scandinave Spa offers hot and cold baths, a waterfall, and a range of therapeutic massages, including Thai, Swedish, and a fusion of the Hawaiian lomilomi and the reharmonizing Japanese shiatsu.

THE NORDIK SPA-NATURE

The Nordik Spa-Nature in the Outaouais region is the largest spa in North America and its vast catalog of facilities impress. It's got 10 outdoor baths, nine saunas, an infinity pool, a saltwater flotation pool, a yoga and meditation room. It also boasts four restaurants, including a biergarten with an outdoor terrace and panoramic view.

SPA NORDIQUE LE GERMAIN

Part of Le Germain Hotel in Charlevoix's Baie St-Paul, Spa Nordique Le Germain provides the usual menu of thermal, hydrotherapy, and beauty treatments, but you'll also find a Nordic shower and a "Snow Fountain" producing finely crushed ice that you rub all over your body.

Best Side Trips from Montréal and Québec City

FARM-HOPPING ON ÎLE D'ORLÉANS

Thousands of tourists and Québec City residents visit this cornucopia of an island each year to go farm-hopping. Along the way they savor the local bounty—maple syrup, fruit jams, apple cider, wine, black currant liqueur, chocolate, bread, pastries, and more.

WENDAKE, HURON-WENDAT NATION VILLAGE

Just half an hour outside Québec City, the village of Wendake, along with its hotel, museum, and traditional longhouse, transport you to the world of the Huron-Wendat Nation before colonization.

EASTERN TOWNSHIPS VILLAGES

The area is known for its green mountains and forests, spas, wineries, ski hills, and charming Loyalist-era towns and villages strung like pearls along the Québec-Vermont border.

ROUTES DES VINS

The official Route des Vins organization includes 22 wineries, four scenic road trip itineraries, and four cycling routes.

CHUTE MONTMORENCY

Plunging 272 feet from the top of a cliff, the spectacular Montmorency Falls stand a full 98 feet higher than Niagara Falls. Daredevils and more active types may prefer to tackle rather than simply admire the falls, and can do so by zip line, *via ferrata*, or the stairway climbing up the side of the promontory.

KAMOURASKA AND THE BAS ST-LAURENT

With its expansive meadows and farmlands sweeping down to the water, brightly painted Victorian homes, and a lively main street, Kamouraska is without a doubt the prettiest village in this seaside region.

CHARLEVOIX AND THE NORTH SHORE

The Charlevoix is a year-round destination blessed with painterly landscapes, a lively maritime atmosphere in summer, and a ski resort in winter. It's also known as a whale-watching destination and is beloved for its epicurean trail, La Route des Saveurs.

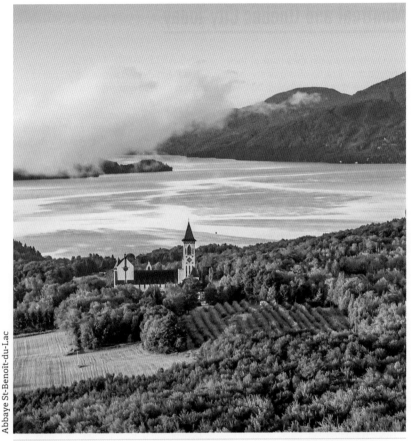

Abbaye St-Benoît-du-Lac

ABBAYE ST-BENOÎT-DU-LAC

Built by the Benedictines in 1912 on a wooded peninsula overlooking Lac Memphrémagog, the abbey is inhabited by more than 50 monks. Plan a retreat, pick your own apples in season, take a tour of the abbey, shop the delicious homemade cheeses and jellies, and hike the trails.

THE OUTAOUAIS

Less than two hours northwest of Montréal lies the Outaouais region, a 33,000-square-mile natural playground numbering 20,000 lakes, 249 miles of hiking trails, and countless rivers. It's beautiful year-round but easier to explore in summer. Be sure to visit Gatineau Park and the iconic Château Montebello log house hotel.

ASTROLAB IN PARC DU MONT-MÉGANTIC

Located in a wild and mountainous area, the Parc du Mont-Mégantic features 31 miles of hiking, snowshoeing, and cross-country skiing trails and the most powerful observatory in Canada. In 2007, the remote park became the world's first-ever International Dark Sky Reserve.

Montréal and Québec City Today

Ask Quebecers what they think of their city, and they'll rattle off a grocery list of things to improve: potholes, bureaucratic corruption, chronic road work, snow removal, icy sidewalks, parking tickets—the list goes on. Then ask them if they would move anywhere else in the world, and the answer is almost always a resounding no. Any indication that the snow and cold weather are gone, and Quebecers will head to an outdoor terrace (or *terrasse,* pronounced terr-*ass* by anglophone Quebecers) or patio.

THERE'S MUSIC IN THE AIR

As far back as native son Leonard Cohen singing about "Suzanne" in the 1960s, Montréal has been known for its indie music scene. More recently, with Montréal band Arcade Fire's Grammy win in 2010, international record labels began paying more attention to the city. Artists like Milk and Bone, Half Moon Run, Grimes, Kaytranada, Shay Lia, NOBRO, and Béatrice Martin, better known as Coeur de Pirate, are making Montréal concert halls the place to be.

QUÉBEC POLITICS

Politics in Québec can be as entertaining as hockey. In 2018, businessman François Legault's Coalition Avenir Québec ended nearly 50 years of two-party rule in the province. With the CAQ firmly entrenched in its second term, the controversial language bill, Bill 96, passed into law in May 2022. Meant to slow the perceived decline of the French language across Québec, Bill 96 also states that Québec is a nation, not just a province, and that the official and common language of this nation is French, thus unilaterally modifying the Canadian Constitution.

THE ARTS MAKE A SPLASH

The Place des Arts' new C$34 million social-minded esplanade is now complete. The expansive outdoor space at the heart of the Quartier des Spectacles links all of Place des Arts' venues. The space hosts Montréal's biggest festivals, cultural activities, and popular events year-round: the Festival International de Jazz de Montréal, Les Francofolies, Montréal Complètement Cirque (circus festival), Just for Laughs, Montréal en Lumière, the Grand Marché de Noël, and more. Families will appreciate the splash pad in summer and the refrigerated outdoor ice rink in winter.

In and around Old Montréal, be sure to look out for the Cité Mémoire project, an outdoor video-projection installation that recounts the stories of celebrated and lesser-known Montrealers who have helped shape the city's history and identity. Films are projected onto building façades, windows, towers, and even trees around Old Montréal.

Québec City, for its part, has been emerging as a premier stop for summer concerts and festivals. On the Plains of Abraham, outdoor performances accommodate more than 250,000 spectators, and people come from all over to watch under the stars. Past performers including Madonna, Céline Dion, Paul McCartney, Rush, and Lady Gaga have helped put Québec City on the entertainment map.

SPORTS FANS IN HIGH PLACES

Montréal's soccer team, CF Montréal (Club de Foot Montréal, formerly known as the Impact) began competing in Major League Soccer in 2012, which helped solidify its fan base. The 2023 additions of top American and international players Aaron Herrera, George Campbell, and Ilias Iliadis means soccer is continuing to grow as a spectator sport and local attraction.

Montréal lost its beloved baseball in 2004. Judging by the number of people who still wear Expos baseball caps, one would think the team had never left. Every few years, there is renewed talk of the return of a major league baseball team to Montréal. The last time was 2021. That year, a wealthy local businessman had proposed to buy a team but Mayor Valérie Plante, along with many other Montrealers, agreed that taxpayers should not be paying for a new stadium, nor should one be built on the site that had been proposed for social housing. One idea that was floated around was that the Tampa Bay Rays could split their time between Tampa Bay and Montréal. That possibility remains to be seen.

Former Québec City mayor Régis Labeaume, still sore that his city lost its hockey team in 1995, decided that one of his priorities was to get an NHL team back in town. He built a C$400 million stadium, which opened in September 2015 and has been prospected as a potential venue for a new NHL team in the city. Up to now there is still no hockey team in Québec's capital. But one can still hope.

PEDAL POWER

Montréal has come a long way since its 2009 introduction of BIXI, a bike-sharing scheme similar to those in New York City, London, Chicago, and many other cities. Using the system, you pay to take a bicycle from a rental station and then leave it at a station near your destination. Every year more bike paths are added to city streets (there are at least 500 km [300 miles] of them now), much to the chagrin of some drivers. In 2019, the scheme enjoyed a record-breaking year, with rides per day increasing from around 31,000 per day in 2018 to more than 36,000 per day in 2019. Since late that year BIXI has been adding more electric bikes to its fleet, and they have proven at least 75% more popular than the regular bicycles. So popular in fact that despite the 700-plus new e-bikes added in summer 2021, 500 in 2022, and 250 in 2023, they are rarely available.

Montréal and Québec City with Kids

There's no shortage of fantastic activities in Montréal and Québec City for kids. Here's a sampling of what the little ones might enjoy during a visit.

Montréal with Kids

Montréal's popular rent-a-bicycle system, **BIXI**, is a great way for families to see the city. The expanding network of car-free cycling paths now meanders around Parc du Mont-Royal and through Old Montréal, across Parc Jean-Drapeau on Île Notre-Dame, and along the Lachine Canal.

Kids who've had their fill of churches and museums can expend some pent-up energy at the adjacent **Old Port,** which has boats to pedal, a clock tower to climb, and a maze. There's also a water-front beach, but alas, no swimming is allowed.

For culturally adventurous youngsters, there are outdoor dance and theater presentations at **Parc Lafontaine.** Kids can also explore the mysteries of bonsai trees and Chinese gardens at the **Jardin Botanique**.

What soccer is to Brazilians and baseball is to Americans, hockey is to Canadians. It's not a game, it's a religion! If you can score tickets (best to order in advance), catch a **Montréal Canadiens** game at Centre Bell. A night with the "Habs" and their lively fans is a riveting family experience. Alternatively, take a one-hour tour (ages five and up) of **Centre Bell**, which includes access to the Canadiens dressing room.

On hot summer days, spend some time at the Quartier des Spectacles, where the large fountains spread along the street will provide some fun and surely cool off your kids. You may even see some adults jumping in, too.

Québec City with Kids

Ice-cream stands, street performers, and (in winter) a steep, thrilling toboggan run make **Terrasse Dufferin** as entertaining for children as for adults, as do the **Plains of Abraham's** open spaces.

Place Royale in the Lower Town brings the 17th and 18th centuries to life for even the youngest children.

La Citadelle's Changing of the Guard ceremony, complete with the Royal 22nd Regiment's mascot, Batisse the Goat, has lots of kid appeal. The hands-on exhibits at the **Musée de la Civilisation** and the 19th-century jail cells preserved in the **Musée de Québec** are both must-see attractions.

Outside Montréal and Québec City with Kids

In the Laurentians, the gentle rides of the **Au Pays des Merveilles** (Wonderland) and the **Village du Père Noël** (Santa's Village) are perfect for younger children. There are plenty of thrills at the **Water Parks** at Mont-St-Sauveur in the Laurentians and Bromont in the Eastern Townships.

Montmorency Falls, on the Côte-de-Beaupré, aren't as grand as Niagara, but they're higher, and crossing the suspension bridge above the spectacular chutes of water is a thrill. Farther along the St. Lawrence coast in **Tadoussac,** you can take a boat ride for an encounter with whales (be careful not to get salt water in your camera or phone).

Free and Cheap

There might be no such thing as a free lunch in Montréal or Québec City, but plenty of other things are free, or nearly so.

ART

Admission to the permanent collections of Montréal's Musée des Beaux-Arts (⊕ www.mbam.qc.ca/en) and Québec City's Musée National des Beaux-Arts (⊕ www.mnbaq.org) is always free. The Musée d'Art Contemporain (⊕ macm.org/en), temporarily housed at Place Ville Marie, is half-price on Wednesday night. Every summer the city of Montréal mounts an outdoor exhibit of art or photographs on the sidewalks of avenue McGill College between rues Ste-Catherine and Sherbrooke.

CONCERTS

Montréal's Christ Church Cathedral (⊠ 635 rue Ste-Catherine Ouest ☎ 514/843–6577), a magnificent neo-Gothic treasure, offers free concerts most Saturday afternoons at 2.

Les Petits Chanteurs du Mont-Royal, one of the finest boys' choirs in North America, sings the 11 am mass at the Oratoire St-Joseph (⊠ 3800 chemin Queen-Mary ☎ 514/733–8211) every Sunday from March to December 24. They also perform several free concerts throughout the year.

Montréal's annual Festival International de Jazz (late June to early July) and Québec City's Festival d'Été in July have dozens of free, open-air concerts. These huge happenings bring thousands, and tens of thousands, of revelers to the streets.

FIREWORKS

From mid-June through July, the sky comes alive with light and color on most Wednesday and Saturday evenings when fireworks teams from around the world compete in the spectacular L'International des Feux Loto-Québec. You can pay for a seat at La Ronde amusement park, or join thousands of Montrealers in the Old Port, on the Jacques Cartier Bridge, and in Parc Champlain on the South Shore and watch for free.

POLITICS

Political junkies can join free guided tours of North America's only French-speaking legislature, the Assemblée Nationale du Québec (☎ 418/643–7239). The parliamentary debates take place Tuesday to Thursday from August to November and February to May.

SCIENCE

McGill University's Redpath Museum (⊠ 859 rue Sherbrooke Ouest ☎ 514/398–4086) houses an eclectic collection of dinosaur skeletons, seashells, fossils, minerals, Egyptian mummies, and Stone Age tools in a beautiful 19th-century building. Watch for free lectures.

SIGHTSEEING

For one of the best views of Québec City, take the C$3.95 ferry (⊠ 10 rue des Traversiers ☎ 418/643–8420) for a mini cruise across the St. Lawrence River to Lévis and back. Or for C$5 ride the Funiculaire du Vieux-Québec (⊠ 16 rue du Petit-Champlain ☎ 418/692–1132), the sharply vertical railway that creaks along the cliff from Lower Town to Upper Town.

What to Read and Watch

THE APPRENTICESHIP OF DUDDY KRAVITZ BY MORDECAI RICHLER

Duddy Kravitz is a scrappy kid, determined to fight his way out of the Jewish tenements of 1950s Montréal, and this novel is full of colorful characters and classic Montréal neighborhood institutions. The book covers much of the city and expanses of Québec countryside, from the "cold-water flats" of rue St-Urbain to the lakes of Québec's Laurentians region. A 1974 movie version stars Richard Dreyfuss. Another of Mordecai Richler's novels, *Barney's Version,* is set in Montréal as well, and was adapted into a movie with Paul Giamatti and Rosamund Pike.

SWEET AFFLICTION BY ANNA LEVENTHAL

A series of interweaving, loosely connected stories make up this fresh, funny work of fiction, starring a youthful cast of characters quintessential to Montréal: members of the LGBTQ+ community, writers, artists, bohemians, and anarchists. Here you'll get slices of Montréal contemporary life, such as in "Moving Day": a story dedicated to Montréal's unique tradition and once-official law in the province, decreeing that any lease in Montréal must end on July 1, Canada Day—thus forcing all of the city's residents to share the same moving day.

MĀN BY KIM THÚY

Like Thúy's first novel *Ru, Mān* is about the Vietnamese immigrant experience in Montréal, this time with an intimate personal story centered largely around cooking and food. Aside from writing fiction, author Kim Thúy has been a lawyer, cookbook author, and restaurant owner, and her restaurant Ru de Nam was a longtime favorite Vietnamese eatery in Montréal. Ru de Nam is no longer open, but this novel is sure to get you excited about the other great choices in Montréal's Vietnamese dining scene—only some of the great international eating experiences the city has to offer.

THE ARMAND GAMACHE SERIES BY LOUISE PENNY

Chief Inspector Armand Gamache is the hero of Louise Penny's popular mystery crime series about a provincial police chief solving crimes in the fictional Québec village of Three Pines. The author herself is a longtime resident of Québec's Eastern Townships, just outside Montréal, and bases the series' setting on her own rustic life. Penny's books are a bountiful reading choice for the traveler to Québec, as there are 18 total installments in the series, including the most recent, *A World of Curiosities. Three Pines*, the television series based on Penny's books, was released by Amazon Prime in December 2022.

A PEOPLE'S HISTORY OF QUÉBEC BY JACQUES LACOURSIÈRE AND ROBIN PHILPOT

A concise, well-written account of Québec's colonial history, this book is great preparation before exploring the region. The book touches on the main lives and historical events in this province's rich and complicated past, spanning over 450 years of history: from early French explorers arriving to the Gaspé Peninsula in the 16th century (and their dealings with the Iroquois, Cree, and other First Nations), to the forming of a constitution, ongoing fights for sovereignty, and the creation of a modern society.

COCKROACH BY RAWI HAGE

Canadian author Rawi Hage's second novel is about a cynical, downtrodden man living in Montréal, who often feels—both (meta)physically and metaphorically—as if he is a cockroach. Hage, born in Beirut, introduces the reader to a community of Middle Eastern and European immigrants making life in their adopted city. The story is told through the narrator's dark wit and dry humor, as he struggles with hunger and poverty, desire and pain—and the long, unforgiving Montréal winter.

JESUS OF MONTRÉAL

Jesus of Montréal—along with *The Fall of the American Empire, The Decline of the American Empire, Barbarian Invasions*, and *Testament*—is just one of several great films from acclaimed Québécois director Denys Arcand, who makes French-language movies that deal in smart social commentary and Montréal-area settings. In this film, a group of actors are hired by the Catholic Church to create a modernized "Passion of the Christ" play—and end up radicalizing themselves and the audience more than was intended.

LÉOLO

Touching and surreal, this Québécois film has plenty of fantasy and enjoyable strangeness (backed up by a Tom Waits soundtrack), telling the story of a boy named Léolo as he comes of age in a very chaotic family. Based in Montréal's Mile End neighborhood, where Léolo's family lives, this critically acclaimed film is full of symbolism and spirituality, with some more realistic commentary on mental illness and familial relations.

THE SCORE

The plot formula in *The Score* will seem familiar: a lone wolf, a convincing rogue sidekick, the big, last job before getting out "for good"—but typical elements are pulled off well here, with plenty of action and entertainment. The target of this classic heist movie (starring Robert De Niro as a Montréal jazz club owner and grand thief) is a $4 million French sceptre stored in the basement of the Montréal Customs House, the most guarded building in Québec, according to the script. Marlon Brando makes a great cameo as an old-time Montréal gangster, and Angela Bassett and Edward Norton complete the cast, in a now-old (2001) picture with plenty of shots of Montréal's Downtown.

HEATHER O'NEILL

Montrealer Heather O'Neill first came to the attention of Canadian literary circles in 2006 with her Montréal-set novel, *Lullabies for Little Criminals*, the story of Baby, a 13-year-old who is drawn into the seedy Montréal underworld of a local pimp. Other novels, also set in Montréal, soon followed: *The Girl Who Was Saturday Night*, about the gorgeous twin children of a famous Québécois folk singer, and *The Lonely Hearts Hotel*, which follows two orphan artists who start a circus. O'Neill's latest novel, *When We Lost Our Heads*, tells the story of two best friends in 19th-century Montréal whose intense friendship changes the course of history.

C.R.A.Z.Y.

Often considered one of the most popular Canadian films of all time, this colorful drama was directed by the late Jean-Marc Vallée (director of *Dallas Buyers Club, Big Little Lies, Sharp Objects*, and *Wild*). It's about a young homosexual man growing up in a conservative Catholic francophone family in the 1960s and '70s. This poignant coming-of-age tale is uniquely Québécois—but the late '60s fashion and soundtrack strike a more universal note.

How to Speak Québécois

EN FRANÇAIS, S'IL VOUS PLAÎT

Anytime you visit a foreign country, being familiar with the local language is sure to win you friends. Learn a few phrases, regardless of whether you pronounce them correctly, and the locals will appreciate it. Around 75% of Quebecers claim French as their mother tongue, and while many Quebecers are bilingual or know at least a little English, plenty more don't, especially east of Downtown Montréal and the less touristy areas of the province. Rest assured that you will come across more than a few unilingual francophones.

As in France, accents and colloquialisms vary widely from region to region. Still, there are several commonly used, uniquely Québécois words and expressions.

EVERYDAY TERMS

For starters, Montréal's subway system is known as *le métro*. If you go around asking francophone Quebecers where the closest subway station is, you'll likely be greeted with a blank stare followed by a "*Désolée, mais je ne parle pas l'anglais*" ("I'm sorry, but I don't speak English"). Similarly, don't go looking for a "convenience store" when you need some last-minute item. Here, even anglophones call them *dépanneurs*, or "deps" for short.

While here you'll probably spend a lot of time in the *centre-ville* (Downtown) checking out splendid sights like the Palais de Justice (not a palace at all, but a courthouse). Except in order to do so you're likely going to need some *argent* (money), or better, *un peu de cash*, which is franglais (a curious yet distinct local hybrid of French and English) for "a bit of money." And where will you be getting that money? Nowhere if you start asking people for the closest ATM. In Québec a bank machine is called a *guichet* (the *gui* pronounced like in guitar, the *chet* like "shea").

DINING OUT

Of course, many things in Québec, like the menus in most restaurants in Montréal, will be in both French and English, but you'll win points with the waitstaff if you order a steak frites *avec un verre de vin rouge* when you want steak with French fries and a glass of red wine. Later, when you ask for *la facture* or *l'addition* (your bill), and your server inquires if you've enjoyed your meal, tell them it was *écoeurant* (the literal translation is "disgusting," or "nauseating," but it's akin to saying something is "sick" for great) and you'll likely see a big amused grin come over their face. It's the rare tourist who's in the know when it comes to Québécois slang and/or colloquialisms, so locals will certainly be impressed if they hear you coming out with the occasional *mon char* (my car) when talking about your wheels, or *ma blonde* or *ma copine* (girlfriend) when introducing somebody to your female significant other. Conversely, if you're talking about a boyfriend, *mon chum* or *mon copain* is how the locals would say it.

HOLY SWEAR WORDS

Almost all Québécois profanities—aka *sacres*—come courtesy of the Catholic Church, so while the literal translation of words like *tabarnac* (tabernacle) or *câlice* (chalice) might seem pretty tame or nonsensical in English, here they're the equivalent of the dreaded F-word.

Chapter 2

TRAVEL SMART

Updated by
Marie-Ève Vallières

POPULATION
Montréal: 1,700,000

Québec City: 500,000

LANGUAGE
French

$ CURRENCY
Canadian dollar

AREA CODE
Québec has nine area codes:
354, 367, 418, 438, 450, 514,
579, 581, 819, 873.

⚠ EMERGENCIES
911

🚗 DRIVING
On the right

⚡ ELECTRICITY
110-120V/60Hz; electrical
plugs have two flat prongs
and a round prong in a V

⊙ TIME
Same as New York

⊕ WEB RESOURCES
www.mtl.org/en
www.quebec-cite.com/en
www.mtlblog.com

Know Before You Go

You know about poutine and Céline Dion—what else is there? Well, the Canadian province fascinates with a rich culture and history that's been earnestly preserved. Here's what you should know to make the most of your visit.

HISTORY = CONTEXT

The short version: After the English victory in 1759, the francophone people became a minority in the New World. During the 1960s Quiet Revolution, they resolved to uphold their unique culture or risk it being forgotten—defining Québécois identity as separate from that of either English-speaking Canada or France. Quebecers are fiercely proud and protective of their traditions as a result. Remembering this helps to put a lack of English representation into perspective.

BRUSH UP ON YOUR FRENCH

For historical reasons, Québec is very conscious of retaining its language. According to law, French must be the predominant language on retail and road signs, and shop and restaurant employees must greet customers first in French (usually with the ubiquitous "Bonjour/Hi!"). Particularly in rural areas, you may encounter people who speak little to no English. In Montréal, however, bilingualism is more common and most people will quickly

switch to English for you. Nonetheless, attempting a few French phrases is appreciated by locals, and might make traveling easier.

Much like American English is different from standard British English, the French spoken in Québec is slightly different from the French you'll hear on the streets of Paris. Mostly it comes down to intonation, accent, and cultural nuances, but there are also many uniquely Québécois idioms and vocabulary that reflect the province's particular history, social influences, and local linguistic evolution.

TIPS ARE APPRECIATED

Servers earn minimum wage, so tips make all the difference. In Québec, tipping is generally 15%—the same amount as the local GST and QST taxes, which makes it easy to just quickly match whatever appears under that amount on your bill. Feel free to tip up to 20% for exceptional service; that would generally be the maximum. A 10% tip is usually customary for taxi drivers.

DOWNLOAD A RIDE-SHARING APP

In Montréal, having Uber or its local competitors Téo Taxi or Eva apps on your smartphone will save you a little money and a lot of peace of mind. Montréal's subway only runs until 1 am on weekdays and 1:30 am on weekends; it resumes service at 5:30 am daily. In Québec City, bus and express shuttle service ends at midnight. Visitors who find themselves puzzled by the French-only signs on public transportation can download the mobile app of the local taxi company, Taxi Coop.

BRACE YOURSELF FOR BAD ROADS AND CONSTRUCTION

Québec's roads are in abominable shape. In 2018, it was estimated that over C$15 billion in repairs were necessary. The government is set to invest C$135 billion into infrastructure projects such as roads until 2031, so it will take some time for those cracks and potholes to disappear. Drive carefully, particularly in winter when weather and road conditions are even worse, and in spring when the snow starts melting. In summer, factor road closures and construction detours into itineraries.

NO RIGHT-ON-RED IN MONTRÉAL

The island of Montréal is the only place in North America besides New York City where it's illegal to turn right on red. Changing the law is still being debated by the local government, but that won't save you from a fine of up to C$200. Elsewhere in the province, right turns on red are allowed (unless otherwise indicated), but not mandatory. In fact, it's a driver's right not to. Honking at someone for staying put can also rack up a C$200 fine on top of the previous one!

DRINKING IN PUBLIC ISN'T ALWAYS ILLEGAL
Unlike the rest of Canada, you can drink alcohol in public in Québec—but not everywhere. The rule is that you must be in a public park and consuming food at the same time, so that the alcohol accompanies your meal. However, the law doesn't clearly define what exactly constitutes a meal. This caveat is somewhat lax, however; as long as you're behaving respect-fully, the authorities will usually turn a blind eye.

GET OUTDOORS IN WINTER
Don't shy away from the chills, as some of Québec's finest joie de vivre happens at -30°C (-22°F). There's skating on the St. Lawrence or at rinks, and festivals like the famed Carnaval de Québec or Igloofest, an electronic music party where guests sport neon snowsuits. Wonderful memories are to be made in the cold.

DRESS FOR THE ELEMENTS—AND COBBLESTONE
Loading up on layers is essential as you never know what Mother Nature's up to. Temperatures can start to plummet as early as October and linger on until March. Québec winter is notorious for gusty winds and icy sidewalks. Slipping and falling is a Montrealer's rite of passage, but can be avoided by a pair of sturdy shoes. Similarly, the cobble-stoned streets in historic areas can wreak havoc on high heels, so you may just be better off with flats.

THERE'S AN UNDERGROUND CITY
Montréal's mammoth Underground City—known locally as the RÉSO—connects museums, universities, office towers, shopping plazas, trendy food halls, entertainment venues, and hotels while providing a welcome escape from the cold or heat and serving as a transport link for 500,000 people per day beneath the city's streets. As well as linking major landmarks such as Centre Bell and Time Out Market, the 20 miles of underground are typical of the city and its northern character. Look for the Art Souterrain festival, which showcases contemporary art every February in the corridors of Montréal's Underground City.

QUÉBEC BEER IS BOOZIER
Québec beers are probably stronger than you're used to unless you're already a craft beer enthusiast. Local and regional microbreweries are known for producing brews with a considerably higher alcohol level, such as darker beers that make the cheeks rosy during winter. Typically, these local beers can be 6% and even rise into the double digits. Know your tipsy limit!

THE LEGAL DRINKING AGE IS 18
In Québec and one other Canadian province, Alberta, the drinking age is 18. That makes Québec a destination for partying, particularly for those who haven't had too much practice doing it yet. Of course, bars and nightclubs cater to differ-ent age demographics and crowds—do your research in case you aren't up for getting rowdy.

HAVE THE RIGHT DOCUMENTS
Those with non-U.S. citizenship will likely need to apply for an Electronic Travel Authorization (eTA) from the Canadian government's website. Nationalities that are not eligible for eTAs must apply for visas. Naturalized U.S. residents should carry their naturalization certificate and passport. Permanent residents who aren't citizens should carry their green card. U.S. residents entering Canada from a third country must have a valid passport, naturaliza-tion certificate, or green card. Regardless of nation-ality, everyone entering Canada must also download and submit information via the ArriveCAN app to meet the latest COVID-19 health requirements.

Getting Here and Around

✈ Air

Flying time (gate to gate) to Montréal is about one and a half hours from New York, two and a half hours from Chicago, four hours from Dallas, and six hours from Los Angeles. Flying time to Québec City is about two hours from New York, three hours from Chicago, five hours from Dallas, and seven hours from Los Angeles.

Trudeau Airport offers self-serve check-in and boarding passes at electronic kiosks throughout the airport. Make sure you arrive at the airport two hours before your flight's scheduled departure.

Security measures at Canadian airports are similar to those in the United States.

AIRPORTS

For service to Montréal, Montréal–Pierre Elliott Trudeau International Airport is 20 km (12.5 miles) west of the city. Québec City's Jean Lesage International Airport is about 13 km (9 miles) northwest of Downtown. Both airports handle domestic and international flights.

GROUND TRANSPORTATION

In Montréal, a taxi from Trudeau International to Downtown costs C$48. All taxi companies must charge the same rate for travel between the airport and Downtown. Taking an Uber might be slightly cheaper.

The least expensive way to get from Trudeau International Airport into the city is to take the 747 Express Bus, operated by Société de Transport de Montréal. Shuttles leave from Montréal Central Bus Station, which is connected to Berri–UQAM *métro* station. They run 24/7—from noon to midnight they leave every 10 minutes or less, while you may wait up to an hour in the early morning hours. The cost is C$11 one-way, payable by card from automated dispensers in the international arrivals area or on the bus in coins only (no bills). The ticket is valid for unlimited travel on the entire Montréal bus and métro system for a 24-hour period.

In Québec City, taxis are available immediately outside the airport exit near the baggage-claim area. A ride into the city costs a flat rate of C$41.40. Taxi Coop Québec is the largest taxi company in the city.

FLIGHTS

All the major U.S. airlines, including American, Delta, and United, serve Montréal and Québec City.

Regularly scheduled flights from the United States to Montréal and Québec City as well as flights within Canada are available on Air Canada and the regional airlines associated with it. Porter Airlines also has connecting service to Montréal and Québec City from select U.S. cities, via Toronto's Billy Bishop Airport. With regular flights from Florida and California to Montréal, Air Transat is another airline to consider.

🚲 Bicycle

Québec continues to expand its Route Verte (Green Route), North America's largest network of bike trails totaling over 5,000 km (more than 3,100 miles). Covering the southern half of the province, the bikeways link to Canadian provinces Ontario and New Brunswick, as well as New England and New York. For information and a route planner, head to Route Verte's website or contact Vélo Québec.

BIKE-SHARING SYSTEMS

Montréal's BIXI offer more than 10,000 bikes (including 2,600 e-bikes) at 865 self-service stations throughout the city, complementing the extensive Réseau

Express Vélo (REV) lanes. Users can conveniently rent bikes for short trips at competitive rates starting at C$1.25 per trip plus 15¢/min for regular bikes and 30¢/min for e-bikes. Download the BIXI app for station locations and bike availability.

Québec City also has a similar but more modest system called àVélo, with 74 stations and 780 e-bikes. Rides cost C$5.25 for each half hour of use.

🚢 Boat and Ferry

The Québec–Lévis ferry, which crosses the St. Lawrence River, gives you a magnificent panorama of Old Québec on its trips to and from Lévis. Although the crossing takes only 12 minutes, the waiting time can increase the trip to an hour. The cost is C$3.95. The first ferry from Québec City leaves weekdays at 6:20 am from the pier at rue Dalhousie, opposite Place Royale. Crossings run every half an hour during weekdays until 6:30 pm. It then runs hourly until 2:20 am. On weekends and holidays, the ferry leaves hourly from 6:30 am to 2:20 am. Schedules can change, so be sure to check the ferry website or call ahead.

🚌 Bus

Several private bus lines serve the province. Orléans Express is probably the most convenient, with regular service between Montréal and Québec City and clean, comfortable buses with individual power outlets. The trip takes a little over three hours. Limocar, another bus line, serves the Eastern Townships, while Greyhound Lines provides interprovincial service. Megabus offers somewhat more luxurious service to New York and Toronto.

Bus terminals in Montréal and Québec City offer service all week. In some small towns the bus station is simply a counter in a local gas station.

Buses from Montréal to Québec City depart nine times daily between 7 am and 9:30 pm. A one-way ticket booked at least a week in advance starts at C$50. All intercity bus lines servicing Montréal arrive at and depart from the city's Downtown bus terminal, the Gare d'Autocars de Montréal, which is conveniently located next to the Berri-UQAM métro station.

Many bus companies offer discounts if you book in advance, usually either 7 or 14 days ahead. Discounts are available for kids.

Most bus lines don't accept reservations for specific seats. You should plan on picking up your tickets at least 30 minutes before the bus's scheduled departure time.

🚗 Car

Montréal is accessible from the rest of Canada via the Trans-Canada Highway, which crosses the southern part of the island as Autoroute 20, with Autoroute 720 leading into Downtown. From New York, take Interstate 87 north until it becomes Autoroute 15 at the Canadian border; continue for another 47 km (29 miles) to the outskirts of Montréal. From Interstate 91 through Massachusetts via New Hampshire and Vermont, you can take Route 55 to Autoroute 10.

■TIP➜ At the border you must clear Canadian customs, so be prepared with your passport and car registration. On holidays and during the peak summer season, expect to wait a half hour or more at the

Getting Here and Around

major crossings. **Border wait times can be checked on the Transport Québec website.**

Montréal and Québec City are linked by Autoroute 20 on the south shore of the St. Lawrence River and by Autoroute 40 on the north shore. On both highways, the ride between the two cities is about 240 km (149 miles) and takes about three hours.

In Québec the road signs are in French, but the important ones have pictograms. Keep in mind the following terms: *centre-ville* (downtown), *arrêt* (stop), *détenteurs de permis* (permit holders only), *gauche* (left), *droit* (right), *ouest* (west), and *est* (east).

Drivers must carry vehicle registration and proof of insurance coverage, which is compulsory in Canada. Québec drivers are covered by the Québec government no-fault insurance plan. Drivers from outside Québec can obtain a Canadian Non-Resident Inter-Provincial Motor Vehicle Liability Insurance Card, available from any U.S. insurance company, as evidence of financial responsibility in Canada. The minimum liability in Québec is C$50,000. If you are driving a car that isn't registered in your name, carry a letter from the owner that authorizes your use of the vehicle.

CAR RENTAL

Rates in Montréal start from about C$40 a day for an economy car with air-conditioning and unlimited kilometers. If you prefer a manual-transmission car, check whether the rental agency offers stick shifts; many agencies in Canada don't.

You must be at least 21 years old to rent a car in Québec, and some car-rental agencies don't rent to drivers under 25. Most rental companies don't allow you to drive on gravel roads. Child seats are compulsory for children ages five and under.

Rentals at the airports near Québec City and Montréal are usually more expensive than neighborhood rentals.

GASOLINE

Gasoline is always sold in liters; 3.8 liters make a gallon. As of this writing, gas prices in Québec were around C$1.75 per liter (this works out to about US$6.60 per gallon). Fuel comes in several grades, denoted as *regulière, supérieure,* and *premium.* Major credit cards are widely accepted.

PARKING

Expect on-street parking in Montréal to be hard to find; your best bet is to leave the car at your hotel garage and take public transportation or a cab. If you must drive, ask your concierge to recommend a garage near your destination. Be extra careful where you park if it snows, to avoid getting towed. Parking in Québec City is much less stressful, although it's also advisable to leave the car at the hotel and walk—especially if you're heading to Vieux-Québec.

The narrow streets of the Old City leave few two-hour metered parking spaces available. Nevertheless, several parking garages at central locations charge about C$12 a day on weekdays or C$7 for 12 hours on weekends. Main garages are at Hôtel de Ville (City Hall), Place d'Youville, Edifice Marie-Guyart, Place Québec, Château Frontenac, rue St-Paul, and the Old Port.

ROAD CONDITIONS

In Montréal and Québec City the jumble of bicycle riders, delivery vehicles, taxis, and municipal buses can be chaotic. In the countryside at night, roads are lighted at exit points from major highways but are otherwise dark. Roads in the province aren't very good, especially during the spring pothole season—be prepared for some spine-jolting bumps and potholes, and check tire pressure once in a while.

In winter, Montréal streets are kept mostly clear of snow and ice, but outside the city the situation can deteriorate. Locals are notorious for exceeding the speed limit, so keep an eye on your mirrors. For up-to-date reports on road conditions throughout the province, go to Transport Québec's website.

ROADSIDE EMERGENCIES

Dial 911 in an emergency. Contact CAA, the Canadian Automobile Association, in the event of a flat tire, dead battery, empty gas tank, or other car-related mishap. Automobile Association of America membership includes CAA service.

RULES OF THE ROAD

By law, you're required to wear seat belts even in the back seat. Infant seats also are required. Radar-detection devices are illegal in Québec; just having one in your car is punishable by a fine. Speed limits, given in kilometers, are usually within the 90 kph–100 kph (50 mph–60 mph) range outside the cities.

Right turns on a red light are allowed in most of the province, the island of Montréal being the notable exception, where they're prohibited. Driving with a blood-alcohol content of 0.08% or higher is illegal and can earn you a stiff fine and jail time. Headlights are compulsory in inclement weather. Drivers aren't permitted to use handheld cell phones. The laws here are similar to the rest of North America.

🚆 Train

Amtrak offers its daily Adirondack service from New York City's Penn Station to Montréal, although the train sometimes arrives too late to make any connecting

trains that evening. Connections are available, often the next day, to Canadian rail line VIA Rail's Canadian routes. The ride takes up to 11 hours, and one-way tickets start at C$140.

VIA Rail trains run from Montréal to Québec City in three hours, arriving at the 19th-century Gare du Palais in Lower Town. Trains on the Montréal–Québec City route run five times daily on weekdays, three to four times daily on weekends. Tickets can be purchased in advance at the station prior to departure or on the VIA Rail website. If you're lucky you can sometimes find discounted fares online for as little as C$50. They are usually nonrefundable.

Business-class tickets start at C$150 each way and include early boarding, seat selection, and a three-course meal with wine.

To save money, look into rail passes. But be aware that if you don't plan to cover many miles, you may come out ahead by buying individual tickets. Senior citizens (60 and older), children (11 and under), and students are often entitled to discounts.

The Train de Charlevoix train system takes you from Québec City to La Malbaie and stops in between, including Baie St-Paul and the new Club Med Québec-Charlevoix, priced at C$199 round-trip. The small villages and rugged natural beauty along the route, which follows the twists and turns of the St. Lawrence River, are impressive to say the least and offer some of the most spectacular maritime landscapes in the province.

Essentials

🏃 Activities

BASEBALL

There is currently one major league baseball team in Canada, the Toronto Blue Jays, founded in 1977. Canada's first major league team, the Montréal Expos, formed in 1969, relocated to Washington, D.C., in 2005. There are proposals to bring the Expos back to Montréal, even part-time, but in the meantime, baseball fans can take in a Capitales game at Québec's Canac stadium. Games are affordable and lively, and the stadium, built in 1939, is set in the middle of the city and has trees that are over 200 years old in the outfield. There's also an inflatable dome, affordable concessions, and nice views. ⊕ *capitalesdequebec.com.*

BIKING

Weather permitting, one of the best ways to discover Montréal is on a bicycle. This is an incredibly bike-friendly metropolis, and there are thousands of designated bike paths connecting diverse neighborhoods across the island, running along the river, and through parks and forests. The most popular cycling trail on the island begins at the Old Port and winds its way to the shores of Lac St-Louis in Lachine. Pack a picnic lunch; there are plenty of green spaces where you can stop and refuel along the way. If you like to bike but would rather not do it on city streets, ferries at the Old Port can take you to Île Ste-Hélène and the south shore of the St. Lawrence River, where riders can connect to hundreds of miles of trails in the Montérégie region.

GOLF

Montréal golf enthusiasts have several excellent golf courses available to them, many less than a half-hour drive from Downtown. If you're willing to trek a bit farther (about 45 minutes), you'll find some of the best golfing in the province.

For a complete listing of the many golf courses in the area, Tourisme Québec is the best place to start.

HIKING

Canada's second-largest province is packed with hiking trails revealing nature's splendor. The Eastern Townships have a good mix of paths for all fitness levels, including over mountain landscapes with campsites or inns along the way. National parks like La Mauricie and Forillon offer more challenging, remote treks, while the Magdalen Islands are perfect for those seeking short and scenic routes.

HOCKEY

Ice hockey is nothing short of an institution in Montréal, the city that arguably gave birth to the sport back in the late 19th century. Although variations of the game are said to have been played in other U.S. and Canadian cities as early as 1800, the first organized game of modern hockey was played in Montréal in 1875, and the first official team, the McGill University Hockey Club, was founded in Montréal in 1880. The city's beloved Montréal Canadiens (⊕ *canadiens.nhl. com*) is the oldest club in the National Hockey League and, as Montrealers are keen to tell you, one of the most successful teams in North American sports history. Tickets tend to sell out well before the game—especially if the Habs, as they're nicknamed, play their archrivals, the Toronto Maple Leafs. You can buy tickets on the NHL website starting from C$60 or show up to Centre Bell on game day, when scalpers usually drop stubs to half price after the puck drops.

SKIING AND SNOWBOARDING

Skiing makes for a great day trip from either Montréal or Québec City. Near Montréal are Ski Bromont, a year-round resort with runs for different experience levels, and Mont-St-Sauveur, offering night skiing. As for cross-country skiing, you needn't even leave the city to find choice locations to pursue the sport. There's a network of winding trails stretching throughout Parc du Mont-Royal, and the Lachine Canal offers a 12-km (7-mile) stretch of relatively flat terrain, making for both a scenic and relatively simple cross-country excursion. There are pros and cons to skiing in the Eastern Townships and the Laurentians. The slopes in the Townships are generally steeper and slightly more challenging, but it requires more time to get out to them. Also, the Townships' centers tend to be quieter and more family oriented, so if it's après-ski action you're looking for, you might prefer heading out to a Laurentian hill like Mont-St-Sauveur where, for many, partying is as much the experience as is conquering the slopes.

Québec City has several lodges only an hour's drive or less from Old Québec. Le Relais, Club Med Québec-Charlevoix, and Le Massif de Charlevoix are popular with locals, particularly families, while Stoneham Mountain Resort features challenging freestyle runs and outdoor hot tubs for a soothing après-ski.

SWIMMING

Most of the city's municipal outdoor pools are open from mid-June through August. Admission is free on weekdays. On weekends and holidays there's a small fee of no more than C$4 at some pools, depending on the borough. The city's man-made beach, Plage Jean-Doré, probably has the cleanest water (tested and monitored) in Montréal. It's a great place to take kids, too, with Parc Aquazilla and its massive floating structures.

⊚ Customs and Duties

U.S. Customs and Immigration has preclearance services at **Pierre Elliott Trudeau International Airport,** which serves Montréal. This allows U.S.-bound air passengers to depart their airplane directly on arrival at their U.S. destination without further inspection and delays.

American visitors may bring in, duty-free, for personal consumption, 200 cigarettes, 50 cigars, 7 ounces of tobacco, and one bottle (1.5 liters or 40 imperial ounces) of wine or liquor, respectively, or up to 8.5 liters of beer or ale. Any alcohol and tobacco products in excess of these amounts are subject to duty, provincial fees, and taxes. You can also bring in gifts for friends or family duty-free, as long as each gift does not exceed C$60 in value.

Cats and dogs must have a certificate issued by a licensed veterinarian that clearly identifies the animal and vouches that it has been vaccinated against rabies during the preceding 36 months. Certificates aren't necessary for Seeing Eye dogs. Plant material must be declared and inspected. There may be restrictions on some live plants, bulbs, and seeds. You may bring food for your own use, as long as the quantity is consistent with the duration of your visit, and restrictions or prohibitions on some fruits and vegetables are observed.

Canada's firearms laws are significantly stricter than those in much of the United States. All handguns and semiautomatic and fully automatic weapons are prohibited and cannot be brought into the country. Sporting rifles and shotguns may be imported, provided they are to be used for sporting, hunting, or competing while in Canada. All firearms must be declared to Canada customs at the first point of entry. Failure to declare firearms will result in their seizure, and criminal

Essentials

charges may be made. Regulations require visitors to have a confirmed Firearms Declaration to bring any guns into Canada; a fee of C$25 applies, valid for 60 days but good for one year if renewed before it expires. For more information, contact the Canadian Firearms Centre.

🍴 Dining

French Canadian fast food follows the same concept as American fast food. Local chains to watch for include St-Hubert, which serves rotisserie chicken; Chez Cora or L'Oeufrier, which specialize in hearty breakfasts; and La Belle Province, Lafleur, and Valentine, all of which serve hamburgers, poutines, hot dogs, and fries.

Many restaurants post their menu du jour outside, so you can stroll along and let your cravings guide the way. Nevertheless, bear in mind that reservations are a must at most restaurants during holidays and events and all throughout the summer months, when the coveted outdoor terraces open. The table d'hôte, a cost-cutting special, is a regular at many restaurants in both Québec City and Montréal.

WINE, BEER, AND SPIRITS

Embedded in Québec's vibrant social fabric and affinity for culinary delights, the liquor industry thrives here, fueled by a deep-rooted appreciation for quality and conviviality.

The province's regulated alcohol supplier, the SAQ, carries a wide selection of wines (with a strong emphasis on those from France), mixers, and spirits; most SAQ stores are open during regular business hours. Supermarkets and grocery stores carry lower-end wines at significantly higher prices as well as a wide selection of affordable local beers; they can sell alcohol until 11 pm (long after SAQ stores close). The legal drinking age in the province of Québec is 18.

Beer: With a selection ranging from fruity sour beers to heavy stouts and everything in between, some of the best local microbreweries in the province include Dieu du Ciel!, Menaud, Brasserie Dunham, Le Trou du Diable, Brasserie Harricana, Brasserie du Bas-Canada, and Brasserie Auval, to name a few. The Association des Microbrasseries du Québec and its interactive map (🌐 *ambq. ca*) is a good place to start your search.

Wine: Although most of the wine consumed in Québec is imported, the southern half of the province is home to a burgeoning and promising wine industry. Wine makers take great pride in their craft and demonstrate a commitment to sustainable practices and unique terroir. Notable vineyards include Domaine du Nival, Les Pervenches, Pinard et Filles, and Domaine Bergeville.

Cider: There is also no shortage of cider. Québec's exceptional reputation for cider is due to its ideal climate, fertile soils, and traditional apple varieties. The result is a diverse, flavorful and aromatic selection of still, sparkling, and even ice ciders. Look out for cider makers like Fleuri, La Cabane d'à Côté, Polisson, Domaine Lafrance, Cidrerie Milton, and Union Libre.

Liquor: Québec's distilled-spirits scene, and especially its gin production, stands out for its diversity and craftsmanship. Local distillers make use of top-quality ingredients and skilled techniques to create high-quality spirits that reflect their Nordic terroir. Most distilleries offer tours and tastings; some of the most popular choices are Distillerie du St-Laurent, Menaud, Les Subversifs, Les Herbes Folles, Distillerie du Fjord, and Distillerie de Montréal.

➕ Emergencies

All embassies are in Ottawa. The U.S. consulate in Montréal is open weekdays from 7:30 am to 5 pm, while in Québec City it's open weekdays 9 to 4. The U.S. consulate maintains a list of medical specialists in the Montréal area.

In Montréal, the main English-language hospital is the Montréal General Hospital (McGill University Health Centre). Many pharmacies in Montréal stay open until midnight, including Jean Coutu and Pharmaprix stores. Some are open around the clock, including the Pharmaprix on chemin de la Côte-des-Neiges.

In Québec City, the Centre Hospitalier Universitaire de Québec is the city's largest institution and incorporates the teaching hospitals Pavillon CHUL in Ste-Foy and Pavillon Hôtel-Dieu, the main hospital in Vieux-Québec. Most outlets of the big pharmacy chains in the region (including Jean Coutu, Brunet, and Uniprix) are open every day and offer free delivery.

📅 Holidays

Canadian national holidays are as follows: New Year's Day (January 1), Good Friday (late March or early April), Easter Monday (the Monday following Good Friday), Victoria Day (called Fête des Patriotes in Québec; late May), Canada Day (July 1), Labor Day (early September), Thanksgiving (mid-October), Remembrance Day (November 11), Christmas, and Boxing Day (December 26). St-Jean-Baptiste Day (June 24) is a provincial holiday.

🛏 Lodging

In Montréal and Québec City you have a choice of luxury hotels, moderately priced modern properties, and small older hotels with fewer conveniences but sometimes more charm. Options in small towns and in the country include large, full-service resorts; small, privately owned hotels; roadside motels; and bed-and-breakfasts. Even outside the cities it's a good idea to make reservations.

Expect accommodations to cost more in summer than in the colder months (except for places such as ski resorts, where winter is high season). When making reservations, ask about special deals and packages. Big-city hotels that cater to business travelers often offer weekend packages, and many city hotels offer rooms at up to 50% off in winter. If you're planning to visit Montréal or Québec City or a resort area in high season, book well in advance. Also be aware of any special events or festivals that may coincide with your visit and fill every room for miles around.

APARTMENT AND HOUSE RENTALS

Airbnb (⊕ www.airbnb.com) has a wide selection of cabins and chalets for rent.

BED-AND-BREAKFASTS

B&Bs, which are also known as *gîtes* in Québec, can be found in both the country and the cities. For assistance in booking these, be sure to check out B&B websites (⊕ www.bedandbreakfast.com is a good resource for B&Bs throughout the province). Room quality varies from house to house as well, so ask to see a few rooms before making a choice.

Essentials

The nonprofit organization Association de l'Agrotourisme et du Tourisme Gourmand du Québec has extensive listings of B&Bs, both urban and rural, as well as farms that take paying guests.

HOTELS

Canada doesn't have a national rating system for hotels, but Québec's tourism ministry rates the province's hotels and B&Bs; the stars are more a reflection of the number of facilities and amenities than of the hotel's performance. Hotels are rated zero to three stars (B&Bs, zero to four suns), with zero stars or suns representing minimal comfort and few services and three stars or four suns being the very best. All hotels listed have private baths unless otherwise noted.

Montréal is always hosting a festival or an international convention, so the hotels are consistently booked. This takes visitors by surprise. Many of the quaint auberges have a small number of rooms, so they fill up fast. It's necessary to book months ahead for the Grand Prix, Jazz Fest, and all holiday weekends.

💲 Money

Throughout this book, prices are given in Canadian dollars, which at this writing are worth roughly 75¢ to the American dollar. The price of a cup of coffee can be C$4 or more, depending on how upscale or downscale the place is; beer costs C$5 to C$9 in a bar; a smoked-meat sandwich costs about C$13; and museum admission can cost anywhere from nothing to C$20.

∎TIP→ **Prices throughout this guide are given for adults. Substantially reduced fees are almost always available for children, students, and senior citizens.**

CURRENCY AND EXCHANGE

U.S. dollars are sometimes accepted in Canada, especially in communities near the border. Major U.S. credit cards are accepted in most areas.

The units of currency in Canada are the Canadian dollar (C$) and the cent, in almost the same denominations as U.S. currency ($5, $10, $20, 5¢, 10¢, 25¢, etc.). The exception is 1¢ coins, which are no longer minted and circulated, so expect to pay and receive change rounded up or down by 5¢ accordingly. The C$1 and C$2 bills are also no longer used in Canada; they have been replaced by C$1 and C$2 coins (known as "loonies," because of the loon that appears on the coin, and "toonies," respectively).

At the time of writing, the exchange rate is US$1 to C$1.25.

Bank cards are widely accepted in Québec and throughout Canada.

🍸 Nightlife

If nightlife in Montréal could be distilled into a cocktail, it would be one part sophisticated New York club scene (with the accompanying pretension), one part Parisian joie de vivre (and, again, a dash of snobbery), and one part Barcelonese stamina (which keeps the clubs booming until dawn). Montréal's nightlife swings with a robust passion. From the early-evening *cinq à sept* (five to seven) after-work cocktail circuit, to the slightly later concerts and supper clubs (restaurant–dance club hybrids where people dance on the tables after eating off of them), on into the even later dance club scene, all tastes, cultural backgrounds, and legal ages join the melee. Clubbing is, to say the least, huge in Montréal.

Some restaurants are even installing discotheques in their basements.

Québec City has a wide variety of cultural institutions for a town of its size, from the symphony to small theater companies. To sample the nightlife, you'll need to head to the clubs and cafés of rue St-Jean, avenue Cartier, and Grande Allée, as well as Lower Town. Most bars and clubs stay open until 3 am.

🔲 Packing

If you're visiting Montréal anytime between November and May, be sure to bring some warm clothes, or be prepared to purchase some while you're here. Come winter Montréal gets cold—very cold—with temperatures almost always dipping below the freezing mark from December until late March. A good winter coat, scarf, hat (locally called a *toque*), gloves, and warm winter boots are pretty much a necessity in Québec if you want to be comfortable going outside in the winter months. In summer, however, temperatures regularly rise above 30°C (86°F), and Downtown Montréal, in particular, can get very humid, so bring a few pairs of shorts, sandals, and warm-weather clothes.

🌐 Passports and Visas

All travelers will need a passport or other accepted secure documents to enter or reenter the United States. Naturalized U.S. residents should carry their naturalization certificate. Permanent

residents who aren't citizens should carry their green card. U.S. residents entering Canada from a third country must have a valid passport, naturalization certificate, or green card.

■ TIP→ **All American visitors require an Electronic Travel Authorization (eTA) if arriving by plane (an eTA is not necessary if arriving by land or sea).**

➕ Safety

Montrealers are keen to boast they can walk the streets of their city at any time of day or night without fear of incident. And although both Montréal and Québec City are among the safest cities in North America, travelers should nevertheless be on their guard for pickpockets and other petty criminals, especially when traveling on Montréal's often-crowded métro system.

💲 Tipping

Tips and service charges aren't usually added to a bill in Canada. In general, tip at least 15% of the total bill. This goes for waiters and waitresses, barbers and hairdressers, and taxi drivers. Porters and doormen should get about C$2 a bag. For maid service, leave at least C$2 per person a day (C$3 to C$5 in luxury hotels).

Essentials

Tours

DAY TOURS AND GUIDES

In Montréal, from May through October, Bateau-Mouche runs four harbor excursions and an evening supper cruise daily. The boats are reminiscent of the ones that cruise the canals of the Netherlands—wide-beamed and low-slung, with a glassed-in passenger deck. Boats leave from the Jacques-Cartier Pier in the Vieux-Port.

Gray Line has nine different types of tours of Montréal from June through October and one tour the rest of the year. There are also day trips to Mont-Tremblant and Québec City. The company offers pickup service at the major hotels and at Centre Infotouriste (✉ *1001 Square Dorchester*).

Local food tours are available in both Montréal and Québec City, and, as the name suggests, focus on the gourmet traditions of several underrated yet fascinating neighborhoods.

In Québec City, Unitours runs bus tours of the city, departing across the square from the Hôtel Château Laurier (✉ *1230 pl. George V*); you can buy tickets at most major hotels. The company runs guided tours in a minibus as well as tours of Côte-de-Beaupré and Île d'Orléans, and whale-watching excursions to Tadoussac. Tours run year-round and cost C$36–C$140. Call for a reservation, and the company will pick you up at your hotel.

Croisières AML has day and evening cruises, some of which include dinner, on the St. Lawrence River aboard MV *Louis-Jolliet*. The crusies run 1½ to 4 hours from May through mid-October and start at C$60 plus tax.

Visitor Information

Tourist Welcome Office in Old Montréal has extensive tourist information on Montréal. It's open daily from 10 to 6, May 1 to June 15 as well as September 1 to October 31; daily from 9 to 7, June 16 to August 31; and from Thursday to Monday from 10 to 6, November 1 to April 30, closed between December 24 and January 3.

In Québec City, Centre Infotouriste de Québec in Old Québec, across from Château Frontenac, is open daily from 9 to 5.

Montréal and Québec City's Best Festivals

Citizens of Montréal and Québec City always find a good reason to party. Québec City celebrates its long winters with a carnival that includes a boat race across a frozen river. And Montréal holds February's cold at bay with a sizzling food extravaganza. Throughout the province, the rest of the year is full of festivals celebrating jazz, folklore, film, classical music, theater, fireworks, comedy, and hot-air balloons.

JANUARY AND FEBRUARY

Carnaval de Québec *(Québec Winter Carnival).* The biggest winter carnival in the world takes place on the Plains of Abraham over two weekends in early February, with winter sports competitions, ice sculpture contests, and parades. ⊠ *Parc de la Francophonie, Québec City* ☎ *418/626–3716* ⊕ *www.carnaval.qc.ca.*

Fête des Neiges de Montréal. Over four weekends from mid-January to mid-February, Montréal celebrates its winter festival at Parc Jean-Drapeau across the port from Old Montréal. Hockey games, tubing, skiing, dog sledding, and a Himalayan zip line are perfect activities to enjoy in the cold winter weather but don't forget your toque, pronounced *took* with long O's. ⊠ *The Islands* ⊕ *www. parcjeandrapeau.com/events/fete-des-neiges-de-montreal* Ⓜ *Jean-Drapeau.*

Montréal en Lumière *(Montréal Highlights).* This festival brightens the bleak days of February with fabulous food and cultural activities. Leading chefs from around the world give demonstrations and take over the kitchens of top restaurants for special dinners. "Nuit Blanche," held on the last Saturday of this festival, lets you explore the city until the wee hours of the morning. Many of the events are free, and there are shuttle services to take you to the locations. Dress extra warmly. ⊠ *Downtown* ⊕ *www.montrealenlumiere.com* Ⓜ *Place-des-Arts.*

Igloofest. Igloofest, Montréal's winter electronic music festival, turns the Old Port into an icy dance paradise. With world-class DJs, dazzling lights, and ridiculously layered outfits to keep warm, it's a celebration that captures the city's love of music and winter, creating an unforgettable fusion of sound and snow. From mid-January to mid-February each year. ⊠ *Old Montréal* ⊕ *igloofest.ca* Ⓜ *Champ-de-Mars.*

MARCH

Art Souterrain. Art Souterrain offers an annual free exhibition of contemporary art in an unlikely place: the public corridors of Montréal's Underground City. The ingenious location puts art in front of a prospective daily audience of the nearly 500,000 people that walk beneath Downtown Montréal through vast corridors that connect office towers, shopping centers, hotels, food halls, universities, museums, and entertainment venues. Art Souterrain exhibits 70 contemporary works in various mediums (sculpture, performance, photography, video, audio, painting), all tied together by a theme that addresses a modern-day social issue. ⊠ *RÉSO Underground City, Downtown* ⊕ *artsouterrain.com* Ⓜ *McGill.*

MAY

Mondial de la Bière. Mondial de la Bière is a captivating event where more than 100 Québécois microbreweries and North American craft beer staples come together. Each May, this popular festival offers visitors an exclusive opportunity to expand their palates, understand beer production, meet artisans, and discover new flavors. ⊠ *Gare Windsor, 1100 av. des Canadiens-de-Montréal, Downtown* ⊕ *festivalmondialbiere.qc.ca/en* Ⓜ *Bonaventure.*

Montréal and Québec City's Best Festivals

JUNE

Fringe Festival. Taking place over the first three weeks of June, Fringe Montréal embraces playwrights, acting troupes, dancers, comics, and musicians. Revered for its avant-garde and thought-provoking essence, the festival offers an uncurated stage to 700 artists with absolute autonomy over their performances. ⊠ *The Plateau* ⊕ *www.montrealfringe.ca.*

Francos de Montréal. Francos de Montréal is one of the city's cultural beacons, offering a range of free grand-scale outdoor performances mixed with ticketed shows in stunning indoor venues. More than 1,000 musicians, many from France, Belgium, Senegal, and Haiti, weave the rich tapestry of the French-speaking world with rock, hip-hop, jazz, funk, and Latin performances, alongside Québec household names such as Daniel Bélanger, Robert Charlebois, Coeur de Pirate, and Charlotte Cardin. ⊠ *Downtown* ⊕ *francosmontreal.com/en-CA* Ⓜ *Place-des-Arts.*

MURAL. MURAL Festival transforms Montréal's streets into a sprawling open-air gallery, showcasing vibrant, large-scale murals by international and local artists. The event is held on a pedestrianized boulevard St-Laurent and complemented by a lively street fair and live musical performances, fusing creative marketplaces and interactive engagements. ⊠ *The Plateau* ⊕ *muralfestival.com* Ⓜ *Mont-Royal.*

JULY

Fantasia. Fantasia is Montréal's premiere genre film festival, showcasing a diverse range of films spanning horror, fantasy, sci-fi, and more. It's a platform for innovative storytelling that attracts cinephiles and creators alike to explore cutting-edge narratives and imaginative worlds. ⊠ *Downtown* ⊕ *fantasiafestival.com/en.*

Festival d'Été de Québec *(Québec City Summer Festival).* This exuberant 11-day music extravaganza in Québec City features some of the biggest names in contemporary music, with recent performances by Paul McCartney, Foo Fighters, and Radiohead. The main concerts rock nightly with 10 indoor and outdoor stages in early July in or near Old Québec, including one on the Plains of Abraham. ⊠ *Plains of Abraham, Upper Town* ⊕ *feq.ca/en.*

Festival International de Jazz de Montréal *(Montréal International Jazz Festival).* This major event, held since 1978, attracts more than 1,000 musicians for more than 400 concerts held over a period of nearly two weeks from the end of June through the beginning of July. Past stars have included B.B. King, Ella Fitzgerald, Lauryn Hill, Norah Jones, and Canada's most famed singer-pianist, Diana Krall. You can also hear blues, Latin rhythms, gospel, Cajun, and world music. ⊠ *Downtown* ⊕ *montrealjazzfest.com/en* Ⓜ *Place-des-Arts.*

Just for Laughs. Montréal's world-famous comedy festival hosts international comics, in French and English, from the second through third weeks of July. There are tons of shows to watch, in venues from big concert halls to quaint bars. Walk around the Quartier des Spectacles during the festival and giggle your way from one outdoor act to another. The twins parade is not to be missed. ⊠ *2101 boul. St-Laurent, Downtown* ⊕ *montreal. hahaha.com/en* Ⓜ *St-Laurent.*

AUGUST

International des Montgolfières St-Jean-sur-Richelieu *(St-Jean-sur-Richelieu Hot-Air Balloon Festival).* This colorful airborne event, the largest gathering of hot-air balloons in Canada, takes flight about 25 minutes' drive southeast of Montréal. The balloons are so vivid and plentiful that you can sometimes see them from Downtown. On top of balloon rides, there is a selection of food trucks on-site, as well as musical performances and family-friendly activities. ✉ *5 chemin de l'Aéroport, St-Jean* ⊕ *en.montgolfieres.com.*

International First Peoples Festival. Artists from Indigenous communities from all over the Americas come to this festival, which presents a dynamic multidisciplinary program of concerts, international film competitions, traditional dances, exhibitions, and seminars over 10 days in Montréal's premiere cultural venues. Come watch Place des Festivals being transformed into a vibrant space that reflects the worldview of the First Peoples, with teepees, a longhouse, and contemporary Indigenous arts. ✉ *Downtown* ⊕ *presenceautochtone.ca/en* Ⓜ *Place-des-Arts.*

Les Fêtes de la Nouvelle-France *(New France Festival).* During this five-day festival, in early to mid-August, Québec City's centuries-old heritage comes alive. The streets of Lower Town are transported back in time, and events range from an old-time farmers' market to games and music—all done in period costume. ✉ *Lower Town* ⊕ *nouvellefrance.qc.ca/en.*

Osheaga. Montréal's premier English-speaking music event draws music enthusiasts to Parc Jean-Drapeau for an experience akin to Coachella without the heat or Glastonbury without the mud. A three-day celebration dedicated to music and visual arts, featuring top-tier international acts across various genres such as Kendrick Lamar, Radiohead, and Dua Lipa. ✉ *The Islands* ⊕ *osheaga.com/en* Ⓜ *Jean-Drapeau.*

OCTOBER

Gardens of Light. In the Montréal Botanical Garden, numerous vibrant silk lanterns in the Chinese garden offer enchanting evenings. Every autumn, from September 1 to October 31, these immersive sensory encounters blend art, science, technology, and emotion seamlessly, providing a captivating experience. ✉ *Montréal Botanical Garden, 4101 rue Sherbrooke Est, Rosemont* ☎ *855/868-3000* ⊕ *espacepourlavie.ca/en* 🎫 *Starting at C$23* Ⓜ *Pie-IX.*

NOVEMBER AND DECEMBER

Marché de Noël Allemand de Québec *(German Christmas Market of Québec City).* In the large plaza fronting city hall, neat rows of darling little wooden huts exactly like those you'd find in Germany offer steaming hot pretzels, gingerbread, mulled wine, roasted chestnuts, and other aromatic foods, while jewelry designers, wood sculptors, glassmakers, and other artisans chat animatedly with customers, as German Christmas carols play in the background. If you can't get to Europe for the holidays, this market is probably the most magical and most authentic you'll find in North America. It market opens in the third week of November and lasts until December 23. ✉ *Upper Town* ⊕ *mnaq.ca/en.*

MTLàTable. Featuring bespoke prix-fixe menus at renowned restaurants, this is the flagship event of the Montréal culinary scene. This beacon of terroir gastronomy beckons foodies to discover exclusive dining experiences throughout the city. For those on a smaller budget, it's an excellent opportunity to dine at high-end restaurants and fork out just a fraction of the usual damage. ✉ *Montréal* ⊕ *mtlatable.mtl.org/en.*

Helpful French Phrases

BASICS

Hello	Bonjour	bohn- zhoor
Yes/No	Oui/non	wee/nohn
Please	S'il vous plaît	seel voo play
Thank you	Merci	mair- see
You're welcome	De rien	deh ree- ehn
I'm Sorry (apology)	Pardon	pahr- don
Good morning	Bonjour	bohn- zhoor
Good evening	Bonsoir	bohn- swahr
Goodbye	Au revoir	o ruh- vwah
Mr. (Sir)	Monsieur	muh- syuh
Mrs.	Madame	ma- dam
Miss	Mademoiselle	mad-mwa- ze
Pleased to meet you	Enchanté(e)	ohn-shahn- tay
How are you?	Comment allez-vous?	kuh-mahn- tahl-ay voo

NUMBERS

one-half	un demi	uhn de-mee
one	un	uhn
two	deux	deuh
three	trois	twah
four	quatre	kaht-ruh
five	cinq	sank
six	six	seess
seven	sept	set
eight	huit	wheat
nine	neuf	nuf
ten	dix	deess
eleven	onze	ohnz
twelve	douze	dooz
thirteen	treize	trehz
fourteen	quartorze	kah-torz
fifteen	quinze	kanz
sixteen	seize	sez
seventeen	dix-sept	deez-set
eighteen	dix-huit	deez-wheat
nineteen	dix-neuf	deez-nuf
twenty	vingt	vehn
twenty-one	vingt-et-un	vehnt-ay-uhn
thirty	trente	trahnt
forty	quarante	ka-rahnt
fifty	cinquante	sang-kahnt
sixty	soixante	swa-sahnt
seventy	soixante-dix	swa-sahnt-deess
eighty	quante-vingts	kaht-ruh-vehn
ninety	quatre-vingts-dix	kaht-ruh-vehn-deess
one hundred	cent	sahn
one thousand	mille	meel
one million	million	meel-ion

COLORS

black	noir	nwahr
blue	bleu	bleuh
brown	brun	bruhn
green	vert	vair
orange	orange	o-rahnj
red	rouge	rouge
white	blanc	blahnk
yellow	jaune	zhone

DAYS OF THE WEEK

Sunday	Dimanche	dee-mahnsh
Monday	Lundi	luhn-dee
Tuesday	Mardi	mahr-dee
Wednesday	Mercredi	mair-kruh-dee
Thursday	Jeudi	zhuh-dee
Friday	Vendredi	vawn-druh-dee
Saturday	Samedi	sahm-dee

MONTHS

January	Janvier	zhahn-vee-ay
February	Février	feh-vree-ay
March	Mars	marce
April	Avril	a-vreel
May	Mai	meh
June	Juin	zhwehn
July	Juillet	zhwee-ay
August	Août	ah-oo
September	Septembre	sep-tahm-bruh
October	Octobre	oc-to-bruh
November	Novembre	no-vahm-bruh
December	Décembre	day-sahm-bruh

USEFUL WORDS AND PHRASES

Do you speak English?	Parlez-vous anglais?	par-lay voo ahn-glay
I don't speak [Language].	Je ne parle pas …	zhuh nuh parl pah
I don't understand	Je ne prends pas.	zhuh nuh kohm-prahn pah
I don't know.	Je ne sais pas.	zhuh nnuh say pah
I understand.	Je comprends	zhuh kohm-prahn
I'm American.	Je suis américain.	a-may-ree-kehn
I'm British.	Je suis anglais.	ahn-glay
What's your name?	Comment vous appelez-vous?	ko-mahn voo za-pell-ay-voo
My name is …	Mon nom est...	zhuh ma-pell
What time is it?	Quelle heure es-il	kel air eh-teel
How?	Comment?	ko-mahn
When?	Quand?	kahn
Yesterday	Hier	yair

Today	Aujourd'hui	o-zhoor-dwee
Tomorrow	Demain	duh-mehn
This morning	Ce matin	suh mah-tin
This afternoon	Cet après-midi	set a-pray mee-dee
Tonight	Ce Soir	suh swahr
What?	Quoi?	kwah
What is it?	Qu'est-ce que c'est?	kess-kuh-say
Why?	Pourquoi?	poor-kwa
Who?	Qui?	kee
Where is ...	Où est	oo ay
...the train station?	la gare?	la gar
...the subway station?	la station de metro?	la sta-syon duh may-tro
...the bus stop?	l'arrêt de bus?	la-ray duh booss
...the airport	l'aéroport?	la-ay ro-porr
...the post office?	la poste?	la post
...the bank?	la banque?	la bahnk
...the hotel?	l'hôtel?	lo-tel
...the museum?	le musée?	luh mew-zay
...the hospital?	l'hôpital?	lo-pee-tahl
...the elevator?	l'ascenseur?	la-sahn-seuhr
Where are the restrooms?	Où sont les toilettes?	oo sohn lay twah-let
Here/there	Ici/là	ee- see /la
Left/right	à gauche/à droite	a goash/a draht
Is it near/far?	Est-ce que c'est près/loin?	say pray/lwehn
I'd like ...	Je voudrais...	zhuh voo- dray...
...a room	une chambre	ewn shahm-bruh
...the key	la clé	la clay
...a newspaper	un journal	uhn zhoor- nah
...a stamp	un timbre	uhn tam-bruh
I'd like to buy ...	Je voudrais acheter...	zhuh voo- dray ahsh-tay...
...a city map	un plan de la ville	uhn plahn de veal
...a road map	une carte routière	ewn cart roo-tee- air
...a magazine	une revue	ewn reh- vu
...envelopes	des enveloppes	dayz ahn-veh- lope
...writing paper	du papier à lettres	dew pa-pee- ay a let-ruh
...a postcard	une carte postale	ewn cart pos- tahl
...a ticket	un billet	uhn bee-yeah
How much is it?	C'est combien?	say comb-bee- ehn
It's expensive/ cheap	C'est cher/pas cher	say sher/pa sher
A little/a lot	Un peu/ beaucoup	uhn peuh/bo- koo
More/less	Plus/moins	plus/mwehn

Enough/too (much)	Assez/trop	a-say/tro
I am ill/sick	Je suis malade.	zhuh swee ma- lahd
Call a doctor	Appelez un docteur	a-play uhn dohk- tehr
Help!	Au secours!	o suh- koor
Stop!	Arrêtez!	a-reh- tay

DINING OUT

A bottle of ...	une bouteille de...	ewn boo- tay duh
A cup of ...	une tasse de...	ewn tass duh
A glass of ...	un verre de...	uhn vair duh
Beer	une bière	ewn bi- yair
Bill/check	l'addition	la-dee-see- ohn
Bread	du pain	dew pan
Breakfast	le petit-déjeuner	luh puh- tee day-zhuh- nay
Butter	du beurre	dew burr
Cocktail/apéritif	un apéritif	uhn ah-pay-ree- teef
Coffee	un café	uhn ca- fay
Dinner	le dîner	luh dee- nay
Fixed-price menu	la table d'hôte	la ta- bleh doe- teh
Fork	une fourchette	ewn four- shet
I am a vegetarian	Je suis végétarien(ne)	zhuh swee vay-zhay-ta-ree- en
I cannot eat ...	Je ne peux pas manger de...	zhuh nuh puh pah mahn- jay deh
I'd like to order ...	Je voudrais commander...	zhuh voo- dray ko-mahn- day...
Is service included?	Est-ce que le service est compris?	ess kuh luh sair- veess ay comb-b- pree
I'm hungry/ thirsty	J'ai faim/soif	zay fehn / sua- f
It's good/bad	C'est bon/ mauvais	say bohn/mo- vay
It's hot/cold	C'est chaud/froid	say sho/frwah
Knife	un couteau	uhn koo- toe
Lunch	le déjeuner	luh day-zhuh- nay
Menu	la carte	la cart
Napkin	une serviette	ewn sair-vee- et
Pepper	du poivre	dew pwah-vruh
Plate	une assiette	ewn a-see- et
Please give me ...	Donnez-moi...	doe-nay- mwah...
Salt	du sel	dew sell
Spoon	une cuillère	ewn kwee-air
Tea	du thé	dew tay
Water	de l'eau	duh lo
Wine	du vin	dew vehn

Great Itineraries

Montréal in a Day

Start with a stroll to the peak of Mont-Royal, the city's most enduring natural symbol. Afterward, wander south on rue Peel and through McGill University's leafy campus to Downtown. The Musée des Beaux-Arts de Montréal, on rue Sherbrooke, was once the bastion of the Anglo-Canadian establishment and is worth a visit.

For a more francophone perspective, walk from Mont-Royal (the mountain) along Mont-Royal (the avenue) to discover the Plateau, Montréal's most artsy neighborhood, lined with cafés, vintage boutiques, and bookstores. This is a good place to get to know the more local side of the city, to stroll through its tree-lined streets, and to take in its colorful architecture.

Head down to Old Montréal and pop into the Basilique Notre-Dame-de-Montréal before getting in some nightlife, as in the summer months the Old City is one of the most popular places to party. There are dozens of restaurants to choose from, as well as clubs and bars.

Day Trips and Overnights from Montréal

If you have only a couple of days for a visit and you need to concentrate on one area, the Laurentians are a good choice. Less than an hour's drive from Downtown Montréal, this resort area has recreational options (depending on the season) that include golf, hiking, and superb skiing, both Alpine and cross-country.

Pick a town to stay in and use that as a base for visiting some of the surrounding towns. Each town has its own style and appeal: St-Sauveur-des-Monts is lively, Morin Heights is tranquil, and Ste-Adèle, along with the nearby towns of Val-Morin and Val-David, is a center of gastronomy. Mont-Tremblant, a sophisticated ski and golf resort, is worth a trip, particularly for the picturesque gondola ride to the summit.

You can combine a taste of the Eastern Townships with a two-day visit to the Laurentians. After an overnight stay in the Laurentians, head back south of Montréal to the Townships, which extend to the east along the border with New England. Overnight in quaint, walkable villages such as Sutton for a true local experience.

The next day, you can shop in attractive Knowlton (look for signs to Lac Brome) and explore regional history in such towns as Valcourt. Spend a night or two in a cabin by the water in North Hatley or at one of Canada's most prestigious resorts, Ripplecove Hôtel and Spa. Enjoy outdoor activities, whether it's golfing, skiing, biking, or hiking. Foodies should set aside some time for the many wineries, cider houses, and gourmet tables in the area.

Québec City in a Day

It's inspiring to start your day in Québec's Lower Town, the earliest site of French civilization in North America. Stroll along the narrow streets of the Quartier Petit-Champlain, visit the Maison Chevalier, and browse the craft stores and boutiques. From there, head to Place Royale, making a stop at the Église Notre-Dame-des-Victoires, and continue upward to

Terrasse Dufferin. In the afternoon, when the crowds thin out, check out the Musée de la Civilisation or the brand-new, almost futuristic wing of the Musée National des Beaux-Arts du Québec.

Catch a gorgeous sunset from the Plains of Abraham—site of the battle that ended France's colonial dreams in North America and marked the beginning of British rule in Canada—before dining anywhere on rue St-Jean, one of the best streets in the city for restaurants and nightlife.

Day Trips and Overnights from Québec City

If you want to get out of Québec City for a day or two, take a 20-minute drive to Île d'Orléans, a picturesque island called the "Garden of Québec." In summer, you can explore this idyllic island's boutiques, galleries, and food stands. Stay over in a cozy B&B, or continue on Route 138 northeast to Côte-de-Beaupré. Here you can visit the impressive Mont-morency Falls and the ornate shrine at Ste-Anne-de-Beaupré.

Another option is to take the Train du Massif de Charlevoix, which departs from the spectacular Parc de la Chute-Montmorency outside Québec City. It follows the St. Lawrence shore and the dramatic mountainous land-scapes of Charlevoix. You'll visit the artistic community of Baie St-Paul, the impressive mountain Le Massif, and the cliff-top village of La Malbaie. You can do the two-segment rail trip in one day or stay overnight at the castle-like Fairmont Le Manoir Richelieu.

From La Malbaie, it's an hour by car to Tadoussac, at the confluence of the Saguenay and St. Lawrence Rivers, where you can hop on a boat for a whale-watching excursion.

Québec City is also the gateway to some of the province's most stunning national parks. Hikers will be delighted by the opportunity to hike in the Grands Jardins or the Acropole des Draveurs, both of which offer rewarding views that are well worth the effort. For a truly unforgettable overnight experience in the boreal forest, check out Huttopia's cabins through the provincial national park agency, SÉPAQ.

A Food Lover's Tour of Montréal

Many Montrealers are true gourmets, or at least enthusiastic food lovers. And, indeed, the city has thousands of restaurants, markets, and food boutiques catering to just about every conceivable taste, from Portuguese barbecue to Tonkinese soup. Most menus are posted outside.

OLD MONTRÉAL

You can't go wrong starting the day with a bowl of steaming latte and a croissant at **Crew Collective and Café**, a stunning café set on the ground floor of the former Royal Bank of Canada building.

DOWNTOWN

For something a little different head over to Chinatown for a dim sum breakfast at **Maison Kam Fung,** a neighborhood institution.

THE PLATEAU

Walk up through the streets of the Latin Quarter on rue St-Denis and you'll hit Square St-Louis. Admire the Victorian-era buildings as you get to boulevard St-Laurent; turn right. Stop at the iconic **Schwartz's Delicatessen** and split one of the world's best smoked-meat sandwiches, served piled high on rye (it's best slathered with spicy deli mustard), with your walking companion.

Next work up an appetite for lunch with a walk. Head east along avenue Duluth and take a stroll through Parc Lafontaine. There are two options for a bite to eat: exit the park on the southwest corner to rue Rachel and turn left for **La Banquise,** one of Montréal's top poutine spots (so popular you may have to wait in line to get in); or go northwest on rue de la Roche until you reach avenue Mont-Royal, a spirited stretch of *terrasses*, tattoo parlors, and thrift shops. Stop for a bagel sandwich on a hot and sweet Montréal-style bagel at **St-Viateur Bagel and Café.**

A Food Lover's Tour of Montréal

HIGHLIGHTS
A fat smoked-meat sandwich at Schwartz's Delicatessen; walking around the Marché Jean-Talon tasting vendors' samples

WHERE TO START
Rue St-Jacques in Old Montréal, amid the former tallest skyscrapers and financial hub of Canada

LENGTH
About 5.5 km (3.5 miles) walking, plus the métro from Laurier to Marché Jean-Talon on the Orange Line

WHERE TO END
Little Italy. From here, you can walk back to the Orange Line that runs through Downtown.

BEST TIME TO GO
Busy summer Saturday (the crowds are half the entertainment)

WORST TIME TO GO
Dull winter Monday

EDITOR'S CHOICES
Walking up boulevard St-Laurent, peeking in the delis and offbeat boutiques; the colorful streets of the Plateau; creative ales at the women-owned Harricana brewery

LITTLE ITALY

Hop on the métro at Mont-Royal station and head north to the Jean-Talon stop for an afternoon visit to one of Canada's best markets, **Marché Jean-Talon.** You can spend hours browsing fish, sausage, and cheese shops and sampling everything from smoked buffalo to seasonal produce like heirloom tomatoes.

Why not treat yourself to something sweet before dinner? Head over to the **Pasticceria Alati-Caserta** for some earth-shatteringly good cannolis.

There's no leaving this area without stopping for dinner, so again, stroll over

to boulevard St-Laurent and find a place to eat in Petite-Italie (Little Italy). Two restaurants to try are **Impasto** and **Bottega Pizzeria**, both of which should be booked in advance.

Finish with a bracing espresso at **Caffé Italia,** where neighborhood men huddle around the TV to watch soccer, or with something stronger at **Brasserie Harricana,** a trendy microbrewery with a surprising interior.

From here, it's an easy walk back to the Jean-Talon métro stop for a ride back to Old Montréal or Downtown.

A Walk through Québec City's History

Exploring Québec City's history can be an all-consuming pastime—and a rewarding one. The walk outlined here takes you through much of it, but feel free to pursue the Old City's inviting little detours.

OUTSIDE THE OLD CITY

The best place to begin a journey through the history of New France is at the end. Start your tour at the **Wolfe-Montcalm Monument,** on the far west side of the **Plains of Abraham.** It was here in 1759 that British general James Wolfe extinguished France's dreams of a North American empire and set off the English-French divergence that has both enriched and plagued Canada's history.

The Plains of Abraham was where the famous Battle of Québec (also called Battle of the Plains of Abraham) took place, in which General Wolfe's forces were victorious against Marquis de Montcalm's surprised French troops. Today this hilltop patch of green is a pleasant and expansive city park with trees, lawns, and meandering paths with sweeping views of the St. Lawrence River.

Make your way over to the Fortifications and the Old City via the northern side of the Plains of Abraham, along the **Grande Allée,** through the residential neighborhood of **Montcalm,** home to gorgeous 19th-century neo-Gothic and Queen Anne–style mansions and **Hôtel du Parlement.**

THE FORTIFICATIONS

The end of the Grand Allée is Porte St-Louis. Turn right down côte de la Citadelle, which leads to **La Citadelle.** Something of a microcosm of Canada's sometimes contrarian cultural character, the fortress is home to the Royal 22nd Regiment, a crack military unit

A Walk through Québec City's History

HIGHLIGHTS
Exploring La Citadelle; leisurely strolling along the Terrasse Dufferin; walking along rue du Petit-Champlain in the Old City

WHERE TO START
The Wolfe-Montcalm Monument, on the far western side of the Plains of Abraham outside the walls of the city

LENGTH
About 3 km (2 miles)

WHERE TO END
On rue du Petit-Champlain, in the Lower Town section of the Old City

BEST TIME TO GO
A weekday summer morning

WORST TIME TO GO
A cold winter day

EDITOR'S CHOICE
Strolling along the tree-lined streets off Grande Allée in Montcalm; riding the funicular from Upper Town to Lower Town; standing in historic Place Royale

that speaks French but dresses in the bearskin hats and red tunics of a British guards unit for ceremonial parades. Don't miss the daily Changing of the Guard ceremony.

UPPER TOWN

Beyond **Porte St-Louis,** you can imagine yourself in 17th- and 18th-century France. Steep-roofed houses with small windows crowd a tangle of narrow, curving streets and the rattle of horse-drawn carriages on ancient cobblestones adds to the illusion.

The **Maison Jacquet** on rue St-Louis looks exactly as it did when it was built in 1677, and the **Maison Kent** was once the home of Queen Victoria's father, the Duke of Kent. **Le Couvent des Ursulines** at 12 rue Donnacona has a museum featuring an exhibit of magnificent lace embroidery created by Ursuline nuns in the 19th and early 20th centuries.

Québec City's most famous building, the **Fairmont Le Château Frontenac,** is at the beginning of **Terrasse Dufferin,** which is worth a stroll for sweeping views of the St. Lawrence River before you get on the funicular to reach Lower Town.

LOWER TOWN

Once at the base of this cable-connected elevator, you end up in the 17th-century **Maison Louis-Jolliet,** built before he paddled off to explore the Mississippi River. From here, it's a short walk to **Place Royale,** a square graced by a statue of the Sun King Louis XIV, and considered to be the birthplace of New France. The last jaunt is along **rue du Petit-Champlain,** the oldest street in the city, lined with shops and cafés.

Montréal and Québec City's Best Walking Tours

Beyond the Bagel Tour. Montréal's renowned Jewish cuisine comes alive in Mile End and Plateau with this walking tour led by the Museum of Jewish Montréal. Delve into traditional and modern flavors, uncover historical secrets, and savor classics like smoked meat and bagels. ✉ *5220 boul. St-Laurent, Mile End* ☎ *514/840-9300* ⊕ *museemontrealjuif.ca/beyond-the-bagel* 🖳 *Starting at C$95* Ⓜ *Mont-Royal.*

Circuit des Fantômes du Vieux-Montréal *(Old Montréal Ghost Trail).* From May to October, you can join these street theater walking tours through the Old City, where a host of spirits are said to still roam the streets. Tours begin at 8:30 pm and the haunted journey lasts about 90 minutes. Reservations are required. ✉ *360 rue St-François-Xavier, Old Montréal* ☎ *514/844-4021* ⊕ *fantomesmontreal.com* 🖳 *Starting at C$29* Ⓜ *Place-d'Armes.*

Ghost Tours of Québec. Costumed actors lead ghoulish 90-minute evening tours of Québec City murders, executions, and ghost sightings. The tours are available in English or French, from May through October. After the walk, you can buy a copy of *Ghost Stories of Québec,* which has stories not told on the tours. ✉ *34 boul. Champlain, Lower Town* ☎ *855/692-9770* ⊕ *ghosttoursofquebec. com* 🖳 *Starting at C$25.*

Guidatour. Explore the historic, cultural, or architecturally heritage of diverse areas such as Old Montréal, the Underground City, the Christmas Secrets of Old Montréal, and the elite 19th-century

neighborhood known as the Golden Square Mile. Reservations are required. ✉ *360 rue St-François-Xavier, Suite 400, Old Montréal* ☎ *800/363-4021* ⊕ *www. guidatour.qc.ca/en* 🖳 *Starting at C$29* Ⓜ *Place-d'Armes.*

Local Food Tours. Discover the gourmet heritage of well-known and some lesser-known neighborhoods with these expert-led food tours that superbly weave history, gastronomy, and culture in these one-of-a-kind experiences. Offered in both Montréal and Québec City. ⊕ *localfoodtours.com* 🖳 *Starting at C$52.*

Spade and Palacio. Discover the hidden gems of Montréal on these highly curated, small-group guided tours. The two-hour Murals Tour, a colorful and vibrant walk down Canada's premier street art corridor, is truly a must. ✉ *3801 rue St-Denis, Suite B, The Plateau* ☎ *514/806-3263* ⊕ *spadeandpalacio.com* 🖳 *Starting at C$40* Ⓜ *Sherbrooke.*

Tours Voir Québec. This tour company offers English- and French-language (and Spanish from June to September) walking tours of the Old City. Other tours include a "Bury Your Dead" murder mystery tour based on the novels of Louise Penny, as well as a popular food tour with tastings at various establishments for C$55. Self-guided audio tours are also available. ✉ *12 rue Ste-Anne, Upper Town* ☎ *418/694-2001* ⊕ *www.toursvoirquebec.com* 🖳 *Starting at C$28.*

Contacts

Air

AIRLINE CONTACTS Air Canada. ☎ 888/247–2262 ⊕ www.aircanada. com. **American Airlines.** ☎ 800/433–7300 ⊕ www. aa.com. **Air Transat.** ⊕ www.airtransat.com. **Delta Airlines.** ☎ 800/221–1212 for U.S. reservations, 800/241–4141 for international reservations ⊕ www.delta.com. **Porter Airlines.** ☎ 888/619–8622 ⊕ www.flyporter.com.

AIRPORT INFORMATION Jean Lesage International Airport. (YQB). ⊠ 505 rue Principale, Québec City ☎ 418/640–3300, 877/769–2700 ⊕ www. aeroportdequebec.com. **Montréal–Pierre Elliott Trudeau International Airport.** (YUL). ⊠ 975 boul. Roméo-Vachon Nord, Dorval ☎ 800/465–1213, 514/633–3333 ⊕ www. admtl.com.

AIRPORT SECURITY ISSUES Canadian Air Transport Security Authority. ⊕ catsa-acsta.gc.ca.

GROUND TRANSPORTATION Société de transport de Montréal. ⊠ Montréal ☎ 514/786–4636 ⊕ www. stm.info. **Taxi Coop Québec.** ☎ 418/525–5191 ⊕ www. taxicoop-quebec.com.

Bicycle

BIXI. ⊠ Montréal ⊕ bixi. com/en.

Bus

Gare d'autocars de Montréal. ⊠ 1717 rue Berri, Montréal ☎ 514/842–2281 ⊕ www. gamtl.com. **Gare du Palais Bus Station.** ⊠ 320 rue Abraham-Martin, Québec City ☎ 418/525–3000 ⊕ www.orleansexpress. com. **Greyhound Lines.** ☎ 800/231–2222 in the U.S., 800/661–8747 in Canada ⊕ www.greyhound. com. **Limocar.** ☎ 866/692–8899, 819/562–8899 ⊕ www.limocar.ca. **Orléans Express.** ☎ 833/449–6444, 450/640–1477 ⊕ www. orleansexpress.com.

Car

EMERGENCY SERVICES CAA. ☎ 800/222–4357, 800/686–9243, 800/222–4357 Roadside assistance ⊕ www.caaquebec.com.

MAJOR RENTAL AGENCIES Alamo. ☎ 844/357–5138 ⊕ www.alamo.com. **Avis.** ☎ 800/879–2847 ⊕ www.avis.com. **Budget.** ☎ 800/268–8900 from Canada, 800/218–7992 from U.S. ⊕ www.budget. com. **Hertz.** ☎ 800/654–3001 ⊕ www.hertz.com.

National Car Rental. ☎ 844/382–6875 in the U.S., 844/307-8014 in Canada ⊕ www.national-car.com.

Emergencies

FOREIGN EMBASSIES AND CONSULATES U.S. Consulate General. ⊠ 1155 rue St-Alexandre, Montréal ☎ 514/398–9695 ⊕ ca.usembassy.gov/ embassy-consulates/ montreal. **U.S. Consulate General.** ⊠ 2 pl. Terrasse Dufferin, Québec City ☎ 418/692–2095 ⊕ ca. usembassy.gov/embassy-consulates/quebec. **U.S. Embassy.** ⊠ 490 Sussex Dr., Ottawa ☎ 613/688–5335 ⊕ ca.usembassy.gov.

HOSPITALS Centre Hospitalier Universitaire de Québec. ⊠ 2705 boul. Laurier, Ste-Foy ☎ 418/525–4444 ⊕ www. chudequebec.ca. **Centre Hospitalier Universitaire de Québec, Pavillon Hôtel-Dieu.** ⊠ 11 côte du Palais, Upper Town ☎ 418/525–4444, 418/691–5042 emergencies ⊕ www. chudequebec.ca/centre-hospitaliers/l'hotel-dieu-de-quebec.aspx. **Montréal General Hospital (McGill University Health Centre).** ⊠ 1650 av. Cedar, Downtown ☎ 514/934–1934 ⊕ www.muhc.ca/ mgh Ⓜ Guy-Concordia.

Contacts

Lodging

BED AND BREAKFASTS
Association de l'Agrotourisme et du Tourisme Gourmand du Québec. ☎ 514/252–3138 ⊕ www.agrotourismeettourismegourmand.com. **BB Canada.** ⊕ www.bbcanada.com. **Bed and Breakfasts Québec.** ⊕ www.bedbreakfastsquebec.com. **Vrbo.** ☎ 877/202–9331 ⊕ www.vrbo.com.

$ Money

CURRENCY CONVERSION
Oanda.com. ⊕ www.oanda.com. **XE.com.** ⊕ www.xe.com.

🪙 Taxes

INFORMATION Canada Customs and Revenue Agency. ✉ Summerside Tax Centre, 275 Pope Rd., Suite 104, Summerside ☎ 800/668–4748 in Canada, 902/432–5608 ⊕ www.ccra-adrc.gc.ca.

🧭 Tours

CONTACTS Bateau-Mouche. ☎ 514/849–9952, 800/361–9952 ⊕ www.bateaumouche.ca.
Croisières AML. ✉ 10 rue Dalhousie, Lower Town

☎ 866/856–6668 ⊕ www.croisieresaml.com. **Fitz Montréal.** ✉ 1251 rue Rachel Est, The Plateau ⊕ fitzmontreal.com Ⓜ Mont-Royal. **Gray Line.** ✉ Montréal ☎ 800/472–9546 ⊕ www.grayline.com. **Unitours.** ☎ 800/267-8687 ⊕ www.toursvieuxquebec.com/en/home.

🚆 Train

INFORMATION Amtrak. ☎ 800/872–7245 ⊕ www.amtrak.com. **Train de Charlevoix.** ☎ 844/737–3282, 418/240–4124 ⊕ www.traindecharlevoix.com. **VIA Rail Canada.** ☎ 888/842–7245 from U.S. ⊕ www.viarail.ca.

📍 Visitor Information

CONTACTS Association Touristique des Cantons de l'Est. ✉ 20 rue Don Bosco Sud, Sherbrooke ☎ 866/963–2020 administration, 800/355–5755 ⊕ www.cantonsdelest.com. **Association Touristique des Laurentides.** ✉ La Porte-du-Nord rest area, Autoroute des Laurentides, Exit 51 ☎ 450/224–7007, 800/561–6673 ⊕ www.laurentides.com.

Association Touristique Régionale de Charlevoix. ✉ 495 boul. de Comporté, La Malbaie ☎ 418/665–4454, 800/667–2276 ⊕ www.tourisme-charlevoix.com. **Canadian Tourism Commission.** ☎ 604/638–8300 ⊕ www.travelcanada.ca. **Centre d'Interpretation de la Côte-de-Beaupré.** (Beaupré Coast Interpretation Center). ✉ 7976 av. Royale, C.P. 40, Château-Richer ☎ 418/824–3677, 877/824–3677.

Centre Info-Touriste. ✉ 1255 rue Peel, Suite 100, Downtown ☎ 514/873–2015, 877/266–5687 ⊕ www.bonjourquebec.com Ⓜ Peel or Bonaventure. **Parks Canada.** ☎ 819/420–9486, 888/773–8888 ⊕ www.pc.gc.ca. **Québec City Tourist Information.** ✉ 12 rue Ste-Anne, Upper Town ☎ 418/641–6290, 877/266–5687 ⊕ www.quebec-cite.com/en. **Sépaq.** ☎ 800/665–6527 ⊕ www.sepaq.com. **Terroir & Saveurs.** ✉ Montréal ☎ 514/252–3138 ⊕ www.terroiretsaveurs.com. **Tourisme-Montréal.** ☎ 877/266–5687 ⊕ www.mtl.org/en/contact-us. **Tourisme Québec.** ✉ 1001 rue du Square Dorchester, Suite 100, C.P. 979, Downtown ☎ 877/266–5687, 514/873–2015 ⊕ www.bonjourquebec.com.

Chapter 3

MONTRÉAL

Updated by
Elizabeth Warkentin

3

 Sights
★★★★★

 Restaurants
★★★★★

 Hotels
★★★★★

 Shopping
★★★★★

 Nightlife
★★★★★

WELCOME TO MONTRÉAL

TOP REASONS TO GO

★ **Browse public markets:** Amble through Marché Atwater, one of the city's oldest public markets, and the bustling Marché Jean-Talon, the largest open-air market in North America.

★ **Check out the nightlife:** Enjoy Canada's unrivaled party capital at famous nightlife spots that include rue Crescent, boulevard St-Laurent, and the Latin Quarter, as well as Old Montréal and the Village, Montréal's epicenter of gay life.

★ **Get a dose of multiculturalism:** Explore ethnic neighborhoods and sample global cuisine.

★ **Celebrate Jazz Fest:** Montréal's biggest musical event, Jazz Fest, happens every year from late June to early July. Reserve early: hotels book up months in advance.

★ **Stroll Old Montréal:** Historic Vieux-Montréal has cobblestoned streets, a great waterfront, fine restaurants and bed-and-breakfasts, and the Old Port, which buzzes with nightlife.

1 **Old Montréal (Vieux-Montréal).** The oldest part of the city.

2 **Downtown.** Montréal's largest shopping district.

3 **Westmount.** An affluent "suburb," or independent municipality within the city.

4 **The Latin Quarter.** People-watching is the order of the day here.

5 **The Village.** Lively, diverse, and great nightlife.

6 **The Plateau Mont-Royal and Mile End.** Trendy cafés and upscale boutiques and galleries.

7 **Outremont.** Chic fashion boutiques and stylish cafés.

8 **Little Italy.** All the best Italian pastry shops and grocery stores.

9 **Parc du Mont-Royal.** The Central Park of Montréal.

10 **Côte-des-Neiges.** A vibrant and ethnically diverse neighborhood.

11 **Hochelaga-Maisonneuve.** The site of the 1976 Olympics.

12 **Sud-Ouest and Lachine.** A magnet for creatives and foodies.

13 **The Islands.** Île Ste-Hélène and Île Notre-Dame.

KEY

Ⓜ Métro Stations

🚲 Route Verte Bike Route

LITTLE ITALY

8 Marché Jean-Talon

r. De Bellechasse

BEAUBIEN

av. du Parc

r. St-Denis

r. De St-Vallier

r. Boyer

OUTREMONT

OUTREMONT

7 rue Bernard

av. St-Viateur

blvd. St-Laurent

Côte-Ste-Catherine

ROSEMONT

UNIVERSITÉ-DE-MONTRÉAL

ÉDOUARD-MONTPETIT

blvd. Mont-Royal

av. Fairmont

av. Laurier

LAURIER

av. de Lorimier

Partenais

av. Papineau

1e Av.

r. de St-Joseph

LAURIER

MILE END

r. Villeneuve

MONT-ROYAL

6

r. Fabre

blvd. St-Joseph

Cimetière Mont-Royal

av. du Parc

av. du Mont-Royal

MONT-ROYAL

Route Verte Bike Route

r. De Biébeuf

r. de Lanaudière

Chemin Remembrance

Voie C. Houde

St-Urbain

r. Marie-Anne

THE PLATEAU

Parc Lafontaine

r. de Lorimier

r. Chapleau

Côte-des-Neiges

Parc du Mont-Royal

av. du Parc

r. Duluth

av. Papineau

Parc-Lafontaine

av. Calixa-Lavallée

r. Rachel

r. Hochelaga

r. Hogan

9

PARC DU MONT-ROYAL

av. Cedar

de Bullion

r. Laval

St-Denis

rue Berri

r. Roy

r. Fabre

r. Papineau

r. Sherbrooke

av. des Pins

av. Docteur-Penfield

r. Prince-Arthur

Jeanne-Mance

r. Milton

SHERBROOKE

r. Amherst

r. Beaudry

r. de Lorimier

Partenais

r. Bercy

r. Peel

PLACE-DES-ARTS

ST-LAURENT

r. Ontario

BERRI-UQÀM

BEAUDRY

FRONTENAC

ATWATER

GUY-CONCORDIA

PEEL

MCGILL

blvd. de Maisonneuve

PAPINEAU

r. Atwater

du Fort

r. St-Marc

r. St-Mathieu

r. Crescent

Beaver Hall

r. Ste-Catherine

HOCHELAGA-MAISONNEUVE

autoroute Ville-Marie

DOWNTOWN

2

blvd. René-Lévesque

THE VILLAGE

5

11

GEORGES-VANIER

LUCIEN-L'ALLIER

BONAVENTURE

SQ.-VICTORIA-OACI

CHINATOWN

de la Gauchetière

CHAMP-DE-MARS

4

LATIN QUARTER

autoroute Ville-Marie

r. Notre-Dame

côte du Beaver Hall

r. St-Jacques

r. St-Jacques

PL.-D'ARMES

1

OLD MONTRÉAL

Jacques-Cartier

Pont Jacques-Cartier

La Ronde

Lachine Canal

r. St-Patrick

r. Ctre

r. Island

r. Mullins

r. Shearer

r. Wellington

r. D'Hibernia

Peel

autoroute Bonaventure

r. Mill

OLD PORT

av. Pierre-Dupuy

Route Verte Bike Route

ÎLE STE-HÉLÈNE

JEAN-DRAPEAU

THE ISLANDS

13

Pont de la Concorde

Parc Jean-Drapeau

112

Parc Leber

St. Lawrence River

ÎLE NOTRE-DAME

Casino de Montréal

Parc Floral

15/20

Pont Victoria

20

0   1/2 mile

0   500 meters

Canada's second-most diverse metropolis, after Toronto, Montréal is an island city that favors style and happiness over order or even prosperity, a city where past and present intrude on each other daily. In some ways it resembles Vienna—well past its peak of power and glory, perhaps, yet still vibrant and grand.

But don't get the wrong idea. Montréal has always had a bit of an edge. During Prohibition, thirsty Americans headed north to the city on the St. Lawrence for booze, music, and a good time, and people still come for the same things. Summer festivals celebrate everything from comedy and French-language music and culture to the circus arts and fireworks, and, of course, jazz. And on those rare weeks when there isn't a planned event, the party continues. Clubs and sidewalk cafés are abuzz from late afternoon to the early hours of the morning. Montréal is also a city that knows how to mix it up even when it's 20 below zero. Rue St-Denis is almost as lively on a Saturday night in January as it is in July, and the festival Montréal en Lumière, or Montréal Illuminated, enlivens the dreary days of February with concerts, balls, and fine food.

Montréal takes its name from Parc du Mont-Royal, a stubby plug of tree-covered igneous rock that rises 764 feet above the surrounding cityscape.

Although its height is unimpressive, "the Mountain" forms one of Canada's finest urban parks, and views from the Chalet du Mont-Royal atop the hill provide an excellent orientation to the city's layout and major landmarks.

Old Montréal is home to museums, the municipal government, and the magnificent Basilique Notre-Dame-de-Montréal within its network of narrow cobblestoned streets. Although Montréal's centre-ville, or Downtown, bustles like many other major cities on the surface, it's active below street level as well, in the Underground City—the underground levels of shopping malls and food courts connected by pedestrian tunnels and the city's subway system, or métro. Residential Plateau Mont-Royal and trendy neighborhoods like Griffintown/ St-Henri thrum with the kinetic energy of restos, boîtes de nuit (nightclubs), bars, art galleries, and cafés. The greener areas of town include Parc du Mont-Royal, Parc Lafontaine, and the Jardin Botanique.

Planning

When to Go

To avoid crowds and below-freezing temperatures, Montréal's short spring, which typically starts in late April or early May but doesn't normally end until early June, is ideal. Fall is gorgeous—and touristy—when the leaves change color, so expect traffic on weekends. Early September after Labor Day until the end of the month is another good time to visit.

Planning Your Time

Put Old Montréal and the Old Port at the top of your sightseeing list. Spend a full day walking around this area, head back to your hotel for a late-day break, and return for dinner. Aside from finding several of the city's top restaurants here, city hall, Marché Bonsecours, and other grand and charming buildings are illuminated at night. Also dedicate a full day to wandering around Downtown, rue Ste-Catherine, and Chinatown. Visit the Latin Quarter and the area around McGill University—both have a busy student ambience, but shouldn't be dismissed as places where only under-twenties frequent. Even if you're too tired to go out on the town, take a nighttime walk down rue Crescent or rue St-Denis for a taste of the city's joie de vivre.

For browsing, shopping, and dining out, explore Outremont, Mile End/the Plateau, Griffintown/St-Henri, and Westmount. For kid-friendly activities, check out Hochelaga-Maisonneuve and the Islands for the Biôdôme, La Ronde, and the Jardin Botanique.

A city landmark not to miss is St. Joseph's Oratory, Canada's largest church, in the west end of the city.

Getting Here and Around

AIR

Montréal's Trudeau International Airport (also often referred to by its previous name, Dorval) is about 24 km (15 miles) west of the city center.

GROUND TRANSPORTATION

The easiest way to get in is to take a cab for a fixed fare of C$48.40, unless your hotel provides transportation. The cheapest way to get into town is the 747 express bus, a 24-hour shuttle service from the airport to the main bus terminal with stops at the Lionel-Groulx métro station and several additional stops near Downtown hotels. The one-way fare is C$11 (accepted in coins only)—with 24 hours of unlimited bus and métro travel included in the price. Plan on it taking about a half hour outside rush hour to get to Downtown from the airport. Another alternative is the 204 bus, with a one-way fare of C$3.25, taking you from the Dorval train terminal straight to the airport.

BICYCLE

An extensive network of bike paths and (mostly) relatively flat terrain means Montréal is ideal for bicycles. The BIXI (a contraction of "bicycle" and "taxi") system—with more than 10,000 sturdy aluminum-frame bikes (including 2,600 electric BIXIs) and almost 800 credit card–operated stands throughout the city (or you can download the app on your phone)—makes two-wheel exploring easy. There's a one-way unlocking fee of C$1.25, plus C15¢ a minute for a regular bike and C30¢ a minute for an e-bike.

CAR

If you're driving in to the city, take I–91 or I–89 from Vermont, I–87 from New York, and Autoroute 20 (also known as Autoroute Jean-Lesage) from Québec City.

Having a car Downtown isn't ideal—garages are expensive and on-street parking can be a hassle. The city has a diligent tow-away and fine system for double-parking or sitting in no-stopping zones during rush hour, and ticket costs are steep. In residential neighborhoods, beware of alternate-side-of-the-street-parking rules and resident-only parking. In resident-only parking, residents' cars will bear a special sticker in the upper left-hand corner of the back window. In winter, street plows are ruthless in dealing with parked cars in their way. If they don't tow them, they'll bury them.

PUBLIC TRANSPORTATION

The Société de transport de Montréal (STM) operates both the métro (subway) and the bus system. The métro is quiet (it runs on rubber tires), and will get you to most of the places you want to visit. For those few places that are more than a 15-minute walk from the nearest métro station, bus connections are available.

Métro hours on the Orange, Green, Blue, and Yellow Lines are weekdays 5:30 am to 12:30 am and weekends 5:30 am to 12:30, 1, or 1:30 am (it varies by line). Trains run every three minutes or so on the most crowded lines—Orange and Green—at rush hours. The cash fare for a single ticket is C$3.75. One- and three-day unlimited-use cards are also available for C$11 and C$21.25.

TAXI

Taxis in Montréal all run on the same rate: C$4.10 minimum and C$2.05 per kilometer (roughly ½ mile). They're usually easy to hail on the street, outside train stations, in shopping areas, and at major hotels. You can also call a dispatcher to send a driver to pick you up at no extra cost. A taxi is available if the white or orange plastic rooftop light is on.

⇨ *For more information on getting here and around, see Travel Smart.*

Activities

Most Montrealers would probably claim they hate winter, but the city is full of cold-weather sports venues—skating rinks, cross-country ski trails, and toboggan runs—that see plenty of action. During warm-weather months, residents head for the tennis courts, bicycle trails, golf courses, and two lakes for boating and swimming.

You don't have to travel far from Montréal to find good downhill skiing or snowboarding. The many ski centers in the Laurentians and Eastern Townships are within an hour's drive from the city. As for cross-country, excellent trails can be found right in Parc du Mont-Royal, or on the Islands (Île Ste-Hélène and Île Notre-Dame).

Despite the often bitter winters (or perhaps because of them), Montréal has fallen in love with the bicycle, with enthusiasts cycling year-round. More than 900 km (372 miles) of bike paths crisscross the metropolitan area, and bikes are welcome on the first car of métro trains during off-peak hours. And with winters becoming increasingly milder, BIXI decided, in 2023, to keep bikes available for rental year-round.

The city is truly passionate about Canada's national sport, hockey. If you're here during hockey season, try to catch a Montréal Canadiens game at Centre Bell, or at the very least find yourself a good sports bar.

Where Should I Stay?

	Neighborhood Vibe	Pros	Cons
Old Montréal	Cobblestone streets, boutique hotels, designer clothes, and historic architecture; very touristy, especially at the eastern end, although it quiets down at night.	Quaint; easy access to bike paths; nice to walk along the water-front; hip restaurants and mixology options are in the Old Port.	Can be desolate in the late evening outside hotel lobbies; parking is scarce; depending on the exact location, métro and bus access can be limited.
Downtown	Montréal's center for hustle and bustle, mostly on rue Sherbrooke, rue Ste-Catherine, and boulevard de Maisonneuve.	Extremely convenient; big-name hotel chains and luxury hotels; central location; pools; garage parking; perfect for families as well as business travelers; near the outdoor Quartier des Spectacles.	Traffic congestion is relentless; not as many dining options as other neighborhoods, and what is there tends to be at either extreme—fast food or very pricey (and not always worth it).
The Latin Quarter	Hopping with university kids and moviegoers, this area boasts a crazy mix of cafés, bars, handmade-chocolate shops, and folks carrying library books.	Festival central; easy métro access; right between the Plateau and Downtown; local characters abound.	Uneven gentrification means dodgy pockets; litter; bad roads.
The Plateau Mont-Royal and Mile End	Scattered auberges, Airbnb rentals, and B&Bs host the artsy crowd and academics, with streets filled with local boutiques and hip restaurants; perfect for strolling.	Stumbling distance to the best bistros and pubs; unique shopping that focuses on local designers and craftspeople.	Limited métro and taxi access; limited hotel options; can be noisy at night; panhandlers galore.

3

Montréal **PLANNING**

Hotels

Montréal is a city of neighborhoods with distinct personalities, which creates a broad spectrum of options when it comes to deciding on a place to stay. The Downtown core has many of the big chain hotels you'd find in any city, but also several luxury hotels, such as the Ritz-Carlton and the Four Seasons. Old Montréal, the Plateau, and other surrounding areas have unique auberges (inns) and boutique hotels.

Most of the major hotels in Downtown—the ones with big meeting rooms, swimming pools, and several bars and restaurants—are ideal for those who want all the facilities along with easy access to the department stores and malls on rue Ste-Catherine, the museums of the Golden Square Mile, and nightlife on rues Crescent and de la Montagne. If you want something a little more historical, consider renting a room in one of the dozen or so boutique hotels that occupy the centuries-old buildings lining the cobbled streets of Old Montréal. Most of them offer all the conveniences along with the added charm of stone walls, casement windows, and period-style furnishings.

If your plans include shopping expeditions to avenue Mont-Royal and rue Laurier with maybe a few late nights at the jazz bars and dance clubs of boulevard St-Laurent and rue St-Denis, then the place to bed down is in one of Plateau Mont-Royal's small but comfortable hotels. Room rates in the area tend to be quite reasonable, but be careful: the hotels right in the middle of the action—on rue St-Denis, for example—can be noisy, especially if you get a room fronting the street.

⇨ *Hotel reviews have been shortened. For full information, visit Fodors.com. Hotel prices are the lowest cost of a standard double room in high season.*

WHAT IT COSTS in Canadian Dollars			
$	$$	$$$	$$$$
HOTELS			
under C$200	C$200–C$300	C$301–C$400	over C$400

Nightlife

If nightlife in Montréal could be distilled into a cocktail, it would be one part sophisticated New York club scene (with the accompanying pretension), one part Parisian joie de vivre (and, again, a dash of snobbery), and one part Barcelonese stamina (which keeps the clubs booming until dawn).

Hot spots are peppered throughout the city. There are compact clusters along rue Crescent, boulevard St-Laurent (known as "The Main"), avenue Mont-Royal, and rue St-Denis. Prominent rue Ste-Catherine plows through town, connecting most of these nighttime niches, and farther east, near Beaudry métro station,

it becomes the main drag for the Village, also called the Gay Village. For whatever reason, the streets named after saints contain most of the clubs: rue Ste-Catherine, boulevard St-Laurent, rue St-Paul, and rue St-Denis. The Old Port/Old Montréal is currently Montréal's hottest neighborhood. Before COVID, a steady stream of chic venues were opening in this cobblestoned district.

Montréal's nightlife swings with a robust passion. From the early evening "5 à 7" (*cinq à sept*) after-work cocktail circuit, to the slightly later concerts and supper clubs (restaurant–dance club hybrids where people dance on the tables after eating off them), on into the even later dance club scene, all tastes, cultural backgrounds, and legal ages join the melee. Clubbing is, to say the least, huge in Montréal, with some restaurants even installing discotheques in their basements.

The bars stop serving around 3 am and shut down shortly thereafter (with the exception of sanctioned "after-hour" haunts). On the weekends, expect them to be packed to the gills until closing. The club scene picks up right after the bars close, and then extends until dawn.

Performing Arts

Montréal is the home of nearly a dozen professional companies and several important theater schools, but there's also a lively English-language theater scene and one of the few remaining Yiddish theaters in North America. As for venues, the Quartier des Spectacles is a 70-acre entertainment district in Downtown with stages for outdoor performances and nearly 80 venues for dance, music, theater, and art.

For a city its size, Montréal offers a remarkable number of opportunities for fans of classical music to get their fill, from operas and symphonies to string quartets.

As for dance, there are several modern dance companies of note, including Montréal Danse and Québec's premier ballet company, Les Grands Ballets Canadiens.

Restaurants

Montréal has one of North America's most cosmopolitan restaurant scenes, with trendy new eateries popping up regularly, their menus heavily influenced by flavors from around the globe, and often with an added touch of French or Québecois flair.

Montréal's top dining destinations are plentiful, especially as young chefs move to hip destinations in Mile End, the Plateau, and the Griffintown/St-Henri areas to open new restaurants. Downtown, convenient to many hotels, finds most of its restaurants clustered between rues Guy and Peel and on the side streets that run between boulevard René-Lévesque and rue Sherbrooke. Rue St-Denis and boulevard St-Laurent, between rues Sherbrooke and Jean-Talon, have long been convenient and fashionable areas, with everything from sandwich shops to high-price gourmet shrines. Old Montréal, too, has a collection of well-regarded restaurants, most of them clustered on rue St-Paul, avenue McGill, and place Jacques-Cartier.

You can usually order à la carte, but make sure to look for the table d'hôte, a two-to-four-course package deal. It's often more economical, offers interesting specials, and may also take less time to prepare. For a splurge, consider a *menu dégustation*, a five-to-seven-course tasting menu that generally includes soup, salad, fish, sorbet (sherbet, to cleanse the palate), a meat dish, dessert, and coffee or tea. A menu dégustation for two, along with a good bottle of wine, will cost around C$250.

Most restaurants will have an English menu or, at the very least, a bilingual menu—but some may only be in French. If you don't understand what a dish is, don't be too shy to ask; a good server will be happy to explain. If you feel brave enough to order in French, remember that in Montréal an *entrée* is an appetizer, and what Americans call an entrée is a *plat principal,* or main dish.

⇨ *Restaurant reviews have been shortened. For full information, visit Fodors. com. Restaurant prices are the average cost of a main course at dinner or, if dinner is not served, at lunch.*

WHAT IT COSTS in Canadian Dollars			
$	$$	$$$	$$$$
RESTAURANTS			
under C$12	C$12–C$20	C$21–C$30	over C$30

Shopping

Montrealers *magasinent* (shop) with a vengeance, whether they're scurrying down busy rue Ste-Catherine in Downtown, checking out department store bargains, hunting for Danish mid-century antiques in the Gay Village, browsing designer wares on St-Laurent, or sampling gourmet eats at one of the city's markets. For many locals, doing the *magasinage* is practically an art form.

Yet, even before COVID-19 struck, one of North America's top shopping cities was in a state of flux. Where, until recently, boulevard St-Laurent and rue St-Denis were the "it" streets to shop, this honor is now shared with Old Montréal. In the decade before the pandemic, Montréal's patron saint of shopping streets, Ste-Catherine, was undergoing a metamorphosis as a significant cohort of young, educated professionals moved into Downtown condos and retailers scrambled to meet their needs

Money-Saving Tips

There are several good ways to save money during your trip. If you'll be visiting three or more of the city's museums, consider buying a museum pass for $C75 for three consecutive days or the Excursion+ card for an adult and up to four children (rates vary depending on the number of children. ⊕ *museesmontreal.org/en/ museums-cards*.

Tourist transit passes, which give you unlimited access to the transit system, also may be worth your while; one-day passes are C$11, while three-day passes will set you back C$21.25. Weekly passes cost C$30, but they're loaded electronically on a special nonrefundable Opus card that costs C$6. ⊕ *www.stm.info/en#view-tariffs*.

Hitting the town earlier in the evening is a good way to save as well, by stopping into cafés and bars for food and drink specials offered during cinq à sept (5 to 7), Québec's happy hour.

and tastes. Along with the pandemic, the changing face of retail and the prevalence of online shopping have also contributed to the transformation of Ste-Catherine and other Downtown streets, with the corresponding downward slide of many traditional brick-and-mortar stores. That being said, Montréal's most important shopping street has also welcomed new arrivals such as the trendy Vancouver-based Aritzia; Lolë, Montréal's answer to Lululemon; an elegant Club Monaco spread out over two floors of the Beaux-Arts-style Dominion Square Building; and a branch of hip Montréal brand Frank and Oak, initially an online-only retailer. And, after years of talk, the city's two luxury department stores, Ogilvy and Holt Renfrew, merged in early 2020 into one giant upmarket department store directly attached to the stylish and impossibly modern Four Seasons Hotel, opened in summer 2019.

Meanwhile, the iconic rue Ste-Catherine is currently in Phase 2 of a major infrastructure and street design facelift. According to the City of Montréal website, the usually congested thoroughfare will consist of only a single traffic lane, with wide sidewalks on either side and the addition of numerous trees, placing pedestrians at the heart of the new public space. The plan is also to create cool spaces for locals during the city's oppressive heat waves by connecting and consolidating existing green spaces in the Downtown core and increasing plant cover. Plans may also include heated sidewalks in winter, an idea that has been under discussion for many years.

Old Montréal (Vieux-Montréal)

Old Montréal, which was once enclosed by thick stone walls, is the oldest part of the city. It runs roughly from the waterfront in the south to ruelle des Fortifications in the north and from rue McGill in the west to rue Berri in the east. The churches and chapels here stand as a testament to the religious fervor that inspired the French settlers who landed here in 1642 to build a "Christian commonwealth" under the leadership of Paul de Chomedey, Sieur de Maisonneuve, and the indomitable Jeanne Mance, a French nurse. Stone warehouses and residences are reminders of how quickly the fur trade commercialized that lofty ideal and made the city one of the most prosperous in 18th-century Nouvelle-France. And finally, the financial houses along rue St-Jacques, bristling with Victorian ornamentation, recall the days when Montrealers controlled virtually all the wealth of the young Dominion of Canada.

History and good looks aside, however, Old Montréal still works for a living. Stockbrokers and shipping companies continue to operate out of the old financial district. The city's largest newspaper, *La Presse,* has its offices here. Lawyers in black gowns hurry through the streets to plead cases at the Palais de Justice or the Cour d'Appel; the city council meets in the Second Empire city hall on rue Notre-Dame; and tech innovators and creatives in film, animation, visual effects, and video gaming hustle off to meetings in airy lofts and ornate coworking spaces.

GETTING HERE AND AROUND

The easiest way to get from Downtown to Old Montréal is aboard Bus 515, a shuttle that provides a quick direct link to several sites in the Old City and Old Port. It runs from 7 am to midnight on weekdays and until 1 am on weekends. You can also take the métro's Orange Line to the Place-d'Armes and Square-Victoria stations, or you can walk, but the primary routes from Downtown go through some drab and somewhat seedy, although not especially dangerous, areas. If you feel like biking, it's better to rent a BIXI bicycle at a Downtown stand and drop it off at one in Old Montréal. Biking to Old Montréal is a breeze because it's all downhill, but the return trip to is a challenging workout, unless you can snag an e-bike.

Taxis can whisk you here from Downtown in about 10 minutes.

The best way to get around the Old City is on foot, but wear good shoes because the cobbles can be hard on the feet.

TIMING

Having enough time to see the sights, stroll around, and try some of the area's notable restaurants means dedicating at least one day. If it's your first time in the city and you're only here for an extended weekend, consider staying in one of Old Montréal's auberges or boutique hotels.

◉ Sights

★ **Basilique Notre-Dame-de-Montréal** (*Our Lady of Montréal Basilica*)
CHURCH | Few churches in North America are as wow-inducing as Notre-Dame. Everything about the Gothic Revival–style church, which opened in 1829, seems designed to make you gasp—from the 228-foot twin towers out front to the tens of thousands of 24-karat gold stars that stud the soaring blue ceiling.

Nothing in a city renowned for churches matches Notre-Dame for sheer grandeur—or noisemaking capacity: its 12-ton brass bell is the largest in North America, and its 7,000-pipe Casavant organ can make the walls tremble. The pulpit is a work of art in itself, with an intricately curving staircase and fierce figures of Ezekiel and Jeremiah crouching at its base. The whole place is so overwhelming it's easy to miss such lesser features as the stained-glass windows from Limoges and the side altars dedicated to St. Marguerite d'Youville, Canada's first native-born saint; St. Marguerite Bourgeoys, Canada's first schoolteacher; and a group of Sulpician priests martyred in Paris during the French Revolution.

For a peek at the magnificent baptistery, decorated with frescoes by Ozias Leduc, you'll have to tiptoe through the glassed-off prayer room in the northwest corner of the church. Every year dozens of brides—including Céline Dion, in 1994—march up the aisle of Chapelle Notre-Dame-du-Sacré-Coeur (Our Lady of the Sacred Heart Chapel), behind the main altar, to exchange vows with their

Did You Know?

In the evening, the nave of Basilique Notre-Dame-de-Montréal is darkened for *Aura*, a light-and-sound show that depicts the city's history and showcases the church's art.

grooms before a huge modern bronze sculpture that you either love or hate.

Notre-Dame is an active house of worship, so dress accordingly. The chapel can't be viewed weekdays during the 12:15 pm mass, and is often closed Saturday for weddings. ■TIP➔ Don't miss the 45-minute multimedia spectacle, *Aura*, which celebrates the basilica's exquisite features through light and sound. See website for schedule (⊕ *www.aurabasilique-montreal.com/en*). ✉ *110 rue Notre-Dame Ouest, Old Montréal* ☎ *514/842–2925, 866/842–2925 for Aura tickets* ⊕ *www. basiliquenotredame.ca/en* ✆ *Self-guided tour C$15, multimedia show Aura C$34* ⌖ *Reserve online or by phone* Ⓜ *Place-d'Armes.*

Centre des Sciences de Montréal

CHILDREN'S MUSEUM | FAMILY | You—or more likely, your kids—can design an energy-efficient bike, create a television news report, explore the impact that manufacturing one T-shirt has on the environment, find out what it's like to ride a unicycle 20 feet above the ground, create an animated film, or just watch an IMAX movie on a giant screen at Montréal's interactive science center. Games, puzzles, and hands-on experiments make it an ideal place for rainy days or even fair ones. The center also has a bistro serving light meals, a coffee and pastry shop, and a food court. ✉ *Quai King Edward, Old Montréal* ☎ *514/496–4724, 877/496–4724* ⊕ *www.centredessciencesdemontreal.com* ✆ *Exhibitions C$27, IMAX C$12.75* Ⓜ *Place-d'Armes.*

Chapelle Notre-Dame-de-Bon-Secours (*Our Lady of Perpetual Help Chapel*)

CHURCH | Mariners have been popping into Notre-Dame-de-Bon-Secours for centuries to kneel before a little 17th-century statue of the Virgin Mary and pray for a safe passage—or give thanks for one. Often, they've expressed their gratitude by leaving votive lamps in the shape of small ships, many of which still hang from the barrel-vaulted ceiling. This is

why most Montrealers call the chapel the Église des Matelots (the Sailors' Church), and why many people still stop by to say a prayer and light a candle before leaving on a long trip.

These days, the statue of Our Lady of Perpetual Help guards the remains of St. Marguerite Bourgeoys, who had the original chapel built in 1657 and is entombed in the side altar next to the east wall of the chapel. The current chapel dates from 1771; a renovation project in 1998 revealed some beautiful 18th-century murals that had been hidden under layers of paint.

The 69-step climb to the top of the steeple is worth the effort for the glorious view of the angels overlooking the harbor as is the steep climb down to the archaeological excavations under the chapel for a glimpse into the history of the chapel and the neighborhood. The dig is accessible through the adjacent Musée Marguerite Bourgeoys, which also has exhibits on the life of St. Marguerite and the daily lives of the colonists she served. ✉ *400 rue St-Paul Est, Old Montréal* ☎ *514/282–8670* ⊕ *marguerite-bourgeoys.org/en* ✆ *Museum (includes archaeological site) and tower C$14, chapel free* ⊘ *Closed Mon. mid-Oct.–mid-May* Ⓜ *Champ-de-Mars.*

Centre PHI pour l'Art Contemporain

ART GALLERY | Currently housed in two heritage buildings, this nonprofit organization aims to showcase compelling contemporary art from around the world. The foundation presents two to three major exhibitions a year in addition to a series of public events, special collaborative projects, and a forward-thinking education program. A free app takes you through the exhibits, and podcasts provide a fascinating look at the artists themselves. ■TIP➔ Check the website or call before you visit as the Fondation PHI closes regularly for installations. PHI will have a new space in 2026, consolidating the PHI Foundation and the PHI Centre under one roof.

Old Montréal
(Vieux-Montréal)

Sights ▼

1 Basilique Notre-Dame-de-Montréal.............. E6
2 Centre des Sciences de Montréal F7
3 Centre PHI pour l'Art Contemporain D6
4 Chapelle Notre-Dame-de-Bon-Secours I5
5 Hôtel de Ville H5
6 Maison St-Gabriel A9
7 Marché Bonsecours ... H6
8 Musée d'Archéologie et d'Histoire Pointe-à-Callière (PAC) D7
9 Musée du Château Ramezay H5
10 Old Port H7
11 Place d'Armes E5
12 Place de la Grande-Paix............. D7
13 Place Jacques-Cartier H5
14 Place Royale E6
15 Square Victoria B4

Restaurants ▼

1 Bloom C7
2 Brasserie 701............. E5
3 Brit & Chips.............. B6
4 Club Chasse et Pêche H5
5 Garde Manger D6
6 Le Cartet B8
7 Le Serpent............... A7
8 Monarque B5
9 Olive + Gourmando C6
10 Restaurant Helena...... B6
11 SeaSalt................... E6
12 Toqué!.................... C4

Quick Bites ▼

1 Crew Collective and Café...... C5
2 Le Petit Dep D6
3 Pâtisserie Végania...... D5

Hotels ▼

1 Auberge du Vieux-Port G6
2 Hôtel Bonaparte D6
3 Hôtel Épik Montréal D6
4 Hôtel Gault............... C6
5 Hôtel Nelligan............ E6
6 Hôtel St. Paul............ B7
7 Hôtel Uville D7
8 Hôtel William Gray...... G5
9 InterContinental Montréal.................. C4
10 Le Petit Hôtel............. D6
11 Le Place d'Armes Hôtel and Suites E5
12 Le Saint-Sulpice E6
13 LHotel C5
14 SpringHill Suites by Marriott............... F5
15 W Montréal............... B4

✉ *451 rue St-Jean, Old Montréal*
☎ *514/225-0525, 855/526-8888* ⊕ *phi. ca/en/foundation* 🎟 *Exhibition prices vary, otherwise free* 🕙 *Closed Mon. and Tues.* ☞ *Tickets can be purchased online or by phone at 514/225-0525.* Ⓜ *Square-Victoria.*

Hôtel de Ville (*City Hall*)

GOVERNMENT BUILDING | President Charles de Gaulle of France marked Canada's centennial celebrations in 1967 by standing on the central balcony of Montréal's ornate city hall on July 24 and shouting "*Vive le Québec libre*" ("Long live free Québec"), much to the delight of the separatist movement and to the horror of the federal government that had invited him over in the first place. Perhaps he got carried away because he felt so at home: the Second Empire–style city hall, built in 1878, is modeled after the one in Tours, France. ✉ *275 rue Notre-Dame Est, Old Montréal* ☎ *514/872–0311* ⊕ *www.ville. montreal.qc.ca* ☞ *The building has been closed to the public since 2019 due to a massive heritage restoration and modernization project. It is slated to reopen in late 2023.* Ⓜ *Champ-de-Mars.*

Maison St-Gabriel

HISTORIC HOME | Thick stone walls, a steep roof, and mullioned windows mark the Maison St-Gabriel as one of Montréal's rare surviving 17th-century houses. But it's the interior and the furnishings that will sweep you back to the colonial days when St. Marguerite Bourgeoys and the religious order she founded used this house to train *les filles du roy* (king's daughters) in the niceties of home management. Les filles were young women without family or fortune but plenty of spunk who volunteered to cross the Atlantic in leaky boats to become the wives and mothers of New France. It wasn't an easy life, as the Maison's hard narrow beds, primitive utensils, and drafty rooms attest—but it had its rewards, and the prize at the end was a respectable, settled life. St. Marguerite also had some

state-of-the-art domestic equipment— the latest in looms and butter churns, labor-saving spit turners for roasting meat, and an ingenious granite sink with a drainage system that piped water straight out to the garden. Located on the little island of New France and deep in the gentrifying working-class neighborhood of Pointe-St-Charles, Maison St-Gabriel is off the beaten path, but it's well worth a 10-minute taxi ride from Old Montréal. ✉ *2146 pl. Dublin, Pointe-St-Charles* ☎ *514/935–8136* ⊕ *www.maisonsaintgabriel.ca/en* 🎟 *C$15 weekdays, C$17 summer* 🕙 *Closed Mon. and Tues.* ☞ *Guided tours Wed.–Fri. at 1 or 3 in French, at 2 in English; weekends at 10, 1, or 3 in French, at 11 or 2 in English* Ⓜ *Square-Victoria, then Bus 61.*

Marché Bonsecours (*Bonsecours Market*)

NOTABLE BUILDING | You can't buy fruits and vegetables in the Marché Bonsecours anymore, but you can view an exhibit; shop for local fashions, crafts, and souvenirs in the row of upscale boutiques that fill its main hall; lunch in one of the cafés or restaurants; or grab a craft beer. But the *marché* is best admired from the outside. Built in the 1840s as the city's main market, it is possibly the most beautifully proportioned neoclassical building in Montréal, with its six cast-iron Doric columns and two rows of meticulously even sash windows, all topped with a silvery dome. Perhaps the marché was too elegant to be just a farmers' market. ✉ *350 rue St-Paul Est, Old Montréal* ☎ *514/872–7730* ⊕ *www.marchebonsecours.qc.ca* Ⓜ *Champ-de-Mars.*

★ Musée d'Archéologie et d'Histoire Pointe-à-Callière (PAC) (*Pointe-à-Callière Archaeology and History Museum*)

RUINS | A modern glass edifice built on the site of Montréal's first European settlement, the PAC impresses. The museum presents new local and international temporary exhibitions each year, but the real reason to visit the city's most ambitious archaeological museum is to

Built on the actual foundations of the city, the impressive Pointe-à-Callière museum takes visitors back in time to 17th-century Montréal.

take the elevator ride down to the 17th century.

It's dark down there, and just a little creepy thanks to the 350-year-old tombstones teetering in the gloom, but it's worth the trip. This is a serious archaeological dig that takes you to the very foundations of the city. A more lighthearted exhibit explores life and love in multicultural Montréal. For a spectacular view of the Old Port, the St. Lawrence River, and the Islands, ride the elevator to the top of the tower, or stop for lunch in the museum's glass-fronted café. In summer there are re-creations of period fairs and festivals on the grounds near the museum.

The Fort Ville-Marie pavilion showcases the remains of the forts and artifacts from the first Montrealers. The 360-foot underground William collector sewer, built in the 1830s and considered a masterpiece of civil engineering at that time, connects the original museum space with the new pavilion and features a sound-and-light show projected onto

the walls of the collector sewer. ✉ *350 pl. Royale, Old Montréal* ☎ *514/872–9150* 🌐 *www.pacmusee.qc.ca* ✉ *C$26* Ⓜ *Place-d'Armes.*

Musée du Château Ramezay

HISTORIC HOME | Claude de Ramezay, the city's 11th governor, was probably daydreaming of home when he built his Montréal residence, now one of the UNESCO-listed "1001 Historic Sites You Must See Before You Die." Its thick stone walls, dormer windows, and steeply pitched roof make it look like a little bit of 18th-century Normandy dropped into the middle of North America—although the round, squat tower is a 19th-century addition. The extravagant mahogany paneling in the Salon de Nantes was installed when Louis XV was still king of France. The British used the château as headquarters after their conquest in 1760, and so did the American commanders Richard Montgomery and Benedict Arnold. Benjamin Franklin, who came north in a failed attempt to persuade the locals

Montréal's History

Montréal is the second-largest French-speaking city in the Western world, but it's not only francophone culture that thrives here. About 13% of the 4.3 million people who call Greater Montréal home claim English as their mother tongue.

Yet the two cultures are not as separate as they once were. Chatter in the bars and bistros of rue St-Denis east of boulevard St-Laurent still tends to be in French, and crowds in restaurants on rue Crescent in the Downtown core speak English. But the lines have blurred, with more conversations taking place in a uniquely Montréal mixture of the two languages.

Both linguistic groups have had to come to grips with no longer being the only player. So-called allophones—people whose mother tongue is neither French nor English—make up 20% of the city's population.

The first European settlement on the island of Montréal was Ville-Marie, founded in 1642 by 54 men and women under the leadership of Paul de Chomedey, Sieur de Maisonneuve, and Jeanne Mance, a French noblewoman, who hoped to create a new Christian society. The settlement's location near the confluence of the St. Lawrence and Ottawa Rivers also meant a lucrative trade in beaver pelts, as the fur was a staple of European hat fashion for nearly a century.

The French regime in Canada ended with the Seven Years' War, also known as the French and Indian War. The Treaty of Paris ceded all of New France to Britain in 1763. American troops under Generals Richard Montgomery and Benedict Arnold occupied the city during their 1775–76 campaign to conquer Canada, but their efforts failed and troops withdrew. Soon invaders of another kind—English and Scottish settlers—poured into Montréal. By 1832, the city became a colonial capital. But 1837 brought anti-British rebellions, and this led to Canada's becoming a self-governing dominion in 1867.

The city's ports continued to bustle until the St. Lawrence Seaway opened in 1957, allowing ships to sail from the Atlantic to the Great Lakes without having to stop in Montréal to transfer cargo.

The opening of the métro in 1966 changed the way Montrealers lived, and the next year the city hosted the World's Fair. But the rise of Québec separatism in the late 1960s under René Lévesque created political uncertainty, and many major businesses moved to Toronto. By the time Lévesque's separatist Parti Québécois won power in Québec in 1976—the same year the summer Olympics came to the city—Montréal had become Canada's No. 2 city.

Uncertainty continued through the 1980s and '90s, with the separatist Parti Québécois and the federalist Liberals alternating in power in Québec City. Since 1980, the city has endured two referenda on the future of Québec and Canada. In the cliffhanger of 1995, just 50.58% of Quebecers voted to remain part of Canada. Montréal bucked the separatist trend and voted nearly 70% against independence.

to join the American Revolution, stayed here during that winter adventure.

Most of the château's exhibits are a little staid—guns, uniforms, and documents on the main floor and tableaux depicting colonial life in the cellars—but they include some unexpected little eccentricities that make it worth the visit. Head outside, through the back door, and you'll enter gardens full of 18th-century tranquility. ⊠ *280 rue Notre-Dame Est, Old Montréal* ☎ *514/861–3708* ⊕ *www.chateauramezay.qc.ca/en* ☒ *C$13.50* ⊘ *Closed Mon. late Oct.–late May* Ⓜ *Champ-de-Mars.*

Old Port (*Vieux Port*)
CITY PARK | FAMILY | Montréal's favorite waterfront park is your ideal gateway to the St. Lawrence River. Rent a pedal boat, take a ferry to Île Ste-Hélène, sign up for a dinner cruise, or, if you're really adventurous, ride a raft or a jet boat through the turbulent Lachine Rapids. If you're determined to stay ashore, however, there's still plenty to do, including riding the Grande Roue, the tallest Ferris wheel in Canada; soaking in the rays at the Clock Tower Beach (you can't swim, though); and enjoying street performances, sound-and-light shows, or art displays and exhibitions.

Visiting warships from the Canadian navy and other countries often dock here and open their decks to the public. You can rent a bicycle or a pair of in-line skates at one of the shops along rue de la Commune and explore the waterfront at your leisure. In winter, rent a pair of skates and glide around the outdoor rink. You can also, quite literally, lose the kids in Shed 16's Labyrinthe, a maze of alleys, surprises, and obstacles built inside an old waterfront warehouse. With the rope and aerial courses aboard life-size replicas of pirate and royal ships, kids will also go crazy for the Voiles en Voiles adventure park. ⊠ *Old Montréal* ☎ *514/496–7678, 800/971–7678* ⊕ *www.*

oldportofmontreal.com Ⓜ *Place-d'Armes or Champ-de-Mars.*

Place-d'Armes
PLAZA/SQUARE | When Montréal was under attack, citizens and soldiers would rally at Place-d'Armes, but these days the only rallying is done by tourists, lunching office workers, and flocks of voracious pigeons. The pigeons are particularly fond of the triumphant statue of Montréal's founder, Paul de Chomedey, with his lance upraised, perched above the fountain in the middle of the cobblestoned square. Tunnels beneath the square protected the colonists from the winter weather and provided an escape route; unfortunately, they are too small and dangerous to visit. ⊠ *Bordered by rues Notre-Dame Ouest, St-Jacques, and St-Sulpice, Old Montréal* Ⓜ *Place-d'Armes.*

Place de la Grande-Paix
PLAZA/SQUARE | If you're looking for peace and quiet, the narrow strip of grass and trees on Place d'Youville just east of Place Royale is an appropriate place to find it. It was here, after all, that the French signed a major peace treaty with dozens of aboriginal nations in 1702. It was also here that the first French colonists to settle in Montréal landed their four boats on May 17, 1642. An obelisk records the settlers' names. ⊠ *Between pl. d'Youville and rue William, Old Montréal* Ⓜ *Place-d'Armes.*

Place Jacques-Cartier
PLAZA/SQUARE | The cobbled square at the heart of Old Montréal is part carnival, part flower market, and part sheer fun. You can pause here to have your portrait painted, buy an ice cream, or watch the street performers. If you have more time, try to get a table at one of the sidewalk cafés, order a beer or a glass of wine, and watch the passing parade. During the holiday season you can order a mulled wine or hot cider in the market and warm up by one of the wood-burning stoves from your perch on an Adirondack

chair. At the top of the slope, you'll notice a monument to Lord Nelson. It honors Nelson's victory over Napoléon Bonaparte's French navy at Trafalgar and is a source of anger for some modern-day Québec nationalists. The campaign to raise money for the 1809 monument was led by Sulpician priests, who were engaged in delicate land negotiations with the British government at the time and were eager to show what good subjects they were. ⊠ *Bordered by rues Notre-Dame Est and de la Commune, Old Montréal* Ⓜ *Champ-de-Mars.*

Place Royale

PLAZA/SQUARE | The oldest public square in Montréal, dating to the 17th century, was a market during the French regime and later became a Victorian garden. ⊠ *Bordered by rues St-Paul Ouest and de la Commune, Old Montréal* Ⓜ *Place-d'Armes.*

Square Victoria

PLAZA/SQUARE | Although Square Victoria officially lies within the Quartier International, or International District, Montrealers consider it a part of Old Montréal. The square nicely blends its French and English heritage with an 1872 statue of Queen Victoria on one side and an authentic Parisian métro entrance and a flower market on the other. Both are framed by a two-block stretch of trees, benches, and fountains that makes a pleasant place to relax and admire the handsome 1920s office buildings on the east side. The art nouveau métro entrance, incidentally, was a gift from the French capital's transit commission. ⊠ *Rue du Square Victoria, between rues Viger and St-Jacques, Old Montréal* Ⓜ *Square-Victoria.*

🍴 Restaurants

Old Montréal is home to some of the city's most en vogue bistros and fine-dining establishments—all tucked into gorgeous heritage buildings. Foodies eat wild game, fresh seafood, and inventive plant-based dishes while tasting local and imported wine. Daily changing menus written on chalkboards are a common sight, since market-fresh food is popular.

Bloom

$$$ | VEGETARIAN | A relatively new addition (opened in late 2019) to the plant-based sushi zeitgeist, Bloom on rue St-Paul aims to prove that it's possible to enjoy sushi without harming our oceans and the fish that live in them. With its white-painted brick and stone walls, blond wood surfaces, and low-hanging cloth lamps, this gorgeous resto is like a cross between a spa and a traditional Japanese restaurant. **Known for:** New Delhi roll, a fried roll with crispy tempeh, avocado, sweet potato, shibazuke, and curry aioli; crispy avocado rolls (fried rice paper, crispy onion, and crispy puffed rice with a spicy sauce); wheat-free rolls and the pretty Moulin Rouge (rice paper, beets, rice, avocado, green onion, apple, and yuzu sauce). Ⓢ *Average main: C$24* ⊠ *368 rue St-Paul Ouest, Old Montréal* ☎ *514/906–2005* ⊕ *bloomsushi.com/en/ restaurants/bloom-st-paul* ⊗ *Closed Mon. No lunch* Ⓜ *Square-Victoria.*

Brasserie 701

$$$$ | BRASSERIE | Inspired by Paris's golden-age brasseries, Brasserie 701's spectacular setting features high ceilings, neoclassical architecture, giant arched windows, and lovely chandeliers. The menu incudes the usual suspects expected at a brasserie, from tartares to filet mignon, escargot, and foie gras. **Known for:** salmon or beef tartare; homemade wild mushroom ravioli; being packed with locals. Ⓢ *Average main: C$35* ⊠ *701 côte de la Place-d'Armes, Old Montréal* ☎ *514/904–1201* ⊕ *www.brasserie701. com/en* Ⓜ *Place-d'Armes.*

Brit & Chips

$$ | BRITISH | FAMILY | There's no need to cross the pond to find perfectly battered fish and delicious chips, as they can be found right here in Old Montréal. The cod is a staple, but the salmon dipped in beer batter is also a menu favorite, and for a Canadian touch, try the haddock covered in golden maple syrup batter. **Known for:** maple syrup batter; popcorn shrimp; sticky toffee pudding. $ *Average main: C$16* ⊠ *433 rue McGill, Old Montréal* ☎ *514/840–1001* ⊕ *www.britandchips. com* Ⓜ *Square-Victoria.*

Club Chasse et Pêche

$$$$ | CANADIAN | Despite the name— French for "Hunting and Fishing Club"—this isn't a hangout for the local gun-and-rod set. Impeccable service and top-notch ingredients have made this one of the best restaurants in the city; the name is simply referencing the wood-and-leather décor. **Known for:** chasse (filet mignon) et pêche (lobster) dish; hamachi with rhubarb, crème fraîche, sunflower, and marigold; terroir cuisine. $ *Average main: C$50* ⊠ *423 rue St-Claude, Old Montréal* ☎ *514/861–1112* ⊕ *www. leclubchasseetpeche.com* ☾ *Closed Sun.–Tues. No lunch* Ⓜ *Champ-de-Mars.*

Garde Manger

$$$$ | CANADIAN | Blink and you'll miss it. While the address is written on the building's façade, the restaurant's non-descript exterior and lack of a sign mean you may be searching for a while. **Known for:** seafood bar; seasonal chef's menu experience; celebrity chef. $ *Average main: C$60* ⊠ *408 rue St-François-Xavier, Old Montréal* ☎ *514/678–5044* ⊕ *garde-manger.ca* ☾ *Closed Sun.–Tues. No lunch* Ⓜ *Place-d'Armes.*

Le Cartet

$$ | FRENCH | As a gourmet grocery shop, take-out counter, and French restaurant rolled into one, this splendid space was quickly adopted by local foodies. Instead of being dejected by the brunch queues on Saturday and Sunday, visitors should take advantage of that time to browse the restaurant's inviting grocery shop for gourmet souvenirs to take home. **Known for:** brunch canton or toscan; mimosas; gazpacho. $ *Average main: C$20* ⊠ *106*

rue McGill, Old Montréal ☎ *514/871–8887* ⊕ *www.lecartet.ca* ☾ *No dinner* Ⓜ *Square-Victoria.*

★ Le Serpent

$$$$ | MODERN ITALIAN | The expertise and irreproachable service at Le Serpent truly make it an essential stop on any Montréal foodie itinerary. The industrial-looking space caters to trendy diners, and almost paradoxically, serves sublime Italianate plates that could be mistaken for comfort food if they weren't so elegantly presented. **Known for:** oysters doused in maple mignonette sauce; industrial-chic vibe; friendly service. $ *Average main: C$43* ⊠ *257 rue Prince, Old Montréal* ☎ *514/316–4666* ⊕ *www. leserpent.ca* ☾ *Closed Sun. and Mon. No lunch* Ⓜ *Square-Victoria.*

Monarque

$$$$ | CANADIAN | For fine dining in Old Montréal, head to this elegant contemporary restaurant and brasserie serving expertly presented Canadian fare, from oysters to Prince Edward Island *côte de boeuf*. A chic, illuminated bar showcases the wine collection, with 400 selections including some Québécois bottles. **Known for:** classic salle à manger; top-notch service; wine and cheese selection. $ *Average main: C$50* ⊠ *406 rue St-Jacques, Old Montréal* ☎ *514/875–3896* ⊕ *restaurantmonarque.ca/en* ☾ *No lunch weekends* Ⓜ *Square-Victoria-OACI.*

★ Olive + Gourmando

$$ | CAFÉ | FAMILY | Influential types arrive at lunchtime en masse for a table at this bustling bakery and sandwich shop where vegetables are organically grown in a nearby garden. Crowd pleasers include Le Cubain panini (pancetta, roasted pork, Gruyère with lime, cilantro, and chipotle) and the #24 salad (mixed vegetables, pickled daikon, peanuts, fried shallots, roasted marinated tofu, fresh herbs, and soba noodles) mixed with a sweet-and-sour dressing. **Known for:** organic produce; hot sandwiches; popular brunch and all-day breakfast.

3

Montréal OLD MONTRÉAL (VIEUX-MONTRÉAL)

Montréal's Chinatown

Sandwiched between Downtown and Old Montréal, the center of the action in Montréal's Chinatown is at the intersection of rue Clark and rue de la Gauchetière, where part of the street is closed to traffic. On weekends, especially in summer, it's particularly busy, crowded with tourists as well as residents shopping in the Asian markets for fresh produce, meat and fish, and health supplements.

Chinese immigrants first came to Montréal in large numbers after 1880, following the construction of the transcontinental railroad, and there's been a steady influx of people from Asia and Southeast Asia—including the Vietnamese—since then. These days the city's Chinatown covers about an 18-block area between boulevard René-Lévesque and avenue Viger to the north and south, and near rue de Bleury and avenue Hôtel de Ville to the west and east.

The best way to enter Chinatown is through the ornate gates on boulevard St-Laurent—Place-d'Armes is the closest métro station—then head for the hub at rue de la Gauchetière at the intersection of rue Clark. Chinatown has four gates, or *paifangs*. The most prominent one is probably the South Gate at the corner of boulevard St-Laurent and avenue Viger.

Where to Eat

Maison Kam Fung. This family-run restaurant in existence for three generations offers more than 60 dishes on rotation on any given day, making this *the* place for dim sum feasts. Waiters clatter up and down the aisles pushing a parade of trolleys bearing such treats as firm dumplings stuffed with pork and stir-fried squid and shrimp. **Known for:** steamed and fried dim sum; Peking duck; Cantonese and Szechuan dishes. ⊠ *1111 rue St-Urbain, Suite M05, Chinatown* ☎ *514/878–2888* ⊕ *www.restaurantchinatownkimfung. com* Ⓜ *Place-d'Armes.*

Noodle Factory. The dining room is small and not much to look at, but no matter—the food here is the main attraction, and locals come in droves for the homemade noodles and dumplings. If you time your visit right, you might see the staff through the huge kitchen window working on the dough. **Known for:** cash only; ma-po tofu; homemade noodles and dumplings. ⊠ *1018 rue St-Urbain, Chinatown* ☎ *514/868–9738* ⊕ *www. restonoodlefactory.com* ⊟ *No credit cards* ☽ *Closed Mon.* Ⓜ *Place-d'Armes.*

Qing Hua Dumplings. Groups of students and other budget-conscious connoisseurs of hearty chow crowd the tables at this hole-in-the-wall restaurant for traditional Chinese *jiaozi*, or soup dumplings, just like they make them in northeast China, with a price that's right: just C$12 to C$16 for 15 dumplings. Among the 40 or so varieties of dumplings here, there are also vegetarian versions, including tofu and vegetables, zucchini and vegan "salami," cabbage and Texas "sausage," and pumpkin. **Known for:** peanut butter and pork dumplings; cash only; affordable eats. ⊠ *1019 boul. St-Laurent, Chinatown* ☎ *514/903–9887* ⊕ *qinghuadumpling.com* ⊟ *No credit cards* Ⓜ *Place-d'Armes.*

$ *Average main: C$20* ✉ *351 rue St-Paul Ouest, Old Montréal* ☎ *514/350–1083* ⊕ *www.oliveetgourmando.com* ⊘ *Closed Mon. and Tues. No dinner* Ⓜ *Square-Victoria.*

Restaurant Helena

$$$$ | PORTUGUESE | Housed inside a welcoming space with alcove windows and stone walls, this airy, colorful restaurant serves traditional upscale Portuguese cuisine with plenty of seafood dishes. Share a few tapas plates, like the grilled sardines fillets, cod fritters, grilled asparagus, or baby potatoes with herbs before delving into the main course. **Known for:** historic building; Portuguese tapas; caldo verde. $ *Average main: C$45* ✉ *438 rue McGill, Old Montréal* ☎ *514/878–1555* ⊕ *www.restauranthelena.com* ⊘ *Closed Sun. No lunch Sat.* Ⓜ *Square-Victoria.*

SeaSalt

$$$$ | SEAFOOD | The perfect seafood spot for the summer with impeccable views of the Vieux Port, SeaSalt is a great place to stop for lunch or dinner while walking around Old Montréal. Start off with one of the amazing tartares and try not to miss out on the maple-and-rose-crusted salmon with carrot and yuzu cream, lobster bisque sauce, and a kale and lemon salad on the side. **Known for:** fresh oysters; lobster rolls; refreshing cocktails. $ *Average main: C$30* ✉ *351 pl. Royale, Old Montréal* ☎ *514/937–6555* ⊕ *seasalt-montreal.ca* Ⓜ *Place-d'Armes.*

★ Toqué!

$$$$ | CANADIAN | Frequently named one of Montréal's best restaurants and Canada's third best by Canada's 100 Best (⊕ *canadas100best.com*), a meal at Toqué! is not so much about sustenance but rather about experience. **Known for:** tasting menu; market cuisine; wine pairings. $ *Average main: C$66* ✉ *900 pl. Jean-Paul-Riopelle, Old Montréal* ☎ *514/499–2084* ⊕ *www.restaurant-toque.com* ⊘ *Closed Sun. and Mon. No lunch Sat.* Ⓜ *Square-Victoria.*

☕ Coffee and Quick Bites

★ Crew Collective and Café

$ | CAFÉ | Undoubtedly the most strikingly beautiful café in Montréal, perhaps even in North America, Crew Collective and Café is housed inside a former 1920s-era bank that's fitted with 50-foot-high vaulted ceilings, intricate tiling, and bronze chandeliers. It's no wonder *Forbes* named it one of the five most beautiful coworking spaces in the world. **Known for:** architectural, lavish space; curated coffee beans; cold brew. $ *Average main: C$7* ✉ *360 rue St-Jacques, Old Montréal* ☎ *514/285–7095* ⊕ *crewcollectivecafe.com* Ⓜ *Place-d'Armes.*

★ Le Petit Dep

$ | CANADIAN | You'll want to keep coming back again and again to this adorable little gourmet convenience store and café with its mint-green façade and single-origin coffee. Le Petit Dep proudly stocks local products, including *prêt-à-manger* (ready-to-eat) soups, salads, and comfort foods such as chili, pasta, and vegan shepherd's pie. **Known for:** prêt-à-manger meals; quaint setting; delicious sweets. $ *Average main: C$9* ✉ *179 rue St-Paul Ouest, Old Montréal* ☎ *514/284–9162* ⊕ *www.lepetitdep.ca* Ⓜ *Place-d'Armes or Square-Victoria.*

Pâtisserie Végania

$ | CANADIAN | Initially an artisanal frozen dessert brand, Végania unveiled its sit-down patisserie-boutique in August 2022, mere steps from Basilique Notre-Dame-de-Montréal. Chef-pâtissier owner Justine's plant-based, mostly gluten-free desserts, made with cashew nuts, Québec maple syrup, and organic ingredients, marry gourmandise with healthy eating. **Known for:** exquisite almond cake; velvety chocolate cheesecake topped with chocolate brownie chunks; new skin care product line. $ *Average main: C$8* ✉ *216 rue Notre-Dame Ouest, Old Montréal* ⊕ *www.veganiadesserts.com* ⊘ *Closed Mon.–Wed.* Ⓜ *Place-d'Armes.*

🛏 Hotels

Let's start with the name. Nobody says "Old Town." That's an American phrase. You may call it Old Montréal, but street signs are in French and say "Vieux-Montréal." Either way, it's full of charm—from narrow, cobblestoned streets to quaint outdoor terraces, or *terrasses* in French. You can find boutique hotels, auberges, and cozy B&Bs nestled inside heritage buildings. Most properties have exposed beams, stone walls, wooden floors, and thick casement windows. History buffs find this area pleasing, as do people who want to wander around boutiques and art galleries. But know that this is no place for stilettos. Bring your walking shoes and expect to stumble upon film crews and the occasional Hollywood actor taking a smoke break. We're talking to you, Brad Pitt.

★ Auberge du Vieux-Port

$$$ | B&B/INN | This showcase for 19th-century architecture—think casement windows, exposed beams, and brick—is the gold standard for intimate boutique hotels, attracting A-listers and well-heeled romantics with its mix of old-world charm and modern comfort. **Pros:** loft options offer more space and high ceilings; expansive rooftop deck; some rooms have decks and fireplaces. **Cons:** sometimes noisy in street-facing rooms; some rooms are very small; breakfast not included in base price. $ *Rooms from: C$390* ✉ *97 rue de la Commune Est, Old Montréal* ☎ *514/876–0081, 888/660–7678* ⊕ *www.aubergeduvieuxport.com* 🛏 *45 rooms, plus apartments and lofts in other buildings* ⦿ *No Meals* Ⓜ *Place-d'Armes or Champ-de-Mars.*

Hôtel Bonaparte

$$$ | B&B/INN | Housed inside a 19th-century building, the Hôtel Bonaparte is a gem. **Pros:** excellent location; breakfast included in room rate; perfect for theater lovers—the Centaur Theatre is next door. **Cons:** downstairs restaurant can be a bit noisy on weekends; not family friendly; parking lot is down the street. $ *Rooms from: C$340* ✉ *447 rue St-François-Xavier, Old Montréal* ☎ *514/844–1448, 514/844–4368 for restaurant* ⊕ *www.bonaparte.com* 🛏 *36 rooms, 1 suite* ⦿ *Free Breakfast* Ⓜ *Place-d'Armes.*

Hôtel Épik Montréal

$$$ | B&B/INN | With its rustic stone walls and exposed beams, this inn was the first of its kind in the Old Port when it opened in the late 1980s, and the new owners continue to honor its tradition of calm excellence while adding modern comfort and contemporary design accents throughout. **Pros:** sunny garden terrace; soundproof shutters; bountiful breakfast. **Cons:** rooms need to be booked far in advance; rooms could use an update; no elevator. $ *Rooms from: C$350* ✉ *171 rue St-Paul Ouest, Old Montréal* ☎ *514/842–2634, 877/841–2634* ⊕ *www.epikmontreal.com* 🛏 *10 rooms* ⦿ *Free Breakfast* Ⓜ *Place-d'Armes.*

★ Hôtel Gault

$$$ | HOTEL | Once a cotton factory in the 1800s, this five-story heritage boutique hotel has loftlike rooms, suites, apartments, and terrace-suites with soaring ceilings, French windows, cast-iron columns, and an artsy vibe that doesn't sacrifice comfort for style. **Pros:** some rooms have private terraces; 24/7 room service; quiet location. **Cons:** a bit hard to find; C$40 valet; no pool. $ *Rooms from: C$390* ✉ *449 rue Ste-Hélène, Old Montréal* ☎ *514/904–1616, 866/904–1616* ⊕ *www.hotelgault.com* 🛏 *30 suites* ⦿ *No Meals* Ⓜ *Square-Victoria.*

Hôtel Nelligan

$$$ | HOTEL | This boutique hotel, named for Québec's most passionate poet, Émile Nelligan, is known for its lobby atrium and rooftop terrace offering views of Old Montréal and the harbor. **Pros:** cozy rooms, many with with exposed brick walls, king-sized beds, and large bathrooms, some with whirlpool bathtubs

and showers; in summer, breakfast or cocktails with a view on rooftop terrace; Le Labo toiletries. **Cons:** popular event space; pricey valet parking; some rooms can be noisy. $ *Rooms from: C$375* ✉ *106 rue St-Paul Ouest, Old Montréal* ☎ *514/788–2040, 877/788–2040* ⊕ *www.hotelnelligan.com* ⇄ *105 rooms* ⦿ *No Meals* Ⓜ *Place-d'Armes.*

Hôtel St. Paul

$$$ | HOTEL | Forget fussy oil paintings or rococo furniture—behind its 19th-century Beaux-Arts façade, the St. Paul boasts a chic lobby furnished with jewel-toned velvet sofas and a giant alabaster fireplace built of backlit blocks of "ice." Rooms have also undergone a redo with an airier, more contemporary feel and design in line with the lobby. **Pros:** pets allowed (C$75 per night); designer lobby; kooky bar, Bar @Pol. **Cons:** underlighted hallways and elevators can be spooky; modern furniture and bright colors not for everyone; no pool. $ *Rooms from: C$358* ✉ *355 rue McGill, Old Montréal* ☎ *514/380–2222, 866/380–2202* ⊕ *www.hotelstpaul.com* ⇄ *119 rooms* ⦿ *No Meals* Ⓜ *Square-Victoria.*

★ Hôtel Uville

$$$ | HOTEL | Opened in 2019, this retro boutique hotel-slash-museum is an ode to the Montréal of the 1960s and '70s, when the city hosted Expo '67 and stood at the forefront of the art, culture, and design scenes in North America. **Pros:** pet-friendly; nice lounge bar serving cocktails, coffees and light plates; friendly, knowledgeable service. **Cons:** a bit removed from the main sights and more popular venues; rooms are a little compact; bed linens could be higher quality. $ *Rooms from: C$350* ✉ *204 pl. d'Youville, Old Montréal* ☎ *514/289–4044* ⊕ *uvillehotelmontreal.com* ⇄ *33 rooms* ⦿ *Free Breakfast* Ⓜ *Place-d'Armes.*

Hôtel William Gray

$$$ | HOTEL | Popular with A-listers and creatives, the Hôtel William Gray marries the deep history and contemporary cool of Old Montréal, with its two 18th-century stone buildings topped by an eight-story glass tower. **Pros:** magnificent views of Old Montréal and Jacques Cartier bridge from popular rooftop terrace; small, tranquil outdoor pool, a rarity in Old Montréal hotels; Himalayan salt room in the spa. **Cons:** older travelers may not appreciate the trendy scene in the restaurant or two rooftop bars; pool too small for laps; most rooms don't have bathtubs. $ *Rooms from: C$390* ✉ *421 rue St-Vincent, Old Montréal* ☎ *514/656–5600, 844/576-5600* ⊕ *www.hotelwilliamgray.com* ⇄ *127 rooms* ⦿ *No Meals* Ⓜ *Champ-de-Mars.*

InterContinental Montréal

$$$ | HOTEL | After extensive room renovations in 2016, the InterContinental definitely got its groove back, catering to a variety of travelers—from families and their pets, to the business and fitness cliques. **Pros:** saltwater swimming pool; easy underground access to shopping and nightlife; outdoor terrace on sixth floor. **Cons:** gets the convention crowd; dull ground-floor entry; 1990 building lacks character. $ *Rooms from: C$345* ✉ *360 rue St-Antoine Ouest, Old Montréal* ☎ *514/987–9900, 877/660–8550* ⊕ *www.montreal.intercontinental.com* ⇄ *357 rooms* ⦿ *No Meals* Ⓜ *Square-Victoria or Place-d'Armes.*

Le Petit Hôtel

$$$ | HOTEL | FAMILY | Little sister of Auberge du Vieux-Port, this boutique hotel marries creative design with old stone walls, exposed beams, a narrow lobby with a counter coffee bar and a 7-foot orange sculpture, and—contrary to its name—not-so-petite rooms. **Pros:** a few bicycles to borrow; elevator; cribs, playpens, and babysitters available. **Cons:** small bathrooms have no tubs and some can be cramped; steep fee for valet parking; lobby not especially elegant or cozy. $ *Rooms from: C$348* ✉ *168 rue St-Paul Ouest, Old Montréal* ☎ *514/405–3729, 877/530–0360* ⊕ *www.*

petithotelmontreal.com ⬐ *28 rooms* ⫶◯⫶ *Free Breakfast* Ⓜ *Square-Victoria.*

★ Le Place d'Armes Hôtel and Suites

$$$$ | **HOTEL** | **FAMILY** | Four splendidly ornate neoclassical commercial buildings were merged to create Old Montréal's largest boutique hotel, pleasing honeymooners and business execs alike with its old-fashioned grandeur, exposed brick walls in rooms, hammam (Middle Eastern–style steam bath), rooftop terrace, and unobstructed views of the Basilique Notre-Dame-de-Montréal. **Pros:** best (Turkish) spa in town; Japanese tavern with hamachi bibimbap (marinated yellowtail); rooftop bar. **Cons:** late sleepers may be disturbed by the noontime Angelus bells at the basilica; steep approach from métro is slippery in winter; rooms in new building have no bathtubs, only multi–jet showers. ⑤ *Rooms from: C$425* ⊠ *55 rue St-Jacques, Old Montréal* ☎ *514/842–1887, 888/450–1887* ⊕ *www.hotelplacedarmes.com* ⬐ *169 rooms* ⫶◯⫶ *No Meals* Ⓜ *Place-d'Armes.*

Le Saint-Sulpice

$$$ | **HOTEL** | With its sought-after address beside the basilica's chapel, this boutique hotel is blessed with a magical garden terrace, luxurious suites—both in space and décor—artwork by Québec designer Jean-Claude Poitras, and a lively lobby restaurant with one of the city's best menus. **Pros:** in-room massage service; rooms tend to be a bit more spacious than other Old Montréal properties; casement windows that open. **Cons:** church bells may disturb late sleepers; furnishing could use updating; pricey summer rates. ⑤ *Rooms from: C$370* ⊠ *414 rue St-Sulpice, Old Montréal* ☎ *514/288–1000, 877/785–7423* ⊕ *www.lesaintsulpice.com* ⬐ *108 rooms* ⫶◯⫶ *No Meals* Ⓜ *Place-d'Armes.*

LHotel

$$$ | **HOTEL** | Housed in a stately 19th-century bank in the financial district, the dignified façade accurately suggests the grand interior with its high ceilings,

antique furnishings, and large windows. **Pros:** Botero bar-lounge has distinct character; spacious high-ceiling rooms; excellent art collection and close to other galleries. **Cons:** some rooms are dated; buffet continental breakfast is pricey and not included; rue St-Jacques is dull after 6 pm. ⑤ *Rooms from: C$370* ⊠ *262 rue St-Jacques Ouest, Old Montréal* ☎ *514/985–0019, 877/553–0019* ⊕ *www.lhotelmontreal.com* ⬐ *59 rooms* ⫶◯⫶ *No Meals* Ⓜ *Square-Victoria.*

SpringHill Suites by Marriott

$$ | **HOTEL** | **FAMILY** | Convenient and quiet, with large rooms and underground parking—rarities in Old Montréal—this all-suites hotel attracts families and business travelers who return for the free breakfast buffet, lobby market, saltwater pool, and fitness center. **Pros:** free, bountiful breakfast with healthy options; saltwater pool; well-stocked lobby store. **Cons:** popular with families, so pool can be crowded; difficult access on a narrow street; poor views. ⑤ *Rooms from: C$295* ⊠ *445 rue St-Jean-Baptiste, Old Montréal* ☎ *514/875–4333, 866/875–4333* ⊕ *www.marriott.com/en-us/hotels/yulsh-springhill-suites-old-montreal/overview* ⬐ *124 rooms* ⫶◯⫶ *Free Breakfast* Ⓜ *Champ-de-Mars.*

W Montréal

$$$$ | **HOTEL** | A chic showcase for your Prada luggage, the W Montréal lives up to the brand's reputation for a hip take on luxury and style, providing its A-list clientele with excellent service and sleek, modern decor, notably peekaboo bathrooms, a trendy bar, and a lobby designed for lingering and entertaining. **Pros:** bright, airy rooms; well-connected concierge; Bluetooth speakers in rooms. **Cons:** nonmember fee for in-room Wi-Fi (free in the lobby); lobby noisy at night; showers afford no privacy. ⑤ *Rooms from: C$470* ⊠ *901 Square Victoria, Old Montréal* ☎ *514/395–3100, 888/627–7081* ⊕ *www.marriott.com/en-us/hotels/*

yulwh-w-montreal/overview ⤳ *152 rooms* ❖❘ *No Meals* Ⓜ *Square-Victoria.*

 Nightlife

Once a tourist trap full of overpriced, tacky souvenir shops, Old Montréal is now home to a mix of top-notch restaurants and chic lounges. During the summer you can enjoy stunning views of the river from some of the city's best rooftop terraces. Excellent dining can be found along rue St-Paul, while rue McGill is a big part of the 5 à 7 scene.

BARS AND LOUNGES
Coldroom

BARS | No advertised street number. A secret, nondescript steel door in the back. Imaginative, award-winning mixologists. A cocktail selection that changes with the seasons. Twists on old classics (think: an old-fashioned with mezcal). Clear, no-nonsense house rules:

"Act your age, or you'll be required to be accompanied by a parent or guardian."

"For all make out purposes, may we suggest our next door neighbour The William Gray hotel? Get a room."

And just for the men: "Know your alcohol limits. Stay classy."

"Erase the word 'slut' and 'gay' and any other abusive language from your vocabulary."

"Learn some dance moves. If you need help, ask our manager Dan."

To be admitted, simply push the button and wait for the light to flicker red. What more could you want in a speakeasy? ✉ *401A rue St-Vincent, Old Montréal* ⟷ *Adjacent to El Pequeño Bar (same owners). The entrance is via the large black door with "Sortie" written above it. Press the doorbell. Be patient* ☎ *514/294–6911* ⊕ *www.thecoldroom-mtl.com* Ⓜ *Champ-de-Mars.*

★ El Pequeño Bar

BARS | Owned by the same people who run Coldroom, El Pequeño Bar really lives up to its name: the bar seats only nine, it's that small. For all its diminutive size El Pequeño packs a big punch, having been named one of Canada's top 50 bars in early 2020, ranking at no. 4. Adorned with an ornate glass chandelier, white marble countertops, and dozens of Caribbean rum bottles behind the bar, this pocket-sized spot is an homage to the 1920s Havana hotel lobby bar. Gifted *cantineros* (bartenders) specialize in mixing Cubanos and other rum-based cocktails while recounting tales of Ernest Hemingway in his Havana period. In summer, there's a good-sized terrace outside. ✉ *401A rue St-Vincent, Old Montréal* ☎ *514/294-6911* ⊕ *www.elpequenobar. com* Ⓜ *Champ-de-Mars.*

Maison St-Paul

WINE BAR | Sharpen your swords! This chic bar for Champagne and other bubblies is the perfect place to break open a bottle—literally. The staff like to open the bottles of Champagne with sabers, a practice that adds an element of fun and drama to an accessible venue. Finger foods include oysters, steak (and other kinds of) tartares, and caviar. ✉ *343 rue St-Paul Est, Old Montréal* ☎ *514/903–9343* ⊕ *www.maisonsaintpaul.ca* ⊖ *Closed Mon.* Ⓜ *Champs-de-Mars.*

Philémon Bar

WINE BAR | You can grab a glass of one of Philémon's well-priced private import Cavas, Proseccos, or Champagnes to accompany the menu at this sleek bar, which serves more than the usual pub fare (oysters, anyone?). It's packed with locals Thursday through Saturday—in fact, it's become quite the singles hangout. Bouncers keep the ratio of guys to gals at a comfortable level. ✉ *111 rue St-Paul Ouest, Old Montréal* ☎ *514/289–3777* ⊕ *www.philemonbar. com* Ⓜ *Place-d'Armes.*

Terrasse sur l'Auberge
BEER GARDENS | For an unbeatable view of the Old Port and numerous Montréal landmarks, head to this unpretentious patio on the roof of the Auberge du Vieux-Port hotel. Open from the end of May through mid-October (2–11 weekdays, 1–11 on weekends), it's a great place to watch the International Fireworks Festival—if you're early enough to snag a table—and enjoy cocktails and a light tapas menu. ■ **TIP**→ **Try the clear sangria (made with peach Ciroc, Cointreau, white wine, and Sprite).** ⊠ *Auberge du Vieux-Port, 97 rue de la Commune Est, Old Montréal* ☎ *514/419–1349* ⊕ *www.terrassesurlauberge.com* Ⓜ *Place-d'Armes or Champ-de-Mars.*

LIVE MUSIC
Lola Lola Lolita
LIVE MUSIC | A relatively new addition to Old Montréal, Lola Lola Lolita opened in 2021. The club hosts reggaeton nights on Fridays and big bands on Saturdays, playing bachata, merengue, salsa, and the occasional mariachi. Drinks range from beers to sangrias and classic Latin cocktails such as mojitos, margaritas, and Caipirissimas, as well as virgin cocktails. Tasty appetizers like ceviche, guacamole, Colombian empanadas, chicken wings, and *mamalon* tacos are also on offer. ⊠ *60 rue St-Jacques, Old Montréal* ⊕ *www.lolalolalolitamtl.com* ☞ *There's a C$15 cover charge for live music* Ⓜ *Place-d'Armes.*

Modavie Wine Bar
WINE BAR | With a French and Mediterranean menu, an attractive sidewalk terrasse, and a sophisticated interior that contrasts dark wood against stone walls, this jazz bar is pleasing to the eyes *and* ears. Despite being spread out over two floors, the space still feels cozy. Live duos play during the first part of the week, while weekends showcase full bands. There's never a cover charge. ⊠ *1 rue St-Paul Ouest, Old Montréal* ☎ *514/287–9582* ⊕ *www.modavie.com* Ⓜ *Champ-de-Mars.*

Performing Arts

THEATER
Centaur Theatre
THEATER | Montréal's best-known English-language theater company stages everything from frothy musical revues to serious works and prominently features works by local playwrights. Its home is in the former stock exchange building in Old Montréal. ⊠ *453 rue St-François-Xavier, Old Montréal* ☎ *514/288–3161* ⊕ *www.centaurtheatre.com* Ⓜ *Place-d'Armes.*

Centre Phi
PERFORMANCE VENUES | Packed with intimate screening rooms, recording facilities, exhibition spaces, and a performance space, this center promotes artist-driven film, design, and music from locals as well as international artists. Films are in English and French. ⊠ *407 rue St-Pierre, Old Montréal* ☎ *514/225–0525, 855/526–8888* ☞ *info.centre@phi.ca* ⊕ *phi.ca/en/centre* Ⓜ *Place-d'Armes or Square-Victoria.*

🛍 Shopping

The historic part of the city still has its fair share of garish souvenir shops, but there remain a few fashion boutiques and shoe shops with low to moderate prices lining rues Notre-Dame and St-Jacques, from rue McGill to place Jacques-Cartier. However, with gentrification in the west end of the area, this is increasingly the exception rather than the norm as high-end fashion boutiques and spas, especially along rue St-Paul Ouest, oust the last holdouts out of business. The area is also rich in art galleries and crafts shops along rue St-Paul and tucked inside the narrow rue des Artistes. Use the Place-d'Armes, Champ-de-Mars, or Square-Victoria métro stations.

Top Montréal Shopping Experiences

Some of the best deals can be found at **La Maison Simons** department store, where there's something cheap and chic for everyone, from teeny-boppers to mesdames and messieurs, on a budget. Montréal's luxury lane runs from **Holt Renfrew Ogilvy**, the Saks 5th Avenue of Montréal, on rue Ste-Catherine, and north up rues de la Montagne and Crescent to rue Sherbrooke, with local designer fashions such as **Marie Saint Pierre** and **Arthur** lining the route.

The path of luxury continues west along rue Sherbrooke, where you'll find the Montréal Museum of Fine Arts, as well as high-end galleries and antiquarians such as **Le Petit Musée** and **Galerie Alan Klinkhoff.**

Funky fashionistas will want to hit Mile End and the Plateau. In Mile End, hipster territory includes **General 54** and **Unicorn**, with **Citizen Vintage** for recycled fashions. Moving down Montréal's beloved Main—boulevard St-Laurent—check out vintage, décor, fashion, and design shops.

Closer to Downtown, **Boutique 1861** and **M0851** are worth the walk. One-of-a-kind independent shops line avenue Mont-Royal and rue St-Denis.

ART

Galerie Bloom

ART GALLERY | Located in an attractive space featuring wood floors and brick and gray-stone walls, Galerie Bloom is a family affair specializing in contemporary Canadian art. Owners Julien Michaud and Stéphanie Rivet are known for providing knowledgeable, individualized service and making modern art more accessible to the general public. ⊠ *224 rue St-Paul Ouest, Old Montréal* ☎ *514/419–2233* ⊕ *galeriebloom.com/en* ⊘ *Closed Wed.* Ⓜ *Place d'Armes.*

Images Boréales

ART GALLERY | If the friendly and knowledgeable staff don't win you over, the vast collection of Inuit art certainly will. Images Boréales represents the best-known Inuit artists while also making a point of working with young, emerging Inuit talent with strong potential. With more than 2,000 pieces of sculpture in soapstone and serpentine, the biggest challenge at this gallery-boutique will be deciding what to buy. ⊠ *4 rue St-Paul Est, Old Montréal* ☎ *514/439–1987* ⊕ *www.imagesboreales.com* Ⓜ *Champ-de-Mars.*

CLOTHING

Boutique Anne de Shalla | Signatures Québécoises

CLOTHING | Housing a streamlined selection of Québécois fashion designers, the loftlike space inside Marché Bonsecours sells luxe lines that include Ricardo, Christian Chenail, and the fanciful creations of Ophelie Hats. But it's the owner's own exotic kimonos that steal the show. ⊠ *Marché Bonsecours, 350 rue St-Paul Est, Old Montréal* ☎ *514/398–0761* ⊕ *www.facebook.com/boutiqueannedeshalla* Ⓜ *Champ-de-Mars.*

Boutique Denis Gagnon

CLOTHING | This innovative designer, whose creations have been exhibited at the Montréal Museum of Fine Arts, is much loved on the Montréal fashion scene. In this sleek boutique, Gagnon's couture designs stand alongside his ready-to-wear collection. He's also well known for his shoes. More recently he added the "bazaar," a collection of vintage tableware, furniture, and curios. ⊠ *170 rue St-Paul Ouest, Old Montréal* ☎ *514/935–6360* ⊕ *www.denisgagnon.ca* Ⓜ *Place-d'Armes.*

Montréal's Best Shopping Streets

Most visitors to Montréal will have Downtown and Old Montréal on the itinerary, but for an authentic experience à la Montréalaise you should also venture into some of the other neighborhoods.

Avenue Laurier Ouest. Shops and boutiques along the eight blocks between boulevard St-Laurent and chemin de la Côte-Ste-Catherine sell medium- to high-end fashions, home furnishings, decorative items, artwork, books, kitchenware, gourmet food, and children's items. There are plenty of restaurants, bars, and cafés in which to rest your feet and admire your purchases. The street is about a 10-minute walk from the Laurier métro station.

Boulevard St-Laurent. Affectionately known as The Main, boulevard St-Laurent has restaurants, boutiques, and nightclubs that cater mostly to an upscale clientele. Still, the area has managed to retain its working-class immigrant roots and vitality to some degree: high-fashion shops are interspersed with ethnic-food stores, hardware stores, and secondhand clothing and décor boutiques. A trip up this street takes you from Chinatown to Little Italy.

Rue Atateken. Mid-century antiques shops began springing up in the Gay Village in the early 1990s, most of them on rue Atateken between rues Ste-Catherine and Ontario. Use the Beaudry métro station.

Rue Bernard Ouest. Only a few blocks from the Outremont métro station, this chic village-like street in the Outremont neighborhood

is well worth a detour. The street boasts many sidewalk patios—called terrasses in local parlance—for fine or casual dining, as well as specialty food stores, décor shops, and some of the best ice cream in Montréal at Le Glacier Bilboquet.

Rue Chabanel. The eight-block stretch of Chabanel just west of boulevard St-Laurent is the heart of the city's garment district. The goods seem to get more stylish and more expensive the farther west you go. If you're lucky, you might come across signs for designer sample sales. Many of the city's furriers have also moved into the area. From the Crémazie métro station, take Bus 53 north.

Rue Notre-Dame Ouest. The fashionable place for antiquing is a formerly run-down five-block strip of Notre-Dame between rue Guy and avenue Atwater. Most of the action is at the western end of the strip, as are many of the restaurants and cafés that have sprung up to cater to shoppers. Walk east from Lionel-Groulx métro station.

Victoria Village. The carriage-trade area for wealthy Westmount citizens, who live on the leafy slopes of Mont-Royal, has morphed into a shopping destination for all Montrealers with an eye for style. While high-end chain stores are increasingly dominating the neighborhood, a few independent boutiques still offer distinctive home décor, shoes, gifts, stationery, and fashion along rues Victoria and Sherbrooke, with the epicenter between Victoria and Claremont. Vendôme is the closest métro station.

★ Maison Pepin

HOUSEWARES | Talented owner and painter Lysanne Pepin has an eye for design. Her boutiques, located a few addresses apart on the same block, are beautiful and intriguing spaces to explore. They are filled with romantic clothes, funky shoes, and a carefully edited mix of local and international labels, as well as eclectic housewares and furniture for home and office. ⊠ *350 and 378 rue St-Paul Ouest, Old Montréal* ☎ *514/844–0114* ⊕ *the-pepinshop.com* ⊙ *Closed Mon. and Tues.* Ⓜ *Square-Victoria.*

U&I

CLOTHING | Stylish locals flock to this boutique in Old Montréal, which is stocked with avant-garde finds from North America and Europe, with an emphasis on Montréal and Canadian brands. Here, Cydwoq and Canada Goose hang alongside coats from the sleek Montréal label Mackage and pieces from U&I's own label. ■**TIP→ The two other locations of U&I are also in Old Montréal: U&I Man at 215 rue St-Paul Ouest and U&I Dream at 445 rue St-Sulpice.** ⊠ *235 rue St-Paul Ouest, Old Montréal* ☎ *514/508–7704* ⊕ *www. boutiqueuandi.com* ⊙ *Closed Sun.* Ⓜ *Place-d'Armes.*

SHOES
John Fluevog

SHOES | Unusually curved lines, from the heels of his shoes to the interior design of his funky boutique, have cultivated a devout following for the Canadian shoe designer. Belts and bags are also available, letting you create a quirky yet coordinated outfit. Look to the soles for curious and inspiring messages. ⊠ *180 rue St-Paul Ouest, Old Montréal* ☎ *514/379–1970* ⊕ *www.fluevog.com* Ⓜ *Place d'Armes.*

SKINCARE
Maison Margan

SKINCARE | A portmanteau of the words *Morocco* and *oil of argan*, Margan's argan-oil-based skin care products are made in Québec with natural and organic ingredients that are sustainably sourced and prepared without animal cruelty. The pretty boutique in dusty rose tones envelops you in its intoxicating Moroccan-inspired fragrances the moment you walk in. With a sink built into its rose marble island counter, you'll want to test out the new brand's rich serums in different scents, luscious creams, and gorgeous soap bars in the same hue as the décor. Margan also makes scented candles, perfect for accompanying your bath ritual. ⊠ *370B pl. Royale, Old Montréal* ⊹ *A block from Pointe-à-Callière museum* ☎ *514/987–4300* ⊕ *maisonmargan.com/en* Ⓜ *Place d'Armes.*

Activities

BOATING

In Montréal, you can climb aboard a boat at a Downtown wharf and be crashing through Class V white water minutes later.

Lachine Rapids Tours (*Jet Boating Montréal*)

BOATING | FAMILY | Discover the rapids aboard a large jet boat—and be sure to bring a change of clothes. There are daily departures (every two hours) May through October from the Clock Tower Pier in the Old Port. The price includes all gear, and the trip lasts an hour. Another option is a 20-minute ride in a 12-passenger boat that reaches speeds up to 80 kph (50 mph). Boats leave the Old Port's Jacques-Cartier Pier every half hour between 10 am and 6 pm from May to October. Trips are narrated in French and English. ■**TIP→ Bring a change clothes for the jet boat or wear a bathing suit and bring a dry bag for your clothes.** ⊠ *47 rue de la Commune Ouest, Old Montréal* ☎ *514/284–9607* ⊕ *jetboatingmontreal. com* ⌖ *Jet boat C$70, 20-minute speedboat ride C$35, 45-minute panoramic trip (much calmer) C$45* Ⓜ *Champ-de-Mars.*

Biking in Montréal

Weather permitting, one of the best ways to discover Montréal is on a bicycle. This is an incredibly bike-friendly metropolis, and there are thousands of designated bike paths connecting diverse neighborhoods across the island, running along the river, and through parks and forests. If you like to bike but would rather not do it on city streets, ferries at the Old Port can take you to Île Ste-Hélène and the south shore of the St. Lawrence River, where riders can connect to hundreds of miles of trails in the Montérégie region.

Fitz Montréal. This company's bike tour of Montréal highlights is popular, but go deeper and try "Hoods & Hidden Gems" to really learn what makes the city tick. They also offer bike rentals, walking tours, and snow tours in winter. ☒ *1251 rue Rachel Est, The Plateau* ☎ *438/792–6480* ⊕ *fitzmontreal. com* Ⓜ *Bus 11, 97, or 30 from Mont-Royal station.*

Go Bike Montréal Festival. The biggest bike celebration in North America, Féria de Vélo de Montréal includes the Tour la Nuit, a 22-km (14-mile) nighttime ride through the city. The weeklong festival culminates in as many as 50,000 cyclists taking over the streets for the Tour de l'Île, a 50-km (31-mile) ride along a route encircling Montréal. ☒ *Montréal* ☎ *514/521–8356, 800/567–8356 ext. 504* ⊕ *www.velo.qc.ca/en/event-category/go-bike-montreal-festival.*

Lachine Canal. The most popular cycling trail on the island begins at the Old Port and winds its way to the shores of Lac St-Louis in Lachine. Pack a picnic lunch; there are plenty of green spaces where you can stop and refuel along the way. ☒ *Montréal.*

Le Pôle des Rapides. This 100-km (62-mile) network of bicycle trails follows lakefronts, canals, and aqueducts. The trails are open April 15 to October 15. ☒ *Montréal* Ⓜ *Verdun, Angrignon, LaSalle, Charlevoix, or Lionel-Groulx.*

SPAS
Bota Bota, Spa sur l'Eau
SPA | A unique concept in this northern city, this spa is set on a repurposed ferryboat in Old Montréal. The floating spa features a garden, pool, terraces, and hammocks. Other facilities include a sauna, steam room, and water circuit (cold bath, exterior cold shower, lukewarm bath, jet bath). Silence and/or whispering is required everywhere on the boat. ☒ *Old Port of Montréal, McGill entrance, Corner of rue de la Commune and rue McGill, Old Montréal* ☎ *514/284–0333, 855/284–0333* ⊕ *botabota.ca/en* Ⓜ *Square-Victoria.*

Le Scandinave Les Bains Vieux-Montréal
SPA | A bastion of urban chic in historic Old Montréal, this spa is especially popular on cold winter days. Inspired by the age-old tradition of public baths, the Scandinave prides itself on offering guests an authentic yet contemporary experience with an accent of privacy and total relaxation. The posh interior of slate, marble, and wood contrasts nicely with the bubbling pool and misty steam rooms. The ultimate wind-down is the zero-stress chamber of absolute quiet and darkness to intensify the peacefulness. All you need to bring along is your bathing suit; the spa provides sandals, bathrobes, and towels. For extra

relaxation, sign up for a massage with one of their professional masseuses. ✉ *71 rue de la Commune Ouest, Old Montréal* ☎ *844/220–2009 reservations, 844/220–2009* ⊕ *www.scandinave.com* Ⓜ *Place-d'Armes.*

Downtown

Downtown Montréal took a serious hit during the pandemic and has yet to to fully recover. With high numbers of Montrealers continuing to work from home and many office buildings largely vacant, the future of the city center is uncertain.

The heart of Downtown (or *centre-ville* in French)—with its department stores, boutiques, bars, restaurants, theaters, art galleries, bookstores, and even a few churches—runs from avenue Atwater to boulevard St-Denis. Rue Ste-Catherine is also the main drag of the Quartier des Spectacles, which runs west to east from rue Bleury to rue St-Hubert. Inside this arts and entertainment district are the Place des Arts and several other cultural venues; it also serves as the Downtown home to most of Montréal's many summer festivals.

Walk farther north on rue Crescent to rue Sherbrooke and the lower slopes of Mont-Royal and you come to what was once the most exclusive neighborhood in Canada—the **Golden Square Mile.** During the boom years of the mid-1800s, baronial homes covered the mountain north of rue Sherbrooke. Many are gone, replaced by high-rises or modern town houses, but there are still plenty of architectural treasures to admire, most of them now foreign consulates or university institutes.

And underneath it all—the entire Downtown area and then some—is Montréal's **Underground City,** a vast network of more or less anything you'd find on the street above.

GETTING HERE AND AROUND

Getting to and around Downtown is easy, thanks to the métro. There are several stations along boulevard de Maisonneuve, which is a block away from and runs parallel to rue Ste-Catherine. Many of them link directly to the Underground City.

Sights

Arsenal Art Contemporain

ART GALLERY | Housed in a repurposed shipyard boasting 80,000 square feet of exhibition space, Arsenal Art Contemporain dedicates itself to the support, promotion, and development of contemporary art and has been credited with helping revitalize the old industrial area of Griffintown. The largest private art center in Canada, it was originally founded in Montréal in 2011 but also has locations in Toronto and New York City. ✉ *2020 rue William, Griffintown* ☎ *514/931–9978* ⊕ *www.arsenalcontemporary.com/mtl/ home* 🖃 *C$15* 🕙 *Closed Mon.* Ⓜ *Georges-Vanier or Lionel-Groulx.*

Cathédrale Marie-Reine-du-Monde (*Mary, Queen of the World Cathedral*)

CHURCH | The best reason to visit this cathedral is that it's a quarter-scale replica of St. Peter's Basilica in Rome—complete with a magnificent reproduction of Bernini's ornate baldachin (canopy) over the main altar and an ornately coffered ceiling. When Bishop Ignace Bourget (1799–1885) decided to build his cathedral in the heart of the city's Protestant-dominated commercial quarter, many fellow Catholics thought he was crazy. But the bishop was determined to assert the Church's authority—and its loyalty to Rome—in the British-ruled city. Bourget didn't live to see the cathedral dedicated in 1894, but his tomb holds a place of honor among those of his successors in the burial chapel on the east side of the nave. ✉ *1085 rue de la Cathédrale, Downtown* ✛ *Enter through main doors on boul. René-Lévesque*

Did You Know?

The baroque-style Cathédrale Marie-Reine-du-Monde, or Mary, Queen of the World Cathedral in English, is the third-largest church in Québec. It is a quarter-scale replica of St. Peter's Basilica in Rome.

☎ 514/866–1661 ⊕ microsites.diocesemontreal.org/microsites/cathedralecatholiquedemontreal (French only) ✉ Free Ⓜ Bonaventure.

Centre Bell
SPORTS VENUE | FAMILY | The Montréal Canadiens haven't won the Stanley Cup since 1993, though they came very close in June 2021, ultimately losing the finals against Tampa Bay. Most of the team's fans can't remember the golden 1960s and '70s, when Les Glorieux virtually owned the trophy. The superstitious blame the team's fallen fortunes on its 1996 move from the hallowed Forum to the brown-brick Centre Bell arena. Still, Montréal is a hockey-mad city and the Habs, as locals call the team, are still demigods here, and there are even university courses based on this superstar team. (When it celebrated its 100th season in 2009–10, the city changed the name of the strip of rue de la Gauchetière in front of the Centre Bell to avenue des Canadiens-de-Montréal.) Centre Bell is also a venue for blockbuster acts like Coldplay, Drake, Trevor Noah, and Cirque du Soleil. ✉ 1260 av. des Canadiens-de-Montréal, Downtown ☎ 877/668–8269, 855/310–2525 for hockey tickets ⊕ www.centrebell.ca ✉ Tours C$20 Ⓜ Bonaventure or Lucien-l'Allier.

★ Christ Church Cathedral
CHURCH | The seat of the Anglican (Episcopalian) bishop of Montréal offers downtown shoppers and strollers a respite from the hustle and bustle of rue Ste-Catherine, with free Saturday afternoon concerts. Built in 1859, the cathedral is modeled on Snettisham Parish Church in Norfolk, England, with some distinctly Canadian touches. The steeple, for example, is made with aluminum plates molded to simulate stone, and inside, the Gothic arches are crowned with carvings of the types of foliage growing on Mont-Royal when the church was built. The stained-glass windows behind the main altar, installed in the

early 1920s as a memorial to the dead of World War I, show scenes from the life of Christ. On the wall just above and to the left of the pulpit is the Coventry Cross; it's made of nails taken from the ruins of Britain's Coventry Cathedral, destroyed by German bombing in 1940. ■**TIP→ Free Saturday group tours can be arranged by calling the office.** ✉ 635 rue Ste-Catherine Ouest, Downtown ☎ 514/843–6577 ext. 241 ⊕ www.montrealcathedral.ca ✉ Free Ⓜ McGill.

Church of St. Andrew and St. Paul
CHURCH | Montréal's largest Presbyterian church—sometimes affectionately called the A&P—is worth a visit, if only to see the glorious stained-glass window of the risen Christ that dominates the sanctuary behind the white-stone communion table. It's a memorial to members of the Royal Highland Regiment of Canada (the Black Watch) who were killed in World War I. ✉ 3415 rue Redpath (main entrance on rue Sherbrooke), Downtown ☎ 514/842–3431 ⊕ www.standrewstpaul.com ✉ Free ☞ In July and Aug. visitors are welcome to visit or join tours weekdays between 10 am and 3 pm. Rest of the year, phone ahead to make arrangements. Ⓜ Guy-Concordia.

McCord Stewart Museum (McCord Museum of Canadian History)
HISTORY MUSEUM | David Ross McCord (1844–1930) was a wealthy pack rat with a passion for anything that had to do with Montréal or Canadian history. His collection of paintings, costumes, toys, tools, drawings, and housewares provides a glimpse of what city life was like for all classes in the 19th century. If you're interested in the lifestyles of the elite, however, you'll love the photographs that William Notman (1826–91) took of the rich at play. One series portrays members of the posh Montréal Athletic Association posing in snowshoes on the slopes of Mont-Royal, all decked out in Hudson Bay coats and woolen hats. Each of the hundreds of portraits

3

Montréal DOWNTOWN

Downtown and Westmount

Sights ▼

1 Arsenal Art
   Contemporain **A8**
2 Cathédrale Marie-Reine-
   du-Monde **D5**
3 Centre Bell **B5**
4 Christ Church
   Cathedral **E3**
5 Church of St. Andrew
   and St. Paul **A2**
6 McCord Stewart Museum|
   Musée McCord
   Stewart **E2**
7 McGill University **D1**
8 Musée des Beaux-Arts
   de Montréal **B2**
9 Place des Arts **H3**
10 Place Ville Marie **E4**
11 St. George's
   Anglican Church **C5**
12 Saint Patrick's
   Basilica **F5**
13 Square Dorchester
   and Place du Canada ... **C4**
14 The Underground
   City **G6**

Restaurants ▼

1 Aux Vivres **A2**
2 Bouillon Bilk **I3**
3 Café Ferreira **C3**
4 Café Parvis **F3**
5 Chez Nick **A2**
6 Deville Dinerbar **C3**
7 Escondite Cervecería
   de Barrio **E4**
8 Kazu **A4**
9 Le Taj **C2**
10 LOV **B4**
11 Mandy's **B2**
12 Park **A2**
13 Petros **A2**
14 Ryū **C3**
15 Time Out Market
   Montréal **E3**

Quick Bites ▼

1 Café Bazin **A2**
2 Café Myriade **A3**
3 Caffettiera **C2**

Hotels ▼

1 Château Versailles **A2**
2 Delta Montréal **F2**
3 Fairmont Le Reine
   Elizabeth **D5**
4 Four Seasons
   Montréal **B3**
5 Hôtel Birks **F4**
6 Hôtel Bonaventure
   Montréal **E6**
7 Hôtel Chez Swann **B3**
8 Hôtel HONEYROSE
   Montréal **G3**
9 Hôtel Humaniti
   Montréal **G5**
10 Hôtel Le Germain **D2**
11 Hôtel le Square-
   Phillips et Suites **F4**
12 Le Centre Sheraton **C4**
13 Le Marriott
   Château Champlain **C6**
14 Le Mount Stephen
   Hotel **B3**
15 Le St-Martin Hôtel
   Particulier **D3**
16 Ritz-Carlton
   Montréal **B2**
17 Sofitel Montréal **C2**
18 Vogue Hotel
   Montréal Downtown ... **B3**
19 Warwick Le Crystal
   Montréal **B4**

was shot individually in a studio and then painstakingly mounted on a picture of the snowy mountain to give the impression of a winter outing. The McCord Stewart Museum's mission is to present life in Montréal, past and present. There are guided tours (call for schedule), a reading room, a documentation center, a gift shop, a bookstore, and a café. ⊠ *690 rue Sherbrooke Ouest, Downtown* ☎ *514/861–6701* ⊕ *www.musee-mc-cord-stewart.ca/en* ⊠ *C\$20* ⊗ *Closed Mon.* ☞ *Wed. after 5 pm: "Indigenous Voices of Today" and "Swallowing Mountains," free; "Hochelaga—Evolving Montréal" and "Becoming Montréal: The 1800s," \$C10* Ⓜ *McGill.*

McGill University

COLLEGE | Merchant and fur trader James McGill would probably be horrified to know that the university that he helped found in 1828 has developed an international reputation as one of North America's best party schools. McGill also happens to be one of the two or three best universities in Canada, and certainly one of the prettiest. Its campus is an island of grass and trees in a sea of traffic and skyscrapers. The statue of James McGill himself was removed in Summer 2021 after several bouts of vandalism aimed at the representation of the deceased slave owner. Take the time to stroll up the drive that leads from the Greek Revival Roddick Gates to the austere neoclassical Arts Building and meander over to the splendid Romanesque Redpath Hall building. McGill's first dedicated library is now a grand 300-seat concert hall (⊕ *www.mcgill.ca/music/about-us/halls/redpath-hall*), though the newer library building next door still bears the generous benefactor's name. If you have an hour or so, drop into the temple-like Redpath Museum of Natural History (⊕ *www.mcgill.ca/redpath*) to browse its eclectic collection of dinosaur bones, old coins, African art, and shrunken heads. ⊠ *859 rue Sherbrooke Ouest, Downtown* ☎ *514/398–3000 main switchboard,*

514/398–4861 museum ⊕ *www.mcgill.ca* ⊠ *Suggested donation C\$10* Ⓜ *McGill.*

★ Musée des Beaux-Arts de Montréal
(*Montréal Museum of Fine Arts*)

ART MUSEUM | Not surprisingly, Canada's oldest museum has one of the finest collections of Canadian art anywhere. The works of such luminaries as Paul Kane, the Group of Seven, Paul-Émile Borduas, and Marc-Aurèle Fortin are displayed here in the Bourgie Pavilion, a space built onto the back of the neoclassical Erskine and American United Church, one of the city's most historic Protestant churches. The nave has been preserved as a meeting place and exhibition hall and also displays the church's 18 Tiffany stained-glass windows, the biggest collection of Tiffany's work outside the United States. The rest of the museum's permanent collection, which includes works by everyone from Rembrandt to Renoir, is housed in its four other pavilions: the neoclassical Hornstein Pavilion; the modernist 1970s Stewart Pavilion; the glittering, glass-fronted Desmarais Pavilion; and the cantilevered glass and aluminum Hornstein Pavilion for Peace, which looks like an illuminated paper lantern at night. All of the pavilions are linked by tunnels. ■ TIP→ **Admission is half-price from 5 to 9 pm Wednesday.** ⊠ *1380 rue Sherbrooke Ouest, Downtown* ☎ *514/285–2000* ⊕ *www.mbam.qc.ca/en* ⊠ *C\$24; half-price Wed. after 5 pm* ⊗ *Closed Mon.* Ⓜ *Guy-Concordia.*

Place des Arts

PERFORMANCE VENUE | Montréal's primary performing arts complex has been hosting performances since 1963. The glass-walled Maison Symphonique 2,000-seat concert hall is the permanent home of the Montréal Symphony Orchestra; with state-of-the-art acoustics and only 75 feet between the end of the stage and the last row, it's an intimate place for concerts. The Salle Wilfrid Pelletier performance space is used by three resident companies: the Opéra de Montréal, Les

The Musée des Beaux-Arts has one of Canada's largest permanent collections of Canadian art, as well as a gallery where you can buy paintings by local artists.

Grands Ballets Canadiens, and the popular Jean Duceppe theater company. The venue's four other performance spaces host dance, theater, and festival events. Place des Arts is also the centerpiece of the city's Quartier des Spectacles, a square kilometer dedicated to arts and culture, with performance halls, dance studios, broadcasting facilities, and recording studios. The huge plaza, or esplanade, in front of the complex is a favorite gathering place for locals and visitors—especially during the Jazz Festival and Just for Laughs, when it's packed with free concerts, entertainment, and kid-friendly activities. ■ TIP → **Even if you don't have tickets to something, you can walk around the quartier during festival season (pretty much all summer) to take in a variety of shows and concerts for free.** ✉ *175 rue Ste-Catherine Ouest, Downtown* ☏ *514/285–4200 administration, 514/842–2112 tickets* ⊕ *www.placedesarts.com* Ⓜ *Place-des-Arts.*

Place Ville Marie

STORE/MALL | The cross-shaped 1962 office tower of Place Ville Marie was Montréal's first modern skyscraper. The mall complex underneath it was the first link in the Underground City. The wide expanse of the building's plaza, just upstairs from the mall, makes a good place to relax with coffee or a snack. Benches, picnic tables, potted greenery, and fine views of Mont-Royal make it popular with walkers, tourists, and office workers. While there you'll surely want to try out the newish (2019) gastro food pavilion, Le Cathcart Restaurants et Biergarten (⊕ *lecathcart.com/en*). For more opportunities to wine and dine while also enjoying great views of the city, the building's 44th floor is home to a rooftop brasserie, Les Enfants Terribles (⊕ *www.jesuisunenfantterrible.com/place-ville-marie*), which boasts a year-round terrace. And, in August 2023, two new venues opened on PVM's top floors: Rose Orange, advertised as "cocktails with a view," and Hiatus, a French Japanese fusion restaurant/café/bar, located on the

Montréal Jazz Fest offers a series of ticketed concerts that take place at a dozen or so Montréal venues as well as six stages of free, diverse programming in the heart of Downtown Montréal.

44th, 45th, and 46th floors, respectively. ⊠ *Bordered by boul. René-Lévesque and rues Mansfield, Cathcart, and University, Downtown* ☎ *514/861–9393* ⊕ *placeville-marie.com/en* Ⓜ *McGill or Bonaventure.*

Square Dorchester and Place du Canada
PLAZA/SQUARE | On sunny summer days you can join the folks who gather in these two green squares in the center of the city to eat lunch under the trees and perhaps listen to an open-air concert. Dorchester Square features a Victorian-style fountain designed to appear cut in half and two arched footbridges. Even the *vespasienne,* the public toilets built in the 1930s as make-work projects just after the Depression, was restored and turned into a little summer café with outdoor tables. ⊠ *Bordered by boul. René-Lévesque and rues Peel, Metcalfe, and McTavish, Downtown* Ⓜ *Bonaventure or Peel.*

St. George's Anglican Church
CHURCH | This is possibly the prettiest Anglican (Episcopalian) church in Montréal. Step into its dim, candle-scented interior and you'll feel you've been transported to some prosperous market town in East Anglia, England. The double hammer-beam roof, the rich stained-glass windows, and the Lady Chapel on the east side of the main altar all add to the effect. It certainly seems a world away from Centre Bell, the modern temple to professional hockey that's across the street. ⊠ *1001 av. des Canadiens-de-Montréal, Downtown* ☎ *514/866–7113* ⊕ *www.st-georges.org* 🎫 *Free* Ⓜ *Bonaventure.*

★ St. Patrick's Basilica
CHURCH | Built in 1847, this is one of the purest examples of the Gothic Revival style in Canada, with a high vaulted ceiling glowing with green and gold mosaics. The tall, slender columns are actually pine logs lashed together and decorated to look like marble, so that if you stand in one of the back corners and look toward the altar you really do feel as if you're peering at the sacred through a grove of trees. St. Pat's—as most of its parishioners call it—is to

Montréal's Anglophone Catholics what the Basilique Notre-Dame-de-Montréal is to their French-speaking brethren—the mother church and a monument to faith and courage. One of the joys of visiting the place is that you'll probably be the only tourist there, so you'll have plenty of time to check out the old pulpit and the huge lamp decorated with six angels 2 meters (6 feet) tall hanging over the main altar. And if you're named after some relatively obscure saint like Scholastica or Aeden of Fleury, you can search for your namesake's portrait among the 170 painted panels on the walls of the nave. ■ TIP➔ **For a solemn experience, visit on the third Sunday of the month (September through June), when the mass is sung completely in Latin.** ⊠ *454 boul. René-Lévesque Ouest, Downtown* ☏ *514/866–7379* ⊕ *stpatricksmtl.ca* ☞ *Free* ☞ *Free tours are available most Sun. afternoons in summer.* Ⓜ *Square-Victoria.*

The Underground City (*La ville souterraine*)
STORE/MALL | Place Ville Marie, the cruciform skyscraper designed by I. M. Pei, was the tallest structure in the city when it opened in 1962. Located in the heart of Downtown, it signaled the beginning of Montréal's subterranean city. Montrealers were skeptical that anyone would want to shop or even walk around in the new "down" town, but six decades later they can't live without it, especially in winter.

About half a million people use the 32-km (20-mile) Underground City, or *la ville souterraine*, daily. The tunnels link 10 métro stations, seven hotels, 200 restaurants, 1,700 boutiques, and 60 office buildings—not to mention movie theaters, concert halls, convention complexes, Centre Bell, two universities, and a college. In 2004, the Underground City was rebranded as the RESO, a play on the word *réseau,* which means network. You'll see the signs for it in the Downtown area and can find a map of the network online (⊕ *montrealvisitorsguide.com/the-underground-city-map*). ⊠ *Downtown.*

🍽 Restaurants

From top-quality steak to gourmet burgers, there is lots of meat to be found in Downtown. That said, plant-forward restaurants are increasingly stepping onto the scene and making a big splash with meat eaters and vegetarians alike. You'll find everything in Downtown from Indian curries, simple Chinese dumplings, Mexican cauliflower-and-agave tacos to designer veggie burgers, mouthwatering shawarma and falafel, and Mediterranean and Middle Eastern dishes that stretch the definition. The dress code can be as formal as at the Ritz or completely toned down and hip—it all depends on where you go.

Bouillon Bilk
$$$$ | MODERN FRENCH | The décor at this restaurant reflects its philosophy: fresh, thoughtful, and simplified (yet not simple). The market-based menu changes often and includes dishes that are just as beautiful to look at as they are delicious. **Known for:** private-import wines; tasting menu; sleek, minimalist décor. ⑤ *Average main: C$40* ⊠ *1595 boul. St-Laurent, Downtown* ☏ *514/845–1595* ⊕ *www.bouillonbilk.com* ⊗ *No lunch weekends* ☞ *Tasting menu: 5 services C$105, 8 services C$135* Ⓜ *St-Laurent.*

Café Ferreira
$$$$ | PORTUGUESE | The open-concept kitchen in this sleek restaurant is renowned for its for "haute" Portuguese cuisine, including roasted salted cod, seafood bouillabaisse, and a whole array of appetizers like giant shrimp and grilled octopus or roasted sardine fillets. Wine connoisseurs are attracted to the impressive list of Portuguese wines. **Known for:** seafood bouillabaisse; intimate Portuguese experience; ceviche. ⑤ *Average main: C$45* ⊠ *1446 rue Peel, Downtown* ☏ *514/848–0988* ⊕ *www.ferreiracafe.com* ⊗ *No lunch weekends* Ⓜ *Peel.*

The Underground City

Café Parvis

$$$ | **ECLECTIC** | What was once a fur showroom in the 1970s now hosts Café Parvis, a stylish, bohemian eatery with floor-to-ceiling windows, half-stripped mint-green paint, and luxuriant plants hanging from the ceiling. If morning visits are for artisanal coffee and pâtisserie du jour, dinner is for ordering shareable wood-oven-baked pizzas enhanced by fresh salads and the on-point selection of organic wines. **Known for:** quality coffee; wood-oven-baked pizzas; organic wines. $ *Average main: C$22* ⊠ *433 rue Mayor, Downtown* ☎ *514/764–3589* ⊕ *cafeparvis.com* ☉ *Closed Mon. No dinner Sun.* Ⓜ *Place-des-Arts.*

Deville Dinerbar

$$$$ | **DINER** | Located in Montréal's Downtown core, Deville Dinerbar is a fun alternative to the otherwise rather serious dining options in the area. A palette of neon pink, white, and black keeps the dining room vivid and exciting (but not diner-kitschy). **Known for:** Deville Food Cake; funky cocktails; lobster spaghetti. $ *Average main: C$40* ⊠ *1425 rue Stanley, Downtown* ☎ *514/281–6556* ⊕ *www.devilledinerbar.com* ☉ *No lunch weekends* Ⓜ *Peel.*

Escondite Cervecería de Barrio

$ | **MEXICAN** | Escondite's young, ambitious, and talented owners know a good idea when it comes to them. So much so that they now have seven branches across the city since the avenue Union location opened in 2015. **Known for:** guacamole; black cherry pork ribs; Mexican General Tao cauliflower with agave. $ *Average main: C$11* ⊠ *1206 av. Union, Downtown* ☎ *514/419–9755* ⊕ *escondite. ca* ☉ *No lunch weekends* Ⓜ *McGill.*

Kazu

$$ | **JAPANESE** | You could almost walk right by this tiny, unpretentious establishment on this seedier stretch of rue Ste-Catherine, but the line of people waiting to get in is a telltale sign. Locals and visitors alike love Kazu not for its

décor but for its delicious Japanese comfort food. **Known for:** long lines; housemade tofu; housemade soft ice cream (egg- and dairy-free) in a variety of flavors. $ *Average main: C$20* ⊠ *1862 rue Ste-Catherine Ouest, Downtown* ☎ *514/937–2333* ⊕ *www.kazumontreal. com* ☉ *Closed Mon.–Wed. No lunch.* Ⓜ *Guy-Concordia.*

★ Le Taj

$$$ | **INDIAN** | Refined Le Taj carries a piece of Montréal's history with its ornate mud wall originally made for India's pavilion at Expo '67. With northern Indian cuisine in mind, which isn't as spicy as its southern counterpart, *thalis*—platters comprising a variety of curries—are ideal for sampling unfamiliar flavors. **Known for:** vegetarian-friendly dishes; multiflavored platters; samosas and pakoras made with herb-flavored batter. $ *Average main: C$25* ⊠ *2077 rue Stanley, Downtown* ☎ *514/845–9015* ⊕ *www.restaurantletaj. com* ☉ *No lunch* Ⓜ *Peel.*

LOV

$$$ | **VEGETARIAN** | With its airy, all-white-and-green, plant-filled décor, dining at LOV (Local, Organic, Vegan) is like eating in a beautiful greenhouse. This fashionable restaurant is the kind of plant-based establishment that even die-hard carnivores will line up to enter. **Known for:** truffle fries and kimchi fries; great cocktails; biodynamic and natural wines. $ *Average main: C$25* ⊠ *464 rue McGill, Downtown* ☎ *514/287–1155* ⊕ *www.lov. com* Ⓜ *Square-Victoria–OACI.*

Mandy's

$$ | **CONTEMPORARY** | If you're in the mood for a big, nourishing, market-fresh salad served in a colorful ceramic bowl in a pastel setting, Mandy's is the place to go. Choose from among a dozen signature varieties or make your own. **Known for:** delicious salad dressings; attractive setting in soothing colors; always fresh ingredients. $ *Average main: C$17* ⊠ *2067 rue Crescent, Downtown* ☎ *514/419–0779* ⊕ *www.mandys.ca* Ⓜ *Guy.*

Ryū

$$ | JAPANESE | The salmon and avocado tartare is a must at this surprisingly affordable Japanese tapas restaurant and lounge. Vegans and vegetarians will appreciate plates like the shiitake lettuce cups, avocado tacos, and black truffle mushroom dumplings. Carefully selected wines and classic cocktails combine with sleek lighting (the dragon changes color throughout the night) for a memorable dining experience. **Known for:** high-end sushi; traditional and contemporary dishes; omakase. ⑤ *Average main: C$18* ✉ *1468 rue Peel, Downtown* ☎ *514/446–1468* ⊕ *www.ryusushi.ca* ☾ *No lunch* Ⓜ *Peel.*

★ Time Out Market Montréal

$$ | CONTEMPORARY | Time Out Market, the popular "anti–food courts" gastro hall opening in cities around the globe, unveiled its Montréal location just a few months shy of the pandemic lockdowns. The industrial-chic, dimly lit 40,000-square-foot space features a black ceiling, gray and concrete surfaces, and warm, oil-finished maplewood floors. **Known for:** arts and events space; great mocktails; curated selection of some of Montréal's best eateries all under one roof. ⑤ *Average main: C$20* ✉ *Centre Eaton, 705 rue Ste-Catherine Ouest, Downtown* ☎ *514/370–3883* ⊕ *timeoutmarket.com/montreal/en* Ⓜ *McGill.*

☕ Coffee and Quick Bites

Café Myriade

$ | CAFÉ | Aficionados are willing to wait for a seat at this small café, where the foam on your latte or café au lait is artfully arranged in waves, hearts, or curlicues. The gastro coffee is imported from Ethiopia, Guatemala, Brazil, Bolivia, and elsewhere via the famed 49th Parallel Coffee Roasters in Vancouver. **Known for:** high-quality coffee; latte art; baked goods made in house. ⑤ *Average main: C$8* ✉ *1432 rue Mackay, Downtown*

☎ *514/939–1717* ⊕ *www.cafemyriade. com* Ⓜ *Guy-Concordia.*

★ Caffettiera

$ | ITALIAN | Step inside Caffettiera and you just might be convinced you've entered an Italian café circa 1994. Here in this faux-wood-paneled space with its stand-up espresso bar, beige and blue banquettes, and block-color formica tabletops, you're likely to hear native Italians speaking together—just like in Italy. **Known for:** décor; Italian pastries; coffee. ⑤ *Average main: C$8* ✉ *2055 rue Stanley, Downtown* ☎ *514/507–2055* ⊕ *www. caffettiera.ca* Ⓜ *Peel.*

Hotels

The hub for countless festivals, Downtown Montréal is a convenient place to unpack your bags. This is where you'll find the major chain hotels, with underground parking, pools, and all the amenities that families enjoy. Some new boutique and luxury hotels have appeared in recent years, providing more options for couples without kids. From Downtown, it's just a short trip—via bike path, métro, or taxi—to the city's other neighborhoods of interest, so this is a good central point from which to see the city. Traffic often crawls in the city, and since the outdoor festival "quartier," Quartier des Spectacles, was revamped, even more people are attracted to Downtown's hotels. So leave your car at the hotel and go by foot, métro, or BIXI bicycle whenever possible.

Château Versailles

$$ | HOTEL | History lovers—and lovers of the romantic variety, too—appreciate the luxury within the Versailles' two elegant Beaux-Arts mansions, with high ceilings, plaster moldings, antique furnishings, and a twinkling chandelier in the entryway. **Pros:** elaborate décor; spacious rooms with fireplaces; easy access to museum district and to nearby Westmount. **Cons:** at busy intersection; décor and furnishings could use a refresh; no elevator. $ *Rooms from: C$200* ⊠ *1659 rue Sherbrooke Ouest, Downtown* ☎ *514/933–3611, 888/933–8111* ⊕ *chateauversaillesmontreal.com* ⇆ *65 rooms* ¶⊙¶ *Free Breakfast* Ⓜ *Guy-Concordia.*

Delta Montréal

$$$ | **HOTEL** | **FAMILY** | Business travelers and jazz and comedy festival performers cycle through the Delta's airportlike lobby every year, taking advantage of the hotel's minimalist and quiet rooms, saltwater pool, squash courts, high-tech gym, and family-friendly restaurant. **Pros:** two squash courts and saltwater pool; excellent soundproofing; kid- and pet-friendly amenities. **Cons:** drab lobby needs a makeover; fee for a safe in room; restaurant could be improved. $ *Rooms from: C$305* ⊠ *475 av. du Président-Kennedy, Downtown* ☎ *514/286–1986, 844/860–3753* ⊕ *marriott.com/hotels/travel/yuldb-delta-hotels-montreal* ⇆ *456 rooms* ¶⊙¶ *No Meals* Ⓜ *McGill or Place-des-Arts.*

★ Fairmont Le Reine Elizabeth

$$$ | **HOTEL** | Le Reine Elizabeth's 2017 retro-chic makeover boasts contemporary mid-century modern interiors; a huge market and food hall; a gorgeous pool redo and new spa; and creative meeting hubs, all the while preserving the property's iconic heritage (John and Yoko's 1969 "bed-in" suite [1742] has been carefully restored and enhanced with artifacts from the day). **Pros:** craft cocktails at Nacarat Bar and outdoor terrace; excellent dining options; stylish, luxurious rooms. **Cons:** daily fee for Wi-Fi unless you are a member; conventioneers abound; some bathrooms are small. $ *Rooms from: C$390* ⊠ *900 boul. René-Lévesque Ouest, Downtown* ☎ *514/861–3511, 866/540–4483 reservations* ⊕ *www.fairmont.com/queen-elizabeth-montreal* ⇆ *952 rooms* ¶⊙¶ *No Meals* Ⓜ *Bonaventure.*

★ Four Seasons Montréal

$$$$ | **HOTEL** | After a more than two-decade absence, the new Four Seasons Montréal, opened in 2019, offers all you would expect from the iconic brand: world-class design, luxurious rooms, chic social areas, and impeccable service. **Pros:** celebrity chef restaurant and bar, MARCUS; elegant, contemporary bar and lounge; Guerlain spa offers Kneipp hydrotherapy with hot and cold foot baths. **Cons:** only an indoor pool; exorbitant nightly rates; no outdoor spaces. $ *Rooms from: C$750* ⊠ *1440 rue de la Montagne, Downtown* ☎ *514/843–2500* ⊕ *www.fourseasons.com/montreal* ⇆ *169 rooms* ¶⊙¶ *No Meals* Ⓜ *Guy-Concordia or Peel.*

Hôtel Birks

$$$$ | **HOTEL** | Opened in fall 2018, the glamorous Hôtel Birks was once the Canadian headquarters of the Birks jewelry empire, Canada's equivalent of Tiffany's, and it wisely preserved the jewelry store's original stained glass, pendant lamps, and ornate crown moldings. **Pros:** richly appointed lobby in historic building; stunning, atmospheric brasserie popular with locals; many rooms have gas fireplaces. **Cons:** not all rooms have bathtubs; parking can be a challenge; no pool. $ *Rooms from: C$430* ⊠ *1240 rue du Square Phillips, Downtown* ☎ *514/370–3000* ⊕ *www.hotelbirksmontreal.com* ⇆ *132 rooms* ¶⊙¶ *No Meals* Ⓜ *McGill.*

Hôtel Bonaventure Montréal

$$ | **HOTEL** | **FAMILY** | From the Brutalist concrete façade to its modern and fabulous lobby (latest renovation in 2019), the Bonaventure delivers style and value, along with a heated outdoor pool, 2½ acres of rooftop gardens, a pond and waterfalls inhabited by dozens of mallard ducks, and updated bedrooms (most renovated in 2021) with white bedding, gray walls, dark wood, granite countertops, and modern bathrooms. **Pros:** almost every room has a view of the rooftop garden; easy access to the métro and the Underground City; year-round heated pool. **Cons:** high volume of business and

convention traffic; elevator ride to reception is not very welcoming; modernist exterior not for everyone. $ *Rooms from: C$269* ✉ *900 rue de la Gauchetière Ouest, Downtown* ☎ *514/878–2332, 800/267–2575* ⊕ *www.hotelbonaventure.com* ☐ *397 rooms* ⦿ *No Meals* Ⓜ *Bonaventure.*

Hôtel Chez Swann

$$ | **HOTEL** | Drawn to its Baz Luhrmann–style flamboyance, young culture vultures love that Chez Swann fully commits to the idiosyncratic design, with swirly black ceilings in the hallways, original art, custom furniture, textured rugs, sink-in sofas, a spin room, and free calls within North America. **Pros:** eccentric design; on-site Parisian brasserie–style restaurant; central location. **Cons:** no bathtubs; no pets; rooms could be noisy due thin walls. $ *Rooms from: C$285* ✉ *1444 rue Drummond, Downtown* ☎ *514/842–7070, 877/568–7070* ⊕ *www.hotelchezswann.com* ☐ *23 rooms* ⦿ *Free Breakfast* Ⓜ *Peel.*

Hôtel HONEYROSE Montréal

$$ | **HOTEL** | Whether or not you like the art deco style, HONEYROSE is a showstopper. **Pros:** stunning indoor pool; adjacent to the Place des Festivals; many mobility-accessible rooms. **Cons:** décor in common areas a bit kitschy and over the top; buzzy social scene around the fifth-floor Muze Lounge could be irritating; translucent pink shower cubicle out in the open may not be for everyone. $ *Rooms from: C$295* ✉ *355 boul. de Maisonneuve Ouest, Downtown* ☎ *514/470–7673* ⊕ *www.honeyrosemontreal.com* ☐ *143 rooms* ⦿ *No Meals* Ⓜ *Place-des-Arts.*

★ Hôtel Humaniti Montréal

$$$ | **HOTEL** | At the junction of Downtown, Old Montréal, and Chinatown, Humaniti, a member of the Marriott Autograph Collection, is a brand new uber-modern design hotel and condo construction that opened in June 2021. **Pros:** spa; gorgeous lobby filled with artworks by local artists; rooftop pool and poolside bistro and terrace. **Cons:** windows in rooms don't open; pool only open in summer; views not great. $ *Rooms from: C$320* ✉ *40 rue de la Gauchetière Ouest, Downtown* ☎ *514/657–2595* ⊕ *www.humanitihotel.com* ☐ *193 rooms* ⦿ *No Meals* Ⓜ *Place-des-Arts or Champ-de-Mars.*

Hôtel Le Germain

$$$ | **HOTEL** | Le Germain Montréal was popular with creative types and international hipsters who appreciate contemporary design and stylish details even before the 2019 top-to-bottom overhaul. **Pros:** fabulous views, especially from the new glass-walled rooms; stylish French restaurant serving excellent bistro classics; flexible checkout. **Cons:** breakfast no longer included in the rate; parking is scarce, and the valet isn't cheap; glassed-in showers, sometimes visible from the room, are not for everyone. $ *Rooms from: C$300* ✉ *2050 rue Mansfield, Downtown* ☎ *514/849–2050, 877/333–2050* ⊕ *www.germainhotels.com/en/le-germain-hotel/montreal* ☐ *136 rooms* ⦿ *No Meals* Ⓜ *Peel or McGill.*

Hôtel Le Square-Phillips et Suites

$$$ | **HOTEL** | **FAMILY** | Often accommodating movie crews and performers who make themselves at home in the sun-filled laundry room and glassed-in rooftop pool, this apartment-style hotel is full of basic rooms and suites—all with fully equipped kitchens and living rooms with flat-screen televisions. **Pros:** full in-room kitchens; excellent rooftop pool, gym, and sunbathing deck; good shopping nearby. **Cons:** uninspired lobby; drab décor; construction going on behind building (August 2023). $ *Rooms from: C$309* ✉ *1193 pl. Phillips, Downtown* ☎ *514/393–1193, 866/393–1193* ⊕ *www.squarephillips.com* ☐ *164 rooms* ⦿ *Free Breakfast* Ⓜ *McGill.*

Le Centre Sheraton

$$$$ | **HOTEL** | **FAMILY** | Newly renovated in 2022, rooms at the Centre Sheraton are now smart and inviting, with warm wood tones and modern bathrooms fitted with

Old meets new at Le Mount Stephen, where sleek contemporary guest rooms are housed in a grand neoclassical building.

rain shower heads. **Pros:** two outdoor terraces; rooms have views of the mountain or St. Lawrence River; close to Centre Bell. **Cons:** lobby marred by convention signs; lively scene not for everyone; rooms that allow access to Sheraton Club lounge on the 37th floor costs extra. $ Rooms from: C$410 ⊠ 1201 boul. René-Lévesque Ouest, Downtown ☎ 514/878–2000, 888/627–7102 ⊕ www. marriott.com/hotels/travel/yulsi-le-centre-sheraton-montreal-hotel 🛏 825 rooms ⊙| No Meals Ⓜ Bonaventure or Peel.

Le Marriott Château Champlain

$$$ | HOTEL | An icon from Expo '67, this 36-floor skyscraper overlooking Place du Canada is always full of business guests, families, and prom parties, due to its expansive views of the city from its distinctive half-moon windows and the indoor links to the métro and Underground City. **Pros:** expansive views; park-side location; some rooms have Japanese multifunction toilets and shower towers. **Cons:** can be noisy with parties; a/c can be very loud; bathrooms rather plain. $ Rooms from: C$350 ⊠ 1050 rue de la Gauchetière Ouest, Downtown ☎ 514/878–9000, 800/200–5909 ⊕ www. marriott.com/hotels/travel/yulcc-montreal-marriott-chateau-champlain 🛏 614 rooms ⊙| No Meals Ⓜ Bonaventure.

★ Le Mount Stephen Hotel

$$$$ | HOTEL | Set in a restored neoclassical landmark once owned by a Canadian railway pioneer (as well as a new 11-story tower behind the original mansion), this boutique hotel features contemporary guest rooms with state-of-the-art comforts (chromatherapy showers, Japanese [Toto] toilets, heated floors, and Nespresso machines) as well as ornate interiors that include original features, such as 300-year-old stained-glass windows and intricate woodwork. **Pros:** unique historic property with opulent interior; high-end experience; Insta-worthy Bar George popular with locals. **Cons:** not family friendly; rates match the luxury; British-inspired restaurant may be too proper for some. $ Rooms from: C$409 ⊠ 1440 rue Drummond, Downtown

☎ 514/313–1000, 844/838–8655 ⊕ www. lemountstephen.com ⤏ 90 rooms ⧉ No Meals Ⓜ Peel.

Le St-Martin Hôtel Particulier

$$ | **HOTEL** | This tasteful hotel is in a great location for shopping, museums, and restaurants, and made special with features like a year-round heated pool, hardwood accents, fireplaces, soundproofed windows, and a French fusion restaurant. **Pros:** windows are soundproof; soaker tub and TV in bathrooms; good restaurant with stylish décor. **Cons:** reception is just steps from the sidewalk and gets crowded at checkout; small outdoor pool often in shade; guests must be over the age of 25. ⑤ Rooms from: C$295 ✉ 980 boul. de Maisonneuve Ouest, Downtown ☎ 514/843–3000, 877/843–3003 ⊕ www. lestmartinmontreal.com ⤏ 123 rooms ⧉ No Meals Ⓜ Peel.

★ Ritz-Carlton Montréal

$$$$ | **HOTEL** | The legacy, the elegance, the celebrity chef, the pool—all are good reasons to splurge on a room at the Ritz, the city's grandest hotel and icon in the Golden Square Mile, near museums, McGill University, and all the best boutiques. **Pros:** revived style, but still plenty of history; state-of-the-art bathrooms and soundproof windows; indoor saltwater pool with indoor and outdoor patios. **Cons:** poor métro access; rue Sherbrooke can be dull on weeknights; not all rooms have a picturesque view. ⑤ Rooms from: C$750 ✉ 1228 rue Sherbrooke Ouest, Downtown ☎ 514/842–4212, 800/363–0366 ⊕ www.ritzmontreal.com ⤏ 129 rooms ⧉ No Meals Ⓜ Peel or Guy-Concordia.

★ Sofitel Montréal

$$$ | **HOTEL** | At the foot of Mont-Royal, in the heart of Downtown, this stylish 17-story hotel uses its colorful yet understated elegance (if the beautiful lobby carpets, made by the same company that carpeted Versailles for King Louis XIV, can be called understated), excellent service and details, and convenient location to attract a well-heeled international crowd. **Pros:** bright and tailored rooms; chef Olivier Perret helms the exceptional restaurant Renoir; within walking distance of museums, McGill, Centre Bell, and destination boutiques. **Cons:** no pool; scarce street parking; obstructed views in the east-facing rooms. ⑤ Rooms from: C$375 ✉ 1155 rue Sherbrooke Ouest, Downtown ☎ 514/285–9000 ⊕ www. sofitel-montreal.com/en ⤏ 258 rooms ⧉ No Meals Ⓜ Peel.

Vogue Hotel Montréal Downtown

$$$$ | **HOTEL** | Committed luxury shoppers love the location—across the street from the posh Holt Renfrew Ogilvy and steps away from other destination fashion boutiques on rue Ste-Catherine and the Golden Square Mile. **Pros:** fashionable new lobby; accessible amenities and some mobility-accessible rooms; rooftop terrace. **Cons:** no spa; steep valet parking fee; no pool. ⑤ Rooms from: C$405 ✉ 1425 rue de la Montagne, Downtown ☎ 514/285–5555, 844/442–8746 ⊕ www. hilton.com/en/hotels/yulmqqq-vogue-hotel-montreal-downtown ⤏ 142 rooms ⧉ No Meals Ⓜ Peel.

Warwick Le Crystal Montréal

$$$$ | **HOTEL** | The new hotel right across from Centre Bell has a modern and luxurious feel. **Pros:** perfect for the work-from-home crowd; excellent location; all the rooms are suites. **Cons:** surrounding area might get busy from Centre Bell; expensive; may be too modern for some. ⑤ Rooms from: C$550 ✉ 1100 rue de la Montagne, Downtown ☎ 514/657–8111 ⊕ www.warwickhotels.com/warwick-le-crystal-montreal ⤏ 131 suites ⧉ Free Breakfast Ⓜ Lucien-l'Allier.

 ## Nightlife

From expensive restaurants to lowly dive bars, Downtown offers something for every taste and budget. Rue Crescent, with its lively mix of restaurants, pubs, and clubs, is where you'll find most of the action, with neighboring rue Bishop and rue Mackay not far behind.

BARS AND LOUNGES

★ Bar Furco

GATHERING PLACE | Making its name through word of mouth alone, Furco is one of the trendiest Downtown bistro bars. Furco, short for Fur Company since it's housed in an old fur warehouse, is one of those places for which people make reservations—and for good reason. It's all about the industrial-chic interior, the warm amber lighting, and the relaxed, inviting vibe. And a great outdoor terrace. A nice mix of clientele, great food (the menu changes weekly), and good pours also help make this a popular after-work hangout for locals, and the perfect retreat from the Quartier des Spectacles, a stone's throw away. ⊠ *425 rue Mayor, Downtown* ☎ *514/764–3588* ⊕ *www.barfurco.com* ☉ *Closed Sun.* ☞ *They take a small proportion of reservations online; otherwise you'll have to stand in the queue outside* Ⓜ *Place-des-Arts or McGill.*

Brutopia

BREWPUBS | House-brewed concoctions like Raspberry Blond Beer or Mango Session IPA attract locals and tourists alike, and lately the kitchen has been serving up delicious tapas-style pub food, including some healthy vegetarian and vegan options. In addition to the unique brews, check out the sprawling outdoor seating, the art gallery on the third floor, and nightly live music. A typical crowd at Brutopia is under 30, but older folk shouldn't feel out of place. With live music ranging from traditional Irish folk to the occasional punk or psychedelic '60s garage band, this pub serves as a refreshing alternative to the slightly more upscale, trendy bars and nightclubs that mark the Crescent Street strip. ⊠ *1219 rue Crescent, Downtown* ☎ *514/393–9277* ⊕ *www. brutopia.net* Ⓜ *Guy-Concordia.*

Hurley's Irish Pub

PUB | For 30 years this pub has been serving up a bounty of whiskeys and brews (19 different beers on tap), with a healthy dose of Irish atmosphere on the side. Despite its cavernous size, the arrangement of seating areas, flanked by bars, makes it feel cozy, and there's a stage for live entertainment. It still fills up quickly, so unless you don't mind standing while you sip your Guinness, come early to snag a seat. ⊠ *1225 rue Crescent, Downtown* ☎ *514/861–4111* ⊕ *www.facebook. com/HurleysIrishPub* Ⓜ *Guy-Concordia.*

★ Pullman

WINE BAR | At this sophisticated yet relaxed wine bar, let yourself be guided by the expertise of the sommeliers. The tapas-style cuisine is top-notch, and the green beans with truffle oil and roasted almonds are scrumptious. During cooler months things get going at 4:30 pm, but in summer don't arrive until the sun starts to set. ⊠ *3424 av. du Parc, Downtown* ☎ *514/288–7779* ⊕ *www. pullman-mtl.com* ☉ *Closed Sun–Tues.* Ⓜ *Place-des-Arts.*

Taverne Midway

BARS | A Montréal institution for almost a century (it opened in 1927), Taverne Midway has lived through a lot over the years. In its latest incarnation, Midway is one of the trendiest bars to be found at the eastern end of Downtown, with exposed brick walls, wood flooring, and warm Edison bulbs attached to industrial-style wall sconces. It also features an extensive list of beers, wines, and cocktails, as well as a small but appealing selection of finger foods. ⊠ *1219 boul. St-Laurent, Downtown* ☎ *514/398–9669* ⊕ *tavernemidway.com* Ⓜ *St-Laurent.*

COMEDY CLUBS

The Montréal Just For Laughs comedy festival, which takes place every July, has been the largest such festival in the world since its inception back in 1983.

But Montrealers don't have to wait until summer to get their comedy fix, as there are Downtown clubs covering all things funny.

The Comedy Nest

COMEDY CLUBS | For over four decades, this comedy club has been showering Montrealers with humor from some of the biggest names out there: Jim Carrey, Tim Allen, and Russell Peters included. For a mere C$6, Newbie Tuesdays and Comedy Lab Wednesdays, when novice comedians and local comics work out new material, are always good for a laugh and will also secure you one free ticket for a Thursday 8 pm or Friday late show. Arrive early to get a decent spot near the stage (or perhaps away from it). ⊠ *Pepsi Forum, 2313 rue Ste-Catherine Ouest, 3rd fl., Downtown* ☏ *514/932–6378* ⊕ *www.comedynest.com* Ⓜ *Atwater.*

Montréal Improv

COMEDY CLUBS | The heart of the city's improv comedy scene offers shows in both English and French. The Friday night Main Event Smackdowns, where the audience determines the winner, are especially good for a chuckle. ■ TIP→ **Save $C2 on advance tickets; otherwise get here early, as the C$12 tickets usually sell out quickly.** ⊠ *3716 rue Notre-Dame Ouest, Griffintown* ⊕ *www. montrealimprov.com* Ⓜ *Place-St-Henri.*

DANCE CLUBS

Foufounes Electriques

LIVE MUSIC | "Foufs," as it's affectionately known, has been going strong since 1983. Attracting a cult following of alternative rock and heavy metal fans, it gets packed on weekends. You can enjoy a cheap beer on one of two summer terraces under the playful eyes of skulls and spiders. ⊠ *87 rue Ste-Catherine Est, Downtown* ☏ *514/844–5539* ⊕ *www. foufouneselectriques.com* Ⓜ *St-Laurent.*

Salsathèque

DANCE CLUB | Though neon lights and disco balls abound, this flashy club is all about the Latin lover—dance lover, that is. Merengue, bachata, and salsa (of course) are the specialties, but themed evenings keep things interesting with R&B, reggae, and Top 40 hits. Check the website to learn the week's schedule and sign up for the guest list to avoid a cover. ⊠ *1220 rue Peel, Downtown* ☏ *514/875–0016* ⊕ *www.salsatheque.ca* ⊘ *Closed Sun.–Thurs.* Ⓜ *Peel.*

LIVE MUSIC

Club Soda

LIVE MUSIC | The granddaddy of the city's rock clubs has evolved into one of the dominant venues for jazz, reggae, tech-no, and rhythm and blues. Club Soda is a tall, narrow concert hall with high-tech design and 500 seats—all of them with great sight lines. ⊠ *1225 boul. St-Laurent, Downtown* ☏ *514/286–1010, 855/550-7469* ⊕ *www.clubsoda.ca* Ⓜ *St-Laurent.*

McKibbin's Irish Pub

LIVE MUSIC | This beautiful old sandstone mansion includes three floors of food, drink, and good Irish *craic* (a Gaelic term that means having fun with affable companions). This isn't hard to do with more than 20 different stouts, lagers, and ales on tap. There's live entertainment nearly every night of the week, so head to the basement if you're looking for a bit of quiet (or a good chin-wag). The house fries are excellent for noshing, but beware of the Rim Reaper—chicken wings made with the world's hottest pepper. ⊠ *1426 rue Bishop, Downtown* ☏ *514/288–1580* ⊕ *www.mckibbinsirish-pub.com* Ⓜ *Guy-Concordia.*

★ Upstairs Jazz Bar and Grill

LIVE MUSIC | Five nights a week, the cheerful Joel Giberovitch greets you personally near the entrance to his club, which despite the name is actually downstairs. Giberovitch loves what he

Classical Music

The performing arts thrive in Montréal, from dance troupes and classical music groups to theater. Place des Arts, Montréal's main concert hall in Downtown, is a popular venue for large-scale productions, but some groups, such as I Musici, perform at venues throughout town. ■TIP→ Note that many performing arts groups take to the road or are on hiatus in summer.

I Musici de Montréal Chamber Orchestra. Arguably the best chamber orchestra in Canada, I Musici, under the direction of Jean-François Rivest, performs at several venues around town, including the Salle Bourgie at the Musée des Beaux-Arts and the Place des Arts' Nouvelle Salle. ✉ 4672-B rue St-Denis, Montréal ☎ 514/987–6919 ⊕ www. imusici.com.

does, and the constant stream of local and imported jazz musicians makes this the favored jazz hangout in the city. The eclectic menu makes a nice accompaniment to the live music—try the home-cut fries with smoky mayo or the linguine al pesto and portobello mushroom. Cover charge starts at C\$5 and can go up to C\$45 for big-ticket performers during Jazz Fest. The third set is free (usually around 11 pm), and other sets are also free if you sit on one of the cozy terraces. ■TIP→ Parking costs only C\$7. Ask your server for a ticket. ✉ 1254 rue Mackay, Downtown ☎ 514/931–6808 ⊕ www. upstairsjazz.com Ⓜ Guy-Concordia.

🎭 Performing Arts

CLASSICAL MUSIC
Opéra de Montréal
OPERA | This renowned opera company, the largest francophone opera in North America, has a varied schedule of classics, including Le Nozze di Figaro, Rigoletto, and Silent Night. Seventy-five minutes before each show, the "pre-Opera" program, done in French with a summary in English, gives attendees a look at the history, music, and artists of the Opéra de Montréal. ✉ Place des Arts, 260 boul. de Maisonneuve, Downtown ☎ 514/985–2258, 877/385–2222 ⊕ www. operademontreal.com Ⓜ Place-des-Arts.

Orchestre Métropolitain du Grand Montréal
CONCERTS | The Orchestre Symphonique de Montréal may lie in the shadow of the Met, but its talented conductor and artistic director, Yannick Nézet-Séguin, continues to draw the spotlight. He's in high demand across the world; in addition to his role here, he's the musical director at the Philadelphia Orchestra and New York City's Metropolitan Opera, and honorary conductor at the Rotterdam Philharmonic. His charismatic approach has brought in the crowds since 2000 and produced highly acclaimed performances. Most shows take place at Place des Arts or Maison Symphonique de Montréal. ✉ 486 rue Ste-Catherine Ouest, Suite 401, Downtown ☎ 866/842-2112 tickets, 514/842–2112 tickets ⊕ www.orchestremetropolitain.com Ⓜ Place-des-Arts.

★ **Orchestre Symphonique de Montréal**
CONCERTS | Montréal's beloved OSM, under the direction of internationally acclaimed conductor and musical director Rafael Payare, plays programs that include masterful renditions of the classics, with contemporary works thrown into the mix. The orchestra's home, the Maison Symphonique de Montréal, is part of the Place des Arts complex. ✉ 1600 rue St-Urbain, Downtown ☎ 514/842–9951, 888/842–9951 ⊕ www. osm.ca Ⓜ Place-des-Arts.

DANCE

Agora de la Danse

MODERN DANCE | More than just a performance space for contemporary dance, this center actively works in the dance community to encourage creativity and experimentation. Hosting acclaimed artists and companies from around the world, the company is also affiliated with the Université du Québec à Montréal dance faculty. ⊠ *1435 rue de Bleury, Downtown* ☎ *514/525–1500 for tickets* ⊕ *www.agoradanse.com* Ⓜ *Place-des-Arts.*

BJM Danse Montréal

BALLET | Under French artistic director Alexandra Damiani, BJM Danse Montréal fuses contemporary music and visual arts with extraordinary technique. Performances are held at Place des Arts and Agora de la Danse, and there are free shows at Théâtre de Verdure in Parc Lafontaine during the summer months. ⊠ *Downtown* ☎ *514/982–6771* ⊕ *www. bjmdanse.ca.*

La Fondation de Danse Margie Gillis

MODERN DANCE | Margie Gillis, one of Canada's most exciting and innovative soloists, works with her own company and guest artists to stage performances at Place des Arts, Agora de la Danse, and other area venues. ⊠ *Downtown* ☎ *514/845–3115* ⊕ *www.margiegillis.org.*

★ Les Grands Ballets Canadiens de Montréal

BALLET | One of Canada's premier ballet companies, Les Grands have been moving audiences since 1957. Under the artistic direction of Ivan Cavallari, the company has continued to evolve a rich body of both classic and contemporary work. Its annual presentation of *The Nutcracker*, which often sells out, has become a Christmas tradition. Performances take place at the Place des Arts. ⊠ *1435 rue de Bleury, Suite 500, Downtown* ☎ *514/849–0269 tickets* ⊕ *www. grandsballets.com* ☞ *Tickets can be*

purchased online, in person, or by phone Ⓜ *Place-des-Arts.*

Montréal Danse

MODERN DANCE | Lavish sets and dazzlingly sensual choreography have helped make Montréal Danse one of Canada's most popular contemporary repertory companies. It has a busy touring schedule, but also regularly performs at Place des Arts, Agora de la Danse, and the Théâtre de Verdure. ⊠ *Downtown* ☎ *514/871–4005* ⊕ *www.montrealdanse.com.*

Tangente

MODERN DANCE | For more than 40 years, Tangente has hosted weekly performances of contemporary and experimental dance between September and May on various Montréal stages (there are currently three venues in the city). It also acts as an archive for contemporary dance and experimental performance art, with more than 2,000 files focusing on major international dance schools and festivals, companies, and choreographers. Tangente encourages national and international exchanges between dance companies and artists. ⊠ *The Wilder, 1435 rue de Bleury, at rue Ste-Catherine Ouest, Downtown* ☎ *514/525–1500 tickets* ⊕ *www.tangentedanse.ca* Ⓜ *Place-des-Arts.*

FILM

★ Cinéma du Parc

FILM | A favorite of Montréal moviegoers for years, this theater focuses on art films from around the world. Retrospectives based on interesting themes and prominent directors are also screened. Located inside the Galeries du Parc mall, near McGill University, it primarily caters to an Anglophone audience. ■ **TIP→ The cinema offers parking at C$3 for three hours. Just ask for your coupon at the box office.** ⊠ *Galeries du Parc, 3575 av. du Parc, Suite 6100, Downtown* ☎ *514/281–1900* ⊕ *www.cinemaduparc.com* 🎫 *C$14.50* Ⓜ *Place-des-Arts.*

Cinéma Impérial

FILM | Recognized by the Québec government as a historical monument in 2001, this grand Renaissance-style movie theater, complete with ornate ceilings, decorative molding, and red-velvet seats, screens independent films, though on a somewhat irregular basis. It plays host to many cultural events, including the Montréal World Film Festival. ✉ *1432 rue de Bleury, Downtown* ☏ *514/884–7187* ⊕ *www.cinemaimperial.com* Ⓜ *Place-des-Arts.*

THEATER

Black Theatre Workshop

THEATER | The only Black English-language company in Québec (and the longest-running in Canada) continues to support and nourish the careers of many prominent artists on the national scene. Expect innovative new productions performed alongside classic plays such as *A Raisin in the Sun*. Shows take place at the Centaur Theatre and other venues around the city. ✉ *Downtown* ☏ *514/932–1104* ⊕ *www.blacktheatreworkshop.ca.*

Geordie Productions

THEATER | Promoting itself as a theater for all audiences, this accomplished English company has been delighting kids and adults since 1982. Most productions are performed at the Centaur Theatre. ✉ *Downtown* ☏ *514/845–9810* ⊕ *www.geordie.ca.*

Le Monastère – Cabaret de Cirque

CIRCUSES | Before 2019, the Anglican church of St. James the Apostle, like most churches in Québec, was broke and falling into serious disrepair. The solution for St. Jax was to form a partnership. Enter Le Monastère. The nonprofit wanted to offer Québec circus artists a platform to showcase their talents at home and was in need of an appropriate venue. For fours years now, Le Monastère has been putting on mesmerizing circus cabaret performances at St. Jax, underneath its magnificent wooden ceiling complemented by intricate stained-glass windows. The shows vary from month to month and feature different performers, but one thing is certain: an evening out at Le Monastère is an experience you're not likely to forget. ■TIP➔ **In summer, Le Monastère presents outdoor shows in Le Jardin.** ✉ *1439 rue Ste-Catherine Ouest, Downtown* ☏ *438/864-7518 tickets* ⊕ *le-monastere.ca/en* ☑ *$C35–$C75* Ⓜ *Guy-Concordia.*

Monument-National

THEATER | The highly regarded École Nationale de Théâtre du Canada—aka National Theatre School of Canada—supplies world stages with a steady stream of well-trained actors and directors. It works and performs in the historic and glorious old theater that has played host to such luminaries as Edith Piaf and Emma Albani. (Québec's first feminist rallies in the early 1900s also took place here.) Graduating classes perform professional-level plays in both French and English. The theater also plays host to an assortment of touring plays, musicals, and concerts. ✉ *1182 boul. St-Laurent, Downtown* ☏ *866/547–7328, 514/842–7954* ⊕ *ent-nts.ca/en* Ⓜ *St-Laurent.*

★ Théâtre du Nouveau Monde

THEATER | Celebrating 70 years in 2021 on the Montréal theater scene, the Théâtre du Nouveau Monde plans to expand its current space. A season's offerings at this renowned French-language theater might include works by locals Michel Tremblay and Patrice Robitaille, as well as works by Shakespeare, Molière, Camus, Ibsen, Chekhov, and Arthur Miller. ✉ *84 rue Ste-Catherine Ouest, Downtown* ☏ *514/866–8668* ⊕ *www.tnm.qc.ca* Ⓜ *St-Laurent.*

Théâtre Jean Duceppe

THEATER | Named for one of Québec's most beloved actors, this theater makes its home in the smallest and most intimate of the four auditoriums in Place des Arts. It primarily stages major French-language productions. ✉ *175 rue Ste-Catherine*

Ouest, Downtown ☎ *514/842–2112*
⊕ *www.duceppe.com* Ⓜ *Place-des-Arts.*

Shopping

Montréal's largest retail district takes in rues Sherbrooke and Ste-Catherine, boulevard de Maisonneuve, and the side streets between them. Because of the density and variety of the stores, it's the best shopping bet if you're in town overnight or for a weekend. The area bounded by rues Sherbrooke, Ste-Catherine, de la Montagne, and Crescent, anchored by the Museum of Fine Arts to the north and the newly merged luxury department stores Holt Renfrew and Ogilvy (now Holt Renfrew Ogilvy) to the south, is the corridor of chic. You'll find a tempting blend of antiques shops, art galleries, designer salons, and luxury jewelry shops displayed beneath colorful awnings. Rue Ste-Catherine is the main shopping thoroughfare, with most of the chain stores and department stores. To get here, take the métro to the Peel, McGill, or Guy-Concordia stations.

ANTIQUES
Antiquités Pour La Table

ANTIQUES & COLLECTIBLES | Armoires and sideboards brimming with fine crystal and china line the walls at this beautiful shop, while chandeliers, linens, and other vintage pieces make up the rest of the treasures. ■**TIP→ Call or email before you visit, as hours can vary.** ⊠ *762 av. Atwater, Downtown* ☎ *514/989–8945* ⊕ *www.antiquesforthetable.com* ☉ *Closed Sun. and Mon.* Ⓜ *Place-St-Henri.*

Grand Central

ANTIQUES & COLLECTIBLES |"Grand" is the right word to describe this antiques emporium—it's filled to the brim with elegant chandeliers and candelabras, armchairs and secretaries, and other decorative elements from the 18th and 19th centuries. These items would add a touch of refinement to almost any home. ⊠ *2448 rue Notre-Dame Ouest,*

St-Henri, Downtown ☎ *514/935–1467, 514/935–1269* ⊕ *www.grandcentralinc.ca* ☉ *Closed Sun.* Ⓜ *Lionel-Groulx.*

Le Petit Musée

ANTIQUES & COLLECTIBLES | The Kleins have been selling and acquiring exquisite antiques and antiquities from around the globe for four generations. One of Montréal's most prestigious antiques galleries, Le Petit Musée has been a fixture in Downtown's Golden Square Mile for over half a century. The shop, which is housed in a gorgeous graystone on rue Sherbrooke, is a veritable treasure trove covering various rooms over four floors. You'll need a few hours and a lot of stamina to take in the nicely arranged and meticulously cataloged Inuit sculptures, African masks, Chinese bronzes, Japanese screens, Egyptian earthenware, Greco-Roman works, pre-Columbian pottery, Persian textiles, European furniture, oriental jewelry, and more. ⊠ *1494 rue Sherbrooke Ouest, Downtown* ☎ *514/937–6161* ⊕ *petitmusee.com* ☉ *Closed Sat.–Mon.* ☞ *Call or email to make appointment outside business hours* Ⓜ *Guy-Concordia.*

ART
Edifice Belgo

ART GALLERY | Built more than a century ago, Edifice Belgo houses more than two dozen art galleries and artists' studios exhibiting the works of both established and emerging artists. ■**TIP→ Each gallery or atelier maintains different hours, so it's best to call ahead.** ⊠ *372 rue Ste-Catherine Ouest, Downtown* ☎ *514/861–2953* ⊕ *www.thebelgoreport.com/gallery-listing* Ⓜ *Place-des-Arts.*

★ Galerie Alan Klinkhoff

ART GALLERY | From Lawren Harris and Emily Carr to Jean-Paul Riopelle and Jean Paul Lemieux, the Klinkhoffs know art, especially Canadian art. Open since 1950, the gallery showcases several floors of Canadian works from both contemporary and historical artists. ⊠ *1448 rue Sherbrooke Ouest, Downtown*

☎ 514/284–9339, 416/233–0339 Toronto location ⊕ www.klinkhoff.ca ⊙ Closed weekends ☞ Open by appointment outside business hours Ⓜ Guy-Concordia.

BOOKS AND STATIONERY
Paragraphe
BOOKS | This cornerstone of Montréal's English-language literary scene carries the usual selection of mysteries and thrillers, but it also stocks a wide range of Canadian works. It's a favorite with visiting authors, who stop by to read from their latest releases. Sip on a coffee from the adjacent Second Cup coffee shop while you peruse the stacks. ✉ 2220 av. McGill College, Downtown ☎ 514/845–5811 ⊕ www.paragraphbooks.com Ⓜ McGill.

Renaud-Bray
BOOKS | Tucked away in the basement level of the Complexe Desjardins shopping mall, this outlet of the vast French-language book chain is chockablock with French and English books, magazines, and music. ✉ Complexe Desjardins, 150 rue Ste-Catherine Ouest, Downtown ☎ 514/288–4844 ⊕ www.renaud-bray.com Ⓜ Place-des-Arts.

★ The Word
BOOKS | Deep in the heart of the McGill University neighborhood, or the Ghetto as it's known by locals, this award-winning Montréal landmark is bursting with used books (including first editions) and specializes in philosophy, poetry, and literature. Despite its dilapidated appearance, the Lilliputian shop is beloved by locals and visitors alike. As celebrated Montréal novelist Heather O'Neill says, "Everyone says a prayer before walking in so that the roof won't collapse." Open since 1975, the owners shunned modern technology (including a cash register) until just a few years ago. There's not even a sign, so keep your eyes peeled as you walk along Milton, though the bargain books lining the window are a good clue. ■ TIP→ The Word recently made an appearance in the Netflix movie *Pieces of*

a Woman starring Vanessa Kirby and Shia LaBeouf. ✉ 469 rue Milton, Downtown ☎ 514/845–5640 ⊕ www.wordbookstore.ca ⊙ Closed Sun. Ⓜ McGill.

CLOTHING
Aritzia
CLOTHING | At more than 10,000 square feet, Aritzia's gleaming glass-fronted, two-story location on rue Ste-Catherine is the Vancouver brand's largest in Canada. Offering dressy and casual classics in addition to youthful contemporary fashions, this is the place to shop if you're looking for on-trend women's clothing at midrange prices. Along with its own collections, Aritzia also carries popular labels like Mackage, Citizens of Humanity, and AGOLDE. ✉ 1125 rue Ste-Catherine Ouest, Downtown ☎ 514/285–0791 ⊕ www.aritzia.com Ⓜ Peel.

★ Arthur
CLOTHING | Everything about this shop, from the handsome rue Crescent location to the immaculate hardwood floors and the classic bespoke men's suits with damask silk lining and hand-sewn buttonholes, speaks of quality, tradition, and style. Armenian Canadian tailor Arthur Der Shahinian began creating custom-made suits and shirts for men (and some women) since 1978, first from his modest digs at Marché Jean-Talon and later from his elegant atelier-cum-boutique on rue Crescent. Der Shahinian's sons David and John haven't compromised their father's principles of quality and friendly, professional service. The Der Shahinians also custom-make jeans and men's shoes. ✉ 2165 rue Crescent, Downtown ☎ 514/843–0522 ⊕ www.arthurmontreal.com ⊙ Closed Sun. Ⓜ Guy-Concordia.

Café Boutique Eva B
SECOND-HAND | On the secondhand fashion map for decades, Eva B has all kinds of clothes, shoes, jewelry, and even eyeglasses on offer. Budget at least 30 minutes to scour the labyrinth of racks and the "pool," a large platform in the

back where everything is a dollar. Just watch your step; the floor is uneven. If you get hungry in the process, nosh on a samosa or cookie from the in-store café. ■ TIP→ **There is now a second location, Eva D, at 1611 boulevard St-Laurent.** ✉ *2015 boul. St-Laurent, Downtown* ☎ *514/849–8246* ⊕ *boutiqueevab.com* Ⓜ *St-Laurent.*

Editorial Boutique

CLOTHING | Designer duds happily share space with inexpensive but in-vogue items at this low-key Downtown boutique with a devoted cult following. Brands include Citizens of Humanity, Dickies, Dr. Denim, Luv U Always, For Love of Lemons, Brain Dead, and Alltimers. ✉ *1455 rue Stanley, Downtown* ☎ *514/849–3888* ⊕ *www.editorialbou-tique.com* Ⓜ *Peel.*

★ ERA Vintage Wear

CLOTHING | With a reputation as the best vintage shop in the city, this upscale boutique specializes in vintage clothing, shoes, and accessories from the 1920s through the mid-1980s. Each handpicked item is carefully cleaned, repaired, and altered as necessary to give it a more contemporary flair and using no new materials. High-profile clients like Julianne Moore and Cate Blanchett have been known to drop by. This location is bright, spacious, and loaded with irresistible treasures. ✉ *999 rue du College, Suite 41, St-Henri* ☎ *514/543–8750* ⊕ *www.facebook.com/ERAVINTAGEWEAR* ⊗ *Closed Sun. and Mon.* Ⓜ *Place-St-Henri.*

★ Frank and Oak

CLOTHING | From its humble beginnings in a kitchen, this popular Canadian brand outfits young creatives and professionals in casual, contemporary fashions using ecologically friendly fabrics like hemp, kapok, seawool (a yarn made from recycled polyester and oyster shell composites), SeaCell (biodegradable fibers made from renewable raw materials found in seaweed and natural cellulose), and recycled cottons, polyesters, nylons, and wools. ✉ *1420 and 1432 rue Stanley, Downtown* ☎ *514/228–3761 menswear store, 514/360–0553 womenswear store* ⊕ *www.frankandoak.com* ☞ *Menswear at 1420 rue Stanley, womenswear at 1432 rue Stanley* Ⓜ *Peel.*

Harry Rosen

CLOTHING | This is Canada's premier high-end menswear destination. Stocked with both casual and formal attire, wallets, watches, and hats, this 22,000-square-foot flagship store caters to the classically tailored male. Brands include 7 For All Mankind, Michael Kors, Cole Haan, Tom Ford, Giorgio Armani, Brunello Cucinelli, ZEGNA, and BOSS. ✉ *Cours Mont-Royal, 1455 rue Peel, Downtown* ☎ *514/284–3315* ⊕ *www.harryrosen.com* ⊗ *Closed Sat.* Ⓜ *Peel.*

★ Henri Henri

HATS & GLOVES | A Montréal tradition since 1932, the best men's hat store in Canada carries a huge stock of homburgs, fedoras, and derbies, as well as cloth caps and other accessories. Prices range from about C$80 to C$1,000, the top price fetching you a top-of-the-line Panama hat. There are lots of women's hats on offer as well. ✉ *189 rue Ste-Catherine Est, Downtown* ☎ *514/288–0109, 888/388–0109* ⊕ *www.henrihenri.ca* Ⓜ *St-Laurent or Berri-UQAM.*

La Senza

LINGERIE | This Québec-based lingerie chain is known for its bright, cheerful push-up bras, panties, and negligees. It also sells sleepwear and sportswear. ✉ *Place Montréal Trust, 705 rue Ste-Catherine Ouest, Downtown* ☎ *514/288–8775* ⊕ *www.lasenza.com* Ⓜ *Peel.*

Lululemon

CLOTHING | This Canadian sports-and-yoga-wear chain offers plenty of styles, colors, and cuts to please all genders. You'll also find headbands, scarves, jewelry, and more. ✉ *1232 rue Ste-Catherine Ouest, Downtown* ☎ *514/394–0770* ⊕ *www.lululemon.com* Ⓜ *Peel.*

Montréal-based Frank and Oak is hugely successful in Canada with 23 boutiques and a thriving Web presence.

L'Uomo Montréal

CLOTHING | You'll come to this store for the selection of European menswear and accessories, but you'll stay for the impeccable service and attention to detail. Expect suits from Kiton and Borrelli, jeans from Jacob Cohen, shoes from UK brand Edward Green, and bracelets and cuff links from Tate Ossian. ⊠ *1452 rue Peel, Downtown* ☏ *514/844–1008* ⊕ *www.luomo-montreal.com* ♡ *Closed Sun. and Mon.* Ⓜ *Peel.*

★ Marie Saint Pierre

CLOTHING | The leading female designer in Québec (and one who's celebrated throughout Canada), Marie Saint-Pierre is known for her signature pleats and ruffles—think sleek and sophisticated rather than frilly. Now she's lending her avant-garde touch to bridal, with a wedding collection that's available only at this flagship boutique. ⊠ *2081 rue de la Montagne, Downtown* ☏ *514/419–1647* ⊕ *www.mariesaintpierre.com* Ⓜ *Peel or Guy-Concordia.*

Roots

CLOTHING | Bring the great outdoors in, courtesy of this longtime Canadian chain with a beaver emblem. There are lots of casual neutrals for men, women, and kids, with pops of colorful sportswear thrown in for good measure. ⊠ *1025 rue Ste-Catherine Ouest, Downtown* ☏ *514/845–7995* ⊕ *www.roots.com* Ⓜ *Peel.*

★ Tozzi

CLOTHING | Known around Montréal as one of the top menswear destinations, Tozzi is a one-stop shop for the dapper gentleman. Suits, polos, jeans, watches, sunglasses, and cologne—this boutique offers just about everything in a minimalist, serene environment. ⊠ *2085, 2095, 2115, and 2121 rue Crescent, Downtown* ☏ *438/375-9991 café and accessories, 514/285 6364 women's fashions, 514/285–2444 men's fashions* ⊕ *www.boutiquetozzi.com* Ⓜ *Guy-Concordia or Peel.*

Winners

OUTLET | Tucked away on the lowest level of Place Montréal Trust lies this huge discount store stocked with clothing, shoes, housewares—you name it. Allow adequate time if you really want to rummage, but if you're not at leisure, head straight to the runway collections and the sale racks for the best bargains. ■TIP→ **The Alexis Nihon (Atwater métro) location, on the edge of Westmount, can also also be a good bet for snagging a deal on designer labels and Italian shoes.** ✉ *Place Montréal Trust, 1500 av. McGill College, Downtown* ☎ *514/788–4949* ⊕ *www.winners.ca* Ⓜ *McGill.*

DEPARTMENT STORES

Holt Renfrew Ogilvy

DEPARTMENT STORE | These two iconic Canadian luxury department stores (Holt Renfrew and Ogilvy) merged into one brand, undergoing a monumental expansion of the original Ogilvy building. Unveiled as Holt Renfrew Ogilvy in 2019, the posh department store is linked, physically, to the equally glamorous Four Seasons Hotel, also opened in 2019. The exclusive megastore features loads of clean, white-on-white décor (white pillars, white walls, white floors, white marble), showcasing fashions and accessories for men and women from the world's premier designer labels. Many of these are housed in intimate, partitioned boutique settings within the larger department store. On the fifth floor, clients can enjoy a private shopping experience in one of five personal shopping suites. Especially noteworthy is the Café Holt, all 1940s Hollywood-inspired glamour, with a remarkable central light fixture that recalls a solar orb set above a square orange bar, Breccia Pernice marble and chocolate wood surfaces, and gently curved seating in plush orange velvet upholstery. The café menu emphasizes fresh, local ingredients, with the chef highlighting contemporary Canadian cuisine with international influences. ✉ *1307 rue Ste-Catherine Ouest, Downtown*

☎ *514/842–7711* ⊕ *www.holtrenfrew. com/en/stores?location=holtrenfrewogilvy* Ⓜ *Peel.*

Hudson's Bay (formerly La Baie or The Bay)

DEPARTMENT STORE | Hudson's Bay department store is a descendant of the Hudson's Bay Company, the iconic 17th-century fur-trading company that played a pivotal role in Canada's development. The Bay, as it's known by Canadians, has been a department store since 1891 and is known for its duffel coats and signature red-, green-, and white-striped blankets. Besides fashions, housewares, and toys, there's also a beauty salon and spa, an optician, and watch and jewelry repair services. ✉ *585 rue Ste-Catherine Ouest, Downtown* ☎ *514/281–4422* ⊕ *www.thebay.com* Ⓜ *McGill.*

La Maison Simons

DEPARTMENT STORE | Find the trends du jour at a great price from the youth-oriented labels on the ground floor of this bustling department store dating back to 1840. Upstairs, the fare gets more upscale, with designer labels ranging from Balmain to Chloé and Lanvin. The store's fashion-forward men's suits and casual wear are also worth checking out. ✉ *977 rue Ste-Catherine Ouest, Downtown* ☎ *514/289–1840* ⊕ *www.simons. ca* Ⓜ *Peel.*

FOOD

★ **Divine Chocolatier**

CHOCOLATE | Tucked away in a small basement space on rue Crescent, this precious little artisanal *chocolaterie* owned by Belgian *maître* chocolatier Richard Zwierzynski has lived here for over 30 years and been in existence since 1976. With its stuffed teddy bears, shoe- and bottle-shaped chocolate decorations, and antique porcelain plates adorning the walls, a visit to Divine is like stepping into a 19th-century ice-cream parlor. Chocolate massage oil and chocolate tablets made from the mold of an illustration from the *Kama Sutra* will tickle the fancy, but it's the chocolate truffles, assorted chocolates, and the dark-chocolate-ganache cheesecake that will have you returning again and again. ⊠ *2158 rue Crescent, Downtown* ☎ *514/282–0829* ⊕ *www.divinechocolatier.com* ⊗ *Closed Mon. and Tues.* Ⓜ *Guy-Concordia.*

Marché Atwater

MARKET | Heading down avenue Atwater toward Lachine Canal, you can't miss the art deco tower of Atwater Market. This is the best spot to pick up local produce, fresh flowers, and gourmet meats and cheeses. In summer, bring a blanket and enjoy a picnic by the canal or have a drink at the Canal Lounge, a café and bar on a barge. During the winter holidays there is now the added bonus of an outdoor Christmas market. ⊠ *138 av. Atwater, Downtown* ☎ *514/937–7754 for all Montréal's public markets* ⊕ *www.marchespublics-mtl.com* Ⓜ *Lionel-Groulx.*

JEWELRY

Birks

JEWELRY & WATCHES | The Canadian equivalent of Tiffany's (with its own version of the iconic blue box) has been selling diamond engagement rings, exquisite jewelry, and fine crystal since 1879. Recently renovated and redesigned and now part of the new Hôtel Birks, the luxury jewelry store contains partitioned boutiques within a larger boutique and sells items by brands such as Messika, Van Cleef & Arpels, Rolex, Cartier, and Breitling, in addition to Birks' Collections. Even if diamonds or watches aren't on your shopping list, it's still worth a visit to the elegant new hotel and the seriously stunning Henri Brasserie Française (restaurant and bar lounge), serving French-inspired cuisine highlighting seasonal Québec and Canadian products (⊕ *www.restauranthenri.com*). ⊠ *Hôtel Birks, 620 rue Ste-Catherine Ouest, Downtown* ☎ *514/397–2511* ⊕ *www.maisonbirks.com/en_ca/maison-birks-montreal-centre-ville.html* ⊗ *Closed Sun. and Mon.* Ⓜ *McGill.*

Montréal's Markes

Marché Jean-Talon in the north end of the city has an Italian flavor; the surrounding streets are home to some of the finest pizzas and café lattes anywhere. **Marché Atwater** has an indoor hall, packed with eateries, butchers, bakeries, and fine-food emporiums.

The markets are a great place to pick up nonperishables such as jam from Île d'Orléans; cranberries harvested late September to mid-October; or maple syrup and butter year-round.

★ Bleu Comme Le Ciel

JEWELRY & WATCHES | In French they call costume jewelry *bijoux de fantaisie,* and that's exactly what you'll find here: a fantastic array of colorful crystal baubles. Elegant lines from Ginette NY contrast with the bold designs of Reminiscence Paris. The glass-walled boutique is easy to miss, as it blends into the surrounding building. ⊠ *1143 boul. de Maisonneuve Ouest, Downtown* ☎ *514/847–1128* ⊕ *www.bleucommeleciel.com* ⊗ *Closed Sun.* Ⓜ *Peel.*

Château d'Ivoire

JEWELRY & WATCHES | Whether you're considering a watch, diamond bracelet, or engagement ring, Château d'Ivoire might just have what you're looking for (as long as a significant price tag doesn't deter you). Brands at the newly built, ultra modern two-story veneration of all things luxury include Chopard, Piaget, Rolex, IWC, and Cartier, among others. ⊠ *2020 rue de la Montagne, Downtown* ☎ *514/845–4651, 888/883–8283* ⊕ *www.chateaudivoire.com* ⊗ *Closed Sun. and Mon.* Ⓜ *Peel or Guy-Concordia.*

Kaufmann de Suisse

JEWELRY & WATCHES | Walk the red carpet (literally) beyond the black-and-white marble exterior into an elegant room filled with precious jewels. Founded in Montréal more than 60 years ago by a Swiss master jeweler and goldsmith, Kaufmann de Suisse is known for its flowing bands of gold and platinum. The posh yet friendly family-run boutique now also includes a dedicated VIP Philippe Patek corner, showcasing wares from the exclusive Swiss watchmaker. ⊠ *2195 rue Crescent, Downtown* ☎ *514/848–0595* ⊕ *www.kaufmanndesuisse.ca* ⊘ *Closed Sun.* Ⓜ *Guy-Concordia or Peel.*

MALLS AND SHOPPING CENTERS
Les Cours Mont-Royal

MALL | A variety of chic independent boutiques are mixed in with international fashion brands like DKNY, Desigual, and Matinique in this graceful mall, once a grand hotel. Drop by Spa Diva or the top-notch salon Pure if you're in need of a beauty break. The elegant atrium sometimes hosts runway shows. ∎**TIP→ Be sure to stop by the Barbie Expo, a collection of more than 1,000 Barbie dolls rocking some of the biggest names in fashion, including Christian Dior, Donna Karan, Armani, Vera Wang, Oscar de la Renta, Christian Louboutin, Carolina Herrera, and Zac Posen.** ⊠ *1455 rue Peel, Downtown* ☎ *514/842– 7777* ⊕ *www.lcmr.ca* Ⓜ *Peel.*

SHOES
Browns

SHOES | In business since 1940, this local shoe empire stocks fashionable footwear and accessories for men and women. Along with its own label, Browns carries shoes by Michael Kors, Steve Madden, Wishbone, Blundstone, Teva, New Balance, La Canadienne, and more. ⊠ *1191 rue Ste-Catherine Ouest, Downtown* ☎ *514/987–1206, 866/720–7463 customer care* ⊕ *www.brownsshoes.com* Ⓜ *Peel.*

Activities

HOCKEY

Ice hockey is nothing short of a cult in Montréal, the city that arguably gave birth to the sport back in the late 19th century. Although variations of the game are said to have been played in other U.S. and Canadian cities as early as 1800, the first organized game of modern hockey was played in Montréal in 1875, and the first official team, the McGill University Hockey Club, was founded in Montréal in 1877. The city's beloved Montréal Canadiens is the oldest club in the National Hockey League and, as Montrealers are keen to tell you, one of the most successful teams in North American sports history—even though they haven't won the Stanley Cup since 1993!

McGill University Redbirds Hockey

HOCKEY | Formed in 1877, this was the first organized hockey club in Canada. It is now one of the top university men's ice hockey programs in Canada, and the Redbirds were a Canadian University cup finalist in 2011. Games against crosstown rivals, the Concordia Stingers or the UQTR Patriotes, are always emotional duels. Home games take place at Percival Molson Stadium. ∎**TIP→ In 2020, McGill University announced that its sports teams would henceforth be known as the Redbirds (instead of by their former offensive moniker, the Redskins).** ⊠ *475 av. des Pins Ouest, Downtown* ☎ *514/398–7006* ⊕ *mcgillathletics.ca/sports/mens-ice-hockey* Ⓜ *McGill.*

Montréal Canadiens

HOCKEY | The Montréal Canadiens meet National Hockey League rivals at Centre Bell from October through April (and even later if they make the playoffs). The "Habs" (the nickname's taken from Habitants, or early settlers) have won 24 Stanley Cups, although they've been struggling in the standings for several years now and haven't won a cup since the 1992–93 season. (They did make it to

The Route Verte

Stretches of what's called the most extensive route of biking trails in North America pass right through the very heart of Downtown Montréal.

The Route Verte (Green Route) is a free 5,000-km (3,100-mile) network of paths, shared roadways, and paved shoulders that traverse the province of Québec.

The cycling group Vélo Québec first began talking about the possibility of a province-wide bike network back in the 1980s, but it wasn't until 1995 that the government announced it would

fund the C$88.5 million project to be built over the next 12 years.

More than 320 km (200 miles) of the Route Verte cover the streets of the city. It passes through Downtown, stretches up Mont-Royal, hugs the shore near the Lachine Canal, and extends out to Parc Jean-Drapeau, to name just a few of the major areas covered.

For more information, including maps, suggested routes, and other trip-planning tools, visit Route Verte's website (⊕ *www.routeverte.com*).

3

Montréal WESTMOUNT

the finals in July 2021 but lost to Tampa Bay.) Nevertheless, Les Canadiens are a great source of pride to the city's sports fans, and tickets for their local games continue to be a hot commodity. Buy tickets in advance to guarantee a seat. ⊠ *1909 av. des Canadiens-de-Montréal, Downtown* ☎ *877/463–2674, 514/989–2841 Centre Bell* ⊕ *nhl.com/canadiens* Ⓜ *Lucien-l'Allier or Peel.*

ICE-SKATING
Atrium Le 1000 de la Gauchetière
ICE-SKATING | FAMILY | Inside one of the tallest buildings in the city, this skating rink lies under a glass atrium, allowing sunlight to shine down on the rink year-round. After working up an appetite, hit any one of the restaurants in the surrounding food court. ⊠ *1000 rue de la Gauchetière, Downtown* ☎ *514/395–0555* ⊕ *le1000.com/en/skate* ☒ *C$10, skate rental C$9* ☺ *Closed Mon. and Tues.* ☞ *Reservations for groups of 15 or more are essential* Ⓜ *Bonaventure.*

Westmount

The prosperous neighborhood of Westmount is predominantly anglophone, a far cry from the French-speaking Montréal foreigners and people from the ROC (Rest of Canada) often picture. Still, Westmount is changing and more francophones have been moving here.

Around Victoria Village, a shopping area, you'll see Victorian shopfronts frequented by polished moms in Prada sunglasses and Lululemon leggings driving Land Rovers and pushing strollers, as well as dressed-down locals walking their dogs along rue Sherbrooke and avenue Victoria. The largely residential neighborhood has lovely parks for strolling and the homes are beautiful, but there aren't many tourist sights around here. Thanks to inflated property taxes and rents in the last decade, as well as a private management company buying up many of the commercial buildings that make up the neighborhood, many of the more characterful, independent boutiques have been replaced by expensive brands that can be found in Downtown, such as l'Occitane, Sarah Pacini, Aesop, and James Perse,

Ice-Skating in Montréal

Come the winter months and you don't have to look very far to find an ice-skating rink in Montréal. There are municipally run outdoor (some are refrigerated)—and some indoor—rinks in virtually every corner of the city. Outdoor rinks are open from December until mid-March (subject to temperature if not refrigerated) and admission is free, though there is a fee for skate rental. The rinks on Île Ste-Hélène and at the Old Port are large, but note that there is a C$8.25 admission charge (free admission for children under six) to skate at the Old Port one.

All in all, there are at least 195 outdoor and 21 indoor rinks spread across Montréal. So lace up those skates and make some figure eights!

For information on the numerous ice-skating rinks in the city call or check the city's website. ☎ 514/872–1111 ⊕ montreal.ca/en/places?q=skating.

---

in addition to ubiquitous ones such as Starbucks and Lululemon. In spite of this, Westmount is still a good place to go for high-end shopping. Rue Sherbrooke Ouest and avenue Victoria are a pleasant mix of hip shops, fine florists, pâtisseries, cafés, home décor/kitchenware shops, a cookbook store/cooking school, a mom-and-pop hair salon, grocery/produce stores, and a Japanese sushi-cum-grocery shop that's lived on avenue Victoria since the 1970s. The neighborhood also has some interesting dining choices, especially on Victoria.

GETTING HERE AND AROUND

The closest métro to Westmount's Victoria Village is Vendôme. Alternatively, you can take Bus 24 west from Downtown.

🍴 Restaurants

Westmount is a relatively new foodie destination and provides much-needed sustenance after hitting the area's upscale boutiques.

Aux Vivres

$$ | VEGETARIAN | FAMILY | A favorite among vegans, celiacs, and vegetarians (and even omnivores), Montréal's first vegan restaurant serves comfort food dishes and beverages that are creative and delicious—not to mention packed with vitamins. A large chalkboard displays specials of the day. **Known for:** roasted potato wedges; vegan cheesecake (gâteau fauxmage); dal soup. $ Average main: C$19 ⊠ 4896 rue Sherbrooke Ouest, Westmount ☎ 514/842–3479 ⊕ www. auxvivres.com Ⓜ Vendôme.

Chez Nick

$$ | MODERN CANADIAN | Open since 1920, this iconic eatery bordering the eastern edge of Downtown is popular with locals for its old-school diner ambience, friendly staff, and consistent quality of its food. **Known for:** all-day breakfast; huge range of salads, sandwiches, burgers, and pasta dishes; homemade bruschetta. $ Average main: C$17 ⊠ 1377 av. Greene, Westmount ☎ 514/935–0946 ⊕ www.cheznick.ca Ⓜ Atwater.

★ Park

$$$$ | JAPANESE FUSION | Sustainable, organic, and fresh every day is the philosophy of this high-end sushi restaurant. The menu is eclectic, with excellent sashimi, noodles, and some vegetarian-friendly Japanese and Korean dishes mixed with a variety of influences from chef Antonio Park's multiple backgrounds—Korean, Argentinian, and Canadian. **Known for:** kimchi gyoza;

omakase; exquisite desserts. $ *Average main: C$60* ✉ *378 av. Victoria, Downtown* ☎ *514/750–7534* ⊕ *www.parkresto.com* ⊗ *Closed Sun.* Ⓜ *Vendôme.*

Petros
$$$$ | **GREEK** | **FAMILY** | A local favorite in Westmount, this BYOW Greek *estiatorio* (more upscale than a taverna) specializes in seafood and has a warm, welcoming atmosphere. With its Grecian-blue tiles and shutters, white walls, traditional Greek music, and uber-friendly, bona fide Greek waiters, Petros makes you feel as if you've stepped straight onto a Cycladic isle. **Known for:** moussaka; excellent vegan and vegetarian meze; nice little outdoor terrace in summer. $ *Average main: C$40* ✉ *4785 rue Sherbrooke, Westmount* ☎ *514/938–5656* ⊕ *www. restaurantpetros.ca/en* ⊗ *No lunch Sat.– Tues.* Ⓜ *Vendôme, then Bus 24.*

☕ Coffee and Quick Bites

Café Bazin
$$ | **FRENCH** | A mélange of a pâtisserie, a café, and a French bistro, this little restaurant has been a darling of food critics since it opened in 2017. Serving deftly executed French dishes like quiche, vol-au-vent, and tartines niçoises in a fresh, modern setting of white subway tiles, decorative brass struts, richly patinated wooden tables, and mint-green velvet seating, Café Bazin is a little corner of France in the heart of Anglo Westmount. **Known for:** French classics; exquisite pastries; charming décor. $ *Average main: C$16* ✉ *380 av. Victoria, Westmount* ☎ *438/387–3070* ⊕ *www.cafebazin.com* ⊗ *Closed Sun. and Mon.* Ⓜ *Vendôme.*

🛍 Shopping

Stylish locals, quaint architecture, and upscale boutiques make this a chic shopping destination. Victoria Village (rue Sherbrooke Ouest and avenue Victoria) is an eclectic blend of hip shops, fine florists, home décor/kitchenware shops, a cookbook store/cooking school, grocery/produce stores, a Japanese sushi-cum-grocery shop that's lived on avenue Victoria since the 1970s, and midrange to expensive chain brands like Lululemon, Zadig et Voltaire, Roots, and James Perse.

ANTIQUES
Coach Luxury
ANTIQUES & COLLECTIBLES | A fixture on avenue Greene since 1972, Coach Luxury sources antique furniture, decorative items, and paintings from around the world. Their specialty, however, is contemporary and vintage jewelry and they have some fine pieces in their collection. ✉ *1331 av. Greene, Suite 200, Westmount* ☎ *800/717–6191, 514/937–6191* ⊕ *coachluxury.com* ⊗ *Closed Sun.* ☞ *Much of their business is now conducted online, so probably best to call or email ahead* Ⓜ *Atwater.*

ART
Galerie de Bellefeuille
ART GALLERY | This gallery has a knack for discovering important new talents. It represents many of Canada's top contemporary artists as well as some international talents. Its 5,000 square feet hold a good selection of sculptures, paintings, and limited-edition prints. ▦**TIP→ There is another location in Downtown at 1455 rue Sherbrooke Ouest.** ✉ *1366 and 1367 av. Greene, Westmount* ☎ *514/933–4406* ⊕ *www.debellefeuille.com* ⊗ *Closed Sun.* Ⓜ *Atwater.*

CLOTHING
Courval Fine Lingerie
LINGERIE | Whether you're looking for a sheer lace eye mask to enhance your bedroom eyes, a sexy body suit, a sensible bra, or cozy flannel PJs to snuggle up with fireside, Courval, in business since 1918, has it all. ✉ *4861 rue Sherbrooke Ouest, Westmount* ☎ *514/484–5656* ⊕ *courvalfinelingerie.com* ⊗ *Closed Sun.* Ⓜ *Vendôme.*

James

CLOTHING | The home of hippie chic in Montréal, this boutique is packed with flowing tunics, embroidered blouses, and white-cotton dresses. Add a good mix of designer jeans and funky moccasins by Minnetonka and you'll understand why James is a Victoria Village mainstay. ⊠ 4910 rue Sherbrooke Ouest, Westmount ☎ 514/369–0700 Ⓜ Vendôme.

HOUSEWARES

Ben & Tournesol

HOUSEWARES | Open since 1993, this upbeat boutique is the place to go for plush pillows, linens, and duvets from Designers Guild, which may inspire you to redesign your bedroom (if not your whole house). There are also products by Hermès, Fred Perry, Kate Spade, and others. Ask the friendly staff for guidance on the perfect gift. ⊠ 4937 rue Sherbrooke Ouest, Westmount ☎ 514/481–5050 ⊕ www.benandtournesol.com Ⓜ Vendôme.

SHOES

★ Scarpa

SHOES | One of the top shoe stores in Montréal, hands down, Scarpa, which means "shoe" in Italian, has been in business since 2008. From espadrilles, flats, and pumps to winter boots, sneakers, and strappy sandals, Scarpa shoes are always high quality and consistently on point. The company has its own footwear brand and atelier, which aptly enough is called Ateliers. A smaller collection of men's shoes is also available. ⊠ 4901 rue Sherbrooke Ouest, Westmount ☎ 514/484–0440 ⊕ scarpa.ca Ⓜ Vendôme or Bus 24 from Downtown.

TOYS

★ Appetite for Books

BOOKS | Chef and owner Jonathan Cheung not only knows food; he also knows books. The respected chef, author, and CBC Montréal food columnist made a longtime dream come true when he opened his shop, Appetite for Books, in Victoria Village. Here in his kitchen-cum-bookstore he offers private and group cooking classes, private dinners, tasting events, and, of course, a wide selection of cookbooks in both French and English. ⊠ 388 av. Victoria, Westmount ☎ 514/369-2002 ⊕ www.appetitebooks.ca ⊗ Closed Sun. Ⓜ Vendôme.

Les Petits Voyous

CHILDREN'S CLOTHING | Petits voyous, which essentially translates to "little rascals," is a darling children's boutique offering a handpicked selection of fun, educational toys and games, along with playful children's clothing, that appeal to young and old alike. ⊠ 4860 rue Sherbrooke Ouest, Westmount ☎ 514/379-1595 ⊕ lespetitsvoyous.com ⊗ Closed Sun. and Mon. Ⓜ Vendôme.

The Village

Often referred to as the Gay Village, this area is the center of one of the most vibrant LGBTQ+ communities in the world, widely supported by residents of this proudly liberal, open-minded city. In recent years the municipal, federal, and provincial governments have taken it upon themselves to promote the Village and Montréal's LGBTQ+-friendly climate as a reason for tourists to visit, but its restaurants, mid-century modern antiques shops (on rue Atateken), and bars make it a popular destination for visitors of all persuasions. The lively strip of rue Ste-Catherine running east of the Latin Quarter is the backbone of the Village.

In late July, the Village's Pride Parade, widely considered the biggest and most outrageous party of the year, attracts more than a million people.

GETTING HERE AND AROUND

The Village is centered around the Beaudry métro station, which has its entrance adorned with rainbow pillars. Its borders take in rue Ste-Catherine Est from rue Atateken to de Lorimier, and on the north–south axis from boulevard René-Lévesque to rue Sherbrooke.

Sights

Église St-Pierre-Apôtre

CHURCH | The Church of St. Peter the Apostle, built in the Gothic Revival style between 1851 and 1853, is home to the Chapel of Hope, a symbol of unconditional love. Dedicated to the victims of AIDS, it is the only chapel in the world to pay tribute to those who suffered and died from the fatal illness. ⊠ *1201 rue de la Visitation, The Village* ☎ *514/596–6731, 514/596–6485* ⊕ *diocesemontreal.org/ en/lets-connect/churches-parishes/saint-pierre-apotre* ⊙ *Closed outside of mass hours* Ⓜ *Beaudry.*

⏍ Restaurants

A little outside the hustle and bustle of the busy Downtown Montréal core, the Village is quite charming. During the summer months (May to September), rue Ste-Catherine in the Village is closed off to cars, which makes it pleasant to explore the shops and restaurants.

Le Mousso

$$$$ | **MODERN CANADIAN** | Regularly lauded on Canadian best-of dining lists, Le Mousso is run by chef Antonin Mousseau-Rivard, who dreams up exquisitely plated, northern European–inspired dishes that are as much works of art as they are imaginative combinations of flavor and texture for the taste buds. Using mostly local and seasonal ingredients, the seven-course tasting menu might feature dishes such as borscht *décomposé* (beet soup), grilled scallops lightly smoked with fir and served on coals with wild plum butter, or *tataki* Wagyu beef accompanied by cream, New Brunswick caviar, and nasturtium leaves. **Known for:** tasting menus only; minimalist décor; innovative cuisine highlighting terroir. $ *Average main: C$250* ⊠ *1023 rue Ontario Est, The Village* ☎ *438/384–7410* ⊕ *www.lemousso.com* ⊙ *Closed Sun.– Wed. No lunch* ☞ *One service only per evening, starting at 6:30 and ending around 10. Optional wine pairing an additional $C115.* Ⓜ *Berri-UQAM.*

Le Red Tiger – Pub Vietnamien

$$ | **VIETNAMESE** | "The crazier, the merrier"—that's the motto that greets patrons on the neon sign behind the canary yellow counter of this cheerful Vietnamese pub. Serving up authentic yet creative reinventions of Vietnamese street food, the three third-generation Vietnamese Canadian owners of Le Red Tiger have been wooing Montrealers in this quirky, convivial setting since opening in 2015. **Known for:** beef carpaccio with shrimp chips; mini Vietnamese pancakes; great cocktails developed by notable Montréal mixologist Lawrence Picard. $ *Average main: C$16* ⊠ *1201 boul. de Maisonneuve Est, The Village* ☎ *514/439–7006* ⊕ *leredtiger.com/eng* ⊙ *Closed Sun. No lunch* Ⓜ *Beaudry.*

Tendresse

$$ | **VEGETARIAN** | This lovely bistro, with its minimalist interior in coral pink, seafoam green, and golden ochre, attracts locals for its casual yet stylish atmosphere, appetizing vegan cuisine, gourmet cocktails and mocktails, and natural and organic vegan wines. So flavorsome and satisfying are dishes like the seared cauliflower with *panisse* and green goddess sauce, the cabbage and tofu dumplings with sesame sauce, and the sautéed mushroom waffles that even hardcore meat advocates will soon forget they're eating plant-based dishes. **Known for:** inspired cocktails/mocktails and vegan organic wines; some gluten-free dishes; cactus mocktail (with lime, chili syrup, mint, and ginger beer). $ *Average main: C$19* ⊠ *1259 rue Ste-Catherine Est, The Village* ☎ *438/387–1471* ⊕ *bistrotendresse.com* ⊙ *No lunch Mon.–Wed.* Ⓜ *Beaudry.*

Nightlife

Head east along rue Ste-Catherine to enjoy the colorful Gay Village—you'll know you've arrived when you're amid a sea of pretty pink balls and rainbow flags hung in the streets. The village has developed a bit of a foodie reputation as of late, though it's still mainly known as a place for late-night partying.

BARS AND LOUNGES
Club Unity

BARS | Small, semiprivate lounges are scattered throughout the two-story complex, and the beautiful rooftop terrace is one of the finest in the Village. Unity is one of the longest-running, most popular gay dance clubs in town—although, despite some complaints, you'll often find as many straight girls here as you will gay men. Open weekends from 10 pm to 3 am. ⊠ *1171 rue Ste-Catherine Est, The Village* ☎ *514/523–2777* ⊕ *www. clubunity.com* ۞ *Closed Sun.–Wed.* Ⓜ *Beaudry.*

Le Stud

BARS | Once a men-only establishment, Le Stud has been known to let in some women. A small dance floor and trance music have brought in a whole different crowd. It's packed most nights. ⊠ *1812 rue Ste-Catherine Est, The Village* ☎ *514/598–8243* ⊕ *www.studbar.com* Ⓜ *Papineau.*

Renard

BARS | Big brother to the bistro Tendresse, this stylish bar with huge ceiling mirrors that make the space appear twice as large gets packed in the evenings. Despite its prime location in the Gay Village, Renard appeals to a diverse clientele who love its inclusive, convivial atmosphere, festive happy hours, and signature seasonal cocktails. ⊠ *1272 rue Ste-Catherine Est, The Village* ☎ *514/903–0648* ⊕ *bar-renard.com* Ⓜ *Beaudry.*

DANCE CLUBS
Cabaret Mado

CABARET | Makeup, glitter, and glamorous costumes abound at this nightclub with drag-queen entertainment. Mado herself is a Québec celebrity (so much so that she was immortalized in wax at the now-defunct Grévin museum inside Centre Eaton). During karaoke and improv evenings, even the clientele can get involved. ⊠ *1115 rue Ste-Catherine Est, The Village* ☎ *514/525–7566* ⊕ *www. mado.qc.ca* Ⓜ *Beaudry.*

Sky

BARS | This massive complex houses a bar, restaurant, and dance club popular with both gay men and women. Weekly themed events include hip-hop, cabaret, and a Western saloon. The best time to come is during the summer, as the pièce de résistance is the beachlike roof deck with city views and a pool (possibly the hottest destination in the Village). ⊠ *1474 rue Ste-Catherine Est, The Village* ☎ *514/529–6969* ⊕ *www.complexesky. ca/en* Ⓜ *Beaudry.*

Stereo

DANCE CLUB | Some of the most beautiful cross-dressers sashay on the huge dance floor of this converted theater. It's popular with both men and women, straight and gay, and often attracts hip-hop hordes near dawn on Friday and Saturday. Don't even bother arriving before 2 am. ⊠ *858 rue Ste-Catherine Est, The Village* ☎ *514/658–2646* ⊕ *www.facebook.com/ stereomontreal* ☞ *Check Facebook for updated information. For tickets: stereo. tickit.ca* Ⓜ *Beaudry or Berri-UQAM.*

⚪ Shopping

The Gay Village is known for its excellent furniture stores as much as it is for its vibrant nightlife. Rue Atateken counts several antiques shops. Plenty of unique treasures are just waiting to be discovered, most being mid-century modern. The Beaudry métro station is your best bet.

Sights ▼

1 Chapelle Notre-Dame-de-Lourdes . **C4**
2 Église St-Pierre-Apôtre....... **D5**
3 Square St-Louis **B2**

Restaurants ▼

1 Institut de Tourisme et d'Hôtellerie du Québec.. **C2**
2 Labo Culinaire Foodlab **A5**
3 Le Mousso.. **C3**
4 Le Red Tiger - Pub Vietnamien . **D4**
5 Omnivore ... **C4**
6 Sushi Momo **C2**
7 Tendresse .. **D4**

Hotels ▼

1 Hôtel Château de l'Argoat.. **C3**
2 Hotel 10 ..... **A3**
3 Le Loft Hotel......... **B3**

KEY

❶ *Sights*
❶ *Restaurants*
❶ *Hotels*
Ⓜ *Métro Stations*
🚲 *Bike Route*

ANTIQUES

★ Antiquités Curiosités

ANTIQUES & COLLECTIBLES | A sea of chairs, lamps, tables, and other 1930s–1980s furnishings and accessories awaits you at Antiquités Curiosités, but it's the beautifully restored mid-century modern teak pieces that are the biggest draws. Retro curiosities like rotary phones also tickle the fancy. ✉ *1769 rue Atateken, The Village* ☎ *514/525–8772* ⊕ *a-lantiquite-curiosite.business.site* Ⓜ *Beaudry.*

★ Boutique Spoutnik

ANTIQUES & COLLECTIBLES | Mod, space-aged, kitsch—this boutique has it all. From Russell Spanner dressers and vintage needlepoint dog portraits turned cushions to ceramic lamps in atomic designs circa 1950, Spoutnik is a veritable Aladdin's cave of retro treasures. Owner Sylvie Rochon takes her work seriously, carefully curating her collection and adding her own artistic touches to vintage objects. Not surprisingly, her gorgeous boutique has been featured in several Québec home décor publications. ✉ *2120 rue Atateken, The Village* ☎ *514/525–8478* ⊕ *www.boutiquespoutnik.com* ☾ *Closed Sun. and Mon.* Ⓜ *Sherbrooke.*

Espace Vintage

ANTIQUES & COLLECTIBLES | Remember shag rugs? Mushroom lamps? Eero Aarnio ball chairs? Espace Vintage, which specializes in pieces from the 1950s to the 1980s, might just have one in stock, along with other furnishings, lamps, vases, and household collectibles from the era. ✉ *1691 rue Atateken, The Village* ☎ *514/561–8491* ⊕ *espace-vintage.business.site* ☾ *Closed Mon.* Ⓜ *Beaudry.*

The Latin Quarter

The Latin Quarter (Quartier Latin), just south of the Plateau, has been a hub of student life since the 18th century, when Université de Montréal students gave the area its name (courses were given in Latin), and today it continues to infuse the city with youthful energy. When night falls, its streets are filled with multinational hordes—young and not so young, rich and poor, established and still studying.

The Université de Québec à Montréal (UQAM) spreads across the district, along with theaters, bars, bookstores, and movie theaters. Some area businesses cater to a young clientele and their penchant for the loud and flashy, but the Quartier Latin is also home to some of the city's trendiest nightspots. In summer, the streets of the Latin Quarter are busy with summer festival events, such as the Jazz Fest, Montréal Complètement Cirque, and the Just for Laughs Festival.

GETTING HERE AND AROUND

The Latin Quarter is concentrated around boulevard de Maisonneuve and rue St-Denis. The busy Berri-UQAM métro station is the closest.

Sights

Chapelle Notre-Dame-de-Lourdes (*Our Lady of Lourdes Chapel*)
CHURCH | Artist and architect Napoléon Bourassa called his work here *l'oeuvre de mes amours,* or a labor of love—and it shows. He designed the little Byzantine-style building himself and set about decorating it with the exuberance of an eight-year-old making a Mother's Day card. He covered the walls with murals and encrusted the altar and pillars with gilt and ornamental carving. It's not Montréal's biggest monument to the Virgin Mary, but it's the most unabashedly sentimental. ⊠ *430 rue Ste-Catherine*

Est, Latin Quarter ☎ *514/845–8278 ext. 201* ⊕ *www.cndlm.org* ☑ *Free* Ⓜ *Berri-UQAM.*

Square St-Louis
PLAZA/SQUARE | This large, leafy square is an oasis in the middle of Montréal's urban jungle of noise, traffic jams, and chronic road works. Entering the square, which is surrounded by colorful and ornate Second Empire–style graystone homes, feels a little like entering a children's picture book, especially in winter, when the ground and the houses are blanketed with snow and the white stuff muffles all sound. In summer, locals spread out on the grass by the fountain or take a bistro table at the little gray kiosk (a public toilet, once upon a time) café that serves sandwiches, salads, ice cream, and other cold refreshments—it even offers a book exchange. And for an unexpected bonus, some of the lanes to the side and rear of the square's beautiful houses have been lovingly "greened up" with street art and vegetation, thanks to a lot of hard work and effort on the part of the neighbors. ⊠ *Bordered by av. Laval and rue St-Denis between rue Sherbrooke Est and av. des Pins Est, Latin Quarter* Ⓜ *Sherbrooke.*

Restaurants

Institut de Tourisme et d'Hôtellerie du Québec
$$$$ | CONTEMPORARY | Long held in disdain by Montréal food critics, the restaurant at the Institut de Tourisme et d'Hôtellerie du Québec (ITHQ) has upped its epicurean game. These days the restaurant's top-notch cuisine pays homage to Québec's terroir with enticingly presented dishes served in a contemporary yet elegant setting (think white tablecloths, cloche plate covers, and impeccable service). **Known for:** top-drawer cuisine and service; vegan options; nice selection of wines. ⑤ *Average main: C$35* ⊠ *3535 rue St-Denis, Latin Quarter* ☎ *514/282–5155, 855/229–8189 select*

Ruelles Vertes

Almost as emblematic of Montréal as its winding staircases fronting duplexes and triplexes, are the city's back alleys, or ruelles, with their jumble of ramshackle tin and wood sheds, spiral staircases, and rambunctious kids playing hockey. Originally intended for back-door coal and heating oil deliveries, garbage pickups, and telephone line and electrical services, they fell out of use by the 1970s. However, in the last 15 or 20 years, many of these back alleys have been lovingly embellished with plants, flowers, murals, and other artwork, thanks to a lot of hard work and dedication on the part of residents. In some cases, asphalt has given way to grassy paths, giving an even greater impression of being in the countryside. In French, these vibrant and imaginative green spaces are known as *ruelles vertes*. There are currently more than 400 officially designated ruelles vertes, representing about 43 miles in terms of distance, and making Montréal one of the world's top cities for green laneways.

Green laneways and *éco-quartiers* (eco-neighborhoods) can be found all over the city, but the prettiest tend to be located around the Plateau, the Latin Quarter, Mile End, Outremont, Parc Extension, Rosemont–La Petite-Patrie, and NDG. If you're in the Latin Quarter, be sure to visit the one between rues Drolet and Henri-Julien and avenue des Pins and Square St-Louis, or ruelle Demers between rues Henri-Julien and Hôtel-de-Ville. In the Plateau, try ruelle Milton between rues Clark and St-Urbain. More information about the green laneway and éco-quartier citywide initiative can be found, in French only, at ⊕ *www.eco-quartiers.org/les-eco-quartiers.*

option 2 from the voice message menu ⊕ *www.ithq.qc.ca/en/restaurants/restaurant-de-lithq* ☾ Closed Sun. No dinner Mon. No lunch Sat. Ⓜ Sherbrooke.

★ Labo Culinaire Foodlab

$$$$ | ECLECTIC | Take cutting-edge experimental art and mix it up with food and what you get is Labo Culinaire Foodlab. Located on the third floor of Montréal's Society of Arts and Technology, Foodlab is an ongoing culinary experiment with rotating themes that range from destinations (e.g., Jerusalem) to dishes inspired by chefs (e.g., Julia Child's cookbook). **Known for:** trendsetting chefs; lovely terrace; natural wines. ⑤ *Average main: C$45* ⊠ *Société des Arts Technologiques, 1201 boul. St-Laurent, Latin Quarter* ☏ *514/844–2033 ext. 225* ⊕ *sat.qc.ca/en/foodlab* ☾ Closed Sun. and Mon. No lunch Ⓜ St-Laurent.

Omnivore

$$ | LEBANESE | This small, unpretentious, plant-filled eatery serves up the usual Lebanese fare—meze, salads, and pita sandwiches—but the sandwiches come with a variety of twists: Thai, Indian, Latin American, Italian, pescatarian, with grilled veggies, and so on. **Known for:** Beirut, spicy Thai, and Bombay sandwiches; interesting veggie options like the potato sandwich with garlic sauce, ketchup, pickles, and white cabbage; "healthy fast food." ⑤ *Average main: C$14* ⊠ *1633 rue St-Denis, Latin Quarter* ☏ *514/750–4040* ⊕ *www.omnivoregrill.com* Ⓜ Berri-UQAM.

★ Sushi Momo

$$$ | JAPANESE | A darling of Montréal food critics since it opened in 2014, Canada's first vegan sushi restaurant is an innovative twist on the traditional sushi eatery. The setting, fresh from a renovation and redesign in 2021, is replete with brick walls, natural woods, and soothing tones, including a few stunning walls of botanical murals. **Known for:** inventive cuisine; eco-consciousness; soy- and gluten-free options. ⑤ *Average main: C$22* ✉ *3609 rue St-Denis, Latin Quarter* ☎ *514/825–6363* ⊕ *sushimomo. ca* ⊘ *Closed Mon. and Tues. No lunch* Ⓜ *Sherbrooke.*

Hotels

Bustling with moviegoers and university students rushing to cafés and libraries, the Quartier Latin is alive with expectation. No, it isn't as pretty as Old Montréal, since gentrification has been slow and uneven, but it's full of local flavor—artisanal chocolate shops, gastropubs, and hippie shops. The panhandlers tend to be funny, not dangerous, and beg in two languages.

Hôtel Château de l'Argoat
$ | **B&B/INN** | At the nexus of the Plateau, the Quartier Latin, and the Quartier des Spectacles, the Château de l'Argoat consists of two Victorian-era cream-colored stone homes, some of whose original character and gorgeous wood features have been retained. **Pros:** friendly, helpful staff; storage for bicycles, plus tools; free parking for up to 15 cars, with two EV chargers. **Cons:** standard and comfort rooms in need of renovation; no elevator and not really wheelchair accessible; unappealing lobby. ⑤ *Rooms from: C$175* ✉ *524 rue Sherbrooke Est, Latin Quarter* ☎ *514/842–2046* ⊕ *hotel-chateau-ar-goat.com* ⟿ *25 rooms* ⦿ *No Meals* Ⓜ *Sherbrooke.*

Hotel 10
$$ | **HOTEL** | Its exterior may be part art nouveau from 1914 and part modern brick-and-concrete, but the hip clientele, sleek and modern interiors and furnishings, and art throughout make this centrally located hotel *all* cool. **Pros:** rooms are bright and modern; pet spa package that includes Hotel 10 monogrammed pet robe for cats or dogs; proximity to nightlife on the Main. **Cons:** drivers must choose between iffy street parking or C$30 valet parking; weekend party atmosphere can be alienating for some; can be noisy due to traffic outside and hotel's nightclub. ⑤ *Rooms from: C$240* ✉ *10 rue Sherbrooke Ouest, Latin Quarter* ☎ *514/843–6000, 855/390–6787* ⊕ *www.hotel10montreal.com* ⟿ *136 rooms* ⦿ *No Meals* Ⓜ *St-Laurent.*

Le Loft Hotel
$$$ | **HOTEL** | Inside an art deco landmark, this chic hotel has loftlike rooms and apartments with high ceilings and lots of space, as well as sleek IKEA kitchens, king beds, funky art, leather sectionals, and expansive views of the cityscape. **Pros:** 10-foot ceilings; good for longer stays; superior soundproofing. **Cons:** street parking is scarce; a bit hard to find; dark hallway—some complaints about lack of security. ⑤ *Rooms from: C$350* ✉ *334 terr. St-Denis, Latin Quarter* ☎ *514/439–1818* ⊕ *www.lofthotel. ca* ⟿ *30 loftlike rooms or apartments* ⦿ *Free Breakfast* Ⓜ *Berri-UQAM.*

Nightlife

Though tiny, the Quartier Latin is known for its theaters, cafés, and student population since one of the major French-language universities, UQAM, is located here. Concentrated on lower rue St-Denis, there are copious bars if you're looking for some nightlife.

BARS AND LOUNGES
Le Cheval Blanc

BREWPUBS | Unchanged for four decades and showing its age, this hole-in-the-wall-with-atmosphere was Montréal's first artisanal brewpub. It's a lively spot, where music blends with the buzz of arty and political dialogue. There is outdoor seating, and it often hosts art exhibits. ⊠ *809 rue Ontario E, Latin Quarter* ☎ *514/522–0211* ⊕ *www.lechevalblanc.ca* Ⓜ *Berri-UQAM.*

Le 4e Mur

COCKTAIL BARS | "Hint: Find the secret brick to open the door that will take you to le 4e Mur." That's part of the message patrons receive when they become a "member" of the speakeasy in order to get directions to Le 4e Mur (the Fourth Wall). Named one of Montréal's best hidden bars by *Time Out,* this dimly lit Prohibition-style bar mixes some of the city's best cocktails while encouraging customers to play detective to solve a murder mystery game with fun clues. ⊠ *rue St-Denis, Latin Quarter* ⊕ *www.le4emur.com/?lang=en* ⊗ *Closed Mon.* Ⓜ *Berri-UQAM.*

Le Ste-Élisabeth

PUB | In between the Quartier des Spectacles (the local performing arts district) and the Quartier Latin, this European pub is popular in part because of its friendly service and good selection of domestic and imported beers, as well as whiskey and cognac. With one of the city's prettiest backyard terraces, this is a great place to enjoy the fall colors. ⊠ *1412 rue Ste-Elisabeth, Downtown* ☎ *514/286–4302* ⊕ *www.facebook.com/PubSteElisabeth* ⊗ *Closed Sun.* Ⓜ *Berri-UQAM.*

🎭 Performing Arts

FILM
Cinémathèque Québécoise

FILM | With more than 35,000 films in its collection, and a ticket price of just C$10, Montréal's Museum of the Moving Image is the best place in the city to catch a foreign flick in its original language (with subtitles), in addition to Québécois and other Canadian productions. The museum also stocks scripts, television shows, and various new media, with a permanent display of vintage cinema equipment. The Cinémathèque also has a nice café-bar with a large outdoor terrace. ⊠ *335 boul. de Maisonneuve Est, Latin Quarter* ☎ *514/842–9763* ⊕ *www.cinematheque.qc.ca* Ⓜ *Berri-UQAM.*

★ Grande Bibliothèque – Bibliothèque et Archives Nationales du Québec

FILM | Spread over five floors, Montréal's largest public library is a modern, light-filled, and spacious place to while away an afternoon perusing an impressive film collection. With 18 screening stations and new titles acquired monthly, it offers a wide range of genres to suit film buffs. ⊠ *475 boul. de Maisonneuve Est, Latin Quarter* ☎ *514/873–1100* ⊕ *www.banq.qc.ca* ⊗ *Closed Mon.* Ⓜ *Berri-UQAM.*

THEATER
Espace St-Denis

PERFORMANCE VENUES | This is one of several venues hosting events that are part of the Just for Laughs Festival. Touring Broadway productions, concerts, musicals, and dance performances can often be seen here. Formerly known as Théâtre St-Denis, the space expanded in 2023 and is now called Espace St-Denis. The new complex houses the original Théâtre St-Denis, a studio-cabaret for events such as nouveau cirque performances and virtual art shows, a rooftop bar, and the Parisian brasserie–style Le Molière

The projections on the wall at the pavilion of the Université du Québec à Montréal (UQAM) change according to the different festivals happening there year-round.

par Mousso, of Le Mousso restaurant fame. ⊠ *1594 rue St-Denis, Latin Quarter* ☎ *514/849–4211, 514/790–1111 tickets* ⊕ *espacestdenis.com* Ⓜ *Berri-UQAM.*

Théâtre Ste-Catherine

THEATER | With approximately 100 comfortable seats, this independent alternative theater features comedy and improv shows most nights. On Sunday, there's a free improv workshop that's open to all, with participants later showing off what they learned as that evening's entertainment. The theater also houses a café-bar as well as Le Nouveau International, a nonprofit organization run by a thriving community of artists working year-round to produce theater, comedy, improv, films, a bimonthly magazine, and sketch shows. ⊠ *264 rue Ste-Catherine Est, Latin Quarter* ☎ *514/284–3939* ⊕ *www.theatresaintecatherine.com* Ⓜ *Berri-UQAM.*

The Plateau Mont-Royal and Mile End

The Montréal borough of Plateau Mont-Royal—or simply the Plateau, as it's more commonly known—has long been known as a welcoming area for newcomers to Canada. It was a primarily a Jewish area until after the Second World War when Greek immigrants settled around avenue du Parc, followed by Portuguese, Spaniards, and other eastern and southern Europeans.

More recently, the Plateau has been a magnet for immigrants from France. So much so that the neighborhood is often given the sobriquets La Nouvelle France and Le Petit Paris.

There remain few traces of the days when the Plateau was home to Eastern European immigrants. There is still a Portuguese Canadian community here, but gentrification has meant soaring rents, driving many students, immigrant families, and single young graduates to neighborhoods farther north and east. As a result, much of the housing originally built for factory workers has been bought and renovated by professionals, artists, performers, and academics eager to find a place to live close to all the action. The Plateau is always bustling, even in the dead of winter, but on sunny summer weekends it's packed with Montrealers who come here to shop, dine, and people-watch.

Many of the older residences in the Plateau and the nearby neighborhoods have the wrought-iron balconies and spiral staircases that are typical of Montréal. The stairs and balconies, treacherous in winter, are often full of families and couples gossiping, picnicking, and partying come summer. If Montrealers tell you they spend the summer in "Balconville," they mean they don't have the money or the time to leave town and won't get any farther than their balconies.

Blending almost seamlessly with the Plateau is Mile End, one of the hippest neighborhoods in town. This funky area starts buzzing the moment restaurants open for brunch. Historically home to Montréal's working-class Jewish community, it is now full of inexpensive, often excellent restaurants as well as shops selling handicrafts, design furniture, and secondhand clothes. Head east from Parc off streets like Bernard, St-Viateur, and Fairmount. By day it's a great place to take a stroll or sit on a café's terrasse to watch the passersby—from artsy bohemians to Hasidic Jews.

GETTING HERE AND AROUND

The Plateau's most convenient métro station is Mont-Royal on the Orange Line. It's a large district, but relatively flat and easy to walk around. If you want to cover more ground without resorting to a taxi, there are several BIXI bicycle stands in the area and plenty of bike lanes.

Mile End borders the Plateau and Outremont. To reach Mile End by public transit, take the métro's Orange Line to Laurier or Bus 55 from Place-d'Armes métro station; get off at avenue Fairmount or rue St-Viateur and walk west from there. Alternatively, take the métro's Green Line to Place-des-Arts station and hop on Bus 80 going north. Get off at avenue Fairmount, rue St-Viateur, or avenue Bernard and walk east from there.

 Sights

Boulevard St-Laurent

STREET | A walk here is a walk through Montréal's multicultural history. The shops, restaurants, synagogues, and churches that line the 10-block stretch north of rue Sherbrooke reflect the various waves of immigrants that have called it home. Keep your eyes open and you'll see Jewish delis, Hungarian charcuterie shops, Greek restaurants and bakeries, Portuguese rotisseries, Italian cafés, Vietnamese sandwich shops, Spanish tapas bars, and Peruvian eateries. You'll also spot some of the city's trendiest restaurants, cafés, and galleries, as well as the dernier cri in skateboard fashion. The first immigrants to move into the area in the 1880s were Jews escaping pogroms in Eastern Europe. It was they who called the street "the Main," as in Main Street—a moniker that endures to this day. Even francophone Montrealers sometimes call it "La Main." ⊠ *The Plateau* ⊕ *boulevardsaintlaurent.com/en* Ⓜ *St-Laurent, Sherbrooke, or Mont-Royal.*

Musée des Hospitalières de l'Hôtel-Dieu

HISTORY MUSEUM | FAMILY | The nuns of the Religieuses Hospitalières de St-Joseph ran Montréal's Hôpital Hôtel-Dieu for more than 300 years, until the province and the Université de Montréal took it over in the 1970s. The first sisters—girls of good families caught up in the religious fervor of the age—came to New France with Jeanne Mance in the mid-1600s to look after the poor, the sick, and

Art in the Métro

Montréal was ahead of the curve in requiring all construction in the métro system to include an art component, resulting in such dramatic works as Frédéric Back's mural of the history of music in Place-des-Arts and the swirling stained-glass windows by Marcelle Ferron in Champ-de-Mars. The art nouveau entrance to the Square-Victoria station, a gift from the city of Paris, is the only original piece of Hector Guimard's architectural-design work outside the City of Light.

Operating since 1966, the métro is among the most architecturally distinctive subway systems in the world, with each of its 65 stations individually designed and decorated.

The newer stations along the Blue Line are all worth a visit as well, particularly Outremont, with a glass-block design from 1988. Even Place-d'Armes, one of the least visually remarkable stations in the system, includes a treasure: look for the small exhibit of archaeological artifacts representing each of Montréal's four historical eras (Indigenous, French, English, and multicultural).

the dying. The order's museum—tucked away in a corner of the hospital the nuns built but no longer run—captures the spirit of that age with a series of meticulously bilingual exhibits. Just reading the excerpts from the letters and diaries of those young women helps you to understand the zeal that drove them to abandon the comforts of home for the hardships of the colonies. The museum also traces the history of medicine and nursing in Montréal. ■ TIP→ **Tours are also offered on select weekend dates (in French and English). Call for more details or check the website.** ⊠ *201 av. des Pins Ouest, The Plateau* 🕾 *514/849–2919* ⊕ *museedeshospitalieres.qc.ca/en* 🖾 *C$12* ⊙ *Closed 12–1 pm and Mon.* Ⓜ *Sherbrooke, then Bus 144; or Place-des-Arts, then Bus 129 or 80.*

Parc Lafontaine

CITY PARK | You could say that Parc Lafontaine is a microcosm of Montréal: the eastern half is French, with paths, gardens, and lawns laid out in geometric shapes; the western half is English, with meandering paths and irregularly shaped ponds that follow the natural contours of the land. In summer, you can take advantage of bowling greens, tennis courts, an open-air theater (Théâtre de Verdure), where there are free events, and two artificial lakes with paddle boats. In winter, one lake becomes a large skating rink. The park is named for Sir Louis-Hippolyte Lafontaine (1807–64), a pioneer of responsible government in Canada. ⊠ *3933 av. Parc Lafontaine, The Plateau* 🕾 *514/872–6381* Ⓜ *Sherbrooke or Mont-Royal.*

🍽 Restaurants

Peppered with bistros, restos, and cafés, the Plateau has a bohemian edge that can't really be found anywhere else in the city. Chef-owned eateries favor market cuisine served among décor of brick walls and hardwood floors. Noisy French-style bistros, like L'Express, are local institutions, while cafés populated by poets and students with laptops abound. You'll find everything here: old-school Jewish delis, Greek, Peruvian, Italian, Vietnamese, Venezuelan, Colombian, and Thai, along with sushi, vegan haute cuisine, and stubborn little bakeries that refuse to mechanize.

As Montréal's equivalent of Brooklyn and Shoreditch, Mile End caters mostly to hip creatives. Between hipster-run cafés and locally sourced British gastropubs, this neighborhood sets the trends and constantly pushes the limits of culinary experimentation.

Au Pied de Cochon

$$$$ | BISTRO | Not for the timid, the menu at this famous bistro—one of the late Anthony Bourdain's favorites—is an ode to gluttony. Wild restaurateur and chef Martin Picard serves pickled bison tongue, guinea hen liver mousse, duck in a can, a whole pig's head for two, and pork hocks braised in maple syrup. **Known for:** foie gras poutine and other over-the-top foie gras concoctions; difficulty snagging reservations; local celebrity chef. Ⓢ *Average main: C$45* ⊠ *536 av. Duluth Est, The Plateau* ☎ *514/281–1114* ⊕ *www.aupieddecochon.ca* ☉ *Closed Mon. and Tues. No lunch* Ⓜ *Mont-Royal.*

★ Beautys Luncheonette

$$ | DINER | FAMILY | The Schkolnick family has been serving brunch at this Montréal landmark since 1942 and very little here has changed, including the menu. On weekends, the line out front can be daunting. **Known for:** historic venue; bagel with lox; long lines on the weekend. Ⓢ *Average main: C$18* ⊠ *93 av. du Mont-Royal Ouest, The Plateau* ☎ *514/849–8883* ⊕ *www.facebook.com/beautysmtl* ☉ *Closed Tues.* Ⓜ *Mont-Royal.*

Chez Victoire

$$$$ | MODERN FRENCH | A beacon of the French cultural diaspora in Montréal, Chez Victoire is the epitome of Plateau Mont-Royal's joie de vivre and warmth. Fittingly, the creative menu features French-inspired seasonal market cuisine. **Known for:** organic wines; homemade charcuterie; roasted cauliflower and truffles dish. Ⓢ *Average main: C$35* ⊠ *1453 av. Mont-Royal Est, The Plateau* ☎ *514/521–6789* ⊕ *chezvictoire.com* ☉ *No lunch* Ⓜ *Mont-Royal.*

ChuChai

$$$ | THAI | Vegans, vegetarians, and meat eaters alike love this casual Thai restaurant where no meat is served. The chefs prepare meatless versions of such classics as calamari with basil, crispy duck with spinach, chicken with green beans, fish with three hot sauces, and beef with yellow curry and coconut milk—substituting the real thing for soy and seitan. **Known for:** mock duck with soy sauce; miam kram appetizer (coconut, ginger, pepper, nuts, and lime); "Thaïpas" (Thai tapas). Ⓢ *Average main: C$21* ⊠ *4088 rue St-Denis, The Plateau* ☎ *514/843–4194* ⊕ *www.chuchai.ca* ☉ *Closed Sun. and Mon. No lunch* Ⓜ *Mont-Royal.*

HELM Microbrasserie

$$ | CANADIAN | Few places in Montréal are more Québécois than this lively microbrewery/gastropub, where the atmosphere is electrifying on hockey night if the local team, the Canadiens, is playing. With its own set of brews named after iconic Mile End streets and a terroir-inspired, locally sourced menu, HELM (which stands for barley, water, yeast, and malt in French) is in and of itself a vibrant homage to the city's dynamic beer culture. **Known for:** Montréal-inspired microbrews; burgers; dog-friendly. Ⓢ *Average main: C$18* ⊠ *273 rue Bernard Ouest, Mile End* ☎ *514/276–0473* ⊕ *www.helmmicrobrasserie.ca* Ⓜ *Rosemont.*

★ La Banquise

$$ | CANADIAN | FAMILY | Québec is notorious for poutine—French fries topped with cheese curds and gravy—and La Banquise has been the place for an authentic experience since 1968 with an extensive menu featuring 31 varieties. Neophytes might want to stick with La Classique, but mouthwatering novelties like La Taquise (guacamole, sour cream, tomatoes), L'Obélix (smoked meat), La Veggie Reggie (pickles, tomatoes, creamy coleslaw, and Banquise sauce), and La Véganomane (vegan sauce and

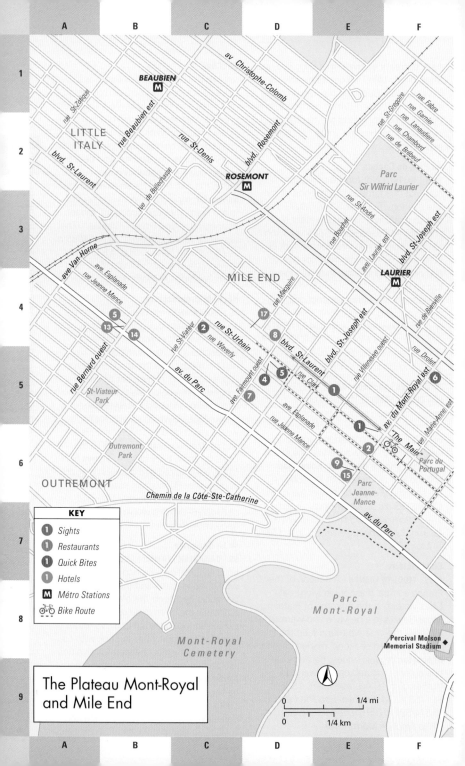

The Plateau Mont-Royal and Mile End

Sights ▼

1 Boulevard St-Laurent **E5**
2 Musée des Hospitalières
 de l'Hotel-Dieu **G7**
3 Parc Lafontaine **I4**

Restaurants ▼

1 Au Pied de Cochon **H5**
2 Beautys Luncheonette............ **E6**
3 Chez Victoire **H3**
4 ChuChai............................ **G5**
5 HELM Microbrasserie............ **B4**
6 La Banquise **H4**
7 La Tamalera **D5**
8 Lawrence........................... **D4**
9 Le Filet **E6**
10 Le Virunga **H5**
11 L'Express........................... **H6**
12 Maison Publique................... **G2**
13 Nouveau Palais **B4**
14 Phyllo Bar Melina's............... **B4**
15 Restaurant Hà...................... **E6**
16 Schwartz's Delicatessen **G7**
17 Sparrow's........................... **D4**
18 Yokato Yokabai **G5**

Quick Bites ▼

1 Boulangerie Hof Kelsten........... **E6**
2 Café Olimpico **C4**
3 Café Replika **G6**
4 Drogheria Fine Conserve **D5**
5 Kem CoBa **D5**
6 Patisserie Au Kouign Amann...... **F5**
7 Pâtisserie Rhubarbe............... **G2**
8 Pâtisserie Végane
 Sophie Sucrée **G7**
9 St-Viateur Bagel & Café **G3**

Hotels ▼

1 Auberge de la Fontaine **H4**

cheese) are quite alluring. **Known for:** open 24 hours; cash only; smoked-meat poutine. $ *Average main: C$14* ⊠ *994 rue Rachel Est, The Plateau* 🕾 *514/525–2415* ⊕ *www.labanquise.com* ═ *No credit cards* Ⓜ *Mont-Royal.*

La Tamalera

$$ | **MEXICAN** | **FAMILY** | The kitschy décor at this cute little Mexican joint includes a display of religious icons as well as vibrantly colorful furniture, while the menu is haute Mexican street cuisine at its best. The food here is simple, but everything is fresh and delicious. **Known for:** corn-based homemade tacos and tortilla chips; homemade beverages; vibrant décor. $ *Average main: C$15* ⊠ *226 av. Fairmount Ouest, Mile End* 🕾 *438/381–5034* ⊕ *www.latamaleramontreal.com* ═ *No credit cards* ⊙ *Closed Mon. No dinner weekends* Ⓜ *Laurier.*

★ Lawrence

$$$$ | **CANADIAN** | There are lines outside this hip establishment before the restaurant even opens. The primarily teal blue and emerald green color palette makes for a soothing ambience—even the menu's binding is a chic peacock blue—the vibe is laid back and the service warm. **Known for:** British-inspired fare; extensive cocktail menu; flawless service with a no-tipping model—all prices include service. $ *Average main: C$34* ⊠ *9 av. Fairmount Est, Mile End* 🕾 *514/796–5686* ⊕ *lawrencemtl.com* ⊙ *Closed Sun.–Wed., No dinner Fri.* Ⓜ *Laurier.*

Le Filet

$$$$ | **MODERN CANADIAN** | A study in contrasts, Le Filet has a discreet blink-and-you'll-miss-it façade with a glitzy black-and-gold interior and a hot-spot buzz. Though it's been around a while, there is no mixed messaging when it comes to the exacting presentation and superb food and wine. **Known for:** voted a top-three seafood restaurant in the city by ThreeBestRated Canada; expert sommeliers; garnished oysters. $ *Average*

main: C$42 ⊠ *219 av. Mont-Royal Ouest, The Plateau* 🕾 *514/360–6060* ⊕ *lefilet. ca* ⊙ *Closed Sun.–Tues. No lunch* Ⓜ *Mont-Royal.*

★ L'Express

$$$ | **FRENCH** | **FAMILY** | This iconic Montréal bistro hasn't changed much since its opening in 1980, and it's just as well—regulars would throw a fit if it did. Quintessential French fare is fairly priced and appetizing, outstanding even, with dishes like steak tartare with fries, salmon with sorrel, and calf's liver with tarragon. **Known for:** steak tartare; lively atmosphere; late-night dining. $ *Average main: C$27* ⊠ *3927 rue St-Denis, The Plateau* 🕾 *514/845–5333* ⊕ *restaurantlexpress. com* ⊙ *Closed Sun.* Ⓜ *Sherbrooke.*

★ Le Virunga

$$$$ | **AFRICAN** | A mother-daughter team helm this delightfully cozy pan-African Québécois fusion restaurant in the Plateau. Innovative and well-executed dishes like cassava couscous with okra and goat stew celebrate local produce and sub-Saharan flavors for an experience you won't soon forget. **Known for:** goat stew; excellent cocktails and South African wine; homey, high-end cooking in an intimate setting. $ *Average main: C$35* ⊠ *851 rue Rachel Est, The Plateau* 🕾 *514/504–8642* ⊕ *www.levirungares-taurant.ca* ⊙ *Closed Sun.–Tues. No lunch* Ⓜ *Mont-Royal.*

Maison Publique

$$$$ | **CANADIAN** | Local celebrity chef Derek Dammann teamed up with famed British chef Jamie Oliver to open this pub-style restaurant that perfectly blends Canadian and British traditions. The interior is dark and cozy; the handwritten menu changes frequently based on what's in season. **Known for:** Welsh rarebit; dishes intended for sharing; celebrity chef owners. $ *Average main: C$40* ⊠ *4720 rue Marquette, The Plateau* 🕾 *514/507–0555* ⊕ *maisonpublique.com* ⊙ *Closed Sun. and Mon.* Ⓜ *Laurier.*

Nouveau Palais

$$ | **CANADIAN** | **FAMILY** | Hipsters head to this laid-back '70s diner for one thing: delicious, classic greasy-spoon dishes with a modern twist (a close second is the décor; think cheap wood paneling and vinyl seats). The Palace Hamburger (Palais Burger) is gaining a reputation among Montrealers as one of the best in the city, and the sweet-potato pie also has fans. ■TIP➔ **On Friday and Saturday the bar is open until 1 am. Known for:** fish-and-chips; house burger (meat and veggie versions); arctic char with fingerling potatoes, leeks, and crème fraîche. $ *Average main: C$18* ⊠ *281 rue Bernard Ouest, Mile End* ☎ 514/273–1180 ⊕ *www.nouveaupalais.com* ⊙ *Closed Mon. No lunch* Ⓜ *Rosemont.*

Phyllo Bar Melina's

$ | **GREEK** | **FAMILY** | It may be in the heart of trendy Mile End, but this "phyllo bar" looks like it was transported directly from Athens, with food arriving on checkered cobalt-blue wax paper. The spanakopita, with a perfect crispy exterior, makes for an excellent lunch on the go, as does the Melina sandwich, with its spicy feta spread, kalamata hummus, cucumbers, tomatoes, and *graviera*. Another must, the *bougatsa*, is a warm custard-filled phyllo pastry with cinnamon. **Known for:** bougatsa pastry; some vegan and vegetarian eats; "evil eye" lemon sugar cookie. $ *Average main: C$9* ⊠ *5733 av. du Parc, Mile End* ☎ 514/270–1675 ⊕ *phyllobarmelinas.com* Ⓜ *Parc.*

Restaurant Hà

$$$ | **VIETNAMESE** | Located at the foot of Mount Royal, this unassuming but contemporary local hot spot serves some of the best Vietnamese fare in the city on one of the most enjoyable patios in Montréal. "Simple yet edgy" are the operative words to describe the menu here. Steamed buns blackened with squid ink, ginger-carrot crispy tofu, and grilled chicken à la *citronnelle* with napa cabbage are among the surprising novelties.

■TIP➔ **There is a second location at 600 rue William in Old Montréal. Known for:** authentic Vietnamese food; lovely terrace; squid-ink steamed buns. $ *Average main: C$25* ⊠ *243 av. Mont-Royal Ouest, The Plateau* ☎ 438/793–5887 ⊕ *www.restirantha.com* ⊙ *Closed Sun. and Mon. No lunch* Ⓜ *Mont-Royal.*

★ Schwartz's Delicatessen

$$ | **JEWISH DELI** | **FAMILY** | Many would say that you simply haven't eaten in Montréal if you haven't eaten at Schwartz's, Canada's oldest deli. This Montréal classic has zero frills on the décor front, yet crowds have been lining up here since 1928 for a thick and legendary smoked-meat sandwich on rye with mustard. **Known for:** local institution; sandwiches with smoked meat marinated in herbs and spices; poutine à la Schwartz's. $ *Average main: C$16* ⊠ *3895 boul. St-Laurent, The Plateau* ☎ 514/842–4813 ⊕ *www.schwartzsdeli.com* Ⓜ *Sherbrooke.*

Sparrow

$$ | **MODERN BRITISH** | Part cocktail bar, part British restaurant, this vintage-inspired spot with wooden pew seats sports a welcoming aviary motif. Dinner favorites are the soba noodles with salmon bok choy, the fried chicken burger, and the portobello burger, while the most popular dishes for brunch include the buckwheat pancakes, the smoked trout, and the Turkish breakfast plate. **Known for:** organic, hormone-free burgers; weekend brunch; basil gimlet. $ *Average main: C$18* ⊠ *5322 boul. St-Laurent, Mile End* ☎ 514/507–1642 ⊕ *www.lesparrowbar.com* ⊙ *No lunch* Ⓜ *Laurier.*

Yokato Yokabai

$$ | **JAPANESE** | Frequently cited as the best ramen house in Montréal bar none, Yokato Yokabai is a discreet restaurant that deserves to be visited by all noodle lovers—especially when temperatures drop below the freezing point here. The décor—dark-wood paneling and minimal knickknacks—immediately transports diners to a Japanese hole-in-the-wall. **Known**

for: sesame and mushroom ramen; atmospheric décor; noodles handmade on-site. ⑤ *Average main: C$18* ✉ *4185 rue Drolet, The Plateau* ☎ *514/282–9991* ⊕ *www.yoka.ca* Ⓜ *Mont-Royal.*

☕ Coffee and Quick Bites

★ Boulangerie Hof Kelsten
$ | BAKERY | The mastermind behind this photogenic bakery had been making bread for Montréal's best restaurants for years before he decided to open up his own place. His own shop is a favorite with locals, who line up every weekend for fresh baguettes. **Known for:** chocolate babka; Jewish cuisine; panettone. ⑤ *Average main: C$10* ✉ *4524 boul. St-Laurent, The Plateau* ☎ *514/649–7991* ⊕ *hofkelsten.com* Ⓜ *Mont-Royal.*

★ Café Olimpico
$ | CAFÉ | FAMILY | Ranked one of the world's best cafés by the United Kingdom's *Telegraph*, this unpretentious 1970s-style café is popular with locals for Italian pastries like cannoli and pistachio bomboloni and, of course, great espresso made from a secret blend of six different coffee beans. It's also a good place to get a feel for authentic Montréal. **Known for:** gourmet coffee; sunny patio; local spot. ⑤ *Average main: C$7* ✉ *124 rue St-Viateur Ouest, Mile End* ☎ *514/495–0746* ⊕ *www.cafeolimpico.com* Ⓜ *Rosemont.*

Café Replika
$ | TURKISH | FAMILY | Students, freelancers, and local hipsters flock to this understated Turkish café for two reasons: the gourmet coffee and the food. Between the Nutella-and-sea-salt cookie, the feta-and-sausage omelet, and the *borek* (a traditional flaky pastry sprinkled with sesame seeds), it's hard to pick just one thing off Replika's menu. **Known for:** latte art; Turkish fare; friendly owners. ⑤ *Average main: C$7* ✉ *252 rue Rachel Est, The Plateau* ☎ *514/903–4384* ⊕ *www.cafereplika.com* Ⓜ *Mont-Royal.*

Drogheria Fine Conserve
$ | ITALIAN | Locals line up outside the window of this shoebox-sized joint, sandwiched between ice-cream shop Kem CoBa and Fairmount Bagel, to get their fix of Nonna Caterina Gattuso's gnocchi topped with her famous Calabrian tomato sauce. It's served in a little cardboard take-out container and costs only C$5. If you ask for parmesan and extra spice it's C$6. ⑤ *Average main: C$5* ✉ *68 av. Fairmount Ouest, Mile End* ☎ *514/588–7477* ⊕ *lasalsadellanonna.com* Ⓜ *St-Laurent, then Bus 55 north.*

★ Kem CoBa
$ | ICE CREAM | FAMILY | Only one word accurately describes the all-natural goodness at this ice-cream and sorbet stand: *yum.* Flavors change frequently based on what chefs find at the market, but the lightly salted butter ice cream is a staple; partner it with the apple sorbet and you'll have yourself an apple pie on a cone. Or, better yet, give the "soft serve of the week" a taste. **Known for:** cash only; inventive soft serve flavors; local favorite. ⑤ *Average main: C$6* ✉ *60 av. Fairmount Ouest, Mile End* ☎ *514/419–1699* ⊕ *www.facebook.com/profile.php?id=100057383353586* ⊟ *No credit cards* ⊗ *Closed Mon. and Oct.–Apr.* Ⓜ *Laurier.*

Pâtisserie Au Kouign Amann
$ | BAKERY | This compact bakery serves some of the best croissants in Montréal, but the specialty here is the eponymous *kouign-amann*, a multilayered butter-and-sugar cake originally from Brittany. The aroma of freshly baked bread is alluring to say the least, and the passion for pastries is evident and sometimes demonstrated by perfectionist owner and native Breton Nicolas Henri. **Known for:** kouign-amman; perfect croissants; tiny gem. ⑤ *Average main: C$6* ✉ *316 av. Mont Royal Est, The Plateau* ☎ *514/845–8813* ⊕ *aukouingamann.com* ⊟ *No credit cards* ⊗ *Closed Sun. and Mon.* Ⓜ *Mont-Royal.*

⭐ Pâtisserie Rhubarbe

$ | **BAKERY** | This small and tastefully decorated bakery is, simply put, a Montréal treasure. Locals come from all over the city to pick up delicious desserts like lemon tarts, Paris-Brest, and the pâtisserie's more modern take on the mille-feuille, all of which taste as good as they look. **Known for:** croissants; dacquoise pistache; Paris-Brest. ⑤ *Average main: C$8 ⊠ 1479 av. Laurier Est, The Plateau* ☎ *514/316–2935 ⊕ www.patisserierhubarbe.com* ⊗ *Closed Mon.–Wed.* Ⓜ *Laurier.*

Pâtisserie Végane Sophie Sucrée

$ | **CAFÉ** | Celebrating its 10th anniversary in 2023, Sophie Sucrée was the first vegan bakery to open in Montréal. Owner Milène Laoun, a self-taught pastry cook, developed her skills by cooking and baking for her loved ones. **Known for:** almond croissant; triple chocolate cake; cherry "cheese" cake. ⑤ *Average main: C$8 ⊠ 3770 boul. St-Laurent, The Plateau* ☎ *514/823–5865 ⊕ www.sophiesucree.com* Ⓜ *St-Laurent.*

St-Viateur Bagel & Café

$$ | **CAFÉ | FAMILY** | Even New Yorkers have been known to (collective gasp!) prefer Montréal's light and crispy bagel to its bulkier Manhattan cousin, due to the dough of the Montréal version being boiled in honey-sweetened water before baking in a wood-burning oven. St-Viateur Bagel & Café is a great place to get them, especially with smoked salmon. **Known for:** delicious bagels; classic and creative options; local favorite. ⑤ *Average main: C$13 ⊠ 1127 av. Mont-Royal Est, The Plateau* ☎ *514/528–6361 ⊕ www.stviateurbagel.com* ▭ *No credit cards* Ⓜ *Laurier.*

Hotels

Chock-full of artists, academics, and creatives, the Plateau and Mile End are bustling neighborhoods with a high density of bistros, brewpubs, martini bars, bakeries, designer boutiques, and parks. This is no place for quiet contemplation. In summer, join the crowds at outdoor markets and street fairs. There aren't many places to stay, but there are a few auberges and B&Bs.

Auberge de la Fontaine

$$ | **B&B/INN | FAMILY** | Built out of two adjoining houses with a signature yellow front door, lacquered-barn-board façade, and welcoming flower boxes, this turn-of-the-20th-century residence overlooks Parc Lafontaine and one of the city's major bicycle trails. **Pros:** near bars and restaurants; most rooms have whirlpool baths; some rooms have private balconies with park views. **Cons:** lobby is serviceable, but lacking glamour; some rooms are unrenovated and quite small; parking can be difficult. ⑤ *Rooms from: C$240 ⊠ 1301 rue Rachel Est, The Plateau* ☎ *514/597–0166, 800/597–0597 ⊕ www.aubergedelafontaine.com* ⇲ *21 rooms* ⊗ *Free Breakfast* Ⓜ *Mont-Royal.*

⑨ Nightlife

The restaurants and bars along St-Denis and Mont-Royal are popular with everyone from rambunctious students to serious food lovers. Boulevard St-Laurent ("The Main"), especially between rue Sherbrooke and avenue des Pins, is home to the see-and-be-seen crowd, with merrymakers spilling out of bars and clubs at all hours of the night.

Mile End has become well-known for inspired cuisine, affordable lounges, and relaxed bars, and is slowly becoming a second village to the hipster gay crowd, who tend to forgo the main Village.

BARS AND LOUNGES
Bar Waverly

BARS | Named for the street that epito-
mizes the Mile End, this neighborhood
bar has a warm staff, friendly atmosphere, and a great selection of Scotch.
Owners Richard Holder and Olivier Farley
have been in the business for years, and
it shows. Nightly DJs provide an edgier
vibe, while huge floor-to-ceiling windows
make it perfect for people-watching.
⊠ 5550 boul. St-Laurent, Mile End
☎ 514/903–1121 ⊕ www.barwaverly.com
Ⓜ Laurier.

Big in Japan Bar

COCKTAIL BARS | Barely noticeable from
the outside, this discreet, dimly lit
cocktail den has won awards for design
and been lauded by critics as one of
the most beautiful bars, if not the most
beautiful, in the city. Heavy drapes and
propane "candles" in small glasses that
reflect the surface of the labyrinthine
wraparound bar imbue this chic space
with a subdued speakeasy feel. Unlike an
izakaya, you don't come here to eat but
to drink, so few snacks are available. The
bar stocks a nice selection of sakes and
sojus, as well as Suntory Toki, a Japanese
whiskey. Beers, killer cocktails, and a
handpicked list of wines round out the
drinks menu. ⊠ 4175 boul. St-Laurent,
Montréal ☎ 438/380–5658 ⊕ www.insta-
gram.com/biginjapan_bar ⊙ Closed Sun.
and Mon. Ⓜ St-Laurent, then Bus 55.

★ Bily Kun

BARS | This Czech-themed bar is a favorite
hangout of Plateau locals. There's live jazz
during the cocktail hour and a DJ or classical performances later in the evening.
Try an absinthe-laced apple cocktail from
the extensive alcohol menu as you nibble
on a few tapas. Bily Kun gets packed,
though the high ceilings help alleviate
the feeling of claustrophobia. ⊠ 354 av.
Mont-Royal Est, The Plateau ☎ 514/845–
5392 ⊕ www.bilykun.com Ⓜ Mont-Royal.

Dieu du Ciel!

BREWPUBS | A chalkboard scribbled
with rotating craft beers and a convivial
atmosphere set the scene for this neigh-
borhood-favorite brewpub, freshly renovated and expanded in 2023. Small bites
such as flatbreads can be ordered to
accompany your IPAs and ales. ⊠ 21 av.
Laurier Ouest, Mile End ☎ 514/490–9555
⊕ dieuduciel.com/en Ⓜ Laurier.

La Buvette chez Simone

WINE BAR | Lively but not obnoxious,
this easygoing wine bar is a great place
to meet up with friends. Arrive early (it
opens at 4 pm but the kitchen only gets
going at 5), because it's always busy and
it doesn't take reservations. Many wines
can be sipped by the glass, in 2- and
4-ounce pours, while you graze on appetizers and cheese/charcuterie boards.
Dress is casual, though the after-work
crowd ups the glam factor. ⊠ 4869 av. du
Parc, Mile End ☎ 514/750–6577 ⊕ buvet-
techezsimone.com ⊙ Closed Sun. and
Mon. Ⓜ Laurier or Mont-Royal.

★ Le Majestique

WINE BAR | With its unappealing store-
front, bric-a-brac décor, retro knick-
knacks, and sceney vibes, Majestique
is a quirky wine bar that's open until the
wee hours with an excellent selection
of small plates. The snazzy surroundings
only add to the charm of this fine-dining-
meets-casual savoir faire; the salmon
confit, foot-long hot dog, quinoa cro-
quette, and rotating choice of fresh oysters are musts. ∎ TIP➜ Note that minors
are not allowed on the premises. ⊠ 4105
boul. St-Laurent, The Plateau ☎ 514/439–
1850 ⊕ www.restobarmajestique.com
⊙ Closed Sun. ☞ Check Facebook for
updated information Ⓜ Mont-Royal.

★ Reservoir

BREWPUBS | It's all about the beer at
this friendly restaurant and bar, where
it's all brewed right on the premises.
Packed almost every night of the week,
this bar has everything from India pale
ales to German-inspired wheat beers.

The upstairs patio is the ideal spot for watching locals stroll along the quaint cobblestoned avenue. ✉ *9 rue Duluth Est, The Plateau* ☎ *514/849–7779* ⊕ *reservoirbrasseur.com* ✆ *Closed Mon.* Ⓜ *Sherbrooke.*

Suwu
BARS | This self-described "hip-hop eatery" and neighborhood bar invites you to relax and pull up a chair or cozy couch in its leafy interior. Simple but intense dishes like truffle-oil popcorn and a grilled cheese mac-and-cheese sandwich (yes, you read that right) are paired with potent cocktails (try the signature Wu-Tang) to help make this one of the hottest destinations on the Main—without any of the usual pretension. Open nightly from 5 to 3. ✉ *3581 boul. St-Laurent, The Plateau* ☎ *438/700–0557* ⊕ *www.suwumontreal. com* ✆ *Closed Mon.* Ⓜ *St-Laurent.*

Whisky Café
BARS | Known for its happy hour, this bar, café, and cigar lounge is elegant but unpretentious—it's the perfect spot for a romantic rendezvous. The selection of more than 150 varieties of Scotch, plus an impressive choice of wines, Champagnes, and ports, leaves most everyone's thirst quenched. ✉ *5800 boul. St-Laurent, Mile End* ☎ *514/278–2646* ⊕ *www.whiskycafe.com* ✆ *Closed Sun.– Tues.* Ⓜ *Rosemont.*

LIVE MUSIC
Barfly
LIVE MUSIC | Fans of blues, punk, country, and bluegrass jam into this tiny hole-in-the-wall, which has some of the cheapest drink prices on boulevard St-Laurent. A very popular hangout for locals, Barfly is arguably the premier dive bar in the city. ✉ *4062-A boul. St-Laurent, The Plateau* ☎ *514/284–6665* ⊕ *www. facebook.com/BarflyMtl* Ⓜ *Sherbrooke or St-Laurent.*

Casa del Popolo
LIVE MUSIC | One of the city's treasured venues for indie rock, jazz, reggae, blues,

folk, and hip-hop, this neighborhood bar is ideal for discovering up-and-coming local acts or forgotten international giants still touring. While you enjoy the music, take a look at the original art and sample some of the tasty vegetarian food. ✉ *4873 boul. St-Laurent, The Plateau* ☎ *514/284–0122 office, 514/284–3804 café* ⊕ *www.casadelpopolo.com* Ⓜ *Mont-Royal.*

🎭 Performing Arts

THEATER
Mainline Theatre
THEATER | Operated by the same people who present the Montréal Fringe Festival every summer, the Mainline opened in 2006 to serve the city's burgeoning Anglo theater community and has been going strong ever since. ✉ *3997 boul. St-Laurent, The Plateau* ☎ *514/849–3378* ⊕ *www.mainlinetheatre.ca* Ⓜ *St-Laurent and Bus 55 or Mont-Royal.*

Théâtre du Rideau Vert
THEATER | The oldest professional francophone theater company in North America, Théâtre du Rideau Vert has been winning over audiences with its contemporary productions since 1948. Many popular francophone actors got their big break here. ✉ *4664 rue St-Denis, The Plateau* ☎ *514/844–1793* ⊕ *www. rideauvert.qc.ca* Ⓜ *Mont-Royal.*

🛍 Shopping

The Plateau has long been recognized as one of North America's hippest neighborhoods, and though trends typically come and go, its certain cachet endures. Rue St-Denis is home to both independent boutiques and chain stores selling local and international fashion, as well as jewelry stores, all at prices for every budget. Boulevard St-Laurent and avenue Mont-Royal both offer opportunities for vintage shopping, with St-Laurent also known for contemporary furniture and décor stores.

Just north of the Plateau, the Mile End offers an eclectic mix of artsy boutiques and shops stocked with up-and-coming Montréal designers.

BOOKS AND STATIONERY

★ Librairie Drawn & Quarterly

BOOKS | If you're a fan of graphic novels, this bookstore has your name on it. Founded in Mile End over 30 years ago, Drawn & Quarterly started out as a magazine and grew into an internationally recognized publisher of the best cartoonists. The company publishes Canadian and international writers and cartoonists like Kate Beaton, Ebony Flowers, Craig Thompson, Tove Jansson, Guy Delisle, Tom Gauld, Astrid Lindgren, Yoshiharu Tsuge, Rutu Modan, Shigeru Mizuki, Zuo Ma, and many more. The cozy shop sells their own publications as well as titles from many other publishers, in addition to hosting authors and book signing events. ⊠ *211 rue Bernard Ouest, The Plateau* ☎ *514/279–2224* ⊕ *drawnandquarterly.com* Ⓜ *Rosemont or Place-des-Arts, then Bus 80.*

CLOTHING

★ atelier b

CLOTHING | Set in an old button factory, this retro, multipurpose space (boutique, design/sewing workshop, and sewing school) makes and sells simple and sustainable clothing for all genders and children, as well as toys, underwear, and homewares. Many of their products, such as pencil cases and bags, are made from recycled scraps of organic cotton and linen, sometimes even turning these into pulp to make lampshades. atelier b also produces made-to-order pieces and does repairs and alterations. ⊠ *5758 boul. St-Laurent, Mile End* ☎ *514/769–6094* ⊕ *atelier-b.ca* Ⓜ *Rosemont.*

Bodybag by Jude

CLOTHING | When Nicole Kidman wore one of this designer's zip denim dresses, Judith Desjardins's star was set. The designer has a penchant for all things British, so look for cheeky checks and plaids. ⊠ *17 rue Bernard Ouest, Mile End* ☎ *514/274–5242* ⊕ *www.bodybagbyjude.com* Ⓜ *Rosemont.*

Boutique 1861

CLOTHING | This boutique stocks romantic, lacy, and affordable finds from local and international designers, including Arti Gogna and Champagne & Strawberry. With everything white—hardwood floors, couches, and armoires—the boudoir vibe is irresistible. Just look for the pink-and-black cameo signage. The name comes from the smaller branch at 1861 rue Ste-Catherine. ■ TIP→ **There is also a "wedding collection" of gowns and dresses for the bride, bridesmaids, mother of the bride, and guests at Boudoir 1861, located on the second floor of 3668 boul. St-Laurent.** ⊠ *3670 boul. St-Laurent, The Plateau* ☎ *844/308–1861, 514/670–6110* ⊕ *www.1861.ca* Ⓜ *St-Laurent.*

Citizen Vintage

SECOND-HAND | If you're a believer in buying stylish upcycled clothing, then this Mile End vintage boutique has your name on it. Bright, spacious, and carefully curated by the owners (who scour North America for their finds), this store makes shopping easy, as everything is arranged by color. The stock changes almost daily, so don't feel you can only visit once. ⊠ *4059 boul. St-Laurent, Mile End* ☎ *438/387–3927* ⊕ *www.citizenvintage.com* Ⓜ *Mont-Royal; or St-Laurent, then Bus 55.*

★ Clark Street Mercantile: Boutique pour Gentlemen

CLOTHING | Featured in publications like the *Guardian*, *GQ,* and *Goop*, this authentically retro locale is a hipster's dream. Little has changed on the building's main floor, with the old, scuffed-up brownish-gray terrazzo flooring still in attendance and few embellishments made to the premises. The focus here is on the clothing and other products like leather goods, apothecary, and homewares, each item handpicked for quality, craftsmanship, and the story behind the brand.

In addition to its own locally produced in-house brand, Clark Street Mercantile sources casual and classic men's clothing from labels like Portuguese Flannel, La Paz, and orSlow; apothecary from Rockwell, Groom, and Baxter; and other lifestyle products, including books, from Barebones, Kinto, and Monocle. ⊠ *5200 rue Clark, Mile End* ☎ *514/508–6090* ⊕ *clarkstreetmercantile.com* ⊘ *Closed Mon.* Ⓜ *Laurier, then Bus 51 west.*

★ Deuxième Peau

LINGERIE | Tucked away in a basement, the tiny "Second Skin" sells a fine assortment of French lingerie. It's hard to miss the curvy mannequins in their ground-floor window, adorned in the likes of Aubade, Chantelle, and Prima Donna. While you're feeling brave and beautiful, kill two birds with one stone and try on a bathing suit from the shop's tasteful collection of French, Spanish, and Australian designers. ⊠ *4457 rue St-Denis, The Plateau* ☎ *514/842–0811* ⊕ *www.facebook. com/boutiqueDeuxiemePeau* ⊘ *Closed Mon.* Ⓜ *Mont-Royal.*

★ Jennifer Glascow Design

CLOTHING | The Mile End neighborhood earned its reputation for all things cool with funky shops like this one. The natural-hue clothes—most by local designers—are feminine and elegant, and owner Jennifer Glasgow sells her eponymous clothing line here. The location on the Main is warm and welcoming, with exposed brick, pendant laps, and an antique display table. ⊠ *5145 boul. St-Laurent, Mile End* ☎ *514/271–2129* ⊕ *www.general54.com* Ⓜ *Laurier.*

Kanuk

CLOTHING | This company's snowy owl trademark has become something of a status symbol among the shivering urban masses. The Québec-made coats and parkas sold are built to keep an Arctic explorer warm and dry. Kanuk has gone fur-free, so gone are the fur-trimmed hoods. While the company still uses duck down, it also makes coats with synthetic insulation. Fifty percent of Kanuk's 2023 collection is made with recycled fabrics, and the company plans to increase this percentage in the coming years. ⊠ *485 rue Rachel Est, The Plateau* ☎ *514/284–4494, 877/284–4494* ⊕ *www.kanuk.com* ⊘ *Closed Mon. and Tues.* Ⓜ *Mont-Royal.*

Mimi & Coco

CLOTHING | You'll want to snap up several of the locally designed T-shirts at Mimi & Coco, perhaps pairing them with luxe knitwear from Italy. Beautiful floor-to-ceiling windows create a bright, inviting interior, even on cloudy days. The shop also sells dog collars and leashes, with profits going to a nonprofit foundation that works to promote animal rescue and adoption. Come at lunchtime and sample one of Mandy's gourmet salads from the in-store counter. ⊠ *5121 boul. St-Laurent, Mile End* ☎ *514/906–0349* ⊕ *www.mimi-coco.com* Ⓜ *St-Laurent, then Bus 55.*

M0851

LEATHER GOODS | Sleek, supple leather clothing and bags from the Québec designer Frédéric Mamarbachi have a cult following from Antwerp to Tokyo. The rough-hewn wood floors and concrete walls of this branch give it an industrial-chic vibe. ⊠ *3526 boul. St-Laurent, The Plateau* ☎ *514/849–9759* ⊕ *www.m0851. com* Ⓜ *St-Laurent or Sherbrooke.*

Mousseline

CLOTHING | With sizes running from 2 to 22, this place makes finding the perfect fit a snap. Choosing from among the casual wear by fashion labels like James Perse, Pas de Calais, Autumn Cashmere, and Odd Mooly might be a bit more difficult. ⊠ *220 av. Laurier Ouest, Mile End* ☎ *514/878–0661* ⊕ *olam-mousseline.com* Ⓜ *Laurier.*

Muse

CLOTHING | Designer Christian Chenail's contemporary take on fashion always has a French twist, and his daring black gowns are showstoppers. His flirty skirts and dresses usually come in cheerful shades of red and blue and call to mind the styles of the '50s. ✉ *4467 rue St-Denis, The Plateau* ☎ *514/848–9493* ⊕ *www.muse-cchenail.com* ⊙ *Closed Sun.* Ⓜ *Mont-Royal.*

Unicorn

CLOTHING | Young Québécois designers like Barilà, Valérie Dumaine, and Mélissa Nepton are the stars of this beautiful Mile End boutique, which also stocks unique national and international labels. All the black and white in the window display hints at the minimalist aesthetic within. ✉ *5135 boul. St-Laurent, Mile End* ☎ *514/544–2828* ⊕ *www.boutiqueunicorn.com* Ⓜ *Laurier.*

WANT Les Essentiels

CLOTHING | Established in Montréal in 2007, WANT's new flagship boutique in hipster Mile End draws inspiration from travel and transitional spaces like airports, train stations, airplane cabins, and Montréal's métro cars, complementing the label's minimalist, gender-neutral clothing, footwear, and bags in muted blacks, whites, and grays. In addition to its own brand, WANT also carries apothecary, jewelry, and accessories from labels such as Grown Alchemist, Susanne Kaufmann, and All Blues, among others. ∎TIP→ **Shoppers can also enjoy a VIP WANT experience by booking an appointment online.** ✉ *5445 av. de Gaspé, Mile End* ⊕ *wantlesessentiels.com* ⊙ *Closed Sun.–Tues.* Ⓜ *Laurier.*

FOOD

★ La Vieille Europe

SPECIALTY STORE | For a taste of the old Main, where generations of immigrants came to shop, look no farther than this deli packed with sausages, cheeses, European chocolates, jams, and loads of atmosphere. Pick up a rich shot of espresso on your way out. ∎TIP→ **Call ahead as hours vary seasonally.** ✉ *3855 boul. St-Laurent, The Plateau* ☎ *514/842–5773* ⊕ *www.facebook.com/LaVieilleEurope* Ⓜ *St-Laurent or Sherbrooke.*

★ Librarie Espagnole

SPECIALTY STORE | A fixture on boulevard St-Laurent since 1964, this is your one-stop shop for all things Spanish and Latin American in Montréal. The name is really a misnomer today since few books are sold here anymore. However, the friendly staff at this unpretentious establishment sell just about everything else from Spanish and Latin American foods to ceramic ware, cookware, flamenco shoes, and a large assortment of espadrilles. ✉ *3811 boul. St-Laurent, The Plateau* ☎ *514/849–3383* ⊕ *lespanola.com* ⊙ *Closed Sun.* Ⓜ *St-Laurent, then Bus 55 north.*

HOUSEWARES
Paul's Boutique

MUSIC | Paul's Boutique, owned by none other than the eponymous and eccentric Paul, is an Aladdin's cave of 20,000-plus rare and used records, with a strong emphasis on hip-hop and vintage 45s. The shop also stocks old DVDs, magazines, and music memorabilia. Housed in a colonial Québec home with dormer windows that's painted canary yellow and fire-engine red—and appears to be caving into itself—it's hard to miss Paul's Boutique. ✉ *112 av. Mont-Royal Est, The Plateau* ☎ *514/284-7773* ⊕ *www.facebook.com/people/Pauls-Boutique-Montreal/100057533916448* ☞ *Hours can vary so best to call ahead* Ⓜ *Mont-Royal.*

★ Zone

HOUSEWARES | This multilevel labyrinth of affordable housewares is filled with fine and stylish designs for the kitchen, bath, and living room. ∎TIP→ **There is also an outpost at 6816 boulevard St-Laurent in Little Italy.** ✉ *4246 rue St-Denis, The Plateau* ☎ *514/845–3530, 877/845–3532* ⊕ *www.zonemaison.com* Ⓜ *Sherbrooke or Mont-Royal.*

Outremont

Above the Plateau and next to Parc du Mont-Royal, Outremont has long been Montréal's more affluent residential francophone enclave (as opposed to Westmount, long stubbornly British right down to its neo-Gothic churches and lawn-bowling club). It has grand homes, tree-shaded streets, perfectly groomed parks, and two upmarket shopping and dining strips along rue Laurier and avenue Bernard. The latter, with wide sidewalks and shady trees, is particularly attractive. The eastern fringes of Outre-mont are home to Montréal's thriving Hasidic community.

GETTING HERE AND AROUND
By métro, take the Blue Line to Out-remont station. You can also get to Outremont from Downtown on Bus 55, which travels along boulevard St-Laurent, or Bus 80, which goes through Parc Mont-Royal along avenue du Parc. Get off at rue Laurier and walk west from there. (Outremont begins on the west side of avenue du Parc; the east side of Parc is Mile End.)

Alternatively, you could stay on the bus for a few more stops until you come to avenue Bernard and then walk west. Both avenues Laurier and Bernard are Outremont's primary hubs for commer-cial activity. The Outremont métro stop lets you off on avenue Van Horne, another commercial hub but without the more attractive boutiques and restaurants of Laurier and Bernard. If you're coming from Downtown and feeling fit, you could walk to Outremont in roughly 30–45 minutes, or, for that matter, just hop on a BIXI bicycle, taking the same route as Bus 80 and getting there in half the time.

◉ Sights

★ Avenue Bernard
STREET | If your taste runs to the chic and fashionable, then there is simply no better street than avenue Bernard, west of avenue Querbes, for people-watching. Its wide sidewalks and shady trees make it ideal for the kind of outdoor cafés and restaurants that attract the bright and the beautiful. And, in summer, the avenue is pedestrianized between avenues Wise-man and Bloomfield, with people walking freely and outdoor patios spilling out into the street. ⊠ *Outremont* Ⓜ *Outremont.*

🍴 Restaurants

Outremont caters to affluent French-speaking professionals with restaurants that look as good as the food being served. There are plenty of charming outdoor terraces in the warm months.

Brasserie Les Enfants Terribles
$$$ | CANADIAN | With its cavernous corner spot on Outremont's trendy avenue Bernard, sophisticated yet playful décor, and artfully prepared comfort food, this brasserie is always a good bet for quality food and excellent people-watching. The menu at Les Enfants Terribles is a mix of high-end cuisine and comfort-food favorites, from salmon tartare with grilled oyster mushroom salad to spaghetti Bolognese, fish-and-chips, and mac and cheese. **Known for:** pouding chômeur cake; mojito d'Outremont; elevated comfort food. ⑤ *Average main: C$30* ⊠ *1257 av. Bernard Ouest, Outremont* ☎ *514/759–9918* ⊕ *www.jesuisunenfant-terrible.com* Ⓜ *Outremont.*

Damas
$$$$ | MIDDLE EASTERN | Colorful and cozy, with beautiful glass lanterns hanging from the red ceiling and meze dishes that are perfect for sharing, this Syrian res-taurant is a treat. Try *fatta* (yogurt, tahini,

pita, pistachios, pine nuts, and herbs), hummus shawarma, hummus with mushrooms, or *moujaddaraa* (braised lentils with bulgur and caramelized onions, tomato salsa, and yogurt mint sauce). **Known for:** authentic Syrian cuisine; safarjal (quince and saffron sorbet with cardamom, honey, pistachio, and mint); Mediterranean wines. $ *Average main: C$40* ⊠ *1201 av. Van Horne, Outremont* ☎ *514/439–5435* ⊕ *www.damas.ca* ⊘ *Closed Mon. No lunch* Ⓜ *Outremont.*

La Chronique

$$$$ | FRENCH | Although La Chronique is indeed an elegant place with white walls and high ceilings flooded with light, people don't come here for the setting; they come for the excellent food. Without fuss or fanfare, La Chronique has remained one of the best French restaurants in town since it opened in 1995. **Known for:** tasting menu; seared foie gras; excellent French cuisine. $ *Average main: C$140* ⊠ *104 av. Laurier Ouest, Outremont* ☎ *514/271–3095* ⊕ *www.lachronique. qc.ca* ⊘ *Closed Sun.–Tues. No lunch* ⌒ *Tasting menu only* Ⓜ *Laurier.*

★ Leméac

$$$$ | BISTRO | Open since 2001, this sophisticated French bistro pleases Montrealers with its flawless classics and its heated wraparound outdoor terrace. Regulars gravitate toward dishes such as the beef or salmon tartare, grilled Cornish hen, asparagus and wild mushroom risotto, mushroom ravioli, and hanger steak—all served with ceremonial aplomb on white linen tablecloths. **Known for:** being busy; salmon tartare; pain perdu (French toast with maple syrup and dulce de leche). $ *Average main: C$40* ⊠ *1045 av. Laurier Ouest, Outremont* ☎ *514/270–0999* ⊕ *www.restaurantleme-ac.com* Ⓜ *Outremont.*

★ Pizzeria 900

$$ | PIZZA | No one does pizza quite like these pizzaiolos; they are, after all, legally certified by the Associazione Vera Pizza Napoletana in Italy. Using all-natural and non-processed ingredients, and adhering to traditional pizza-making methods (like using a 900-degree oven), Pizzeria 900 on avenue Bernard is one of the most sought-after high-end pizza joints in town with one of the most popular patios. **Known for:** 900-degree oven; Neapolitan-style pizza; stylish space. $ *Average main: C$19* ⊠ *1248 av. Bernard Ouest, Outremont* ☎ *438/386–0900* ⊕ *no900. com* Ⓜ *Outremont.*

Coffee and Quick Bites

★ La Croissanterie Figaro

$$ | BISTRO | FAMILY | The self-proclaimed "un coin perdu de Paris" (a lost corner of Paris) is famous for its wraparound patio, Parisian vibe, century-old corner building featuring stained glass and woodwork, an art deco chandelier, and an art nouveau bar. Although this is a full bistro serving three meals every day of the week, it shines brightest in the morning. **Known for:** charming setting; croissant with almond paste; opens early and closes late. $ *Average main: C$13* ⊠ *5200 rue Hutchison, Outremont* ☎ *514/278–6567* ⊕ *www.lacroissanteriefigaro.com* Ⓜ *Outremont.*

★ Le Glacier Bilboquet

$ | ICE CREAM | FAMILY | Families and couples with dogs congregate here on warm summer nights, where the artisanal ice-cream recipes are prepared by hand. Real cream and real milk are the star ingredients, while the sorbets are 80% fruit puree. **Known for:** cranberry sorbet; maple taffy ice cream; late hours in summer. $ *Average main: C$9* ⊠ *1311 av. Bernard Ouest, Outremont* ☎ *514/276–0414* ⊕ *www.bilboquet.ca* ▭ *No credit cards* Ⓜ *Outremont.*

Toi Moi et Café

$$ | BISTRO | Film producers and poets congregate at this corner café-bistro, sitting on the terrace to sip award-winning espresso. Although there's a hearty lunch and dinner menu of salads and grilled meat, brunch is the big draw. **Known for:** single-origin specialty coffees; student and artist crowd; exclusive blends like baklava coffee. $ *Average main: C$15* ✉ *244 av. Laurier Ouest, Outremont* ☎ *514/279–9599* ⊕ *www.toimoicafe.com* Ⓜ *Laurier.*

 # Performing Arts

CLASSICAL MUSIC
Salle Claude-Champagne
MUSIC | This beautiful, modern concert hall hosts more than 150 symphonic and operatic performances every year by the music faculty of the Université de Montréal. The repertoire includes both classic and contemporary works. ✉ *220 av. Vincent-d'Indy, Outremont* ☎ *514/343–6427* ⊕ *musique.umontreal.ca/en/about/our-spaces/concert-halls/salle-claude-champagne* Ⓜ *Édouard-Monpetit.*

THEATER
Théâtre Outremont
PERFORMANCE VENUES | Inaugurated in 1929, this gorgeous art deco theater rapidly became a local favorite and had its heyday in the '70s before it fell into disarray. After reopening its doors in the early '90s, the theater has regained much of its steam with mostly theater and live music acts, but also film screenings, comedy, and circus performances. ✉ *1248 av. Bernard Ouest, Outremont* ☎ *514/495–9944* ⊕ *www.theatreoutremont.ca* Ⓜ *Outremont.*

 # Shopping

Avenue Laurier in Outremont is a good destination for those in pursuit of a little luxury.

CLOTHING
Billie
CLOTHING | One of Montréal's favorite boutiques, Billie has rows of bookcases, drawers, and shelves that give the feeling of raiding your best friend's closet. Look for chic dresses and blouses from Velvet,

cozy sweaters from 360 Cashmere, and eclectic shoes by Inuikii. If you are shopping for kid sizes, visit Billie le Kid at 1001 avenue Laurier Ouest. ✉ *1012 av. Laurier Ouest, Outremont* ☎ *514/270–5415* ⊕ *www.billieboutique.com* Ⓜ *Laurier.*

★ Lyla
LINGERIE | Helping women feel their best since 1982, this lovely shop carries some of the finest lingerie in the city—including brands like Eres and Prima Donna. The staff is extremely helpful in finding what fits and flatters. Two other reasons to stop and shop: exquisite fashions from Europe and a great selection of swimsuits and darling cover-ups. ✉ *400 av. Laurier Ouest, Outremont* ☎ *514/271–0763* ⊕ *www.lyla.ca* ⊙ *Closed Sun.* Ⓜ *Laurier.*

FOOD
Gourmet Laurier
FOOD | Acres of chocolate and candy and the best coffee beans in town draw well-heeled shoppers to this Outremont shop. The colossal assortment of fine cheeses, charcuterie, and other local and imported goodies add to the appeal. ✉ *1042 av. Laurier Ouest, Outremont* ☎ *514/274–5601* ⊕ *www.gourmetlaurier.ca* Ⓜ *Laurier.*

Yannick Fromagerie
FOOD | This gourmet cheese shop is the go-to destination for the city's top chefs and cheese aficionados. Yannick Achim carries 400 varieties, buying from local dairies and stocking an astonishing international selection. You'll find Pikauba cheese from Québec beside pecorino made with raw sheep's milk and laced with black truffles. Cheese lovers here eagerly trade advice on building the perfect after-dinner cheese plate. ✉ *1218 av. Bernard Ouest, Outremont* ☎ *514/279–9376* ⊕ *www.yannickfromagerie.ca* ⊙ *Closed Mon.* Ⓜ *Outremont.*

Sights ▼

1 Avenue Bernard..... **B6**

2 Chiesa della Madonna della Difesa **B3**

3 Marché Jean-Talon **A2**

Restaurants ▼

1 Beaufort Bistro........ **B2**

2 Bottega Pizzeria... **B3**

3 Brasserie Harricana... **A3**

4 Brasserie Les Enfants Terribles..... **B6**

5 Damas...... **A6**

6 Impasto **B3**

7 La Chronique... **D6**

8 Le Petit Alep **A2**

9 Leméac **D7**

10 Montréal Plaza **D3**

11 Mon Lapin .. **B3**

12 Pastaga **B4**

13 Pizzeria Napoletana. **B3**

14 Pizzeria 900........... **B6**

15 Tapeo........ **A1**

Quick Bites ▼

1 Caffè San Simeon...... **B3**

2 Dinette Triple Crown **B4**

3 La Cornetteria.. **B4**

4 La Croissanterie Figaro ... **C7**

5 Le Glacier Bilboquet ... **B7**

6 Toi Moi et Café **D7**

Outrement and Little Italy

KEY

1 Sights

1 Restaurants

1 Quick Bites

M Métro Stations

Little Italy

North of Mile End lies Little Italy, which still serves as HQ to Montréal's sizable Italian community of nearly a quarter of a million people. While families of Italian descent now live all over the greater Montréal area, many come back here every week or so to shop, eat out, or visit family and friends, and the 30-odd blocks bounded by rues Jean-Talon, St-Zotique, Marconi, and Drolet remain its heart and soul. You'll know you've reached Little Italy when the gardens have tomato plants and grapevines, there are sausages and cans of olive oil in store windows, and the heady smell of espresso emanates from cafés.

GETTING HERE AND AROUND

You can take both the Orange and Blue Lines to get to Little Italy: get off at Jean-Talon station and walk six short blocks to get to boulevard St-Laurent. Bus 55, which runs north along St-Laurent, will also get you here fairly quickly from Downtown, or you could just take a BIXI bike and get here in roughly 20 minutes. Once here, you can stop for produce and cheese at the Marché Jean-Talon, and you might just see a wedding party outside the Madonna della Difesa church.

🔘 Sights

Chiesa della Madonna della Difesa

CHURCH | If you look up at the cupola behind the main altar of Little Italy's most famous church, you'll spot Montréal's most infamous piece of ecclesiastical portraiture. Yes, indeed, that lantern-jaw fellow on horseback who looks so pleased with himself is Benito Mussolini, the dictator who led Italy into World War II—on the wrong side. The mural, by Guido Nincheri (1885–1973), was completed long before the war and commemorates the signing of the Lateran Pact with Pope Pius XI, one of II Duce's few lasting achievements. The controversy shouldn't distract you from the beauties of the rest of the richly decorated church. ✉ *6800 av. Henri-Julien, Little Italy* ☎ *514/277–6522* ⊕ *www.facebook.com/MadonnadellaDifesaMTL* ⛪ *Free* ☞ *Call ahead as the church is rarely open outside mass hours* Ⓜ *Beaubien or Jean-Talon.*

★ Marché Jean-Talon

MARKET | The smells of roasting chestnuts and fresh pastries at this market will surely excite your olfactory system. To further delight your senses there are dozens of tiny shops full of Québec cheeses, Lebanese sweets, country pâtés, local wines, and handmade chocolates. Less threatening to the waistline but a feast for the eyes are the huge mounds of peas, beans, apples, carrots, pears, garlic, and other produce on sale at the open-air stands. Visit on weekends during the warm summer months, and it will feel as if all of Montréal has come out to shop. ■TIP→ **During the holiday season there is a Christmas market, which runs from late November until the 23rd of December.** ✉ *7070 av. Henri-Julien, Little Italy* ☎ *514/277–1588* ⊕ *www.marches-publics-mtl.com/en/marches/jean-talon-market* Ⓜ *Jean-Talon.*

🍴 Restaurants

Little Italy offers a nostalgic look back at what La Bella Italia used to be 40 or 50 years ago, as old men congregate in front of their favorite café and chat about politics and last night's soccer game. With its location just steps away from Jean-Talon Market, it's only fitting that the historic Piccola Italia would go on to become the sought-after dining destination that it is today. It's now neighbored by the trendsetting Mile-Ex and Rosemont areas, where chefs, moving away from Old Montréal and Downtown's expensive rents, benefit from splendid spaces and eager locals, which include young professionals and diners hungry for new experiences.

It's well worth the métro ride up to Little Italy's busy Marché Jean-Talon to see Québécois farmers sell their local produce and prepared food.

Beaufort Bistro

$$$ | BISTRO | FAMILY | Beaufort Bistro, a cross between haute cuisine and comfort food, has received a lot of attention since it opened in 2014. Since then, this part restaurant, part busy café-bar has moved to a much larger space to better accommodate more—and more types of—diners. **Known for:** grilled octopus with corn puree, coriander-and-lime sour cream, and chorizo; tartares; Italian coffee. $ *Average main: C$30* ✉ *6653 rue St-Hubert, Rosemont* ☎ *514/274–6969* ⊕ *www.beaufortbistro.ca* ⊗ *Closed Sun. and Mon. No lunch* Ⓜ *Beaubien.*

Bottega Pizzeria

$$$ | PIZZA | FAMILY | Nobody questions the authenticity of the Neapolitan-style pizza here, seeing as there's a nearly 4-ton wood-burning pizza oven made from Vesuvian rock in the kitchen which cooks pizza in 90 seconds flat at 500°C (932°F). There are just a few toppings available, but all are fabulously flavorsome, like fresh tomatoes, vegetables, and top-quality salumi. **Known for:** excellent gelato to go; authentic Neapolitan-style pizza; panozzi, calzoni, and tronchetti. $ *Average main: C$23* ✉ *65 rue St-Zotique Est, Little Italy* ☎ *514/277–8104* ⊕ *www.bottega.ca* ⊗ *Closed Mon. No lunch Sat.– Wed.* Ⓜ *Beaubien.*

★ Brasserie Harricana

$$$ | MODERN CANADIAN | FAMILY | Instagram famous for its dusty pink chairs and pleasing, contemporary space, this seriously cool brasserie is home to 41 home brews—sold by the bottle at the boutique upstairs—and a solid menu that includes monkfish burgers, beer-can roast chicken, and a hearty rib eye. In 2021, a new, larger brewhouse was opened. **Known for:** beer pairings; architectural space; beer-can roast chicken. $ *Average main: C$23* ✉ *95 rue Jean-Talon Ouest, Little Italy* ☎ *514/303–3039* ⊕ *www.brasserieharricana.com* ⊗ *No lunch weekends* Ⓜ *De Castelnau.*

Da Emma

$$$$ | ITALIAN | The cellar of what used to be Montréal's first women's prison hardly sounds like the ideal setting for

an Italian eatery, but Nonna Emma's cuisine shushes any bad vibes from the 1800s. Nonna Emma recently retired, at the age of 80, but today her daughter, Olga Aureli, and her grandson, Luca, the sixth generation of restaurateurs in the family, now helm the well-known institution. **Known for:** abbacchio al forno (roasted lamb); polpette al sugo (meatballs in tomato sauce); rustic, authentic Roman dishes. $ *Average main: C$40* ⊠ *777 rue de la Commune Ouest, Old Montréal* ☎ *514/392–1568* ⊕ *daemma. com* ⊗ *Closed Sun. and Mon. No lunch* Ⓜ *Square-Victoria.*

★ Impasto

$$$ | **MODERN ITALIAN** | This unpretentious, industrial-chic Little Italy restaurant has garnered a great reputation, thanks in part to its celebrity-chef owners, Stefano Faita and Michele Forgione, who make some of the best pasta dishes in town. **Known for:** modern Italian fare; extensive list of Italian wines; ricotta gnocchi. $ *Average main: C$34* ⊠ *48 rue Dante, Little Italy* ☎ *514/508–6508* ⊕ *www.impasto-mtl.ca* ⊗ *Closed Sun. and Mon. No lunch* Ⓜ *Jean-Talon.*

Le Petit Alep

$$ | **MIDDLE EASTERN** | **FAMILY** | This casual Middle Eastern spot is comfortable and homey but still has style, with music, ivy, exposed-stone walls, and a lovely terrace come summer. The menu is perfect for grazing, and excellent sharing options include the *mouhamara* (pomegranate-and-walnut spread), *sabanegh* (spinach, coriander, and onion pie), *fattouche* (a salad with pita chips and mint), and *yalandji* (vine leaves stuffed with rice, chickpeas, walnuts, and tomatoes). **Known for:** Syrian and Armenian cuisine; atmospheric décor; huge selection of mazza (appetizers). $ *Average main: C$17* ⊠ *191 rue Jean-Talon Est, Rosemont* ☎ *514/270–9361* ⊕ *www. petitalep.com* ⊗ *Closed Sun.–Tues. No lunch Sat. and Wed.* Ⓜ *Jean-Talon.*

★ Mon Lapin

$$$$ | **BISTRO** | Voted Canada's best restaurant in 2023 by the prestigious "Canada's 100 Best," Mon Lapin has gone from being a compact wine bar to a full-fledged 70-seater restaurant with a daily-changing menu of small plates emphasizing local, seasonal ingredients and playful flavor combinations that make the mouth sing. Depending on the day and the season, the minimalist menu might feature chicken brined in sourdough; *croque-pétoncle*; white asparagus atop razor clams with elderflower; radish and chicken-liver parfait; barbecued whelks; or Nanaimo bars with chestnuts and amaro. **Known for:** surprising, flavorful dishes; daily-changing menu; exceptional wine list highlighting natural wines. $ *Average main: C$55* ⊠ *150 rue St-Zotique Est, Little Italy* ☎ *514/379-4550* ⊕ *vinmonlapin.com* ⊗ *Closed Sun. and Mon. No lunch* Ⓜ *Beaubien.*

Montréal Plaza

$$$$ | **MODERN CANADIAN** | You won't see anything too familiar on the menu at this fresh, light-filled restaurant with its high ceilings, clean white walls and tablecloths, and modern mix of wood, glass, and sliding industrial windows that open to outdoor seating in summer. You *will* find whimsical yet unpretentious dishes that surprise and delight. **Known for:** five-service sharing menu plus dessert (C$130 per person); creative menu; desserts. $ *Average main: C$37* ⊠ *6230 rue St-Hubert, Rosemont* ☎ *514/903–6230* ⊕ *montrealplaza.com* ⊗ *Closed Sun. and Mon. No lunch* Ⓜ *Beaubien.*

Pastaga

$$$ | **WINE BAR** | Don't be fooled by the name: Pastaga is not a pasta joint; the name is a slang term for alcoholic drinks composed of anise, specifically pastis. Pastaga is best known for its all-natural wine list and small sharing plates. **Known for:** oyster mushrooms with nuoc mam Vietnamese dipping sauce; spicy muhamara dip (walnuts, red bell peppers,

pomegranate molasses); natural wines. $ *Average main: C$29* ✉ *6389 boul. St-Laurent, Rosemont* ☎ *438/381–6389* ☽ *Closed Sun. and Mon. No lunch* Ⓜ *Beaubien.*

Pizzeria Napoletana

$$$ | PIZZA | Pizzeria Napoletana has been at the heart of Montréal's Italian community since 1948. The menu consists of traditional thin-crust pizzas, pastas, and other southern Italian classics, many based on family recipes. **Known for:** nodini all'aglio (knotted bread with garlic and parmesan); melanzane (eggplant) alla parmigiana; delizia al limone (traditional Amalfi Coast dessert) imported from Italy. $ *Average main: C$22* ✉ *189 rue Dante, Little Italy* ☎ *514/276-8226* ⊕ *www.napoletana.com* ☽ *No lunch Mon.–Thurs.* Ⓜ *Beaubien.*

Tapeo

$$$ | TAPAS | Bringing tapas uptown, this Spanish-inspired eatery is a chic yet casual place to drink imported wines and share a few small plates. The Tapeo version of the classic *patatas bravas* served with a spicy tomato sauce and aioli is always a good choice, as are the roasted vine tomatoes and the grilled chorizo. **Known for:** patatas bravas; chef's table experience; house churros. $ *Average main: C$25* ✉ *511 rue Villeray, Villeray* ☎ *514/495–1999* ⊕ *www.restotapeo.com* ☽ *Closed Mon. No lunch weekends. No dinner Tues. and Wed.* Ⓜ *Jarry.*

☕ Coffee and Quick Bites

Caffè San Simeon

$ | CAFÉ | In the heart of Little Italy, this historic caffè filled with regulars chatting away in Italian is one of the city's best non-hipster, non-design places to get some excellent brew, be it an espresso, latte, or cappuccino. There also are a few pastries available. **Known for:** old-school Italian café; Malibu coffee; 6 am opening. $ *Average main: C$7* ✉ *39 rue Dante, Little Italy* ☎ *514/272–7386* ⊕ *www.*

facebook.com/caffe.sansimeon ⊟ *No credit cards* Ⓜ *Jean-Talon.*

★ Dinette Triple Crown

$$$ | SOUTHERN | Dinette Triple Crown is relatively small (a counter with just eight stools), but the real draw here is not indoor dining but taking the comfort food to go. Locals know to ask for a picnic basket (fully equipped with cutlery, dishes, and a tablecloth) that will be enjoyed in Little Italy Park across the street. **Known for:** large selection of bourbon; weekly menus; fried chicken and other Southern fare. $ *Average main: C$22* ✉ *6704 rue Clark, Little Italy* ☎ *514/272–2617* ⊕ *www.dinettetriplecrown.com* ☽ *Closed Mon.–Wed.* Ⓜ *Beaubien.*

La Cornetteria

$ | BAKERY | This lovely little bakery, which magically transports its patrons (or at least their taste buds) to Italy, specializes in the cornetto, the Italian version of the croissant. Freshly baked every morning, these delightful pastries are available plain or filled with Nutella, ricotta cream, or almond paste. **Known for:** Nutella cornetto; traditional cannoli; stracchino sandwiches. $ *Average main: C$6* ✉ *6528 boul. St-Laurent, Little Italy* ☎ *514/277–8030* ⊕ *www.lacornetteria. com* ⊟ *No credit cards* Ⓜ *Beaubien.*

🛍 Shopping

Little Italy is a gourmet shopper's paradise.

FOOD

★ Marché Milano

FOOD | In business since 1954, customers here form long lines for prepared foods at the takeout counter. There's a vast selection of cheeses, oils, vinegars, and baked goods. For some elbow room, go during the week. ✉ *6862 boul. St-Laurent, Little Italy* ☎ *514/273–8558, 833/645-2662* ⊕ *www.milanofruiterie. com* Ⓜ *De Castelnau or Jean-Talon.*

Parc du Mont-Royal

In geological terms, Mont-Royal is just a bump of basalt-like rock worn down by several ice ages to a mere 760 feet. But in the affections of Montrealers it's a Matterhorn. Without a trace of irony, they call it simply *la Montagne* or "the Mountain," and it's easy to see why it's so well loved.

For Montrealers it's a refuge, a slightly tamed wilderness within the city. It's where you go to get away from it all. And even when you can't get away, you can see the mountain glimmering beyond the skyscrapers and the high-rises—green in summer, gray and white in winter, and gold and crimson in fall.

The nearly 500 acres of forests and meadows were laid out by Frederick Law Olmsted (1822–1903), the man responsible for New York City's Central Park. Olmsted believed that communion with nature could cure body and soul, so much of the park has been left as wild as possible, with narrow paths meandering through tall stands of maples and red oaks. In summer, it's full of picnicking families; in winter, cross-country skiers and snowshoers take over, while families skate at Lac aux Castors and ride sleds and inner tubes down groomed slopes. The nonprofit organization Les amis de la montagne (⊕ *lemontroyal.qc.ca/en*) offers year-round outdoor and educational activities for locals and visitors, like rowboat rentals, mountain clean-ups, and guided walks in summer and guided snowshoeing excursions followed by a bone-warming hot chocolate or mulled wine in winter.

GETTING HERE AND AROUND

If you're in good shape, you can walk, uphill all the way, from Downtown. Climb rue Peel to the entrance to Parc du Mont-Royal and then up the steep stairway to the top of the mountain. Or you can simply take the métro to the Mont-Royal station and catch Bus 11. If you have a car, there's paid parking in Parc du Mont-Royal and at the Oratoire St-Joseph (the latter asks for a contribution of C$5 per vehicle Monday to Saturday for anyone not attending a service or coming to pray). Biking up the mountain will test your endurance, but the park has an extensive network of scenic trails.

TIMING

Depending on your interest, you could spend anywhere from a few hours—if you simply just want to see the view—to the entire day here. If you're here for the afternoon, there's a cafeteria at the Beaver Lake pavilion and a café at Smith House, or you can pick up picnic provisions before you set out.

Sights

Chalet du Mont-Royal

VIEWPOINT | No trip to Montréal is complete without a visit to the terrace in front of the Chalet du Mont-Royal. It's not the only place to get an overview of the city, the river, and the countryside beyond, but it's the most spectacular. On clear days you can see not only the Downtown skyscrapers, but also Mont-Royal's sister mountains—Monts St-Bruno, St-Hilaire, and St-Grégoire. These isolated peaks, called the Montérégies, or Mountains of the King, rise up from the flat countryside. Be sure to take a look inside the chalet, especially at the murals depicting scenes from Canadian history. ⊠ *Off voie Camillien-Houde, Parc du Mont-Royal* ☎ *514/843-8240, ext. 0 for Les amis de la montagnes* ⊕ *www.lemontroyal.qc.ca/en* 🎟 *Free* Ⓜ *Mont-Royal, then Bus 11 west.*

★ **Croix sur la Montagne** (*Cross atop Mont-Royal*)

OTHER ATTRACTION | Visible from up to 50 miles away on a clear day, the 98-foot-high steel cross at the top of Mont-Royal has been a city landmark since it was erected in 1924, largely with money raised through the efforts of 85,000

Did You Know?

An artifical basin fitted on a former swamp on Mont-Royal, Beaver Lake is named for an old beaver dam discovered during the work.

high-school students. Once upon a time, it took four hours and the labor of three to replace the 249 electric bulbs used to light the cross; today, the iconic cross is illuminated via a high-tech remote-control LED system. ☒ *Parc du Mont-Royal* ⊕ *www.lemontroyal.qc.ca.*

Lac aux Castors (*Beaver Lake*)
CITY PARK | FAMILY | Mont-Royal's single body of water, actually a reclaimed bog, is a great place for kids (and parents) to float model boats or rent a rowboat in the summertime. In winter, the lake's frozen surface attracts whole families of skaters, and nearby there's a groomed slope where kids of all ages can ride inner tubes. The glass-fronted Beaver Lake Pavilion is a pleasant bistro that serves lunch and dinner. Skate and cross-country-ski rentals are available downstairs. ☒ *Off chemin Remembrance, Parc du Mont-Royal* ⊕ *www.lemontroyal.qc.ca* Ⓜ *Mont-Royal, then Bus 11 west.*

★ **Maison Smith**
SPECIALTY MUSEUM | If you need a map of Mont-Royal's extensive hiking trails or want to know about the animals and more than 180 kinds of birds that make their home in the park, the former park keeper's residence is the place to go. It's also a good spot for getting a snack, drink, or souvenir. The pretty little stone house—built in 1858—is the headquarters of Les Amis de la Montagne (The Friends of the Mountain), a non-profit organization that offers various guided walks—including moonlight snow-shoe excursions and cross-country ski lessons in winter around the mountain and in nearby areas. ☒ *1260 chemin Remembrance, Parc du Mont-Royal* ☎ *514/843–8240* ⊕ *www.lemontroyal. qc.ca* Ⓜ *Mont-Royal, then bus 11 west.*

Observatoire de l'Est
VIEWPOINT | If you're just driving across Mont-Royal, be sure to stop for a few moments at its eastern lookout for a view of the Stade Olympique and the east end of the city. Tourists enjoy the

location as it's a great photo spot. ☒ *Voie Camillien-Houde, Parc du Mont-Royal* Ⓜ *Mont-Royal.*

Côte-des-Neiges

Not too many tourists venture north and east of Parc du Mont-Royal, but the primarily residential neighborhood of Côte-des-Neiges has much to offer.

One of Montréal's most-visited sights—the Oratoire St-Joseph (St. Joseph's Oratory)—sits atop the northern slope of Mont-Royal, dominating the surrounding neighborhood of Côte-des-Neiges. More than 2 million people of all faiths visit the shrine every year. The most devout pilgrims climb the staircase leading to the main door on their knees, pausing on each of its 99 steps to pray.

Even without the Oratoire (as well as the Cimetière de Notre-Dame-des-Neiges, another site worth seeing), Côte-des-Neiges is a district worth visiting. It's also an area where the dominant languages are neither English nor French.

It's largely working-class immigrants who live here—Filipino, Latin American, Southeast and South Asian, West Indian, Arab, Jewish, Chinese, Haitian, and most recently people from Eastern Europe and Africa. It's also home to a sizable number of students, many of whom attend the Université de Montréal, as well as other smaller surrounding colleges and universities.

As a result, if you're looking for inexpensive, authentic world cuisine, there's no better place in Montréal to come to than Côte-des-Neiges. It's teeming with ethnic shops and restaurants—Thai, Russian, Korean, Indian, Peruvian, Filipino, and more. You're as likely to find a falafel joint as a Vietnamese noodle eatery or Haitian street food.

Parc du Mont-Royal and Côte-des-Neiges

A **B** **C** **D** **E**

av. Lajoie
rue Bernard

av. Dunlop
av. Rockland
av. Davaar
av. McEachran
av. Stuart
av. Wiseman
av. Outremont

av. Willowdale

Parc
Beaubien
av. St-V iateur

av. Lacombe
blvd. Édouard-Montpetit

Parc Outremont

M CÔTE-DES-NEIGES
rue Jean-Brillant

M UNIVERSITÉ-DE-MONTRÉAL

av. Vincent d'Indy
av. Claude
Champagne
av. Courcellette
av. Pagnuelo

chemin de la Côte-Sainte-Catherine

OUTRE-MONT

chemin
Queen Mary

Université de
Montréal

ÉDOUARD-MONTPETIT

av. Maplewood

av. Decelles

❶

CÔTE-DES-NEIGES

Cimetière
Mont-Royal

❸

av. McCulloch

TO MILE END,
MONT-ROYAL
STATION →

❽

av. Oakland

❷

Cimetière de
Notre-Dame-des-Neiges

❼

Summit Circle
Summit
Park

chemin Remembrance

voie Camillien-Houde

Sunnyside Circle
Bellevue Cir.

The Boulevard

Lac aux
Castors
❺

❻

❹

King
George
Park

av. Aberdeen
av. Argyle

The Boulevard
av. Cedar
av. Montrose

WESTMOUNT

chemin de la Côte-des-Neiges

Parc du
Mont-Royal
❶

ch. Côte-St-Antoine

av. Clarke
av. Mountain

av. des Pins

Park
Entrance

rue University

av. Metcalfe
av. Kensington

138

rue Sherbrooke
av. Docteur-Penfield

McGill
University

av. Greene
av. Wood

av. Lincoln

rue de la Montagne
rue Peel

rue Sherbrooke
138

M ATWATER
Forum

blvd. Maisonneuve

M PEEL
M MCGILL

av. Atwater

blvd. Dorchester
M GUY-CONCORDIA
rue Ste-Catherine

rue Guy

DOWNTOWN

Autoroute
Ville-Marie

blvd. René-Lévesque

720

M LIONEL-GROULX

0   1/8 mi
0   1/8 km

KEY
❶ Sights
❶ Restaurants
M Métro Stations
🚲 Bike Route

Sights ▼
1 Chalet du
  Mont-Royal............. **D5**
2 Cimetière de
  Notre-Dame-
  des-Neiges.............**C3**
3 Cimetière
  Mont-Royal............. **D3**
4 Croix sur la
  Montagne **E4**
5 Lac aux Castors..........**C4**
6 Maison Smith **D4**
7 Observatoire de l'Est **E3**
8 Oratoire St-Joseph **A3**

Restaurants ▼
1 Duc de Lorraine......... **A2**

GETTING HERE AND AROUND

Côte-des-Neiges is bordered by avenue Decelles to the north and the Cimetière de Notre-Dame-des-Neiges to the south. It's easy to get here by public transit, either the métro to the Côte-des-Neiges station or the 166 bus from the Guy-Concordia métro station to chemin Queen-Mary. If you take a car—which is not a bad idea if you plan to visit the Parc du Mont-Royal as well—it's usually easy to get a parking space at the Oratoire St-Joseph (a contribution of C$5 per vehicle is requested Monday to Saturday, except for those attending services or coming to the Oratoire to pray).

TIMING

Côte-des-Neiges bustles during the day but is a little quieter at night.

 Sights

Cimetière de Notre-Dame-des-Neiges (*Our Lady of the Snows Cemetery*)
CEMETERY | At 343 acres, Canada's largest cemetery is not much smaller than the neighboring Parc du Mont-Royal, and, as long as you just count the living, it's usually a lot less crowded. You don't have to be morbid to wander the graveyard's 55 km (34 miles) of tree-shaded paths and roadways past the tombs of hundreds of prominent artists, poets, intellectuals, politicians, and clerics. Among them is Calixa Lavallée (1842–91), who wrote "O Canada," the country's national anthem.
■ TIP→ **The cemetery offers some guided tours in summer. Phone ahead for details.**
✉ *4601 chemin de la Côte-des-Neiges, Côte-des-Neiges* ☎ *514/735–1361* ⊕ *www.cimetierenotredamedesneiges.ca* Ⓜ *Côte-des-Neiges, then Bus 165 south.*

★ Cimetière Mont-Royal
CEMETERY | If you find yourself humming "Getting to Know You" as you explore Mont-Royal Cemetery's 165 acres, blame it on the graveyard's most famous permanent guest, Anna Leonowens

(1834–1915). She was the real-life model for the heroine of the Rodgers and Hammerstein musical *The King and I*. The cemetery—established in 1852 by the Anglican, Presbyterian, Unitarian, and Baptist churches—is laid out like a terraced garden, with footpaths that meander between crab-apple trees and past Japanese lilacs. Birders and nature photographers love to come to this cemetery for the 150 or so species of birds found here, including chestnut-sided warblers, ruby-throated hummingbirds, bluebirds, tree swallows, cedar waxwings, nuthatches, yellow warblers, woodpeckers, goldfinches, and more. And keep an eye out for the resident groundhogs and raccoons! ✉ *1297 chemin de la Forêt, Côte-des-Neiges* ☎ *514/279–7358* ⊕ *www.mountroyalcem.com* Ⓜ *Mont-Royal, then Bus 11 west.*

Oratoire St-Joseph (*St. Joseph's Oratory*)
RELIGIOUS BUILDING | Each year some 2 million people from all over North America and beyond visit St. Joseph's Oratory. The most devout Catholics climb the 99 steps to its front door on their knees. It is the world's largest and most popular shrine dedicated to the earthly father of Jesus (Canada's patron saint), and it's all the work of a man named Brother André Besette (1845–1937).

By worldly standards Brother André didn't have much going for him, but he had a deep devotion to St. Joseph and an iron will. In 1870 he joined the Holy Cross religious order and was assigned to work as a doorkeeper at the college the order operated just north of Mont-Royal. In 1904 he began building a chapel on the mountainside across the road to honor his favorite saint, and the rest is history. Thanks to reports of miraculous cures attributed to St. Joseph's intercession, donations started to pour in, and Brother André was able to start work replacing his modest shrine with something more substantial. The result, which wasn't completed until after

Saint Joseph's Oratory is Canada's largest church and claims to have one of the largest domes in the world.

his death, is one of the most triumphal pieces of church architecture in North America.

The oratory and its gardens dominate Mont-Royal's northwestern slope. Its copper dome—one of the largest in the world—can be seen from miles away. The interior of the main church is equally grand, although it's also quite austere. The best time to visit it is on Sunday for the 11 am solemn mass, when the sanctuary is brightly lit and the sweet voices of Les Petits Chanteurs du Mont-Royal—the city's best boys' choir—fill the nave with music.

The crypt is shabbier than its big brother upstairs but more welcoming. In a long, narrow room behind the crypt, 10,000 votive candles glitter before a dozen carved murals extolling the virtues of St. Joseph; the walls are hung with crutches discarded by those said to have been cured. Just beyond is the simple tomb of Brother André, who was canonized a saint in 2010. His preserved heart is displayed in a glass case in one of several galleries between the crypt and the main church.

High on the mountain, east of the main church, is a garden commemorating the Passion of Christ, with life-size representations of the 14 stations of the cross. On the west side of the church is Brother André's original chapel, with pressed-tin ceilings and plaster saints that is, in many ways, more moving than the church that overshadows it. Note: the oratoire operates a shuttle bus for visitors who aren't up to the steep climb from the main parking lot to the entrance of the crypt church. The main church is several stories above that, but escalators and two elevators ease the ascent. ■ TIP→ **A major renovation and expansion project is under way, so expect some potential disruption during your visit.** ⌧ *3800 chemin Queen-Mary, Côte-des-Neiges* ☎ *514/733–8211, 877/672–8647* ⊕ *www. saint-joseph.org* ✉ *Free, museum $C3, parking: contribution of $C5 per vehicle requested (except for those attending services or coming to pray)* ☞ *Daily* *guided tours available in summer at 1:30 for C$6* Ⓜ *Côte-des-Neiges.*

🍴 Restaurants

Duc de Lorraine

$$$$ | **CAFÉ** | A light croissant or rich pastry from the city's oldest pâtisserie makes for a nice break after visiting the Parc Mont-Royal or Oratoire St-Joseph. For lunch, try the avocado toast with goat cheese, cherry tomatoes, and olive oil; the onion soup; or the mushroom or lobster risotto, followed by a tartelette *aux abricots* (apricot tart). ■ **TIP→ If you're taking pastries home, try to snag an almond-paste (as opposed to almond-cream) croissant (or roulé) before the shop runs out. Known for:** ample patio; almond-paste roulé; high prices. ⑤ *Average main: C$34* ✉ *5002 Côte-des-Neiges, Côte-des-Neiges* ☎ *514/731–4128* ⊕ *www.ducdelorraine.ca* Ⓜ *Côte-des-Neiges.*

🎭 Performing Arts

Segal Centre for the Performing Arts

THEATER | English-language favorites like *Harvey, Inherit the Wind,* and *Joseph and the Amazing Technicolor Dreamcoat* get frequent billing at this Côte-des-Neiges venue, along with locally written works. The center is best known, however, as the home to the Dora Wasserman Yiddish Theatre, which presents such musical works as *The Jazz Singer* and *The Pirates of Penzance* in Yiddish. ✉ *5170 chemin de la Côte-Ste-Catherine, Côte-des-Neiges* ☎ *514/739–7944* ⊕ *www.segalcentre.org* Ⓜ *Côte-Ste-Catherine.*

Hochelaga-Maisonneuve

The neighborhood of Hochelaga-Maisonneuve, aka HoMa, is one of the best spots to go if you're craving green space, plus it has one of Montréal's top markets. In fact, it's worth the trip on the métro's Green Line just to see the

---

---

five institutions that make up Montréal's Espace pour la Vie (Space for Life), an innovative natural science museum complex—the first in the world to link humans with nature. It includes the Jardin Botanique (Botanical Garden); the Insectarium, which houses the world's largest collection of bugs; the Biodôme, a great place to experience different ecosystems under one roof; the stunning Rio Tinto Alcan Planetarium; and the Biosphère, housed in the spherical former U.S. pavilion during Expo '67, which explores the links between society and the environment by melding art, science, and citizen action.

Parc Maisonneuve is a lovely green area, and an ideal place for a stroll or a picnic. The leaning tower that supports the roof of the Stade Olympique (Olympic Stadium), which played host to the 1976 Summer Olympics, dominates the skyline here. The area is largely working-class residential, but it's becoming a quartier *branché*, or hip 'hood, with some good restaurants and little shops along rue Ontario Est.

Until 1918, when it was annexed by Montréal, the east-end district of Maisonneuve was a city unto itself, a booming, prosperous industrial center full of factories making everything from shoes to cheese. The neighborhood was

3

Montréal **HOCHELAGA-MAISONNEUVE**

Hochelaga-Maisonneuve

also packed with houses for the almost entirely French Canadian workforce, who kept the whole machine humming.

Maisonneuve was also the site of one of Canada's earliest experiments in urban planning. The Dufresne brothers, a pair of prosperous shoe manufacturers, built a series of grand civic buildings along rue Morgan—many of which still stand—including a theater, public baths, and a bustling market, as well as Parc Maisonneuve. All this was supposed to make working-class life more bearable, but World War I put an end to the brothers' plans, and Maisonneuve became part of Montréal, twinned with the east-end district of Hochelaga.

GETTING HERE AND AROUND

It's not necessary to drive to the area, as the Pie-IX and Viau métro stops on the Green Line provide easy access to all the sites, including the Insectarium and the Jardin Botanique. For bikers, it's a straight shot across the path on rue Rachel.

TIMING

If traveling with kids, you'll probably want to dedicate more time to exploring the area to see the sights. One of the city's major markets—Marché Maisonneuve—is on the corner of rue Ontario and avenue Bennett, and is well worth a stop.

⊙ Sights

Château Dufresne

HISTORIC HOME | The adjoining homes of a pair of shoe manufacturers, Oscar and Marius Dufresne, provide a glimpse into the lives of Montréal's francophone bourgeoisie in the early 20th century. The brothers built their Beaux-Arts palace in 1916 along the lines of the Petit-Trianon in Paris, and lived in it with their families—Oscar in the eastern half and Marius in the western half.

Worth searching out are the domestic scenes on the walls of the Petit Salon, where Oscar's wife entertained friends. Her brother-in-law relaxed with his friends in a smoking room decked out like a Turkish lounge. During the house's incarnation as a boys' school in the 1950s, the Eudist priests who ran it covered the room's frieze of nymphs and satyrs with a modest curtain that their charges lifted at every opportunity.

These days, kids and families are encouraged to play "Flair et Luminaires," a detective game activity in which participants are given clues to solve five mysteries within the château. ■ **TIP→ Guided tours in English are available on weekends.** ⊠ 2929 rue Jeanne-d'Arc, Hochelaga-Maisonneuve ☎ 514/259–9201 ⊕ www.chateaudufresne.com ⊠ C$14 ⊗ Closed Mon., Tues., and public holidays Ⓜ Pie-IX.

Insectarium
SCIENCE MUSEUM | FAMILY | After a complete C$38.4 million metamorphosis, the Insectarium, reopened in 2022, now houses more than 3,000 plants of 150 different varieties and approximately 175 species of insects—including up to 80 species of butterflies flitting about any one time. The reconfigured spaces, inspired by real insect habitats, feature chambers, nests, vegetation, galleries, and soil. Immersive educational experiences aim to replicate life as seen and felt by an insect. For instance, the ground vibrates and ultraviolet visual effects mimic a bug's vision. In this way, visitors are encouraged to move around the way an insect would, by, say, having to squeeze through tunnels or hold on to vertical rods meant to imitate blades of grass. With the new Insectarium, the first of its kind in North America, the hope is that this more intimate experience will lead visitors to rethink our

relationships with bugs. The revitalized venue also includes exhibits and a children's activities room. ⊠ 4581 rue Sherbrooke Est, Hochelaga-Maisonneuve ☎ 514/872–1400 ⊕ www.espacepourlavie.ca ⊠ C$22.75 ⊗ Closed Mon. Sept–May Ⓜ Pie-IX or Viau.

★ **Jardin Botanique** (Botanical Garden)
GARDEN | FAMILY | Creating one of the world's great botanical gardens in a city with a winter as harsh as Montréal's was no mean feat, and the result is that no matter how brutal it gets in January there's one corner of the city where it's always summer. With 181 acres of plantings in summer and 10 greenhouses open all year, Montréal's Jardin Botanique is the second-largest attraction of its kind in the world (after England's Kew Gardens). It grows more than 26,000 species of plants, and among its 30 thematic gardens are a rose garden, an alpine garden, and—a favorite with the kids—a poisonous-plant garden.

You can attend traditional tea ceremonies in the Japanese Garden, which has one of the best bonsai collections in the West, or wander among the native birches and maples of the Jardin des Premières-Nations (First Nations Garden). The Jardin de Chine (Chinese Garden), with its pagoda and waterfall, will transport you back to the Ming dynasty. In the fall, all three cultural gardens host magical mixes of light, color, plant life, and sculpture during the annual Gardens of Light spectacle. ⊠ 4101 rue Sherbrooke Est, Hochelaga-Maisonneuve ☎ 514/872–1400 ⊕ www.espacepourlavie.ca ⊠ C$22.75 ⊗ Closed Mon., except during holiday season Ⓜ Pie-IX or Viau.

Maisonneuve
HISTORIC DISTRICT | World War I and the Depression killed early 20th-century plans to turn this industrial center into a model city with broad boulevards, grand public buildings, and fine homes, but just three blocks south of the Olympic

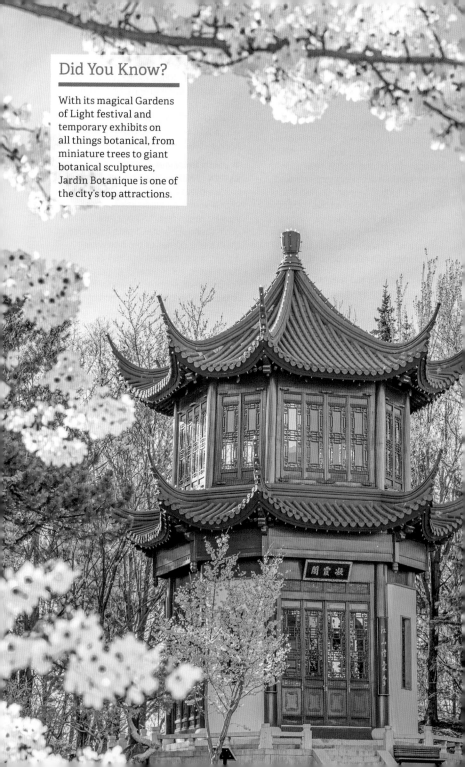

Did You Know?

With its magical Gardens of Light festival and temporary exhibits on all things botanical, from miniature trees to giant botanical sculptures, Jardin Botanique is one of the city's top attractions.

site a few fragments of that dream have survived the passage of time.

A magnificent Beaux-Arts building, site of the old public market, which has a 20-foot-tall bronze statue of a farm woman, stands at the northern end of tree-lined avenue Morgan. Farmers and butchers have moved into the modern building next door that houses the Marché Maisonneuve, which has become one of the city's major markets, along with Marché Jean-Talon and Marché Atwater. The old market is now a community center and the site of summer shows and concerts.

Monumental staircases and a heroic rooftop sculpture embellish the public baths across the street. The Théâtre Denise Pelletier, at the corner of rues Ste-Catherine Est and Morgan, has a lavish Italianate interior; Fire Station No. 1, at 4300 rue Notre-Dame Est, was inspired by Frank Lloyd Wright's Unity Temple in suburban Chicago; and the sumptuously decorated Église Très-Saint-Nom-de-Jésus, has one of the most powerful organs in North America. The 198-acre Parc Maisonneuve, stretching north of the botanical garden, is a lovely place for a stroll. ⊠ *Hochelaga-Maisonneuve* Ⓜ *Pie-IX or Viau.*

Planétarium
OBSERVATORY | FAMILY | In 2013, Montréal got a new, ultramodern, C$48 million planetarium, one of only a handful of planetariums worldwide to have two circular theaters—one for astronomy exhibits and the other a high-tech multimedia venue. Part of the Espace pour la Vie complex, this state-of-the-art facility delivers a futuristic experience unlike any other. The permanent exhibit lets the whole family have fun exploring life on Earth and (perhaps) in the universe through interactive and hands-on stations. ■TIP➔ **Hours vary seasonally.** ⊠ *4801 av. Pierre-de-Coubertin, Hochelaga-Maisonneuve* ☎ *514/868–3000*

⊕ *www.espacepourlavie.ca/en/planetarium* ⊠ *C$22.75* ⊘ *Closed Mon., except for holiday season and in summer* Ⓜ *Viau.*

Stade Olympique
NOTABLE BUILDING | Montrealers finished paying for their Olympic stadium (dubbed the "Big O") in the spring of 2006—30 years after the games for which it was built—but they still call it the "Big Owe," and not very affectionately, either. The architecture is dramatic, squatting like a giant flying saucer in the middle of the east end, but it proved to be unworkable and was abandoned by the sports teams it was supposed to house. It's now used mostly for trade shows. But come on the first Friday of the month in summer, and join the locals who flock to the park outside the stadium to feast from Montréal's food trucks—all of them congregate here for the event (⊕ *lespremiersvendredis.ca*). ■TIP➔ **The tower observatory is closed indefinitely.** ⊠ *4141 av. Pierre-de-Coubertin, Hochelaga-Maisonneuve* ☎ *514/252–4141, 877/997–0919* ⊕ *parcolympique.qc.ca* Ⓜ *Pie-IX or Viau.*

Performing Arts

Théâtre Denise Pelletier
THEATER | With an objective to introduce younger audiences to theater, the Pelletier, which celebrates its 60th year in 2024, puts on French-language productions in a beautifully restored Italianate hall. It's a 15-minute walk from the métro station. ⊠ *4353 rue Ste-Catherine Est, Hochelaga-Maisonneuve* ☎ *514/253–8974* ⊕ *www.denise-pelletier.qc.ca* Ⓜ *Joliette or Pie-IX.*

The Islands

The two islands just east of the city in the St. Lawrence River—Île Ste-Hélène, formed by nature, and Île Notre-Dame, created with the stone rubble excavated from the construction of Montréal's métro—are now used for Montréal's indoor-outdoor playground, Parc Jean-Drapeau.

Expo '67, the World's Fair staged to celebrate the centennial of the Canadian federation, was brought here by the city's then mayor, Jean Drapeau. It was the biggest party in Montréal's history, firmly placing the city on the international map and marking a defining moment in its evolution as a modern metropolis.

The spirit of coming here for excitement and thrills lives on. La Ronde, a major amusement park that has the world's highest double wooden roller coaster, is on Île Ste-Hélène. On Île Notre-Dame, there's Casino de Montréal, which includes gaming tables and more than 3,200 slot machines. The casino might be the only vestige of nightlife on the islands.

Lovers of sports and the outdoors enjoy walking the park's 25-plus kilometers of trails, swimming at the aquatic complex, or practicing open-water swimming in the lake off Île Notre-Dame. In winter, visitors can enjoy skiing, ice-skating, and tobogganing. Nature enthusiasts and photographers love the local wildlife, which includes more than 240 species of birds, as well as groundhogs, squirrels, raccoons, and even red foxes.

GETTING HERE AND AROUND

Both Île Ste-Hélène and Île Notre-Dame are very accessible. You can drive to them via the Pont de la Concorde or the Pont Jacques-Cartier, take the ferry from the Old Port to Île Ste-Hélène (seasonal), or take the métro from the Berri-UQAM station to Jean-Drapeau.

TIMING

If you're traveling with kids, there's enough here to keep them occupied for a full day, especially in nice weather. Because the Islands are so easy to get to with the ferry, visiting can be tacked on to time spent in Old Montréal.

Sights

Biosphère

SCIENCE MUSEUM | **FAMILY** | Nothing captures the exuberance of Expo '67 better than the geodesic dome designed by Buckminster Fuller (1895–1983) as the American Pavilion. It's only a skeleton now—the polymer panels that protected the U.S. exhibits from the elements were burned out in a fire long ago—but it's still an eye-catching sight, like something plucked from a science-fiction movie.

Science of a nonfictional kind, however, is explored in the special environmental center the federal government built in the middle of the dome. It focuses on the challenges of preserving the Great Lakes and St. Lawrence River system, but it has lively and interactive exhibits on climate change, sustainable energy, and air pollution. Kids and others can use games and interactive displays arranged around a large model of the waterway to explore how shipping, tourism, water supplies, and hydroelectric power are affected. ■TIP→ **The Biosphère is now managed by and forms part of Espace pour la Vie, based in Hochelaga-Maisonneuve and which endeavors to bring together art, science, and citizen action.** ✉ *Île Ste-Hélène, 160 chemin Tour-de-l'Île, The Islands* ☎ *514/868-3000* ⊕ *espacepourlavie.ca/en/biosphere* 💰 *C$27.75* ⏱ *Closed Mon., except during summer and the holiday season* Ⓜ *Jean-Drapeau.*

Casino de Montréal

CASINO | You have to be at least 18 to visit Montréal's government-owned casino, but you don't have to be a gambler. The casino is currently home to three bars and four restaurants, ranging from deli style to gourmet. You can even come just to look at the architecture—the main building was the French pavilion at Expo '67. But if you do want to risk the family fortune, there are more than 3,000 slot machines, a keno lounge, a high-stakes gaming area, and 120 tables

The Islands

for playing blackjack, baccarat, roulette, craps, and various types of poker. There is also music, including cabaret. ✉ *Île Notre-Dame, 1 av. du Casino, The Islands* ☎ *514/392–2746, 800/665–2274* ⊕ *www.casino-de-montreal.com* 🎫 *Free* Ⓜ *Jean-Drapeau, then Bus 167.*

La Ronde

AMUSEMENT PARK/CARNIVAL | **FAMILY** | Every year, it seems, this amusement park, at the eastern end of Île Ste-Hélène, adds some new and monstrous way to scare the living daylights (and maybe even your lunch) out of you. The most recent addition is Vipère, a free-fly roller coaster that lifts you 107 feet up and subjects you to unexpected drops, vertical free falls, and 360-degree somersaults. Chaos is a single loop that takes you forward, backward, and upside down while sitting face-to-face with other riders. Titan, a giant swaying pendulum will have you—or the kids—soaring and spinning 148 feet above the park, traveling at speeds up to 70 mph. Demon, an extreme, high-speed ride, twists you, twirls you, and turns you upside down, then douses you with water jets. The park also aims to terrify with such stomach-turning champions as the Endor, the Goliath, the Vampire, Monstre, and Vol Ultime. For the less daring, there are Ferris wheels, boat rides, and kiddie rides. The popular International Fireworks Competition is held here on Saturday and Wednesday in late June and July. ✉ *Île Ste-Hélène, 22 chemin Macdonald, The Islands* ☎ *514/397–2000* ⊕ *www.sixflags.com/larondeen* 🎫 *From C$36 when purchased online at least one day before your visit* ☉ *Hours vary seasonally* Ⓜ *Jean-Drapeau.*

★ **Parc Jean-Drapeau**

CITY PARK | **FAMILY** | Île Ste-Hélène and Île Notre-Dame now constitute a single park named, fittingly enough, for Jean Drapeau (1916–99), the visionary (and spendthrift) mayor who built the métro and brought the city both the 1967 World's Fair and the 1976 Olympics. The park includes La Ronde (a major amusement park), acres of flower gardens, a beach with filtered water, the Formula 1 Grand Prix Circuit Gilles Villeneuve, performance spaces, and the Casino de Montréal. There's history here, too, at the Old Fort, which was built by the British to protect the country from a possible invasion by the United States. In winter, you can skate on the old Olympic rowing basin or slide down iced trails on an inner tube. ✉ *The Islands* ☎ *514/872–6120* ⊕ *www. parcjeandrapeau.com* Ⓜ *Jean-Drapeau.*

Activities

SWIMMING

Parc-Plage l'Île Notre-Dame

(*Plage Jean-Doré*)

SWIMMING | The city's artificial beach on the west side of Île Notre-Dame probably has the cleanest water (tested and monitored) in Montréal. The dress code at the neighboring casino might ban camisoles and strapless tops, but here anything seems to go on hot summer days, when the beach is a sea of oiled bodies. You get the distinct impression that swimming is not uppermost on the minds of many of the scantily clad hordes. If you do want to go in, however, the water is filtered and closely monitored for contamination, and there are lifeguards on duty. A shop rents swimming and boating paraphernalia, and there's a restaurant and picnic areas. ✉ *Île Notre-Dame, The Islands* ☎ *514/872–6120* ⊕ *www.parcjeandrapeau.com* 🎫 *C$9.25* Ⓜ *Jean-Drapeau, then Bus 167.*

Sud-Ouest and Lachine

Lower rents and proximity to Downtown make the Sud-Ouest, a historically industrial, working-class area, an appealing alternative. The area consists of Verdun, St-Henri, Griffintown, and La Petite Bourgogne (aka Little Burgundy). The latter three form what has officially become

Golfing in Montréal

Teeing Up in Montréal

Montréal golf enthusiasts have several excellent golf courses available to them, many less than a half-hour drive from Downtown. If you're willing to trek a bit farther (about 45 minutes), you'll find some of the best golfing in the province. For a complete listing of the many golf courses in the area, Tourisme Québec (⊕ *bonjourquebec.com/en-ca*) is the best place to start.

Club de Golf Métropolitain Anjou (Anjou Metropolitan Golf Club). One of the longest courses in the province, the Championship course features an undulating landscape with five lakes and some tricky bunkers, all calling for accurate shots. Beginners and improvers can hone their skills on the short Executive course. A clubhouse featuring a restaurant, several banquet halls, a pro shop with an indoor practice range (winter only), and an outdoor driving range all serve to make this a top-notch facility. A dress code is in effect. The club is located in Anjou, a 25-minute drive from Downtown Montréal. ⊠ *9555 boul. du Golf, Montréal* ☎ *514/353–5353* ⊕ *www.golfmetropolitainanjou.com* 🖼 *Championship Course C$30–C$51* 🏌️ *Championship Course: 18 holes, 7005 yards, par 3, 4, and 5; Executive Course: 6 holes, 1022 yards, par 3* ☞ *Facilities: Driving range, golf carts, restaurant* Ⓜ *Honoré-Beaugrand.*

Club de Golf du Falcon. Designed by Graham Cooke, this course winds through a verdant, well-wooded landscape dotted with water hazards and sand traps, and offers an exciting challenge. Five sets of tees accommodate different skill levels. It's 25 minutes west of Downtown in the picturesque and largely anglophone village of Hudson (which itself is worth a visit). ⊠ *59 rue Cambridge, Hudson* ☎ *450450/458–1997* ⊕ *www.falcongolf.ca* 🖼 *C$30–C$92* 🏌️ *18 holes, 7096 yards, par 72* ☞ *Facilities: Driving range, putting green, golf carts, rental clubs, lessons, restaurant, clubhouse, practice facilities.*

Golf Dorval. The two original courses here, designed by Graham Cooke, were combined into a single challenging par-72 golf course with a rolling parkland setting. There are four levels of difficulty, finishing with a long, narrow par 4 18th hole with a slope up to the green. There's a dress code. The course is a 20-minute drive from Downtown Montréal. ⊠ *2000 av. Reverchon, Dorval* ☎ *514/631–4653* ⊕ *www.golfdorval.com* 🖼 *C$23–C$117* 🏌️ *18 holes, 6643 yards, par 72* ☞ *Facilities: Driving range, putting green, golf carts, rental clubs, lessons, snack bar.*

Golf Ste-Rose. With lovely views of the Rivière des Mille-Îles, hardwood forests, and myriad ponds, this course may be the most beautiful in Québec. It's a short hop over the bridge to the island of Laval. The course features four sets of tees to accommodate different skill levels. The 18-hole course was designed by John Watson, one of the great names of Canadian golf course architecture. ⊠ *1400 boul. Mattawa, Ste-Rose* ☎ *450/628–6072, 450/628–3573* ⊕ *www.golfsterose.com* 🖼 *C$35–C$57* 🏌️ *18 holes, 6134 yards, par 70* ☞ *Facilities: Driving range, golf carts, rental clubs, restaurant, bar.*

known as Les Quartiers du Canal, or the Canal Neighborhoods, a gentrifying area lining the Lachine Canal that was once home to factory workers, railway workers, and jazz musicians. These days, the area is better known for its small chef-owned restaurants, design boutiques, antiques shops, and condos populated by young professionals and creatives. Take the time to explore the Griffintown Design District, spanning rues Peel, Ann, Wellington, William, and Notre-Dame Ouest, to get a taste of its 50 or so creative furniture design stores, art galleries, architects' ateliers, and trendy cafés and restaurants. The bilingual Design District booklet can be found at ⊕ *lesquartiersducanal.com/en/griffintowndesigndistrict*.

If you want to work up an appetite for lunch—or just get some exercise—rent a bike on rue de la Commune, in Old Montréal, and ride west along the 14-km (9-mile) Lachine Canal through what used to be Montréal's industrial heartland to the shores of Lac St-Louis. You could stop at the Marché Atwater to pick up some cheese, bread, wine, and fruit for a picnic in the lakefront park at the end of the trail. If pedaling sounds too energetic, hop aboard an excursion boat and dine more formally in one of the century-old homes that line the waterfront in Lachine, the historic city borough at the western end of the canal that was once the staging point for the lucrative fur trade.

⊙ Sights

Fur Trade at Lachine National Historic Site
HISTORY MUSEUM | Located in the waterfront park at the end of the Lachine Canal, on the shores of Lac St-Louis, this early 19th-century stone warehouse has been converted into a museum that commemorates the industry that dominated Canada's early history. ⊠ *1255 boul. St-Joseph, Lachine* ☎ *888/773–8888, 514/637–7433* ⊕ *pc.gc.ca/en/lhn-nhs/qc/*

lachine ⊠ *C$4.25* ⊙ *Closed Oct.–May and Mon. and Tues. in summer.*

Lachine Canal National Historic Site
TRAIL | FAMILY | The canal is all about leisure—biking, rollerblading, strolling along the water, and picnicking—but it wasn't always so. Built in 1825 to get boats and cargo around the treacherous Lachine Rapids, it quickly became a magnet for all sorts of industries. But when the St. Lawrence Seaway opened in 1959, allowing large cargo ships to sail straight from the Atlantic to the Great Lakes without stopping in Montréal, the canal closed to navigation and became an illicit dumping ground for old cars and the bodies of victims of underworld killings. The area around it degenerated into an industrial slum.

A federal agency rescued the site in 1978, planting lawns and trees along the old canal, transforming it into a long, narrow park, or *parc linéaire*. Some of the abandoned canneries, sugar refineries, and steelworks have since been converted into desirable residential and commercial condominiums. The bicycle path is the first link in the more than 97 km (60 miles) of bike trails that make up the Pôle des Rapides (☎ *514/364–4490*).

Two permanent exhibits at the Lachine Canal Visitor Services Centre, at the western end of the canal, explain its history and construction. The center also has a shop and lookout terrace. ⊠ *Lachine* ☎ *514/283–6054* ⊕ *pc.gc.ca/en/lhn-nhs/qc/canallachine/visit* ⊠ *Free* Ⓜ *Angrignon, then Bus 195.*

🍽 Restaurants

★ Joe Beef
$$$$ | MODERN CANADIAN | Eating out at this establishment in the St-Henri/Little Burgundy neighborhood is a little like being invited to a dinner party by a couple of friends who just happen to be top-notch chefs. Everything written on the chalkboard menu is simple,

Sud-Ouest and Lachine

KEY

1 Sights
1 Restaurants
1 Quick Bites
1 Hotels
M Métro Stations

hearty, and just delicious, from the fresh oysters to the organic rib steak and the now-famous lobster spaghetti. **Known for:** lobster spaghetti; leafy patio; celebrity chef. ⓢ *Average main: C$55* ✉ *2491 rue Notre-Dame Ouest, St-Henri* ☎ *514/935–6504* ⊕ *www.joebeef.ca* ◷ *Closed Sun. and Mon. No lunch* Ⓜ *Lionel-Groulx.*

★ Le Vin Papillon

$$$ | **MODERN ITALIAN** | First and foremost a wine bar, this atmospheric 30-seat spot also dishes out delicious vegetable-centric, market-based cuisine. The cuisine features local and seasonal ingredients, and the flavors are simple enough to pair well with the stars of the show: the many wines on offer. **Known for:** Italian tapas; Brussels sprouts a la plancha; extensive wine list. ⓢ *Average main: C$24* ✉ *2519 rue Notre-Dame Ouest, Verdun* ☎ *514/439-6494* ⊕ *vinpapillon.com* ◷ *Closed Sun. and Mon.* Ⓜ *Lionel-Groulx.*

Nora Gray

$$$$ | **SOUTHERN ITALIAN** | The crowd that fills this casual and lively spot nightly is hip, and the simple, modern Southern Italian comfort food and impeccable service keeps them coming back. If they're on the menu, start your meal with the fried zucchini flowers stuffed with ricotta, tomatoes, and basil. **Known for:** Southern Italian cuisine; buzzy bar; classic old-world wine list. ⓢ *Average main: C$40* ✉ *1391 rue St-Jacques, St-Henri* ☎ *514/419–6672* ⊕ *noragray.com* ◷ *Closed Sun. and Mon. No lunch* Ⓜ *Lucien L'Allier.*

Restaurant le H4C

$$$$ | **CANADIAN** | Housed inside a stately former bank topped by a clock tower, this well-worth-the-trek restaurant uses the bank's old vault as a walk-in cellar, while the dining room features stone walls and elegant leather chairs. Main dishes are hard to predict because of the product-driven cuisine but regularly feature local and seasonal ingredients such as snow crab, Québec halibut, asparagus, and fiddleheads—but one thing that indeed does not change is the dedication and resourcefulness of the chef. **Known for:** seasonal eight-course or five-course tasting menu only; old bank building; delicious brunch menu. ⓢ *Average main: C$80* ✉ *538 pl. St-Henri, St-Henri* ☎ *514/316–7234* ⊕ *leh4c.com* ◷ *Closed Mon. and Tues. No lunch* ☞ *Brunch service Sun. between 10 and 3* Ⓜ *Place-St-Henri.*

Satay Brothers

$$ | **ASIAN** | Bringing Southeast Asia to southwest Montréal, Satay Brothers is operated by two brothers obsessed with the street foods found in Singapore, Malaysia, Thailand, and Cambodia. The eclectic and oddly charming space— think red walls, illuminated Chinese lanterns, a mishmash of Asian patterns and décor—features communal seating and a long bar facing the kitchen, which fires out steamed pork buns, *laksa* soup, papaya salad, and, of course, satays to keep the constant and lively crowd fed. **Known for:** festive ambience; papaya salad; long lines. ⓢ *Average main: C$16* ✉ *3721 rue Notre-Dame Ouest, St-Henri* ☎ *514/933–3507* ⊕ *www.sataybrothers.com* ◷ *Closed Mon. and Tues. No lunch* Ⓜ *Lionel-Groulx.*

☕ Coffee and Quick Bites

Bernice | Boulangerie et Pâtisserie

$ | **BAKERY** | Opened in 2020, this luminous, inviting bakery in St-Henri has made a name for itself with its old fashioned layer cakes, cookies, and loaves that transport you back to Grandma's kitchen. **Known for:** chocolate dulce de leche cake; vanilla rainbow/funfetti birthday cake; chewy double dark-chocolate-chunk cookies. ⓢ *Average main: C$10* ✉ *5135 rue Notre-Dame Ouest, Verdun* ☎ *514/931-8444* ⊕ *berniceboulangerie.com* ◷ *Closed Sun. and Mon.* Ⓜ *Place-St-Henri.*

Under the Big Tent

Montréal's reinvention of the ancient art of the circus began in the 1980s, when two street performers, Guy Laliberté and Daniel Gauthier, founded the now world-famous Cirque du Soleil. But it didn't stop there. The city is now home to several circus companies and to a circus complex, out beyond Mont-Royal in the St-Michel district, that houses the National Circus School, En Piste (Circus Arts National Network), and Cirque du Soleil's head office. The school attracts budding acrobats and clowns from all over the world, as well as several other smaller schools, and puts on several performances throughout the year at the complex's performance venue, TOHU Cité des Arts du Cirque (⊕ tohu.ca). Montréal has become so synonymous with the circus arts that for 10 days each July, since 2010, the city plays host to Montréal Complètement Cirque (⊕ montrealcompletementcirque.com), a circus festival that transforms theaters, city streets, parks, and sidewalks into stages showcasing high-flying acrobatic performances by talented artists from around the world.

Cirque du Soleil. This amazing circus is one of Montréal's great success stories. The company—founded in 1984 by a pair of street performers— has completely changed people's idea of what a circus can do. Its shows, now an international phenomenon, use no animals. Instead, colorful acrobatics flirt with the absurd through the use of music, humor, dance, and glorious (and often risqué) costumes.

The Cirque has companies in Las Vegas and one each in Orlando and Los Angeles—but none in Montréal (though its HQ and a circus school are located in the northern part of the city). Nevertheless, every year or two, one of its international touring companies returns to where it all began, the Old Port, and sets up the familiar blue-and-yellow tent for a summer of sold-out shows. ⊠ *Montréal* ☎ *844/773-0589* ⊕ *www.cirquedusoleil.com.*

Cirque Éloize. This award-winning troupe has been touring the globe since 1993, and with well over 4,000 performances under its belt, shows no signs of slowing down. Constantly evolving, Cirque Éloize uses artistic mediums like video and music to bring the circus arts to the masses. ⊠ *Montréal* ☎ *514/596–3838* ⊕ *www.cirque-eloize.com.*

Les 7 Doigts de la Main. Literally translated as "the seven fingers of the hand," the name is a play on a French expression about working collectively toward a common goal, and these seven fingers—the seven founding partners of the circus—have done just that, building up a world-renowned circus troupe for over two decades. Combining acrobatics, theater, and dance, they've performed at special events across the globe, including a Royal Variety Performance for Queen Elizabeth II and at the Olympics in Turin and Vancouver. They even made an appearance on *America's Got Talent.* ⊠ *Montréal* ☎ *514/521–4477* ⊕ *www.7doigts.com.*

Cirque du Soleil is Montréal's hometown circus, founded here in 1984. Today there are several troupes across several countries that perform hundreds of shows per year.

 Hotels

ALT Montréal Griffintown

$$ | **HOTEL** | **FAMILY** | This stylish, tech-savvy Griffintown hotel appeals for its affordable set rates, modular loft-style rooms, partially open seventh-floor terrace, light eco-footprint, and the ultimate luxury of no set checkout time. **Pros:** no set checkout time; close to Downtown; underground parking with Tesla charging stations available. **Cons:** minimalist service may not suit those who want more pampering; no restaurant; a bit of a walk to the métro. ⓢ *Rooms from: C$219* ✉ *120 rue Peel, Griffintown* ☎ *514/375–0220, 855/823–8120* ⊕ *www.althotels.com/en/montreal* ➴ *154 rooms* ⏐◯⏐ *No Meals* Ⓜ *Bonaventure, then Bus 107; or Peel.*

 Nightlife

Atwater Cocktail Club

COCKTAIL BARS | Winner of a prestigious Spirited Award for top international bar by the Tales of the Cocktail Foundation, this popular Little Burgundy cocktail club is located at the back end of the restaurant Foiegwa. You enter from the lane through a red-lit unmarked door, behind which lies a dimly lit speakeasy universe of shiny silver leather banquettes, mirrored ceiling, and a gorgeous bar of malachite green marble peopled by thirtysomething scenesters. Kitschy banquettes aside, the drinks, arranged in a paint-chip color palette, are all elegance. The Glitter Green, for instance, is a mix of *blanco* tequila, mezcal, lime, cucumber, jalapeño, and Tajín. The purple Smoke Show artfully blends three-star rum, blackberry liqueur, lemon, thyme, blackberry, and blueberry, while the yellow Mercury mixes pineapple, lime, ginger, orgeat, black walnut bitters, mint, and soda. For growling stomachs, the kitchen serves everything from appetizers such as oysters Rockfeller, fries, and tomato-onion tarts to mains like truffle spaghetti, cheeseburgers, and mushroom-and-lentil-stuffed cabbage. ⊠ *512 av. Atwater, Verdun* ☎ *438/816-8938* ⊕ *atwatercocktailclub.com* ☞ *Reservations not accepted* Ⓜ *Lionel-Groulx.*

Burgundy Lion

PUB | This British pub in St-Henri serves food that's a notch above the usual. Scotch eggs and the ploughman's lunch are paired with an English take on Québec's beloved poutine—with Stilton cheese and caramelized onions—though it's the fish-and-chips that really shine. Be sure to grab a pint of the Burgundy Lion Ale, or any of the many other beers on draft. If you're a whisky aficionado, the Burgundy Lion stocks Québec's largest list of blends, single malts, Scotches, Irish whiskies, bourbons, ryes, and other whiskies from around the globe. Two patios are open in the summer for alfresco drinking. Note that it can get loud in the evenings. ▰ **TIP→ On Sunday afternoons, high tea is served in the true English style in the four-season solarium—by reservation only.** ⊠ *2496 rue Notre-Dame Ouest, Downtown* ☎ *514/934–0888* ⊕ *www.burgundylion. com* Ⓜ *Lionel-Groulx.*

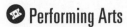

Performing Arts

Théâtre Beanfield

CONCERTS | Built in 1912, this exquisite former cinema and vaudeville theater in the heart of St-Henri has proudly preserved its small stage for the maneuvering of scenery, the artists' lodges under the stage, and the orchestra pit in the foreground. It is the only vintage movie theater in Montréal whose exterior façade and interior have remained almost unchanged. Known as the Corona Theatre until 2023, the Beanfield serves as a concert venue for emerging artists like Milk & Bone, Bobby Bazini, Tom Odell, Kamelot, and Brazilian comedian Rodrigo Marques. ⊠ *2490 rue Notre Dame Ouest, Westmount* ☎ *855/219-0576, 514/492-1775* ⊕ *theatrebeanfield.ca/en* Ⓜ *Lionel-Groulx.*

Shopping

CLOTHING

Harricana

SECOND-HAND | Yesterday's old fur coats and stoles are transformed into everything from car coats and ski jackets to baby wraps and blankets at this designer shop. For summer, vintage scarves become flirty little tops. Old jeans morph into cute little skirts, and tweed jackets are turned into crossover bags. The recycled furs, leather, silks, denims, and woolen items are sold at dozens of shops, but the best place to see what's available is this combination atelier and boutique. ⊠ *3697 rue Wellington, Verdun* ☎ *514/282–1616 ext. 2221* ⊕ *www.harricana.qc.ca* Ⓜ *De l'Église.*

Chapter 4

SIDE TRIPS FROM MONTRÉAL

Updated by
Chris Barry

⦿ Sights   🍴 Restaurants   🛏 Hotels   🛍 Shopping   🍸 Nightlife

★★★★★   ★★★★★   ★★★★★   ★★★★☆   ★★★★★

WELCOME TO
SIDE TRIPS FROM MONTRÉAL

TOP REASONS TO GO

★ **Ski at Mont-Tremblant:**
Heading 150 km (90 miles) north of Montréal takes you to some of the best skiing east of the Rockies, as well as fine hotels and restaurants, a lively ski village, and great golf courses.

★ **Take a driving tour of Eastern Townships wineries:** The vineyards here resemble those in the Niagara Region and Okanagan Valley.

★ **Visit Abbaye St-Benoît-du-Lac:** The Benedictine monks built this splendid church—with its fairy-tale-castle bell tower—on the shores of Lac Memphrémagog.

★ **Spend a night among wolves in Parc Omega:** Go with an experienced guide to explore the lives of these great predators in their natural habitat—the magnificent Outaouais region.

★ **Go leaf-peeping ... anywhere:** From mid-September through mid-October the entire Laurentians, Eastern Townships, and Outaouais are ablaze with spectacular fall foliage.

1 Oka. Oka is most famous for its abbey and provincial park, which also features one of Montréal's only nearby nude beaches.

2 St-Sauveur-des-Monts. The unofficial gateway to the Laurentians.

3 Morin Heights. The small, primarily anglophone hamlet is home to the popular Ski Morin Heights recreational center.

4 Ste-Adèle. With numerous nearby ski hills and dozens of restaurants and hotels, this is the largest village in the Laurentians.

5 Val-David. This village is home to the largest farmers' market in the Laurentians and the hugely successful 1001 Pots ceramics exhibition/workshop.

6 Ste-Agathe-des-Monts. Best known for its ski hills and winter activities, Ste-Agathe also plays host to some of the best beaches in the Laurentians.

7 Mont-Tremblant. Consistently ranked one of the top ski centers in eastern North America.

8 Montebello. Best known for its historic Château Montebello, a spectacular hotel that's also the largest log cabin in the world.

9 Gatineau. Directly across the water from Ottawa, the nation's capital, Gatineau is a large town that's home to the Canadian Museum of History.

10 Bromont. An all-season recreational center offering the only night skiing in the Townships.

11 Knowlton (Lac Brome). The quintessential Eastern Townships resort town.

12 Abbaye St-Benoît-du-Lac. Located on spectacular grounds bordering Lac Memphrémagog, this impressive abbey operates a quaint shop where you can purchase its own sparkling apple wine and outstanding local cheese.

13 Parc du Mont-Orford. One of the top ski centers in the Townships, in addition to being a nature reserve.

14 Magog. A bustling little town located on the banks of Lac Memphrémagog, Magog has one of the nicest beaches in the Townships.

15 North Hatley. One of eastern Québec's prettiest villages.

16 Sherbrooke. This is the Townships' premier "big city," with trendy restaurants and boutiques lining rue Wellington in the downtown core.

17 Notre-Dame-des-Bois. This sleepy one-street village in the shadow of Mont-Megantic has a world-renowned observatory.

In the minds of many who live here, one of Montréal's greatest attributes is its proximity to the sheer physical beauty of the surrounding countryside. From Downtown Montréal you can head in pretty much any direction, and within an hour or so you'll be, if not in the wilderness, then at least in the thick of cottage country. The three most popular side-trip destinations from Montréal are the Laurentians, the Eastern Townships, and the Outaouais—each possessing its own distinct characteristics and flavor.

Most people traveling to this region do so by car, making it easy to spend as much or as little time in any given area as desired. Nevertheless, Québec has created the Route Verte (Green Route), a 5,000-km (3,100-mile) network of bike trails in the southern part of the province. Many of the trails are currently open for access.

MAJOR REGIONS

The Laurentians (les Laurentides) range is a delightful year-round destination for getting outdoors, whether it's for golf and white-water rafting in the summer or skiing and dog sledding in the winter. Along with its stunning natural beauty, it's also known for its authentic Québec food—all of this to be found in little towns like Oka, less than an hour's drive from Downtown Montréal, traffic allowing. The main tourist region, which actually encompasses only a small part

of the Laurentian mountain range, is divided into two major regions: the Lower Laurentians (les Basses Laurentides) and the Upper Laurentians (les Hautes Laurentides). But don't be fooled by the designations; they don't signify great driving distances. The rocky hills here are relatively low, but many are eminently skiable, with a few peaks above 2,500 feet. Mont-Tremblant, at 3,150 feet, is the region's highest. The resort area begins at St-Sauveur-des-Monts (Exit 60 on Autoroute 15) and extends north to Mont-Tremblant. Beyond, the region turns into a wilderness of lakes and forests best visited with an outfitter. Fishing guides are concentrated around Parc du Mont-Tremblant. To the first-time visitor, the hilly areas around St-Sauveur, Ste-Adèle, Morin Heights, Val-Morin, and Val-David up to Ste-Agathe-des-Monts form a pleasant hodgepodge of villages, hotels, and inns that seem to blend one into another. Tourisme Laurentides in Mirabel provides information and offers a daily lodging-booking service. Its main information center is at the Porte du Nord complex at Exit 51 on Autoroute 15.

The Outaouais. First settled in the mid-19th century and long known for its logging, the Outaouais (pronounced ewt-away) region is now a nature lover's paradise as well, with 20,000 lakes, countless rivers, 400 km (249 miles) of hiking trails, and 2,730 km (1,696 miles) of snowmobile trails. To fully experience the majesty of the Outaouais wilderness you could spend close to a week here, but simply driving to any of the region's major provincial parks is a good one-day journey. Montebello, a little country village on the banks of the Ottawa River, is only a 1½-hour drive from Montréal, and is where you'll find Le Château Montebello, the largest log structure ever built. From there you can find excursions to take you to the surrounding countryside, or if you'd prefer, you can simply take in nearby Omega Park, a safari adventure where you'll bear witness to many of the region's creatures interacting within their natural environment. It encompasses an enormous body of land located in the southwest corner of the province. Gatineau, just about two hours outside Montréal, is in another quaint area of Outaouais. Bordering Ontario, and just across the river from Ottawa, this region contains the vast and gorgeous Gatineau Park.

The Eastern Townships (also known as les Cantons de l'Est, and formerly as l'Estrie) refers to the southeast corner of the province of Québec, which borders Vermont, New Hampshire, and Maine, and is known for its mountains, spas, lush forests, and many vineyards. In winter, the Townships are the place to be for serious ski and snowboard enthusiasts, boasting many of the province's highest peaks and most challenging trails. In summer, boating, swimming, sailing, golfing, in-line skating, hiking, and bicycling take over. And every fall the inns are booked solid with visitors eager to take in the brilliant foliage. Fall is also a good time to visit the wineries (although most are open all year). Because of its mild microclimate, the Townships area has become one of the more prominent wine regions in Canada, with a dozen of Québec's 33 commercial wineries.

Planning

When to Go

The Laurentians are a big skiing destination in winter, but the other seasons all have their own charms: you can drive up from Montréal to enjoy the fall foliage; to hike, bike, play golf, camp, or fish; or to engage in spring skiing—and still get back to the city before dark. The only slow periods are early November (aka "mud season"), when there isn't much to do, and June, when the area has plenty to offer but is plagued by black flies. Control programs have improved the situation somewhat.

The Outaouais region is beautiful at any time of year, but unless you're looking to spend several days there it's best to go in summer and stay in the lower region, around Montebello. Making your way up to the provincial parks in the north is a lengthy journey at best, but in winter, potentially hazardous road conditions could well add several more hours to your trip.

The Eastern Townships are best in fall, when the foliage is at its peak; the region borders Vermont and has the same dramatic colors. It's possible to visit wineries at this time, but you should call ahead, since harvest is a busy time.

Getting Here and Around

The Laurentians: Autoroute 15 is the fastest and most direct route from Montréal to the most in-demand spots in the Laurentians. This limited-access highway peters out at Ste-Agathe and morphs into Autoroute 117, which runs all the way to Rouyn-Noranda. Exit numbers on Autoroute 15 reflect the distance from Montréal. Autoroute 15 starts at the New York–Québec border, where it connects to Interstate 87, so it's also the most direct route for most visitors from the United States. The highway crosses into Montréal on the Champlain Bridge and follows the Décarie and Metropolitan Expressways across the island. Visitors arriving from Boston and points east on Interstate 91 can follow Autoroute 55 from the border north to Autoroute 10 (the Autoroute des Cantons de l'Est) and then drive west until it merges with Autoroute 15 at the Champlain Bridge.

The Outaouais: To get to the Outaouais take Autoroute 15 North roughly 40 km (25 miles) until you get to Autoroute 50 West heading toward Lachute. Drive another 70 km (43 miles) past Lachute and you'll soon be in Montebello. Continue on another 15 km (9 miles) to reach Gatineau.

The Eastern Townships: For the Eastern Townships, take Autoroute 10 East (the Autoroute des Cantons de l'Est) from Montréal, or U.S. 91 from New England, which becomes Autoroute 55 as it crosses the border into the Eastern Townships.

Visitor Information

THE LAURENTIANS Tourisme Laurentides (Porte du Nord). ✉ *1000 Autoroute des Laurentides, St-Jérôme* ✛ *Exit 51, Autoroute des Laurentides* ☎ *445/224–7007 from Montréal area, 800/561–6673 from rest of North America* ⊕ *www.laurentides.com.*

THE OUTAOUAIS Tourisme Outaouais. ✉ *103 rue Laurier, Gatineau* ☎ *800/265–7822, 819/778–2222* ⊕ *www.tourisme-outaouais.com.*

THE EASTERN TOWNSHIPS Tourisme Cantons-de-l'Est. ✉ *20 rue Don-Bosco Sud, Sherbrooke* ☎ *819/820–2020, 800/355–5755* ⊕ *www.easterntownships.org.*

Oka

40 km (25 miles) west of Montréal.

If you like apples and delicious cheese, Oka is sure to be a highlight of your trip. It was once the home of Cistercian monks, but the urban sprawl has driven them from their abbey, on the shores of Lac des Deux-Montagnes, to seek solace farther north in St-Jean-de-Matha in the Lanaudière region. However, the cheese they made famous is still produced by a private firm here and is available in local shops. The rolling hills around the little town of Oka are where you'll find many of the apple orchards. If you love cider, follow the Route des Vergers, stopping at various properties along this "Orchard Route" to sample the local wares.

GETTING HERE AND AROUND

To get from Montréal to Oka, take Autoroute 15 North to Autoroute 640 West.

Sights

Hudson

TOWN | A quick detour on the ferry (C$13 one-way) across Lac des Deux-Montagnes brings you to this small town with old houses now used for art galleries, boutiques, and Christmas shops. In winter there's an "ice bridge": basically a plowed path across a well-frozen lake. Taking a walk across the bridge is a singular experience. If you happen to visit on a Saturday from May to October, make a stop at the popular **Finnegan's Market.** Open from 9 to 4, the flea market sells

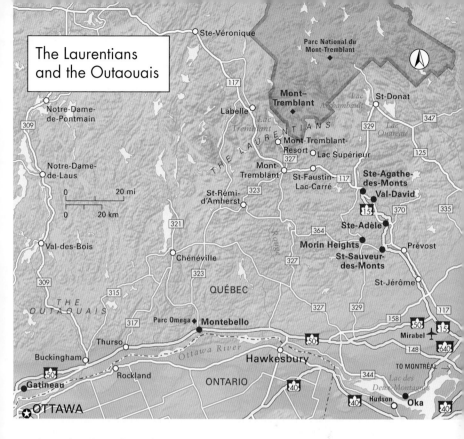

The Laurentians and the Outaouais

antiques, jewelry, crafts, and preserves, among other goods. ⊠ *Hudson* ⊕ *hudson.quebec/en.*

Parc d'Oka (*Oka National Park*)
NATURE SIGHT | Beautifully surrounded by low hills, this park has a lake fringed by a sandy beach and plenty of opportunities for outdoor sports, including hiking and biking trails, kayaking, canoeing, fishing, and, in winter, snowshoeing and cross-country skiing. Locals also consider it to be one of the top camping destinations. Administered by the province along environmentally conscious lines—they implemented the Ecological Integrity Monitoring Program (EIMO) in 2004—it has nearly 900 campsites, and you can rent bicycles, cross-country skis, snowshoes, canoes, and kayaks from the office. Note that the strip at the far

eastern end of the beach is "clothing optional," or, in effect, "clothing non-existent." ⊠ *2020 chemin d'Oka, Oka* ☎ *450/479–8365, 800/665–6527 activities* ⊕ *www.sepaq.com* ⊡ *C$9.55.*

🛍 Shopping

★ Magasin de l'Abbaye d'Oka
SPECIALTY STORE | This shop offers a wide variety of local products, not the least being the abbey's famous Oka cheese. It also has a small dining area where you can dine on Oka cheese poutine and other tasty sundries. ⊠ *1600 chemin d'Oka, Oka* ☎ *450/479–6170* ⊕ *www.abbayeoka.ca.*

St-Sauveur-des-Monts

85 km (53 miles) north of Oka, 63 km (39 miles) north of Montréal.

Just a 45-minute drive from Montréal (or 90 minutes when the traffic's heavy, as it frequently is), St-Sauveur is probably the busiest little town in Québec, especially on weekends. Its rue Principale (basically, Main Street) bristles with bars and restaurants that serve everything from lamb brochettes and spicy Thai stir-fries to steaks and burgers. On summer weekends, the street is so jammed with cars and the sidewalks so packed with visitors that it's sometimes called rue Crescent North after the action-filled street in Montréal. Despite the glitz and the sea of condos that surround it, the town has managed to retain a bit of rural charm in its fine old church and veranda-fronted clapboard homes.

St-Sauveur in winter is no less busy. The "mountains" surrounding the town hardly qualify as Alpine—none has a vertical drop of more than 700 feet—but they're close to Montréal, well serviced by lifts, and lit at night, so the winter sports scene here is very lively. Whether you ski or not, the après-ski scene in St-Sauveur is worth sampling.

GETTING HERE AND AROUND

Take Highway 15 north from Montréal and get off at Exit 60. The best way to explore the main street is to find a parking lot and walk around. Driving through town is difficult in winter and impossible in summer.

VISITOR INFORMATION

CONTACT Tourist Welcome Bureau of Pays-d'en-Haut. ⊠ *1014 rue Valiquette, Ste-Adèle* ☎ *450/229–6637* ⊕ *www. lespaysdenhaut.com.*

Sights

Mont-St-Sauveur Water Park

WATER PARK | FAMILY | Slides, a giant wave pool, a wading pool, and snack bars will all keep the kids occupied here. The river rafting attracts an older, braver crowd; the nine-minute ride follows the natural contours of steep hills. On the tandem slides, plumes of water flow through figure-eight tubes and make for a great time. But if you'd rather stay dry, take an adventure through the trees on the zip line or enjoy a fast ride with the Viking Alpine Coaster. ⊠ *350 av St-Denis, St-Sauveur-des-Monts* ☎ *450/227–4671* ⊕ *www.sommets.com/en* ⊠ *C$51.99.*

Musée du Ski des Laurentides

SPECIALTY MUSEUM | The Laurentians are one of the oldest ski regions in North America, and ski buffs will enjoy this little museum tracing the long history of this area with great photos, artifacts, and some interesting models of early ski lifts. It also houses the Temple de la Renomée du Ski (the Ski Hall of Fame). ⊠ *30 rue Filion, St-Sauveur-des-Monts* ☎ *877/227– 2564* ⊕ *museeduski.com* ⊠ *Free, though donation of C$5 is suggested.*

Hotels

Relais St-Denis

$ | B&B/INN | Once a wartime refuge for well-heeled English children and their governesses, this inn and spa now offers everyone a refuge from everyday stress, with a fireplace and a whirlpool bath in every room and a year-round outdoor heated pool and steam room. **Pros:** variety of spa services and in-room massage packages; kitchenette in all rooms and suites; walking distance to restaurants, outlet shopping, and activities. **Cons:** no restaurant on-site; décor is basic and could use updating; Wi-Fi can be slow. ⑤ *Rooms from: C$125* ⊠ *61 rue St-Denis, St-Sauveur-des-Monts* ☎ *450/227–4766, 888/997–4766* ⊕ *www.relaisstdenis.com* ⇥ *42 rooms* ❤️ *No Meals.*

One of the most popular times to visit the region is in fall, when the mountains are splashed with a spectrum of warm yellows, oranges, and reds.

Shopping

SHOPPING CENTERS

Rue Principale

NEIGHBORHOOD | Small fashion boutiques, restaurant terraces, and cute gift shops in old French Canadian and Victorian homes adorned with bright awnings and flowers line this popular tree-lined shopping street. ⊠ *St-Sauveur-des-Monts*.

Activities

SKIING

Mont-Avila

SKIING & SNOWBOARDING | In St-Sauveur, MSSI's Mont-Avila has 13 trails (two beginner, three intermediate, five difficult, and three extremely difficult), a snow park, and (for those who can't or don't want to ski) a tubing park. ⊠ *500 chemin Avila, Piedmont* ☎ *450/227–4671, 514/871–0101* ⊕ *www.montavila.com.*

Mont-St-Sauveur

SKIING & SNOWBOARDING | Mont-St-Sauveur is the largest of the MSSI properties with a 700-foot vertical drop and 142 acres of skiable terrain. Seventeen of its 38 trails are for beginners and intermediates, 16 are for experts, and five are rated extreme. ⊠ *350 av. St-Denis, St-Sauveur* ⊕ *www.montsaintsauveur.com.*

Sommet St-Sauveur

SKIING & SNOWBOARDING | The hills surrounding St-Sauveur might be relatively low, but this vibrant ski resort is long-established and perennially popular for good reason. It has an extensive skiable area, good snow-making and lift capacity, and many trails that are lit at night, making it possible for energetic Montrealers to drive up after work for a couple of hours of skiing. There are several other hills in the area, but Mont-St-Sauveur is the largest, with a 700-foot vertical drop and 142 acres of skiable terrain. Seventeen of its 38 trails are for beginners and intermediates, 16 are for experts, and five are rated extreme. Mont-Avila has 13 trails (two beginner, three intermediate, five difficult, three extremely difficult), a snow park, a fun tubing park, and the Viking, a toboggan-style ride in a cart that twists and turns on a track through the forest. ⊠ *350 av. St-Denis, St-Sauveur-des-Monts* ☎ *450/227–4671* ⊕ *www.sommets.com.*

Station de Ski Mont-Habitant

SKIING & SNOWBOARDING | More than 60 years in operation, Mont-Habitant is one of the last of the independent ski operations in St-Sauveur. This mountain has always been a favorite with families and with beginner and intermediate skiers because the vertical drop is just 600 feet and the 10 trails are relatively gentle. Mont-Habitant also has St-Sauveur's only beach, which makes it very popular in summer. ⊠ *12 chemin des Skieurs, St-Sauveur-des-Monts* ☎ *450/227–2637, 866/887–2637* ⊕ *www.monthabitant.com* 🍽 *Day pass C$50.*

Morin Heights

10 km (6 miles) west of St-Sauveur-des-Monts, 73 km (45 miles) northwest of Montréal.

If St-Sauveur is too busy and overdeveloped for your liking, Morin Heights is a great alternative, with plenty of restaurants, bookstores, boutiques, and craft shops to explore free from the crowds. The town's British architecture and population reflect its settlers' heritage; most residents here speak English.

In summer, windsurfing, swimming, and canoeing on the area's two lakes—Claude and Lafontaine—are popular. In fall and winter, come for the foliage and the Alpine and Nordic skiing.

GETTING HERE AND AROUND
From Montréal to Morin Heights, take Autoroute 15 North, then take Exit 60.

 Hotels

Morin Heights is true cottage country, and thus options for accommodation are slim. Your best bet might be to rent a cottage, or as they're known by French-speaking locals, a chalet. The Montréal pages are full of posts advertising private chalet rentals in the Laurentians. If you'd prefer to go through a third party, most area real estate agents broker short- and long-term cottage and chalet rentals as well; try Remax Laurentides (☎ *450/227–8411*).

Hotel Alila

$ | B&B/INN | This auberge by the main road is one of the best-equipped spa destinations in the area, and its outdoor terrace is a pleasant place to relax. **Pros:** some rooms have beautiful views of the Rivière du Nord; whirlpool baths and fireplaces in some units; garden has cold-water pools. **Cons:** isolated from village; close to highway; breakfast not included. ⑤ *Rooms from: C$100* ⊠ *500 Rte. 364, Morin Heights* ☎ *450/644–0168* ⊕ *www.alila.ca/Lodging.html* 🛏 *29 rooms* ⓘⓞⓘ *No Meals.*

 Shopping

CRAFTS

Créations d'Aujourd'hui

CRAFTS | Specializing in decorative accessories, unique jewelry, candles, soaps, and natural perfumes, most created by local artists and artisans, many of the items on sale here have been transformed and repurposed by the shop's owner to give them a distinctive second life. ⊠ *910 chemin du Village, Morin Heights* ☎ *450/644–0089* ⊕ *creationsdaujourdhui.weebly.com.*

Activities

SKIING

Ski Morin Heights

SKIING & SNOWBOARDING | FAMILY | This small, family-oriented ski center with 32 trails (for all levels) offers a warm and friendly place to enjoy winter sports. Downhill and cross-country skiing, snowboarding, and snowshoeing are available and free day care is offered to skiers. ✉ *231 rue Bennett, Morin Heights* ☎ *450/227–2020* ⊕ *www.sommets.com/ en/ski-mountains/sommet-morin-heights* 🎿 *Ski day pass C$66.*

SPAS

Amerispa Spa Nordique

SPA | Only 45 minutes outside Montréal, this is a great place to escape and unwind. Hidden in a Laurentian forest of maples, firs, and birches is a beautifully rustic pavilion housing a spa with hot tubs and cold pools, eucalyptus-scented steam baths, and thermal and Nordic waterfalls. The Elixir Ice Cider Massage with companion body wrap is a must. ✉ *160 rue Watchorn, Morin Heights* ☎ *450/226–7722, 866/263–7477* ⊕ *www. amerispa.ca.*

Ste-Adèle

12 km (7 miles) north of Morin Heights, 85 km (53 miles) north of Montréal.

Although Ste-Adèle is not as pretty as St-Sauveur, this town has a lot to offer, with attractions and activities to please families, outdoors enthusiasts, and visitors who want to experience something of the local culture. With a permanent population of more than 10,000, it's the largest community in the lower part of the Laurentians, and has good boutiques, restaurants, summer theater (performed in French), and art galleries. Active types can find horseback riding, golf, and lengthy bike trails in summer and skiing in winter.

GETTING HERE AND AROUND

From Montréal to Ste-Adèle, take Autoroute 15 North and then take Exit 67.

VISITOR INFORMATION

CONTACT Tourist Welcome Bureau of Pays-d'en-Haut. ✉ *1014 rue Valiquette, Ste-Adèle* ☎ *450/229–6637* ⊕ *www. lespaysdenhaut.com.*

Sights

Au Pays des Merveilles

AMUSEMENT PARK/CARNIVAL | FAMILY | Fairy-tale characters such as Snow White, Little Red Riding Hood, and Alice in Wonderland wander the grounds, playing games with children. Small fry may also enjoy the petting zoo, amusement rides, wading pool, and puppet show. A ride called Le Petit Train des Merveilles (the Little Train of Wonders) is a nod to the historic train that launched the tourism industry in the Laurentians. There are 45 activities, enough to occupy those aged two to eight for about half a day. Check the website for discount coupons. The theme park is completely accessible to strollers and wheelchairs. ✉ *3795 chemin de la Savane, Ste-Adèle* ☎ *450/229–3141* ⊕ *www.paysmerveilles.com* 🎫 *C$27.*

🛏 Hotels

Auberge and Spa Beaux Rêves

$ | B&B/INN | With a year-round Nordic spa and outdoor hot tub, hammocks hung all around the property, and a waterfall, relaxation is the order of the day at this rustic riverside retreat. **Pros:** personalized packages tailored to meet specific needs; all rooms overlook the river and have balconies or walk-out terraces; all about "unplugging." **Cons:** can be noisy due to close proximity to the road; no phone or television in rooms; no pool. 🛏 *Rooms from: C$190* ✉ *2310 boul. Ste-Adèle, Ste-Adèle* ☎ *450/229–9226, 800/279–7679, 514/316–7808 from Montréal* ⊕ *www.beauxreves.com* 🛏 *9 rooms, 1 loft* ⑂ *Free Breakfast.*

Hôtel Mont-Gabriel

$ | **HOTEL** | **FAMILY** | At this 1,200-acre resort you can relax in a contemporary room with a valley view or commune with nature in a rustic-style cabin with a fireplace, and there are activities aplenty. **Pros:** beautiful grounds; ski out from many rooms; reasonable packages on offer. **Cons:** rooms are on the small side; can be noisy; some complaints of poor service. ⑤ *Rooms from: C$139* ✉ *1699 chemin du Mont-Gabriel, Ste-Adèle* ☎ *450/229–3547, 800/668–5253* ⊕ *www. montgabriel.com* ⇆ *132 rooms* ⦿ *No Meals.*

 Activities

GOLF

Club de Golf Chantecler

GOLF | Every hole here will provide panoramic views of the surrounding Laurentian scenery. Opened in 1950, this semiprivate club offers a mountainside course with long and narrow fairways and three sets of tees for different skill levels. Just one hour from Montréal, it's easy and convenient for a day-trip. ✉ *2520 chemin du Club, Ste-Adèle* ☎ *450/476–1339, 450/229–3742* ⊕ *www. golflechantecler.com* ✍ *C$30–C$50* ⅄. *18 holes, 6120 yards, par 72.*

SKIING

Ski Mont-Gabriel

SKIING & SNOWBOARDING | Part of Les Sommets chain of ski resorts, Mont-Gabriel has five lifts, 18 superb downhill trails, which are primarily for intermediate and advanced skiers, and a vertical drop of 656 feet. It's about 19 km (12 miles) northeast of Ste-Adèle. ✉ *1501 chemin du Mont-Gabriel, Ste-Adèle* ⊕ *www. sommets.com/en/ski-mountains/som-met-gabriel* ✍ *Ski day pass C$50.*

Val-David

33 km (20 miles) west of Ste-Adèle, 82 km (51 miles) north of Montréal.

Val-David is a major destination for mountain climbers, hikers, and campers. It's also a place that many Québec artists and artisans call home, a fact suggested by the several galleries and marvelous art shops in town.

GETTING HERE AND AROUND

The village is just a couple of kilometers east of Exit N6 on Autoroute 15, making it easy to get to by car, but it's also accessible by bicycle: Le P'tit Train du Nord cycling trail runs right through town.

VISITOR INFORMATION

CONTACT Tourist Bureau of Val-David. ✉ *2525 rue de l'Église, Val-David* ☎ *888/322–7030, 819/324–5678* ⊕ *www. valdavid.com.*

⊙ Sights

Village du Père Noël (*Santa Claus Village*)
OTHER ATTRACTION | **FAMILY** | Santa is not just for Christmas here. In his summer residence kids can sit on his knee and speak to him in French or English, then have fun in the grounds, which contain bumper boats; a petting zoo with goats, sheep, horses, and colorful birds; games; and a large outdoor pool in the summer. There is a snack bar, but visitors are encouraged to bring their own food (there are numerous picnic tables). During the cold winter months, the park transforms into a winter wonderland with skating rinks and tubing fun for the kids. ✉ *987 rue Morin, Val-David* ☎ *819/322–2146, 800/287–6635* ⊕ *www.noel.qc.ca* ✍ *C$26.96.*

Restaurants

★ Au Petit Poucet

$$ | CANADIAN | FAMILY | For a true Québécois treat, stop by this rustic cabin for breakfast or lunch. Founded in 1945, it's a big draw with tourists and locals alike. **Known for:** generous portions; good variety of breakfast options; fresh-baked country bread. ⑤ *Average main: C$20* ✉ *1030 Rte. 117, Val-David* ☎ *819/322–2246, 888/334–2246* ⊕ *www.aupetitpoucet.com* ☾ *No dinner.*

🛏 Hotels

★ La Maison de Bavière

$ | B&B/INN | Walking into this charming bed-and-breakfast is like being transported to a cozy Bavarian mountain inn. **Pros:** directly across from the P'tit Train du Nord cycling and cross-country ski trail; two-minute walk to the village of Val-David; lovely backyard facing the rushing Rivière du Nord. **Cons:** only six rooms; common area is small and right off the bedrooms, so guests need to keep voices down; the bedroom of the efficiency/studio apartment is only accessible by a short ladder. ⑤ *Rooms from: C$190* ✉ *1470 chemin de la Rivière, Val-David* ☎ *819/322–3528, 866/322–3528* ⊕ *www.maisondebaviere.com* 🔖 *6 rooms* 🍽 *Free Breakfast.*

🎭 Performing Arts

★ Le Centre d'Exposition de Val-David

PERFORMANCE VENUES | Showcasing the work of regional and international artists, the nonprofit Le Centre d'Exposition de Val-David is the largest art gallery and exhibition hall in the area. Admission is free. ✉ *2495 rue de l'Eglise, Val-David* ☎ *819/322–7474* ⊕ *centreexpositionvaldavid.com.*

🛍 Shopping

CERAMICS

1001 Pots

CERAMICS | One of the most interesting events in Val-David is this ceramic exhibition, held from July through mid-August, which started in 1988. On view is the Japanese-style pottery of 1001 Pots' founder Kinya Ishikawa—as well as pieces by up to 100 other ceramists. Ishikawa's studio also displays work by his wife, Marie-Andrée Benoît, who makes fish-shaped bowls with a texture derived from pressing canvas on the clay. There are workshops for adults and children throughout the exhibition, and there is always at least one artisan on-site. While you're there, take the time to enjoy tea in one of the three beautiful gardens and learn the art of the Japanese tea ceremony. ✉ *2435 rue de l'Église, Val-David* ☎ *819/322–6868* ⊕ *www.1001pots.com* ☞ *C$4 admission.*

HOUSEHOLD

Atelier Bernard Chaudron

HOUSEWARES | If you're looking for an interesting conversation piece to bring back home with you, check out master craftsman Bernard Chaudron's hand-forged, lead-free pewter household objects that include oil lamps, hammered-silver beer mugs, pitchers, candleholders, and animal-themed knife rests. ✉ *2347 rue de l'Église, Val-David* ☎ *819/322–3944, 888/322–3944* ⊕ *www.chaudron.ca.*

Activities

SKIING

Centre de Ski Vallée-Bleue

SKIING & SNOWBOARDING | Family run and family focused, this ski hill suits everyone, from beginners to advanced-level skiers and snowboarders, with 19 trails, three lifts, and a vertical drop of 365 feet. ✉ *1418 chemin Vallée-Bleue, Val-David* ☎ *819/322–3427, 866/322–3427* ⊕ *www.valleebleue.com* 🎿 *Ski pass from C$32.*

Ste-Agathe-des-Monts

5 km (3 miles) north of Val-David, 96 km (60 miles) northwest of Montréal.

The wide, sandy beaches of Lac des Sables are the most surprising feature of Ste-Agathe-des-Monts, a tourist town best known for its ski hills. Water activities include canoeing, kayaking, swimming, and fishing. Ste-Agathe is also a stopover point on the Linear Park, the bike trail between St-Jérôme and Mont-Laurier.

GETTING HERE AND AROUND
From Montréal to Ste-Agathe-des-Monts, take Autoroute 15 North. Take Exit 89 to reach QC–329 South, and then take QC–117.

VISITOR INFORMATION
CONTACT Tourist Bureau of Ste-Agathe-des-Monts. ⊠ *24 rue St-Paul Est, Ste-Agathe-des-Monts* ☎ *819/326–3731, 888/326–0457* ⊕ *ville.sainte-agathe-des-monts.qc.ca/visiteurs/bureau-daccueil-touristique.*

 Beaches

Major Beach
SWIMMING | FAMILY | The biggest, most popular municipal beach in Ste-Agathe. **Amenities:** lifeguards; parking (no fee); showers; water sports. **Best for:** swimming. ⊠ *1 chemin du Lac-des-Sables, Ste-Agathe-des-Monts* ☎ *819/326–3731, 888/326–0457* ⊕ *ville.sainte-agathe-des-monts.qc.ca/citoyens/batiments-parcs-municipaux/plages-municipales* ⊠ *Full day C$15.*

 Hotels

Hôtel Spa Watel
$ | HOTEL | If you're looking for a room with a double-size Jacuzzi, a fireplace, and a balcony with a superb view of Lac des Sables, try this white-painted, lodge-style hotel, which is also convenient

Camping

In the woods near a lively resort area, Camping Ste-Agathe-des-Monts has activities for all age groups, from sport competitions to outings for the kids. There's a sandy beach where you can rent canoes and kayaks and launch your boat from the town's marina. Reservations for this campground (open mid-May through September) are recommended. ⊠ *2 chemin du Lac-des-Sables, Ste-Agathe-des-Monts* ☎ *819/324–0482, 800/561–7360* ⊕ *www.campingsteagathe.com.*

for the boutiques and cultural activities in Ste-Agathe. **Pros:** adjacent to three beaches; indoor and outdoor pools and Jacuzzis; year-round outdoor spas. **Cons:** not all rooms have a Jacuzzi, fireplace, and lake view; some lake-view rooms are off an enclosed glass balcony, motel style, so they don't receive direct air from outside; the facilities could stand to benefit from a little updating. ⑤ *Rooms from: C$170* ⊠ *250 rue St-Venant, Ste-Agathe-des-Monts* ☎ *819/326–7016, 800/363–6478* ⊕ *www.hotelspawatel.com* ⌁ *31 rooms* ⑩ *Free Breakfast.*

Mont-Tremblant

25 km (16 miles) north of Ste-Agathe-des-Monts, 100 km (62 miles) north of Montréal.

At more than 3,000 feet, Mont-Tremblant is one of the highest peaks in the Laurentians and a major draw for skiers. The resort area at the foot of the mountain (called simply Tremblant) is spread around 14-km-long (9-mile-long) Lac Tremblant and is consistently—and justifiably—ranked among the top ski resorts in eastern North America.

Renting a Ski Chalet in Mont-Tremblant

If you think you'd like to spend more than a few days in the Laurentians you might want to consider renting a chalet from a private owner. There are generally plenty to choose from, and not only is a private rental often less expensive than staying at a hotel, but it's a lot homier as well, especially if you are traveling with children. And even with the many restaurants in Mont-Tremblant, every once in a while it's nice to buy groceries and come home to cook your own dinner.

Options range from cozy little cottages for four to multi-bedroom properties where you could have a real house party with family and friends. If you

fill a place to capacity, the cost can be very competitive, particularly if you don't mind being outside the main hub of the resort or out of the peak season. Some places offer weekend rates as well as renting by the week. Very good sources for chalet rentals in this part of the province are websites, and the Montréal pages are full of posts advertising private chalet rentals in the Laurentians. If you'd prefer to go through a third party, most area real estate agents broker short- and long-term cottage and chalet rentals as well. Try Remax Laurentides at 286 Principal in St-Sauveur (☎ 450/227–8411) for starters.

The hub of the resort is a pedestrians-only village that gives an architectural nod to the style of New France, with dormer windows and colorful steep roofs on buildings that house pubs, restaurants, boutiques, sports shops, a movie theater, self-catering condominiums, and hotels. A historical town this is not: built for the resort, it may strike you as a bit of Disney in the mountains.

GETTING HERE AND AROUND

The easiest way to get here is by car. Drive north on Autoroute 15 until it ends just beyond Ste-Agathe-des-Monts and then continue on Route 117 (a four-lane highway) for another 30 km (18 miles) to the Mont-Tremblant exit (Exit 119). The resort's parking lots are vast, but they fill up quickly. A shuttle bus links them to the main resort and ski area. Mont-Tremblant has two tourist offices, one in the village and one in the downtown area.

VISITOR INFORMATION

CONTACT Tourisme Mont-Tremblant.
✉ 5080 montée Ryan, Mont-Tremblant ☎ 877/425–2434, 819/425–2434 ⊕ www.mont-tremblant.ca.

Sights

La Diable Vistors' Centre

VISITOR CENTER | The park entrance closest to Mont-Tremblant is at La Diable Vistors' Centre, just beyond the village of Lac Supérieur and about a half-hour drive from the resort. ✉ 3824 chemin du Lac Supérieur, Lac Supérieur ☎ 819/688–2281 visitor center, 800/665–6527 Sépaq (government national park agency) ⊕ www.sepaq.com/pq/mot.

★ Parc National du Mont-Tremblant

NATIONAL PARK | **FAMILY** | This vast wildlife sanctuary has more than 400 lakes and rivers and is home to nearly 200 species of birds and animals, so it's great for wildlife-watching. Cross-country skiers, snowshoers, and snowmobilers enjoy the park's trails in winter, and camping, fishing, canoeing, and hiking are the popular summer activities. The park was once the home of the Algonquins, who called this area Manitonga Soutana, meaning "mountain of the spirits." ✉ Mont-Tremblant ☎ 800/665–6527 ⊕ www.sepaq.com ⊡ C$9.25 per day.

Did You Know?

With summer activities like festivals, hiking, biking, zip-lining, and a luge trail, Mont-Tremblant's Alpine pedestrian village is well worth a visit outside ski-season.

Hotels

★ Fairmont Tremblant

$$$ | HOTEL | FAMILY | The centerpiece of the Tremblant resort area takes its cues from the grand 19th-century railroad "castle hotels" scattered throughout Canada. **Pros:** poolside barbecue during the summer; dogs (under 50 pounds) allowed; easy access to ski hills and the village. **Cons:** it's in the fairly busy village rather than more scenic grounds; valet parking C$42 plus tax; public parking is a 10-minute walk away (and fees may apply). ⑤ *Rooms from: C$350* ✉ *3045 chemin de la Chapelle, Mont-Tremblant* ☎ *819/681–7000, 800/257–7544* ⊕ *www.fairmont.com/tremblant* ⟿ *314 rooms* ⏍ *Free Breakfast.*

Le Grand Lodge

$ | HOTEL | FAMILY | At this Scandinavian-style log-cabin hotel, on 13½ acres on the shore of Lac Ouimet, you'll find great year-round amenities and activities for families and sports lovers and a resort-style feel that survives its busy conference trade schedule. **Pros:** peaceful environment amid woods and walking trails; ice rink and ice path in winter; private beach. **Cons:** rooms and suites not very stylish; narrow swimming pool; fireplaces are gas, not wood-burning. ⑤ *Rooms from: C$170* ✉ *2396 rue Labelle, Mont-Tremblant* ☎ *819/425–2734, 800/567–6763* ⊕ *www.legrandlodge.com* ⟿ *112 rooms* ⏍ *Free Breakfast.*

Quintessence

$$$$ | HOTEL | There are spectacular views of Lac Tremblant from every room of this quiet, chic, boutique hotel near the ski slopes. **Pros:** massages in your suite; concierge can provide firewood; lovely garden. **Cons:** very expensive; furnishings could be of better quality; offer of babysitting service for guests, but not all sitters are satisfactory. ⑤ *Rooms from: C$460* ✉ *3004 chemin de la Chapelle, Mont-Tremblant* ☎ *819/425–3400, 866/425–3400* ⊕ *www.hotelquintessence.com* ⟿ *31 suites* ⏍ *Free Breakfast.*

 ## Performing Arts

Festi Jazz

FESTIVALS | Tons of fun and completely free, the very popular five-day jazz festival in early August draws in at least 15,000 tourists and locals to Mont-Tremblant. The concerts take place under the stars on two outdoor stages and in at least 10 restaurants, bars, and hotels in the village or St-Jovite (downtown area). ✉ *Mont-Tremblant* ⊕ *www.jazzmttremblant.com.*

Festival International du Blues de Tremblant

(*Tremblant International Blues Festival*) **CONCERTS |** People don't just flock to Mont-Tremblant for outdoor fun. This place is becoming a music lovers' paradise, especially for 10 days in July when the Blues Festival takes place with more than 130 shows. Artists such as Otis Taylor, JJ Grey & Mofro, and Thornetta Davis entertain fans on outdoor stages and in intimate clubs right in the village. ✉ *Mont-Tremblant* ☎ *819/681–3000 #46643* ⊕ *blues.tremblant.ca/en.*

 ## Activities

GOLF

Mont-Tremblant

GOLF | The same company that operates the ski resort also runs two of the most challenging and popular championship golf courses in Québec. Le Géant (the Giant) was designed by Thomas McBroom to take full advantage of the fantastic scenery. Le Diable (the Devil), with long narrow fairways and strategically placed red sand bunkers, was designed by Michael Hurdzan and Dana Fry. Also at Le Diable, you can find the reputable Tremblant Golf Academy. ✉ *Mont-Tremblant* ☎ *866/356–2233, 866/783–5634* ⊕ *www.tremblant.ca* 🏌 *C$139* 🏌. *Le Diable, 18 holes, 7056* yards, par 71; Le Géant, 18 holes, 6836 yards, par 72.

SKIING

Mont-Tremblant

SKIING & SNOWBOARDING | With a 2,116-foot vertical drop, 654 acres of skiable terrain, 95 trails, 18 acres of ramps and jumps for snowboarders, and enough state-of-the-art snowmaking equipment to blanket a small city, Mont-Tremblant is truly one of the great ski resorts of North America, arguably the best east of the Rockies. Its 14 lifts—including two heated gondolas and five high-speed, four-passenger chairlifts—can handle 27,230 skiers an hour. It has some of the toughest expert runs on the continent, but it also has long, gentle runs like the 6-km (3.7-mile) Nansen and dozens of exciting trails for intermediate skiers. Its altitude and location, as well as all that snowmaking equipment, gives it some of eastern Canada's most reliable ski conditions, especially now that winters are getting warmer. All this doesn't come cheap, mind you. A day lift ticket costs C$119 on weekends, but for serious skiers there is no better mountain in Québec. ⊠ 1000 chemin des Voyageurs, Mont-Tremblant ☎ 866/356–2233, 819/681–3000 ⊕ www.tremblant.ca ☜ One-day lift ticket C$128.

Montebello

130 km (80 miles) west of Montréal.

Located on the banks of the Ottawa River, this little village is best known for the Fairmont Le Château Montebello, a spectacular hotel touted as the largest log cabin in the world. Given the town's relative proximity to Ottawa, the nation's capital, more than a few world leaders and dignitaries have visited Montebello for one of the many international summits hosted by the Château since it was built in 1930. The Outaouais in general is well-known for the rugged beauty of

its wilderness, and even in this more populated southern section of the region there's still excellent fishing, hunting, canoeing, hiking, and wildlife-spotting, with a series of hiking paths starting right beside the Château Montebello. Even if an expedition into the bush isn't quite your thing, you can still get up close to the local wildlife in a more controlled environment at Parc Omega, home to a wide variety of indigenous species and domestic animals.

GETTING HERE AND AROUND

From Montréal, take Autoroute 50 West for 130 km (80 miles); it's about a 90-minute trip.

VISITOR INFORMATION

CONTACT Montebello Tourist Information Office. ⊠ Gare de Montebello, 502-A rue Notre-Dame, Montebello ☎ 819/423–5602 ⊕ www.tourismeoutaouais.com.

Sights

Parc Omega

NATURE PRESERVE | **FAMILY** | In the 1,800 acres of hills, valleys, rivers, and streams that make up the park, visitors drive along designated trails to view wild animals roaming free in their beautiful natural environment. These include bear, Alpine ibexes, buffalo, wolves, elk, and more. There are also walking trails among nonaggressive species like white-tailed deer, with caged golf-cart rental available in summer to save the legwork. Also in summer, you can visit farm animals in the restored 19th-century Léopold's Farm and see a birds of prey show. ⊠ 399 Rte. 323 N, Montebello ☎ 819/423–5487 ⊕ www.parcomega.ca ☜ C$41.

Restaurants

Le Napoleon

$$$$ | **ITALIAN** | In what is basically a one-street town, this restaurant's reputation for serving outstanding food at affordable prices stands out, and the

knowledgeable, personable waitstaff does, too. Though the cuisine is primarily Italian, some Mediterranean, French, and Québécois influences are also in evidence, backed up by a fairly extensive and reasonably priced wine list. **Known for:** great wine list; good food at reasonable prices; beautiful quiet area. ⑤ *Average main: C$32* ⊠ *489 rue Notre-Dame, Montebello* ☎ *819/423–5555* ⊟ *No credit cards* ⊘ *No lunch.*

Hotels

★ Fairmont Le Château Montebello
$$$ | **HOTEL** | **FAMILY** | On a bank of the Ottawa River, with its own marina, this grand log-built hotel provides rustic luxury, local flavor, beautiful grounds, great views, and heaps of activities—no wonder it's an annual family destination for many well-heeled Canadians. **Pros:** great place to bring children; state-of-the-art conference facility; beautiful pool and spa. **Cons:** no nearby restaurants of note; pricey, and a C$35 per-room, per-night resort fee is added to your bill at checkout; carpeting in some rooms looks a bit worn as does some of the furniture in the lounge. ⑤ *Rooms from: C$360* ⊠ *392 rue Notre-Dame, Montebello* ☎ *819/423–6341, 866/540–4462* ⊕ *www.fairmont.com/montebello* ↝ *211 rooms* ⦿❘ *No Meals.*

Gatineau

205 km (127 miles) west of Montréal.

This town on the northern edge of the Ottawa River is best known for the nearby Gatineau Park and the many outdoor activities that can be done here. For more history, visit the Canadian Museum of History, which emphasizes the changes the country has undergone, from the prehistoric past to the present day. From Gatineau, it's a short walk over the Alexandra Bridge to visit Ottawa, the

nation's capital. The view from either side of the river is stunning.

GETTING HERE AND AROUND
From Montréal, take Autoroute 50 West for 205 km (127 miles); it's about a two-hour trip.

VISITOR INFORMATION
CONTACT Gatineau Tourist Information Office. ⊠ *103 rue Laurier, Gatineau* ☎ *819/778–2222, 800/265–7822* ⊕ *www.tourismeoutaouais.com.*

Sights

Canadian Museum of History
HISTORY MUSEUM | **FAMILY** | Formerly known as the Canadian Museum of Civilization, this superb institution officially changed its name in 2013 when it received C$25 million in funding from the Canadian government in order to renovate and expand. More than 50,000 square feet of the existing museum has been renovated, and a Canadian History Hall showcasing the people and events that have shaped Canada over the last 15,000 years. Other highlights include the First Peoples Hall, which has some 2,000 objects on display, and the Children's Museum. ⊠ *100 rue Laurier, Gatineau* ☎ *819/776–7000, 800/555–5621* ⊕ *www.historymuseum.ca* ⊠ *C$22.*

Gatineau Park
NATIONAL PARK | **FAMILY** | This massive park—nearly 364 square km (140 square miles)—brings nature lovers from all over throughout the year. You can hike up King Mountain on a challenging trail that takes you 300 meters (980 feet) above the Ottawa Valley, explore Lusk Cave, go camping, view the Luskville Falls, or swim at one of the six beaches here (there are also 50 lakes). In winter, the cross-country skiing trails cover approximately 200 km (125 miles) of the park. From June to mid-October, you can use the park's south entrance on Taché Boulevard; stop at the reception center for visitor information. ⊠ *Gatineau*

☎ *819/827–2020* ⊕ *www.ncc-ccn.gc.ca/ places/gatineau-park* ✉ *Admission free, parking C$13.50.*

 Hotels

Moulin Wakefield Mill Hotel and Spa
$$ | HOTEL | Part heritage mill with original features, part modern environmentally friendly building, this waterside hotel and spa on the edge of Gatineau Park has lots of character, wonderful views of the MacLaren Falls, and plenty of pampering on offer. **Pros:** walking distance to Gatineau Park; great views; pets allowed. **Cons:** hotel caters mostly to adults; expensive; hardwood floors in rooms in the main building are in need of refinishing. ⑤ *Rooms from: C$240* ✉ *60 chemin Mill, Gatineau* ☎ *888/567–1838, 819/459–1838* ⊕ *www.wakefieldmill.com* ⇱ *42 rooms* ❒ *Free Breakfast.*

Bromont

78 km (48 miles) east of Montréal.

The boating, camping, golf, horse-back riding, swimming, tennis, biking, canoeing, fishing, hiking, cross-country and downhill skiing, and snowshoeing available here make this a place for all seasons. Bromont has the only night skiing in the Eastern Townships—and there's even a slope-side disco, Le Bromontais. The town also has more than 100 km (62 miles) of maintained trails for mountain bikers.

GETTING HERE AND AROUND
Bromont is about one hour from Montréal on Autoroute 10. Get off at Exit 78.

VISITOR INFORMATION
CONTACT Bromont Tourism Office. ✉ *15 boul. de Bromont, Bromont* ☎ *877/276–6668, 450/534–2006* ⊕ *www.tourisme-bromont.com.*

 Sights

★ **Route des Vins** (*Wine Route*)
WINERY | Make sure you bring along a designated driver for this Wine Route, which includes 22 wineries. Map out your chosen stops, and then travel from one to the next to learn about their history and local products and, best of all, sample the wine. Most wineries have an area outdoors where you can enjoy a picnic. ■ TIP→ **Call for hours as they may change from one season to the next.** ✉ *Bromont* ☎ *888/811–4928* ⊕ *www. laroutedesvins.ca/en.*

Vignoble de l'Orpailleur
WINERY | Established in 1982, this vineyard produces 14 wines, including its Double Gold medal–winning ice wine at the Finger Lakes International competition. Guided tours (in French) cost C$15 and are given twice a day during the summer. You can also stop by the boutique for tastings and visit their museum, where you'll learn about the history and production of wine, from the cultivation of the vines to the bottling process. Guided tours given in English need to be reserved well in advance (minimum 12 people). The patio restaurant is a nice place to take a break and open from 11 to 4 every day from mid-June until mid-October. ✉ *1086 rue Bruce (Rte. 202), Dunham* ☎ *450/295–2763* ⊕ *www.orpailleur.ca.*

Vignoble Domaine Côtes d'Ardoise
WINERY | This winery, opened in 1980, was one of the first to set up shop in the area, and is considered to be the oldest vineyard still in operation in Québec. On nearly 30 acres of land, 50,000 vines go to produce some award-winning reds, whites, rosés, and ice wines. Visit for a tasting and enjoy a picnic on the grounds. From July through October, a sculpture garden showcases the works of more than 80 artists, primarily from the area. ✉ *879 rue Bruce (Rte. 202), Dunham* ☎ *450/295–2020* ⊕ *www.cotesd-ardoise.com.*

Did You Know?

Warm summer days and cool nights make this region ideal for producing wine; travelers can visit several vineyards along the Route des Vins in and around the town of Dunham.

Vignoble Les Trois Clochers

WINERY | This lovely winery is another great stop along the wine route. It produces a dry, fruity white from Seyval grapes as well as several other white, red, and ice wines. In addition to the tastings, you can take a tour of the grounds (reservations required), stroll along the trails, and stop for a picnic before you move on to the next stop. ⊠ *341 chemin Bruce (Rte. 202), Dunham* ☎ *450/295–2034* ⊕ *www.3clochers.com.*

Hotels

Hôtel Château Bromont

$ | HOTEL | Massages, algae wraps, and aromatherapy are just a few of the services at this European-style resort, which also includes a large, Turkish-style hammam (steam room) and the Château Bromont Golf Course. **Pros:** outdoor hot tubs; Turkish-style hammam; scenic mountain views. **Cons:** some rooms are small; windows facing the interior courtyard/indoor swimming pool do not open; some rooms are dated. ⑤ *Rooms from: C$124* ⊠ *90 rue Stanstead, Bromont* ☎ *450/534–3433, 888/276–6668* ⊕ *www.chateaubromont.com* ⌁ *166 rooms* ⑪ *Free Breakfast.*

⬤ Shopping

MARKETS

★ Bromont Five-Star Flea Market

MARKET | The gigantic sign on Autoroute 10 is hard to miss. Take Exit 78 to explore more than 1,000 vendors at this indoor flea market selling T-shirts, household gadgets, and much, much more. Shoppers come from as far away as Vermont. ⊠ *16 rue Lafontaine, Bromont* ☎ *450/534–0440* ⊕ *www.mapbromont. com* ⊙ *Closed weekdays and Nov.–Mar.*

Activities

GOLF
Royal Bromont

GOLF | Designed by Graham Cooke, one of the most reputable golf course architects, the Royal Bromont was built in 1992 and is located in the center of Bromont. All 18 holes provide wonderful views of the surrounding mountains and, from novice to expert, this golf course is considered to be one of the top places to play. In 1994, the Royal Bromont hosted the Canadian PGA Championships. ⊠ *400 chemin Compton, Bromont* ☎ *450/534–4653, 888/281–0017* ⊕ *www.royalbromont.com* ⌁ *C$45–C$68* ⚐ *18 holes, 7036 yards, par 72.*

SHOW JUMPING
Parc Équestre Olympique Bromont

SPORTS VENUE | If you love horses and competitions, the Bromont Equestrian Center is the place to visit. Once an Olympic site, it hosts show jumping, dressage, and pony club events, and, in late July, the annual International Bromont Equestrian competition. ⊠ *450 chemin de Gaspé, Bromont* ☎ *450/534-0787.*

SKIING
★ Station de Ski Bromont

SKIING & SNOWBOARDING | FAMILY | Not many metropolises in eastern North America can boast a 1,300-foot ski mountain within an hour's drive of their downtown. That height and proximity has made Bromont very popular with Montréal day-trippers and weekenders. But Bromont's 156 trails (102 of them lighted at night) and nine lifts can handle the crowds quite comfortably. Like many other ski hills, Bromont operates as a year-round resort. In summer and early fall, you can take a mountain bike to the summit aboard a chairlift and test your nerves on one of 19 downhill trails, two of which are labeled "easy"—the rest are "hard" to "extreme." Part of the ski hill is converted into the Bromont Aquatic Park in summer, with a 24,000-square-foot wave pool and 25 rides and slides. ⊠ *150 rue Champlain, Bromont* ☎ *450/534–2200, 866/276–6668* ⊕ *www.skibromont.com* ✉ *Skiing C$42–C$95, aquatic park C$41, mountain biking C$48.*

SPAS

Balnea Réserve Thermale

SPA | Tucked away in a forest and overlooking a lake, this strikingly contemporary spa takes advantage of its location with air beds that float among lily pads, and tiers of sun decks with gorgeous views. In addition to steam rooms, saunas, and baths, Balnea also has 30 body treatments: you can bliss out with the misra herbs and green-tea wrap, a chocolate and grape-seed massage, or yoga by the lake. Full- and half-day spa packages are available. During the summer, Balnea plays host to Summer of Chefs, a gourmet cooking competition that takes places over 10 Sundays and features 10 of Québec's best chefs, who take over the kitchen and create their own menu inspired by ingredients available at the nature reserve. ⊠ *319 chemin du Lac Gale, Bromont* ☎ *866/734–2110, 450/534–0604* ⊕ *www.balnea.ca.*

Knowlton (Lac Brome)

49 km (29 miles) northeast of Bromont, 101 km (63 miles) southeast of Montréal.

Knowlton is the quintessential Eastern Townships resort town, with Loyalist-era buildings, old inns, great antiques shops, and enticing pastry shops. Fortunately, it's managed to retain its particular identity, with a main street full of stores selling antiques, art, clothes, and gifts. Interesting little restaurants have taken residence in renovated clapboard houses painted every color of the rainbow. A frequent feature on most menus here is Brome Lake duck, served in many different ways. These internationally renowned birds are raised at a farm on the shores

of Brome Lake just a few miles outside town. The main regional tourist office is in Foster, one of the other old villages that constitute Lac Brome, but walking maps of Knowlton are available from many local businesses.

GETTING HERE AND AROUND

To get from Montréal to Knowlton, take Autoroute 10 East, head toward Autoroute 15 South, and take Exit 90 for QC–243.

VISITOR INFORMATION

CONTACT Lac Brome Tourism Office. ⊠ *696 rue Lakeside, Lac Brome* ☎ *450/243–1221* ⊕ *www.tourismelacbrome.com.*

 Sights

★ Brome Country Historical Museum

HISTORY MUSEUM | **FAMILY** | Here's a wonderful opportunity to learn about the Loyalists who settled the area after fleeing the American Revolution. Several buildings, including the former county courthouse dating back to 1859, the old firehall (fire station), and a former school, house an eclectic collection that include 19th-century farm tools, Native Canadian arrowheads, and a military collection that includes uniforms and a World War I Fokker aircraft. The museum also maintains the Tibbits Hill Pioneer School, a stone schoolhouse built in 1834 to serve rural families—kids can find out what education was like in the mid-19th century. ⊠ *130 chemin Lakeside, Knowlton* ☎ *450/243–6782* ⊕ *museesbromemissisquoi.com/en/lac-brome-museum* ✉ *C$10* ⊗ *Closed Sun. and Mon.*

🍴 Restaurants

Knowlton Pub

$$ | **CANADIAN** | Serving traditional pub fare, the Knowlton Pub has been around since time immemorial and is one of the best-known establishments in the Eastern Townships. The service is friendly, but diners have been known to wait

The Eastern Townships

Thetford Mines

Lac Saint-François

Lac Mégantic

Notre-Dame-des-Bois

MAINE

NEW HAMPSHIRE

112

Arthabaska

Victoriaville

161

EASTERN TOWNSHIPS

Cookshire

253

30 mi

30 km

216

Sherbrooke

Lennoxville

North Hatley

Lac Massawippi

Ayer's Cliff

Coaticook

55

243

222

Parc du Mont-Orford

Eastman

Magog

55

247

Owl's Head Ski Area

Lac Memphrémagog

91

Drummondville

143

55

222

Valcourt

245

Abbaye St-Benoît-du-Lac

Mansonville

20

TO POINTE-DU-LAC

222

139

Lac Brome

243

Knowlton (Lac Brome)

Sutton

R. Saint-François

112

Bromont

Station de Ski Bromont

202

Dunham

Route des Vins

VERMONT

Lac Saint-Pierre

Granby

10

112

89

R. Richelieu

Chambly

15

Lac Champlain

Fleuve Saint-Laurent

20

MONTÉRÉGIE

10

CANADA U.S.A.

87

25

20

40

MONTRÉAL

20

40

NEW YORK

15

a little longer than they'd like for their food to be served, particularly on dinner theater nights. **Known for:** hearty burgers; unrushed service; local institution. ⑤ *Average main: C$20* ✉ *267 chemin Knowlton, Knowlton* ☎ *450/242–6862* ⊕ *pubknowlton.com* ⊗ *Closed Wed. and Thurs.*

Hotels

★ Auberge Knowlton

$ | **B&B/INN** | A local landmark since 1849, when it was first a stagecoach stop, and later a railway stop, this rustic inn is a special-occasion venue for locals and a delightful option for visitors who relish period style and good regional cuisine. **Pros:** within walking distance of Knowlton's main attractions; storage, repair kits, and so on for bicycles; atmospheric restaurant serving good food. **Cons:** on the main road through town, so not the most scenic location; no elevator; dark, natural light blocked due to veranda roof on second floor. ⑤ *Rooms from: C$160* ✉ *286 chemin Knowlton, Knowlton* ☎ *450/242–6886* ⊕ *www.aubergeknowlton.com* ⌐ *12 rooms* ⍥ *No Meals.*

Domaine Jolivent

$$ | **B&B/INN** | Somewhat hidden away, in the Bondville section of Lac Brome, and on 112 acres of sheer bucolic splendor, is Domaine Jolivent, one of the best kept secrets in the Eastern Townships. **Pros:** plenty of outdoor activities year-round; gorgeous common areas; excellent location. **Cons:** might be noisy from other rooms; no coffee machines in rooms; rooms can be small. ⑤ *Rooms from: C$170* ✉ *667 chemin Bondville, Lac Brome* ☎ *866/525–4272, 450/243–4272* ⊕ *jolivent.ca* ⌐ *12 rooms* ⍥ *No Meals.*

Performing Arts

Théâtre Lac Brome

THEATER | This local theater company stages high-quality productions in both English and French. Under the leadership of executive artistic director Ellen David, TLB is now open year-round and showcases work by local artists in its new lobby. It aims to offer as much and as varied entertainment as possible while reflecting national and regional talent and content. The 175-seat, air-conditioned theater is located behind the Townships' institution, the Knowlton Pub. ✉ *9 chemin Mont-Echo, Knowlton* ☎ *450/242–2270 tickets* ⊕ *www.theatrelacbrome.ca.*

Shopping

ANTIQUES

Camlen

ANTIQUES & COLLECTIBLES | Cameron and Helen Brown (get it? Cam + len) import gorgeous antiques from China and Eastern Europe, create reproductions using old wood, and sell antique Canadian pieces. Their passion for, and dedication to, the art of furniture making is reflected in the high standard of their merchandise. ✉ *110 chemin Lakeside, Knowlton* ☎ *450/243–5785* ⊕ *www.camlenfurniture.ca.*

CLOTHING

Rococo Designer Factory Outlet

CLOTHING | Owners Carla Hadlock and Anita Laurent—the latter a former model—know fashion and style, and have many contacts in the business, so their collection of clothing and accessories includes many items obtained straight from manufacturers. You'll love the prices, too, which are a fraction of what you'd pay in a large retail store. ✉ *293 chemin Knowlton, Knowlton* ☎ *450/243–6948.*

Abbaye St-Benoît-du-Lac

132 km (82 miles) southeast of Montréal.

At this impressive abbey, a bell juts above the trees like a fairy-tale castle. Combine its calm and peaceful surroundings with the chance to pick up some of the products sold here, including sparkling apple wine and some of the best cheese in Québec, and you have an expedition that makes for a very memorable experience.

GETTING HERE AND AROUND

To get to the abbey from Magog, take Route 112 and follow the signs for the side road (Rural Route 2, or rue des Pères) to the abbey.

◉ Sights

★ Abbaye St-Benoît-du-Lac

CHURCH | Built by the Benedictines in 1912 on a wooded peninsula on Lac Memphrémagog, the abbey is home to over 50 monks. They sell apples and sparkling apple wine from their orchards, as well as cheeses: Ermite (which means "hermit"), St-Benoît, and ricotta. Gregorian prayers are sung daily, and some masses are open to the public; call for the schedule. Dress modestly if you plan to attend vespers or other rituals, and avoid shorts. If you wish to experience a few days of retreat, there are guesthouses for both men and women. Reserve well in advance. Overnight visits cost C$65–C$70 per night, which includes three meals. Guided tours of the abbey cost C$14. ⊠ *1 rue Principale, St-Benoît-du-Lac* ☎ *819/843–4080, 819/843–2861 store* ⊕ *www.abbaye.ca* ◷ *Closed major holidays; no guided tours July 11, aka the Feast of Saint Benedict.*

Parc du Mont-Orford

19 km (12 miles) north of Abbaye St-Benoît-du-Lac, 115 km (72 miles) east of Montréal.

In addition to a multitude of year-round outdoor activities, such as hiking, camping, fishing, and snowmobiling, the provincial park here also serves as a nature reserve.

The annual music performances that make up the Festival Orford always draw crowds to the foot of Mont-Orford.

GETTING HERE AND AROUND

From Montréal, go east on Highway 10 (Autoroute des Cantons de l'Est), take Exit 115 onto QC–112 and go north onto QC–141 (chemin du Mont-Orford). Coming from the east, leave Highway 10 at Exit 118 and go north on QC–141.

◉ Sights

Parc du Mont-Orford

NATURE SIGHT | **FAMILY** | The amount of activities seems almost endless at this 58-square-km (22-square-mile) park. Summertime sees hikers, campers, beach lovers, and canoers enjoying the grounds, and in winter, showshoers and cross-country skiers take over. White-tailed deer and blue herons share the park with tourists. The scenery in the fall is spectacular, with vibrant orange, yellow, and red hues spreading across the landscape. ⊠ *3321 chemin du Parc, Orford* ☎ *819/843–9855, 800/665–6527* ⊕ *www.sepaq.com/pq/mor* *C$9.50.*

▥ Hotels

Estrimont Suites and Spa

$ | **HOTEL** | With a Nordic shower, Scandinavian baths, and relaxation yurt, plus nearby golf courses, riding stables, and ski hills, this attractive complex fits the bill for an active or relaxing break. **Pros:** very reasonably priced spa packages;

excellent place for conferences or business retreats; two outdoor hot tubs in scenic surroundings. **Cons:** only one suite is wheelchair accessible; rooms appear dated; children not allowed in spa, yet children were there and noisy. ⑤ *Rooms from: C$195 ⊠ 44 av. de l'Auberge (Rte. 141 N), Orford ☎ 800/567–7320, 819/843–1616 ⊕ www.estrimont.ca ⤳ 95 suites ⦙⦙ Free Breakfast.*

Performing Arts

Festival Orford

MUSIC FESTIVALS | Every summer, from the end of June to mid-August, a celebration of music and art brings classical music, jazz, and chamber orchestra concerts to Parc du Mont-Orford. It's organized by the Orford Arts Centre, which has been teaching students the art of classical music and performance since 1951. ⊠ *3165 chemin du Parc, Orford ☎ 819/843–3981 #232 tickets, 800/567–6155 #232 in Canada ⊕ www.orford.mu/en.*

Magog

11 km (6 miles) south of Parc du Mont-Orford, 118 km (74 miles) east of Montréal.

This bustling town is at the northern tip of Lac Memphrémagog, a large body of water that stretches into northern Vermont. Its sandy beaches are a draw, and it's also a good place for boating, bird-watching, sailboarding, horseback riding, dog sledding, in-line skating, golfing, bass fishing, and snowmobiling. You might even see Memphré, the lake's mythical sea dragon, on one of the many lake cruises—there have been more than 100 sightings since 1816.

In recent years this formerly depressed textile town has enjoyed something of an economic and cultural rebirth, partially due to the substantial number of artists who have chosen to relocate to this welcoming, and relatively inexpensive, region of the province. The streets downtown are lined with century-old houses that have been converted into boutiques, stores, and eateries.

GETTING HERE AND AROUND

From Montréal to Magog, take Autoroute 10 East, keep left toward Autoroute 15 South, and then take Exit 118 for QC–141.

VISITOR INFORMATION

CONTACT Memphrémagog Tourism Office. ⊠ *2911 chemin Milletta, Magog ☎ 819/843–2744, 800/267–2744 ⊕ www.tourisme-memphremagog.com.*

⊙ Sights

Le Cep d'Argent

WINERY | The Scieur brothers, Jean-Paul and François, are sixth-generation winemakers originally from France, who have created their own "Champagne universe" in Québec. Their Selection range of wines includes sparkling, white, and rosé. Red, fortified, flavored, and ice wines are also available. From mid-June to the end of October, they offer the Bubbles, Wines, and Champagne guided tour (but only in French due to the extensive vocabulary of the subject) as well as à la carte tastings of over 10 of their finest wines all for the price of a C$6 souvenir glass. Visitors may also tour the Traditional Method Interpretation Centre to learn about the history of the Scieur brothers or just wander the vineyard and experience a little bit of France in Québec. ⊠ *1257 chemin de la Rivière, Magog ☎ 819/864–4441, 877/864–4441 ⊕ www.cepdargent.com ⤳ Bubbles, Wine, and Champagne tour C$28 ⚠ Reservations are essential and should be made well in advance to guarantee a spot as space is limited.*

Hotels

Ripplecove Lakefront Hotel and Spa

$$$$ | B&B/INN | The accommodations, service, and food at the Ripplecove, 11 km (7 miles) south of Magog, are good enough reason to make the detour. **Pros:** beautiful lakeside setting; first-class dining; spectacular grounds. **Cons:** expensive and a little stuffy; absence of privacy due to thin walls; reports of rude hotel staff. $ *Rooms from: C$300* ⊠ *700 rue Ripplecove, Ayer's Cliff* ☎ *800/668–4296, 819/838–4296* ⊕ *www.ripplecove.com* 🛏 *37 rooms* ¶◯¶ *Free Breakfast.*

Spa Eastman

$$$$ | HOTEL | The oldest spa in Québec, once a simple health center, has evolved into a bucolic haven for anyone seeking rest and therapeutic treatments, including lifestyle and weight-management counseling. **Pros:** dinner included in room rate; stunning surroundings; wheelchair-accessible rooms. **Cons:** no phone or TV might prove too isolating for some; limited dining selection; very pricey. $ *Rooms from: C$525* ⊠ *895 chemin des Diligences, Eastman* ☎ *450/297–3009, 800/665–5272* ⊕ *www.spa-eastman.com* 🛏 *44 rooms* ¶◯¶ *All-Inclusive.*

Nightlife

Auberge des Cantons

BARS | Come by boat and you can moor right alongside this patio bar that overlooks the Magog River. Sometimes there's live entertainment, but when musicians aren't around, the flocks of ducks lining up alongside the café to beg crumbs from patrons' plates keep patrons entertained. ⊠ *20 rue Merry Sud, Magog* ☎ *819/843–9361* ⊕ *www.aubergedescantons.com.*

Café St-Michel

PUB | In a century-old building, this pub, outfitted in shades of charcoal and ebony, serves Tex-Mex food, pasta, fish-and-chips, and local beers. Its patio bar, at Magog's main intersection, may not be peaceful, but it's a great spot to watch the world go by. Chansonniers (singers) belt out popular hits for a full house on Friday and Saturday evening starting at 6. ⊠ *503 rue Principale Ouest, Magog* ☎ *819/868–1062* ⊕ *www.cafestmichel.com* ◯ *Closed Tues.*

Microbrasserie La Memphré

PUB | Named after the monster said to lurk in Lake Memphrémagog, La Memphré dates back to the 1800s, when it belonged to Magog's first mayor, Alvin H. Moore. Now a British-style gastropub, it offers up three styles of cheese fondue alongside Bavarian onion soup, burgers, and all manner of modern pub fare in a non-pub setting. All selections are best accompanied by a cold one of whatever other tempting refreshments are on offer. Making your selection is that much more fun as the beautifully presented menu provides not only mouthwatering descriptions of the food and beverages but also historical information and more. ⊠ *12 rue Merry Sud, Magog* ☎ *819/843–3405* ⊕ *lamemphre.com.*

Performing Arts

Le Vieux Clocher de Magog

MUSIC | Originally built in 1881 as a Methodist church, and converted into a theater by local impresario Bernard Caza 100 years later, this theater headlines well-known francophone comedians and singers such as Claude Dubois and Gilles Vigneault. Most, if not all, performances are in French. ⊠ *64 rue Merry Nord, Magog* ☎ *819/847–0470* ⊕ *www.vieuxclocher.com.*

🏃 Activities

GOLF
Golf Owl's Head

GOLF | This course, close to the Vermont border, has some spectacular views. Laid out with undulating fairways, bent-grass greens, and 64 sand bunkers, Golf Owl's

Head, designed by Graham Cooke, is surrounded by peaceful sloping mountains and evergreens. The clubhouse, a stunning timber-and-fieldstone structure with five fireplaces and 45-foot-high ceilings, is a popular watering hole. ⌧ *181 chemin Owl's Head, Mansonville* ☎ *450/292–3342, 800/363–3342* ⊕ *www.owlshead.com* ✉ *C$55 weekdays, C$65 weekends* 🏌 *18 holes, 6710 yards, par 72.*

Manoir des Sables Golf Course

GOLF | Between Mont-Orford and Lake Memphrémagog, this resort course comes with some of the best scenery in the Eastern Townships and has been voted a clear favorite in Québec. The best views are from the second, third, and fourth holes. Several water hazards are dotted around the course, with streams cutting across more than half the fairways and ponds calling for accuracy on certain greens. ⌧ *90 av. des Jardins, Orford* ☎ *819/847–4299, 800/567–3514* ⊕ *manoirdessables.com* ✉ *C$60 weekdays, C$64 weekends (includes cart)* 🏌 *18 holes, 6352 yards, par 71.*

Mont-Orford Golf Club

GOLF | This venerable course in the heart of the national park winds through forested land, with the peak of Mont-Orford visible from many of its greens. There are some tricky holes—look out for the pond to the right of the fairway and an uphill putt on the fifth, the two streams cutting across the eighth, and the sharp dogleg on the 13th. All in all, it's a satisfying challenge and an exceptionally scenic course to play. ⌧ *3074 chemin du Parc, Magog* ☎ *819/843–5688, 866/673–6731* ⊕ *www.orford.com* ✉ *C$48 weekdays, C$52 weekends* 🏌 *18 holes, 6095 yards, par 72* 🍴 *Facilities: golf carts, rental clubs, pro shop, lessons, restaurant.*

SKIING

★ Owl's Head Ski Area

SKIING & SNOWBOARDING | On the Knowlton Landing side of Lake Memphrémagog, Owl's Head is great for skiers seeking sparser crowds—and the views

from its peak are truly exceptional. It has eight lifts, a 1,772-foot vertical drop, and 50 trails, including a 4-km (2½-mile) intermediate run, the longest such run in the Eastern Townships. For decades, it was one of the least expensive hills in the Townships, but the price of lift tickets have been increasing as the hill grows progressively swankier. Under new management since 2017, the facility has been privy to many recent upgrades, and there are millions more pledged to further modernize the facility throughout 2021. ⌧ *40 chemin du Mont-Owl's Head, Magog* ☎ *450/292–3342, 800/363–3342* ⊕ *www.owlshead.com* ✉ *Ski day pass C$73.*

North Hatley

10 km (6 miles) east of Magog, 133 km (83 miles) east of Montréal.

Along with Frelighsburg and Knowlton, North Hatley is undoubtedly one of Québec's prettiest villages. The small resort town on the tip of Lac Massawippi has a theater as well as some excellent inns and restaurants. Set among hills and farms, it was discovered by rich vacationers in the early 1900s and has been drawing visitors ever since. It was particularly popular with magnates from the American South who were looking for a cool summer refuge that wasn't controlled by the Yankees. The result is that some of the village's most majestic buildings are more reminiscent of Georgia than Vermont.

GETTING HERE AND AROUND

From Montréal to North Hatley, take Autoroute 10 East to Autoroute 15 South, and then take Exit 121 to get onto Autoroute 55 South. Take Exit 29 for QC–108.

Restaurants

Pilsen Pub

$$$ | AMERICAN | Massawippi pale and brown ales and a vast selection of microbrews and imports are all on tap here. Pub food is served both in the upstairs dining room and in the tavern. **Known for:** a vast selection of microbrews and imports on tap; burgers and homemade soups; lively, welcoming atmosphere. ⑤ *Average main: C$30* ⊠ *55 rue Main, North Hatley* ☎ *819/842–2971* ⊕ *www. pilsen.ca.*

🛏 Hotels

★ Manoir Hovey

$$$$ | HOTEL | Overlooking Lac Massawippi, with a private beach, this elegant retreat feels rather like a private estate, with many activities, such as tennis, boating, and bicycling, included in the room rate. **Pros:** secluded, lakeside setting; historic buildings; wheelchair accessible. **Cons:** main restaurant overpriced; grounds often taken over by weddings on weekends; 10% tax added to Saturday-night room rate. ⑤ *Rooms from: C$475* ⊠ *575 chemin Hovey, North Hatley* ☎ *819/842–2421, 800/661–2421* ⊕ *www.manoirhovey.com* ⏎ *36 rooms* ⏏ *No Meals.*

🎭 Performing Arts

★ Piggery

THEATER | Enriching the Townships' cultural landscape since 1965, this theater, in a former pig barn in the mountains, is known for showcasing English-language plays, with a focus on Canadian playwrights. Concerts, magic shows, and comedy acts also feature in a season that runs mid-May through October. ⊠ *215 chemin Simard, North Hatley* ☎ *819/842–2431* ⊕ *www.piggery.com.*

Sherbrooke

21 km (12 miles) northeast of North Hatley, 130 km (81 miles) east of Montréal.

Sherbrooke bills itself as the Reine des Cantons de l'Est (Queen of the Eastern Townships), and with a population of more than 160,000, it's the region's largest and most important city. The Loyalists who founded the city in the 1790s and who named it for Sir John Coape Sherbrooke, one of Canada's pre-Confederation governors-general, used the power of the Rivière St-François to build a strong industrial base. Though the city's economic importance has waned, it still has significant manufacturing and textile plants, and rue Wellington, in the downtown area, is experiencing a significant face-lift, with trendy restaurants, bars, and clubs now occupying once vacant lots.

A highlight of the town is the many beautifully painted murals on the sides of downtown buildings, and you can follow a self-guided 6-km (4-mile) tour of them, starting from the tourist office on rue King.

GETTING HERE AND AROUND

Sherbrooke is easy to get to by car via Autoroute 10. From the United States, it's an easy stop on the way to Montréal if you cross the border via Interstate 91 and take Autoroute 55. There are also frequent bus connections between Montréal and Sherbrooke. The city is large and quite hilly, so getting around on foot can be difficult. But there's a well-developed bus system.

VISITOR INFORMATION

CONTACT Sherbrooke Tourism Office.
⊠ *785 rue King Ouest, Sherbrooke* ☎ *819/821–1919, 800/561–8331* ⊕ *www. destinationsherbrooke.com.*

Sights

Musée de la Nature et des Sciences

SCIENCE MUSEUM | FAMILY | Fun and educational for the whole family, this natural history museum utilizes imaginative multisensory displays with state-of-the-art light and sound effects—the buzzing of mosquitoes may be *too* lifelike—and hands-on displays to enhance the experience. Long-running exhibits include *Terra Mutantes,* a geological experience portraying the birth of the Appalachian Mountains, and *AlterAnima,* a mythical forest featuring hundreds of animals and providing viewers a unique perspective on the world as these animals see and experience it, showing us that it's not always what you see, but what you don't. ⊠ *225 rue Frontenac, Sherbrooke* ☎ *819/564–3200, 877/434–3200* ⊕ *mns2.ca/en* 🖃 *C$15.*

Musée des Beaux-Arts de Sherbrooke

ART MUSEUM | This fine-arts museum has a permanent exhibit on the history of art in the region from 1800 to the present. More than 10 exhibits per year are staged in its three galleries, with an emphasis on artists from the Eastern Townships. ⊠ *241 rue Dufferin, Sherbrooke* ☎ *819/821–2115* ⊕ *www.mbas.qc.ca* 🖃 *C$12* ⊗ *Closed Mon. and Tues.*

Restaurants

Auguste

$$$$ | BISTRO | FAMILY | Auguste placed Sherbrooke on the foodie map when it opened in 2008, and it continues to impress. Local ingredients take pride of place in this minimalist bistro-style restaurant, which features dishes like mushroom risotto or sweet potato ravioli. **Known for:** pouding chômeur (poor man's pudding) drenched in maple syrup; free children's dinner menu Tuesdsay and Wednesday; providing a true gastronomic experience. 💲 *Average main: C$40* ⊠ *82 rue Wellington Nord, Sherbrooke* ☎ *819/565–9559* ⊕ *www.*

auguste-restaurant.com ⊗ *Closed Sun. and Mon. No lunch Sat.*

Performing Arts

Centennial Theatre

THEATER | On the campus of Bishop's University, this 600-seat theater presents a roster of jazz, classical, and rock concerts, as well as opera, dance, mime, and children's theater. ⊠ *2600 rue College, Sherbrooke* ☎ *819/822–9692* ⊕ *www.centennialtheatre.ca* ⊗ *Closed weekends.*

Le Vieux Clocher de l'Université de Sherbrooke

MUSIC | Le Vieux Clocher de l'Université de Sherbrooke presents music, from classical to jazz, and a variety of theater and comedy shows. ⊠ *1590 rue Galt Ouest, Sherbrooke* ☎ *819/822–2102* ⊕ *www.centreculereludes.ca.*

Shopping

La Centrale Métiers d'Art

CRAFTS | Stop into this charming little shop filled with crafts, jewelry, kitchenware, and clothing made by artists from the Eastern Townships. ⊠ *210 rue Wellington Nord, Sherbrooke* ☎ *819/823–0221* ⊕ *www.metiersdartestrie.com* ⊗ *Closed Mon. and Tues.*

Notre-Dame-des-Bois

72 km (43 miles) east of Sherbrooke, 204 km (127 miles) east of Montréal.

Notre-Dame-des-Bois is a sleepy little one-street village just north of the Maine border. It sits in the shadow of one of the region's tallest and steepest mountains—Mont-Mégantic, which soars 576 meters (1,890 feet) above the surrounding plain, with a height of 3,601 feet above sea level. In 2007, the Mont-Mégantic Observatory area was declared the first International Dark Sky Reserve, in recognition

The Mont Mégantic Observatory provides the best views of the beautifully wild and mountainous area that became the first-ever International Dark Sky Reserve.

of the lack of light pollution that provides some of the clearest night skies in Québec, a quality that attracts stargazers, both professional and amateur.

GETTING HERE AND AROUND

Count on a three-hour journey from Montréal, some of it over paved but bumpy secondary roads. To get here, follow Autoroute 10 East past Sherbrooke to its end near Ascot Corner, then follow Route 112 to East Angus, then Route 253 to Cookshire, and finally Route 212 through L'Avenir to Notre-Dame-des-Bois. If you want to make the journey comfortably, plan to stay overnight somewhere rather than just coming for the day.

Sights

Astrolab du Mont-Mégantic
(*Mont-Mégantic Observatory*)
OBSERVATORY | Both amateur stargazers and serious astronomers head to this observatory, located in a beautifully wild and mountainous area that in 2007 became the first-ever International Dark

Sky Reserve. The observatory is at the summit of the Townships' second-highest mountain (3,601 feet above sea level and 1,890 feet above the surrounding landscape), whose northern face records annual snowfalls rivaling any in North America. A joint venture of the University of Montréal and Laval University, the observatory has a powerful telescope, the largest on the East Coast. In the Astrolab's welcome center at the mountain's base, there is an exhibition and multimedia display to provide visitors with information about the night sky. ■TIP➔ **Hours vary depending on the season, so check the website for updated information.** ✉ *Parc du Mont-Mégantic, 189 Rte. du Parc, Notre-Dame-des-Bois* ☎ *819/888–2941, 888/665–6527* ⊕ *www. astrolab-parc-national-mont-megantic. org* ▧ *Observatory and Astrolab C$20.25 daytime, C$22.50–C$26.75 at night. Additional fee of C$9 charged to enter Parc du Mont-Mégantic* ⚓ *Reservations essential.*

Parc du Mont-Mégantic

NATURE SIGHT | If you're short on time
or don't feel like a hike you can take a
shuttle bus to the top of Mont-Mégantic
for spectacular views of Québec, Maine,
New Hampshire, and on really clear days,
Vermont. But if you want the full experience, make the trek by foot. The park has
50 km (31 miles) of hiking trails that are
also open in winter to snowshoers and
cross-country skiers. For a real adventure, you can stay overnight in one of the
park's rustic shelters. ⊠ *189 Rte. du Parc,
Notre-Dame-des-Bois* ☎ *819/888–2941,
800/665–6527* ⊕ *www.sepaq.com/pq/
mme* ⊠ *C$9.55.*

 # Hotels

★ Aux Berges de l'Aurore

$ | B&B/INN | From its lofty perch, this
delightful century-old inn has spectacular views day and night—it's within the
International Dark Sky Reserve—and is
less than a minute's drive from Mont
Mégantic National Park and the Astrolab.
Pros: close to area activities; delicious
breakfasts; hiking trails on the property.
Cons: minimum two-night stay holiday
weekends and some other times; no
shampoo or conditioner provided; some
bathrooms have musty odor. ⑤ *Rooms
from: C$150* ⊠ *139 Rte. du Parc,
Notre-Dame-des-Bois* ☎ *819/888–2715,
514/232–0703* ⊕ *www.auberge-aurore.
qc.ca* ⊃ *5 rooms* ◯ *Free Breakfast.*

Chapter 5

QUÉBEC CITY

Updated by
Marie-Ève Vallières

👁 Sights	🍴 Restaurants	🛏 Hotels	🛍 Shopping	🍸 Nightlife
★★★★★	★★★★☆	★★★★★	★★★☆☆	★★★★☆

WELCOME TO QUÉBEC CITY

TOP REASONS TO GO

★ **See the Château Frontenac:** Even if you're not staying at Québec City's most famous landmark, make sure to pop into one of the world's legendary hotels and admire its French Renaissance architecture.

★ **Dine at world-class restaurants:** High-end bistros, hip cafés, amazing breweries, and wine bars: Québec City has it all.

★ **Explore La Citadelle:** Québec City's pièce de résistance is the largest fortified base in North America and site of the daily Changing of the Guard in summer.

★ **Play on the Plains of Abraham:** This massive waterfront park is a popular place for outdoor fun, from cross-country skiing and sledding in winter to picnicking and concertgoing in summer.

★ **Get festive:** For two weekends in February, the city hosts one of the biggest winter festivals in the world. In July, up to 80,000 people cheer some of the biggest rock and pop stars at the open-air Summer Festival.

1 Upper Town. Crowning Cap Diamant and partially surrounded by the Fortifications, Upper Town hosts the city's main attractions, including the Château Frontenac and La Citadelle. The sweeping views of the St. Lawrence River, the Laurentian Mountains to the north, and the Appalachians to the south are all enchanting.

2 Lower Town. A maze of cobblestoned streets with tucked-away cafés, boutique hotels, antiques shops, and art galleries characterizes Lower Town.

3 Outside the Old City. Rue St-Jean, St-Roch district, avenue Cartier, and the Grande Allée all have restaurants, shops, and nightlife worth checking out.

UPPER TOWN 1

OLD CITY

LOWER TOWN 2

OLD PORT

Séminaire du Québec

Basilique Cathédrale Notre-Dame de Québec

Fairmont Le Château Frontenac

La Citadelle

Parc de l'Esplanade

Jardin des Gouverneurs

Parc Bastion-de-la-Reine

Place de la FAO

St. Lawrence River

rue Abraham-Martin

blvd. Jean-Lesage

rue St-André

rue St-Paul

rue St-Nicolas

rue Vallière

Côte de la Potasse

Côte Dinan

rue des Remparts

Côte De la Canoterie

Côte De la Canoterie

rue St-Paul

rue St-André

rue Sous-le-Cap

rue McMahon

rue St-Jean

rue St-Stanislas

rue Ste-Angèle

rue Cook

rue Dauphine

rue Ste-Anne

rue d'Auteuil

rue Ste-Ursule

rue Charlevoix

rue Couillard

Côte du Palais

Côte de la Fabrique

rue Hamel

rue St-Flavien

rue Ste-Famille

rue Garneau

rue Hébert

r. de l'Université

rue Ste-Anne

rue de Buade

r. du Trésor

r. du Fort

r. Port-Dauphin

r. Ste-Famille

rue St-Louis

rue Donnacona

rue Mont-Carmel

rue des Carrières

rue des Grisons

av. St-Denis

Terrasse Dufferin

rue de Petit-Champlain

Promenade des Gouverneurs

blvd. Champlain

Côte de la Citadelle

r. Sault-au-Matelot

r. St-Pierre

rue Dalhousie

r. Bail

St-Antoine

r. du Porche

r. Notre-Dame

r. Sous-le-Fort

0   1/8 mi

0   1/8 km

Overlooking the St. Lawrence River from the rocky promontory of Cap Diamant, a silent and solemn witness to the development of North America for more than four centuries, Québec City evokes a past marked by military history and European rivalries. At the heart of this complex heritage now thrives one of the largest and most vibrant French-speaking populations outside of France. Visitors come to discover the only walled city north of Mexico, of course, but also the remarkable historical continuity, the seasonal gastronomy, and the irresistible francophone exuberance.

The historic heart of this community is Vieux-Québec (Old City), comprising the part of the Haute-Ville (Upper Town) surrounded by walls and the Basse-Ville (Lower Town), which spreads out at the base of the hill from Place Royale. Visitors can walk downhill (or uphill, as the case may be) from one to the other using the many sets of staircases, or ride the funicular that runs between them. Cobblestoned streets and ornate New France chapels here are charming in all seasons. The Old City earned recognition as an official UNESCO World Heritage site in 1985, thanks largely to city planners who managed to not just update but also fiercely preserve the 400-year-old buildings and attractions without destroying

what made them worth preserving. The most familiar icon of Québec City, the Château Frontenac, is set on the highest point in Upper Town, where it holds court over the entire city.

Sitting proudly above the confluence of the St. Lawrence and St. Charles Rivers, the city's famous military fortification, La Citadelle, built in the early 19th century, remains the largest of its kind in North America. In summer, visitors should try to catch the Changing of the Guard, held every morning at 10; you can get much closer to the guards here than at Buckingham Palace in London.

Enchanting as it is, the Old City is nonetheless just a small part of the true

Québec City experience. Think outside the walls and explore St-Roch's hipster microbreweries, award-winning restaurants, designer boutiques, and third-wave cafés. Meander down the Grande Allée and avenue Cartier to find a livelier part of town dotted with nightclubs and fun, casual eateries. Or while away the hours in St-Jean-Baptiste, a neighborhood with strong literary vibes and colorful architecture.

Planning

When to Go

Winter can be formidable, but the city stays alive—especially during the popular Winter Carnival. Spring is short and sweet with the *cabanes à sucre* (sugar shacks) bringing fresh maple goodies. In summer, the city's terraces and courtyards open and everyone comes out to enjoy the sunshine. In late September and early October, the region's foliage blazes with color.

Getting Here and Around

The Funiculaire du Vieux-Québec, a small elevator up the side of the steep embankment, travels between the Upper and Lower Towns. Another option, and a good workout, is to take one of the sets of stairs that start in Upper Town and end at the Quartier du Petit-Champlain in Lower Town. Renting a car isn't recommended (parking can be a real issue) unless you're taking day-trips outside the city.

AIR

If you're flying in, Jean-Lesage International Airport is about 19 km (12 miles) northwest of downtown. Driving into town, take Route 540 (Autoroute Duplessis) to Route 175 (boulevard Laurier). The ride takes about 30 minutes. Taxis are

available immediately outside the airport exit near the baggage-claim area. A ride into the city costs C$41.40.

BUS

Bus service in Québec City is an effective way to go from the Vieux-Québec to other parts of the city, particularly using the Metrobus lines (those with an 800 number). It is C$9.25 for a one-day ticket or C$3.40 for a one-way trip.

CAR

Montréal and Québec City are linked by Autoroute 20 on the south shore of the St. Lawrence River and by Autoroute 40 on the north shore. On both highways, the ride between the two cities is about 240 km (150 miles) and takes about three hours. U.S. I–87 in New York, U.S. I–89 in Vermont, and U.S. I–91 in New Hampshire connect with Autoroute 20, as does Highway 401 from Toronto. Driving northeast out of Montréal on Autoroute 20, follow signs for Pierre Laporte Bridge (Pont Pierre-Laporte) as you approach Québec City. After you've crossed the bridge, take the exit to boulevard Laurier (Route 175), which becomes the Grande Allée.

TRAIN

VIA Rail, Canada's passenger rail service, has service between Montréal and Québec City. The trip takes less than three hours. One-way tickets cost C$89, but early reservation rates can be as low as C$29. A taxi from the Gare du Palais train station to the Château Frontenac is about C$8.

Hotels

There are over 35 hotels in the Old City alone, with everything from family-run bed-and-breakfasts to household hospitality brands. There truly is something for every taste: modern high-rises outside the ramparts to wake up to spectacular views of Québec City or old-fashioned inns where no two rooms are alike to fully experience the city's historic charm.

In any case, be sure to book well in advance if you plan on visiting during peak season (May through September) or the Winter Carnival (early February), as hotel rates may rise by up to 30%. On the other hand, many lodgings offer weekend discounts and other promotions from November through April.

⇨ *Hotel reviews have been shortened. For full information, visit Fodors.com. Hotel prices are the lowest cost of a standard double room in high season.*

WHAT IT COSTS in Canadian Dollars			
$	$$	$$$	$$$$
HOTELS			
under C$160	C$160– C$200	C$201– C$250	over C$250

Nightlife

In winter, nightlife activity grows livelier as the week nears its end, beginning on Wednesday. As warmer temperatures set in, the café-terrace crowd emerges, and bars are active just about every night. Most bars and clubs stay open until 3 am.

Performing Arts

Québec City has a good variety of cultural institutions for a city of its size, thanks to its renowned symphony orchestra and its many charming venues that welcome (mainly French-speaking) music, theater, comedy, and dance acts.

Restaurants

Bistros, sidewalk cafés, and chic, cutting-edge restaurants make up the dining scene in Québec City. "Grab and go" is more the exception than the rule;

be prepared to eat at a leisurely pace. Québec's culinary scene offers variety, including modern international cuisine and inventive farm-to-table bistros; traditional French dishes like foie gras and escargot; distinctly French Canadian specialties such as tourtière (meat pie); and local fare such as ice cider, poutine, and maple sugar pie.

With so many options, choosing where to go can be difficult. Many establishments post their menu du jour outside, so you can stroll along and let your cravings guide the way. But bear in mind that reservations are a must at most restaurants during holidays, Winter Carnival, and in the summer months, when the coveted outdoor terraces open. When ordering, remember that in this French-speaking province, an *entrée* is an appetizer and the *plat principal* is the main course. Plan to tip at least 15% of the bill.

⇨ *Restaurant reviews have been shortened. For full information, visit Fodors. com. Restaurant prices are the average cost of a main course at dinner or, if dinner is not served, at lunch.*

WHAT IT COSTS in Canadian Dollars			
$	$$	$$$	$$$$
RESTAURANTS			
under C$12	C$12– C$20	C$21– C$30	over C$30

Shopping

On the fashionable streets of Vieux-Québec, shopping has a European tinge. The boutiques and specialty shops clustered along narrow streets such as rue du Petit-Champlain and rues de Buade and St-Jean are especially traditional. For designer brands and curated collections, rue St-Joseph down in the St-Roch neighborhood is the place to be.

Stores are generally open Monday through Wednesday from 9:30 to 5:30, Thursday and Friday until 9, Saturday until 5, and Sunday noon to 5. In summer, most shops have later evening hours.

Visitor Information

CONTACT Québec City Tourist Information. ⊠ *12 rue Ste-Anne, Upper Town* ☎ *418/641–6290, 877/266–5687* ⊕ *www.quebec-cite.com/en.*

Upper Town

No other place in Canada has so much history squeezed into such a small area. Upper Town was a barren, windswept cape when Samuel de Champlain decided to build a fort here over 400 years ago. Now it's a major tourist destination surrounded by cannon-studded stone ramparts.

Home to the city's most famous sites, Upper Town's Old City offers a dramatic view of the St. Lawrence River and the countryside, especially while walking along the Terrasse Dufferin, in front of the Château Frontenac. Historic buildings that house bars, cafés, shops, and hotels line the neighborhood's winding streets. A 3-mile-long wall neatly splices off this section of the city with entrances on rues St-Jean and St-Louis, Vieux-Québec's two main thoroughfares. The wall itself is a national historic monument. It began as a series of earthworks and wooden palisades built by French military engineers to protect the Upper Town from an inland attack following the siege of the city by Admiral Phipps in 1690. Over the next century, the French expended much time, energy, and money to strengthen the city's fortifications. After the fall of New France, the British were equally concerned about strengthening the city's defenses and built an earth-and-wood citadel atop Cap Diamant. Slowly,

the British replaced the palisades that surrounded the city with the massive cut-stone wall that has become the city's trademark attraction. The crowning touch came after the War of 1812, with the construction of the cut-stone, star-shaped citadel, perched high on Cap Diamant.

Like La Citadelle, most of the homes that line the narrow streets in Upper Town are made of granite cut from nearby quarries in the 1800s. The stone walls, copper roofs, and heavy wooden doors on the government buildings and high-steepled churches in the area also reflect the Upper Town's place as the political, educational, and religious nerve center of both the province and the country during much of the past four centuries.

GETTING HERE AND AROUND
Many people begin their tours in Upper Town, taking in the spectacular hilltop views as well as the Château Frontenac, which is probably Québec City's top site. The Fortifications border this section of the city. Walk along rue d'Auteuil, between rues St-Louis and St-Jean, to get a good sense of where the wall divides the Old City.

If you're coming from Lower Town, take the funicular (C$5), or brave one of the many staircases that connect the top of the hill to the bottom. Shops and restaurants provide an opportunity for a quick rest along the way uphill.

TIMING
Plan to spend a whole day visiting the many sights and shops clustered around the Château Frontenac. Rue St-Jean offers many lunch options, or do as the locals do and grab a sandwich and head to a bench in one of the area's parks.

Allot at least a half day for walking the walls of La Citadelle. Set out early in the morning to catch the Changing of the Guard (10 am in summer). Afterward, picnic on the Plains or one of the terraces on the Grande Allée and avenue Cartier.

Upper Town

Sights ▽

1 Basilique Cathédrale Notre-Dame de Québec **F5**
2 Cathedral of the Holy Trinity **E6**
3 Édifice Price **E5**
4 Fairmont Le Château Frontenac **E6**
5 Fortifications of Québec National Historic Site.... **C3**
6 Henry Stuart House **A5**
7 Hôtel du Parlement **A5**
8 Jardin Jeanne-d'Arc ... **A5**
9 La Citadelle **B7**
10 Maison de la Littérature **D4**
11 Monastère des Augustines **F4**
12 Montmorency Park National Historic Site.... **F6**
13 Morrin Cultural Centre **D4**
14 Place d'Armes **E6**
15 Plains of Abraham **A5**
16 Rue du Trésor **E6**
17 Séminaire de Québec **F5**
18 St-Louis Forts and Châteaux National Historic Site **F7**
19 Terrasse Dufferin **E7**
20 Ursuline Chapel **D5**
21 Wolfe-Montcalm Monument **D7**

Restaurants ▽

1 Alphonse **E5**
2 Aux Anciens Canadiens **D6**
3 Café-Boulangerie Paillard **D4**
4 Catherine Méra Pâtisserie **E4**
5 Chez Boulay **D4**
6 Le Champlain **E6**
7 Le Chic Shack **F6**
8 Le Clan **D6**
9 Le Continental **E6**
10 Le Parlementaire **A5**
11 Le St-Amour **C5**
12 L'Entrecôte St-Jean **D4**
13 Sagamité **C5**
14 Sapristi **C4**

Hotels ▽

1 Auberge Place d'Armes **E5**
2 Fairmont Le Château Frontenac **E6**
3 Hilton Québec **B4**
4 Hôtel Cap Diamant **C7**
5 Hôtel Château Bellevue **D7**
6 Hôtel Clarendon **E5**
7 Hôtel du Vieux-Québec **E4**
8 Hôtel Manoir Victoria ... **E3**
9 Hôtel Marie Rollet **D5**
10 Hôtel Nomad **D7**
11 Le Capitole Hôtel **C3**
12 Le Monastère des Augustines **F4**
13 Monsieur Jean **E4**
14 Québec City Marriott Downtown **B3**

Sights

Basilique-Cathédrale Notre-Dame de Québec (*Our Lady of Québec Basilica Cathedral*)

CHURCH | François de Laval, the first bishop of New France and founder of Canada's Catholic Church, once ruled a diocese that stretched to the Gulf of Mexico. Videos and pictures astutely illustrate his life throughout the visit.

Laval's original cathedral burned down and has been rebuilt several times, but the current basilica still has a chancel lamp that was a gift from Louis XIV, the Sun King. The church's interior includes a canopy dais over the Episcopal throne, a ceiling of painted clouds decorated with gold leaf, and richly colored stained-glass windows. A "holy door" was added to the church in 2014. The large crypt was Québec City's first cemetery; more than 900 bodies are interred here, including, perhaps, Samuel de Champlain's; archaeologists have been searching for his tomb since 1950. Guided tours of the cathedral and crypt are available (by appointment only). ⊠ *16 rue de Buade, Upper Town* ☎ *418/692–2533* ⊕ *notre-dame-de-quebec.org* 🖼 *C$5.*

Cathedral of the Holy Trinity

CHURCH | The first Anglican cathedral outside the British Isles was erected in the heart of Québec City's Upper Town between 1800 and 1804. Its simple, dignified façade is reminiscent of London's St. Martin-in-the-Fields, and the pediment, archway, and Ionic pilasters introduced Palladian architecture to Canada. The land on which the cathedral was built was originally given to the Récollets (Franciscan monks from France) in 1681 by the king of France for a church and monastery. When Québec came under British rule, the Récollets made the church available to the Anglicans for services. Later, King George III ordered construction of the present cathedral, with an area set aside for members of

the royal family. A portion of the north balcony is still reserved for the use of the reigning sovereign or his or her representative. The cathedral's impressive rear organ has 3,058 pipes. Even more impressive is the smaller English chamber organ, built in 1790, which was donated to the cathedral for the bicentennial celebrations in 2004. ⊠ *31 rue des Jardins, Upper Town* ☎ *418/692–2193* ⊕ *cathedral.ca* 🖼 *Free.*

Édifice Price

NOTABLE BUILDING | Styled after the Empire State Building, this 17-story art deco structure was the city's first skyscraper when it was built in 1929. It served as headquarters of the Price Brothers Company, a lumber firm founded by Sir William Price, and today is an official residence of the premier of Québec, who uses the top two floors. ⊠ *65 rue Ste-Anne, Upper Town.*

★ Fairmont Le Château Frontenac

HOTEL | The most photographed landmark in Québec City, this imposing turreted castle with a copper roof owes its name to the Comte de Frontenac, governor of the French colony between 1672 and 1698. Samuel de Champlain was responsible for Château St-Louis, the original on the site of the Frontenac, built between 1620 and 1624 as a residence for colonial governors and later restored after burning down in the 1800s. The original portions of the hotel were part of a series of château-style hotels built across Canada to attract wealthy railroad travelers. It was remarkably luxurious for the time: guest rooms contained fireplaces, bathrooms, and marble fixtures, and a special commissioner purchased antiques for the establishment. The current hotel was designed by New York architect Bruce Price, who also worked on Québec City's train station, Gare du Palais. The addition of a 20-story central tower in 1924 completed the hotel. Since then the Château, as it's called by locals, has accumulated a star-studded guest

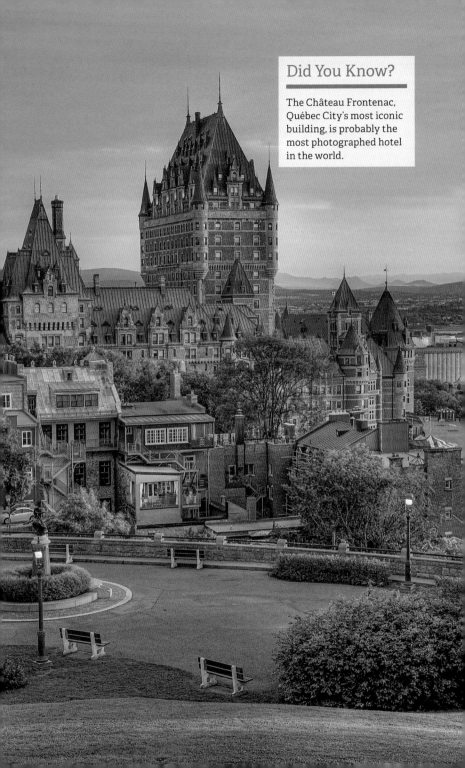

roster, including Prince William and Kate Middleton, Queen Elizabeth II, Princess Grace of Monaco, Alfred Hitchcock, and Ronald Reagan, as well as Franklin Roosevelt and Winston Churchill, who met here in 1943 and 1944 for two wartime conferences.

Those looking to get an in-depth visit can book a guided tour with local operator Québec Cicerone Tours for C$24 per adult and C$12 per child. ⊠ *1 rue des Carrières, Upper Town* ☎ *418/692–3861* ⊕ *fairmont.com/frontenac-quebec*.

Fortifications of Québec National Historic Site
MILITARY SIGHT | Thick stone walls stretch along 5 km (3 miles), connected by four gates and adjoined by forts, bastions, and even a citadel: with such a special and unique landmark, it's not difficult to understand why the Historic District of Old Québec is a UNESCO World Heritage site. These nearly intact ramparts, virtually the only ones of their kind in North America, recall the complex history of the French and British regimes in Québec City. French colonists began building ramparts along the city's cliffs as early as 1690 to protect themselves from the British, but they had trouble convincing the French government to take the threat of invasion seriously. And when the British did invade in 1759, the walls were unsurprisingly still incomplete. The British, despite attacks by the Americans during the American Revolution and the War of 1812, took over a century to finish them—and they never saw armed conflict.

From June to September, two guided tours are offered: one starts at Artillery Park and focuses on the social and architectural heritage of the ramparts, while the other is more military focused and begins at Terrasse Dufferin. Either way, the Dauphine Redoubt in Artillery Park on the northern end of the fortifications should not be missed; it's one of the oldest military buildings in the Americas.

The four gates—St-Jean, St-Louis, Kent, and the more modern Prescott—are well worth a stop, too. ⊠ *2 rue d'Auteuil, Upper Town* ⊕ *parks.canada.ca/lhn-nhs/ qc/fortifications* ☞ *C$8.50* ⊗ *Closed Oct.–May*.

Henry Stuart House
HISTORIC HOME | If you want to get a firsthand look at how the well-to-do English residents of Québec City lived in a bygone era, this is the place. Built in 1849 by the wife of wealthy businessman William Henry, the Regency-style cottage was bought in 1918 by the sisters Adèle and Mary Stuart. Active in such philanthropic organizations as the Red Cross and the Historical and Literary Society, the sisters were pillars of Québec City's English-speaking community. They also maintained an English-style garden behind the house. The home has since been classified a historic site for its immaculate physical condition and the museumlike quality of its furnishings, almost all of them Victorian. Guided tours of the house and garden start on the hour and include a cup of tea and piece of lemon cake. ⊠ *82 Grande Allée Ouest, Montcalm* ☎ *418/647–4347* ⊕ *maisonhenrystuart. qc.ca* ☞ *C$8* ⊗ *Closed Sun. and Mon. and Sept.–late June*.

Hôtel du Parlement
GOVERNMENT BUILDING | The only French-speaking legislature in continental North America, the 125-member Assemblée Nationale du Québec meets behind the stately walls of this Second Empire–style building erected between 1877 and 1886. If the Assemblée is sitting, see if you can get into the visitors gallery to hear heated exchanges between the federalist-leaning Liberals and the secessionist Parti Québécois. Failing that, the buildings themselves, designed by Québec architect Eugène-Étienne Taché, are worth a visit. The façade is decorated with statues of such important figures of Québec history as Cartier, Champlain,

The Fortifications

UPPER TOWN

MONTCALM

Parc de l'Amérique Française

Convention Center

UPPER TOWN

LOWER TOWN

Fairmont Le Château Frontenac

La Citadelle

Plains of Abraham

Parc des Champs-de-Bataille

St. Laurence River

Discovery Pavilion of the Plains of Abraham

0   1/4 mile
0   400 meters

KEY

● Sights
— Ramparts
🛈 Tourist Information

Sights ▶

1 Henry Stuart House **C1**
2 La Citadelle **F3**
3 Musée National des Beaux-Arts du Québec **B2**
4 Parc Jeanne d'Arc **D2**
5 Plains of Abraham **D2**
6 St-Louis Forts and Chateaux National Historic Site **H2**
7 Wolfe-Montcalm Monument **G2**

The History of Québec City

Québec City was founded by French explorer Samuel de Champlain in 1608 and is the oldest municipality in the province. In the 17th century, the first French explorers, fur trappers, and missionaries arrived to establish a colony.

French explorer Jacques Cartier arrived in 1535, and although he did attempt to set up a (short-lived) colony, it was Champlain who founded "New France" some 70 years later and built a fort (called Place Royale today) on the banks of the St. Lawrence.

The British were persistent in their efforts to dislodge the French from North America, but the colonists of New France built forts and other military structures, such as a wooden palisade (defensive fence) that reinforced their position on top of the cliff. It was Britain's naval supremacy that ultimately led to New France's demise. After capturing all French forts east of Québec, General James Wolfe led his army to Québec City in the summer of 1759.

After a months-long siege, thousands of British soldiers scaled the heights along a narrow cow path on a moonless night. Surprised to see British soldiers massed on a farmer's field so near the city, French general Louis-Joseph Montcalm rushed out to meet them in what became known as the Battle of the Plains of Abraham.

The French were routed in the 20-minute skirmish, which claimed the lives of both Wolfe and Montcalm. The battle symbolically marks the death of New France and the birth of British Canada.

British rule was a boon for Québec City. Thanks to more robust trade and large capital investments, the fishing, fur-trading, shipbuilding, and timber industries expanded rapidly.

Wary of new invasions from its former American colonies, the British also expanded the city's fortifications. They replaced the wooden palisades with a massive stone wall and built a star-shaped fortress. Both structures still stand today and are named Fortifications de Québec.

The constitution of 1791 established Québec City as the capital of Lower Canada, a position it held until 1840, when the Act of Union united Upper and Lower Canada and made Montréal the capital. When Canada was created in 1867 by the Act of Confederation, which united four colonial provinces (Québec, Ontario, New Brunswick, and Nova Scotia), Québec City was named the province's capital city, a role it continues to play. In Québec, however, the city is known officially as *la capitale nationale*, a reflection of the nationalist sentiments that have marked Québec society and politics since the 1960s.

Frontenac, Wolfe, and Montcalm. A 30-minute tour (in English, French, or Spanish) takes in the President's Gallery, the Parlementaire restaurant, the Legislative Council Chamber, and the National Assembly Chamber. Tours may be restricted during legislative sessions.

Outdoor tours of the gardens and statues are also available during summer. ✉ *1045 rue des Parlementaires, Upper Town* ☎ *866/337–8837* ⊕ *assnat.qc.ca* 🎫 *Free* ☉ *Closed weekends* � *Reservations are mandatory.*

Kids will love watching the Royal 22nd Regiment's Changing of the Guard every summer day at 10 am, from June 24 until the first Monday in September.

Jardin Jeanne-d'Arc

CITY PARK | Bright with colorful flowers in summer, this urban park is lined with stunning 19th-century mansions and is often adorned with seasonal decorations. It makes for a lovely place to rest between museums. The focus of the park is an equestrian statue of Joan of Arc. A symbol of military courage and of France itself, the statue stands in tribute to the heroes of 1759 near the place where New France was lost to the British. The park also commemorates the Canadian national anthem, "O Canada"; it was played here for the first time on June 24, 1880. ⊠ *av. Wilfrid-Laurier, Upper Town.*

★ La Citadelle

MILITARY SIGHT | Built at the city's highest point, on Cap Diamant, the Citadelle is the largest fortified base in North America still occupied by troops. The 25-building fortress is, quite literally, the star of the Fortifications of Québec National Historic Site. It was intended to protect the port, prevent the enemy from taking up a position on the Plains of Abraham, and provide a refuge in case of an attack.

Since 1920, the Citadelle has served as a base for Canada's most storied French-speaking military formation, the Royal 22nd Regiment, known across Canada as the Van Doos, from the French *vingt-deux* (22). Firearms, uniforms, and decorations from as far back as the 17th century are displayed in the Musée du Royal 22e Régiment in the former powder magazine, built in 1750. Watch the Changing of the Guard, a ceremony in which troops parade before the Citadelle in red coats and black fur hats while a band plays. The regiment's mascot, a well-behaved goat, watches along. The King's representative in Canada, the governor-general, has a residence in the Citadelle, and it's open for tours in summer. You must take a tour to access the Citadelle, since it's a military base. ▦TIP→ **The location—set high above the St. Lawrence River with stunning views of the city and surrounding countryside—is worth a visit even if you don't want to**

Grosse Île Day Trip

For thousands of immigrants from Europe in the 1800s, the first glimpse of North America was the hastily erected quarantine station at Grosse Île—Canada's equivalent of Ellis Island. During the time Grosse Île operated (1832–1937), 4.3 million immigrants passed through the port of Québec. For far too many passengers on disease-racked ships, particularly the Irish fleeing the potato famine, Grosse Île became a final resting place. Several buildings have been restored to tell the story of the tragic period of Irish immigration.

It's necessary to take a boat tour or ferry to visit the park (some day-long cruises depart from Québec City), and you should reserve in advance. Croisières AML offers guided cruises at croisieresaml.com that depart for Grosse Île from Berthier-sur-Mer, 40 minutes east of Québec City on the south shore of the St Lawrence. The six-hour tour, offered from May to October (☎ C$69) includes the short cruise and admission to the island. ☎ *418/234–8841* ⊕ *www.pc.gc.ca/en/lhn-nhs/qc/grosseile.*

pay (or wait) to take a tour. ⊠ *côte de la Citadelle, Upper Town* ☎ *418/694–2815* ⊕ *lacitadelle.qc.ca/en* ☞ *C$18* ☞ *Changing of the Guard at 10 am in summer.*

★ Maison de la Littérature

LIBRARY | Well worth a stop for design, architecture, and book lovers alike, this stunning library houses permanent exhibitions on French Canadian literature. Set in a former 19th-century Methodist church, the now white-washed, design-heavy building was completely revamped a few years ago, winning international acclaim and architecture awards in the process. ⊠ *40 rue St-Stanislas, Upper Town* ☎ *418/641-6797* ⊕ *maisondelalitterature.qc.ca* ⊙ *Closed Mon.*

★ Monastère des Augustines (*Augustinian Monastery and Museum*)

RELIGIOUS BUILDING | Augustinian nuns arrived from Dieppe, France, in 1639 with a mission to care for the sick in the new colony. They established the first hospital north of Mexico, the Hôtel-Dieu, the large building west of the monastery. The complex underwent a complete renovation and expansion, in 2015, and now includes a quiet, health-conscious restaurant (with silent breakfast!), as well

as a holistic spa and accommodations—both contemporary en suite rooms and dormlike rooms with antique furniture—for those looking for a calm retreat. The museum houses an extensive collection of liturgical and medical artifacts of all kinds, and it's also worth visiting the richly decorated chapel designed by artist Thomas Baillairgé, as well as the vaults, which date to 1659 and were used by the nuns as shelter from British bombardments. There is still a small order of nuns living in a section of the monastery. ⊠ *32 rue Charlevoix, Upper Town* ☎ *418/692–2492* ⊕ *monastere.ca* ☞ *C$17* ⊙ *Closed Mon.*

Montmorency Park National Historic Site

CITY PARK | Seemingly floating between Upper and Lower Town, Montmorency Park is a must-see for visitors walking up (or down) côte de la Montagne. The leafy park was home to Parliaments of Lower Canada, Canada East, and Québec from 1791 to 1883; while virtually zero surface structure remains to illustrate this role, it's now a national historic site filled with centenary trees and walkways describing the significance of the site. Along the southeastern edge are the ramparts and defensive walls, from which visitors will find a beautiful panoramic view of the Lower Town and the river. ⊠ *côte de la Montagne, Upper Town* 🎫 *Free.*

Morrin Cultural Centre

ARTS CENTER | This stately graystone building has served many purposes, from imprisoning and executing criminals to storing the national archives. Built between 1808 and 1813, it was the first modern prison in Canada and was converted into Morrin College, one of the city's first private schools, in 1868. That was also when the Literary and Historical Society of Québec, forerunner of Canada's National Archives, moved in. Historical and cultural talks are held in English, and tours of the building, including two blocks of prison cells, the Victorian-era library, and College Hall, are also available. Children and families particularly enjoy this space. ⊠ *44 chaussée des Écossais, Upper Town* 🕾 *418/694–9147* ⊕ *morrin.org/en* 🎫 *C\$17* ⊙ *Closed Mon. and Tues.*

Place d'Armes

PLAZA/SQUARE | For centuries, this wide square was used for parades and military events; today, it's mostly strollers, buskers, and visitors enjoying restaurant terraces. On its west side stands the majestic Ancien Palais de Justice (Old Courthouse), a Renaissance-style building from 1887. The plaza is on land that was occupied by a church and convent of the Récollet missionaries (Franciscan monks), who in 1615 were the first order of priests to arrive in New France. The Gothic-style fountain in the center pays tribute to their arrival. ⊠ *rues St-Louis and du Fort, Upper Town.*

★ Plains of Abraham

HISTORIC SIGHT | This massive urban park is the where the famous Battle of Québec occurred on September 13, 1759, which decided Canada's fate when the French lost the city to the British as part of the acrimonious Seven Years' War. On that date, British soldiers under the command of General Wolfe climbed the steep cliff under the cover of darkness, ultimately defeating the French through a single deadly volley of musket fire, causing the battle to be over within 30 minutes. At the Museum of the Plains of Abraham, check out the multimedia display, which depicts Canada's history, as well as the numerous family-friendly activities at Martello Towers.

Nowadays, locals come here to cross-country ski and admire the St. Lawrence River even as it freezes over in winter; in July, the Summer Festival takes over with tens of thousands of concertgoers. ⊠ *Parc des Champs-de-Bataille, Upper Town* 🕾 *418/649–6157* ⊕ *ccbn-nbc.gc.ca* 🎫 *Museum C\$21.50.*

Rue du Trésor

STREET | In the era of the French Regime, settlers would visit this street to fulfill their tax obligations at the former royal treasury that once stood in this vicinity, which explains the origin of its name, "du Trésor." Now known for its unique cachet, the locale also dubbed "Artists Street" gracefully transforms into an open-air art gallery. Nestled amid historic Château Frontenac and Basilique-Cathédrale Notre-Dame de Québec, this cobblestoned street exudes charm and allure. Here, a multitude of artists gather to display their works every day in the summertime and on long weekends. However, during the shoulder season, the street takes on a quieter, more tranquil ambience. ⊠ *Upper Town.*

Séminaire de Québec

HISTORIC SIGHT | Behind iron gates, next to the Notre-Dame de Québec cathedral, lies a tranquil courtyard surrounded by austere stone buildings with rising steeples, structures that have housed classrooms and student residences since 1663. François de Montmorency Laval, the first bishop of New France, founded the Québec Seminary to train priests in the new colony. In 1852 the seminary gave birth to Université Laval, the first francophone university in North America.

Québec City's Best Walking Tours

Ghost Tours of Québec. Costumed actors lead ghoulish 90-minute evening tours of Québec City murders, executions, and ghost sightings. The tours are available in English or French, from May through October. After the walk, you can buy a copy of *Ghost Stories of Québec*, which has stories not told on the tours. ✉ *34 boul. Champlain, Lower Town* ☎ *855/692–9770* ⊕ *ghosttoursofquebec. com* ⚎ *Starting at C$25.*

Tours Voir Québec. This tour company offers English- and French-language (and Spanish from June to September) walking tours of the Old City. Other tours include a "Bury Your Dead" murder mystery tour based on the novels of Louise Penny, as well as a popular food tour with tastings at various establishments for C$55. Self-guided audio tours are also available. ✉ *12 rue Ste-Anne, Upper Town* ☎ *418/694–2001* ⊕ *www.toursvoirquebec. com* ⚎ *Starting at C$28.*

Today priests still live on the premises, and Québec City's architecture school occupies part of the building. The small Second Empire–style Chapelle Extérieure, at the west entrance of the seminary, was built in 1888 after fire destroyed the 1750 original; its interior is patterned after that of the Église de la Trinité in Paris. ✉ *1 côte de la Fabrique, Upper Town* ⊗ *Closed weekends.*

St-Louis Forts and Châteaux National Historic Site

RUINS | Venture under the Terrasse Dufferin to see archaeological treasures from the official residence and power base of the French and British governors. Massive excavations unearthed artifacts from the first château, built under the direction of Governor Montmagny, to the time the Château St-Louis burned in 1834. Wine bottles, kitchenware—even remains of walls and doorframes—give clues to the luxurious life of the governors, who were among the most powerful men in the nation. Don't miss the guided tours and activities. History buffs might consider attending one of the in-depth archaeology conferences held here. ✉ *Terrasse Dufferin, Upper Town* ☎ *418/648–7016* ⊕ *pc.gc.ca/en/lhn-nhs/qc/saintlouisforts* ⚎ *C$11.25* ⊗ *Closed mid-Oct.–late May.*

★ Terrasse Dufferin

VIEWPOINT | This wide boardwalk with an intricate wrought-iron guardrail has a panoramic view of the St. Lawrence River, the city of Lévis on the opposite shore, Île d'Orléans, the Laurentian Mountains to the north, and the edge of the Appalachians to the south. There are 90-minute tours of the fortifications that leave from here. The Promenade des Gouverneurs begins at the boardwalk's western end; the path skirts the cliff and leads up to Québec's highest point, Cap Diamant, and also to La Citadelle. ✉ *Upper Town.*

Ursuline Chapel

CHURCH | Founded in 1639, the chapel and its Couvent des Ursulines is the oldest institution of learning for women in North America. It houses the finest examples of wood carving anywhere in Québec, gilded by the nuns themselves. The exterior of the Ursuline Chapel was rebuilt in 1902, but the interior contains the original chapel, which took sculptor Pierre-Noël Levasseur from 1726 to 1736 to complete. Following beautification work, the Ursuline Chapel is now reopened to visitors. ✉ *12 rue Donnacona, Upper Town* ☎ *418/694–0694* ⊕ *polecultureldesursulines.ca/en* ⊗ *Closed weekdays Nov.–Apr.*

Wolfe-Montcalm Monument

MONUMENT | Surrounded by a leafy, small park right next to the Château Frontenac, this 50-foot-tall obelisk pays tribute to both a winning (English) and a losing (French) general. More specifically, it marks the place where the British general James Wolfe and French marquis Louis-Joseph Montcalm died during the Battle of Québec in September 1759. Wolfe landed his troops about 3 km (2 miles) from the city's walls; 4,500 English soldiers scaled the cliff and began fighting on the Plains of Abraham. Wolfe was mortally wounded in battle and was carried behind the lines to this spot. Montcalm, who had been famous for winning four major battles in North America, was also fatally injured; he was carried into the walled city, where he died the next morning, essentially marking the end of the French regime in Québec City.

On the south side of the park is avenue Ste-Geneviève, lined with well-preserved Victorian houses dating from 1850 to 1900. Many have been converted to inns, B&Bs, and hotels. ✉ *rue des Carrières, Montcalm.*

Restaurants

In addition to quick to-go *boulangeries* (bakeries), cafés, and diners, Upper Town also has its share of legendary white-tablecloth restaurants (albeit more popular with tourists than locals) known for market-fresh ingredients and legions of creative chefs and sommeliers.

Alphonse

$$$ | MODERN CANADIAN | This sun-drenched, open-space corner bistro, complete with black and dark wood accents for a profoundly Parisian flair, serves local fare in a relaxed yet refined atmosphere. From game meat and seafood (try the gin-sauce scallops) to fresh pasta and revisited classics (try the Brussels sprouts Caesar), along with a string of vegan options, Alphonse certainly aims to please. **Known for:** vegan menu; wonderful cocktails; beautiful space. $ *Average main: C$28* ✉ *19 rue des Jardins, Upper Town* ☎ *418/694–0707* ⊕ *alphonse.ca.*

Aux Anciens Canadiens

$$$ | CANADIAN | Named for a 19th-century book by Philippe-Aubert de Gaspé, who once resided in the 1675 house, this establishment has a modern menu and a good wine list, but most people come for the authentic French Canadian cooking. Servers are dressed in period costume and each of the five dining rooms has a different theme, such as the bright and cheerful *vaisselier* (dish room), featuring colorful antique dishes and a fireplace. **Known for:** tourtière (meat pie); maple pie; historical setting. $ *Average main: C$29* ✉ *34 rue St-Louis, Upper Town* ☎ *418/692–1627* ⊕ *auxancienscanadiens. qc.ca.*

Café-Boulangerie Paillard

$ | BAKERY | FAMILY | This bakery, pastry counter, sandwich bar, pizza shop, and ice-cream parlor is a long-standing local favorite. Long wooden tables, designed to get customers talking to each other, create a convivial atmosphere. **Known for:** efficient service; communal tables; delicious sandwiches and pastries. $ *Average main: C$10* ✉ *1097 rue St-Jean, Upper Town* ☎ *418/692–1221* ⊕ *paillard. ca.*

Catherine Méra Pâtisserie

$$ | BAKERY | This women-owned bakery across the street from Québec City Town Hall serves some of the best French macarons this side of the pond. In addition, every single one of Catherine's pastries is a delicate experience combining refined flavors and architectural marvel— try the swan-shaped *religieuse* pastry or the passionfruit mille-feuille. **Known for:** Ducasse scholar; high-end pâtisseries at low prices; creative, locally-inspired flavors. $ *Average main: C$15* ✉ *40 côte de la Fabrique, Upper Town* ☎ *581/986–1907* ⊕ *catherinemera.com.*

★ Chez Boulay

$$$$ | CANADIAN | Chefs Jean-Luc Boulay and Arnaud Marchand, who are both revered in this town, delight patrons with elegant interpretations of cuisine inspired by northern Québec and made entirely from local ingredients, including reinvented classic desserts, such as iced nougat with cloudberries. A mix of locals celebrating special occasions and tourists fresh from shopping rue St-Jean dine in this elegant dining room on bison tartare, braised beef ravioli with candied red cabbage, and salmon in a flavorful cranberry glaze. **Known for:** signature brunch on weekends; excellent wine list; vegetarian menu. ⑤ *Average main: C$35 ⊠ 1110 rue St-Jean, Upper Town ☎ 418/380–8166 ⊕ chezboulay.com ⊘ Closed Mon. No lunch Tues. and Wed. Brunch only on Sun.*

★ Le Champlain

$$$$ | MODERN CANADIAN | Inside the most romantic dining room at Fairmont Le Château Frontenac is one of the city's top gastronomical tables, showcasing three distinct tasting menus comprising Nordic-inspired ingredients and whimsical presentations. Although service can be a bit stiff, the food is anything but, and the rewards on the plate are definitely worth any formality. **Known for:** creative gastronomy; landmark building; vegetarian tasting menu. ⑤ *Average main: C$119 ⊠ Fairmont Le Château Frontenac, 1 rue des Carrières, Upper Town ☎ 418/692–3861 ⊕ fairmont.com/frontenac-quebec/dining/champlain ⊘ Closed Mon. No dinner Sun.*

Le Chic Shack

$ | FAST FOOD | FAMILY | At this refreshing alternative to the Old City's ubiquitous white-linen bistros, you can get fast food that's also high quality. Burgers made from grass-fed cattle served on soft artisanal brioche buns make this a prime locale for lunch goers. **Known for:** great burgers; quality fast food; delicious milkshakes. ⑤ *Average main: C$11 ⊠ 15 rue du Fort, Upper Town ☎ 418/692–1485 ⊕ lechicshack.ca.*

Poutine Stop

As far as fast food goes, nothing is more Québécois than poutine, that rough-and-ready dish made of fries, cheese curds, and gravy. In Québec City, regional chain Chez Ashton, founded in 1969, is the local favorite for hurried lunchers and late-night snackers. Also well worth trying here is a hot-dog *du lac*, a "steamie" (steamed hot dog) with mayo, cabbage, and a few fries on top. ⊠ *54 côte du Palais ⊕ chezashton.ca.*

Le Clan

$$$$ | MODERN CANADIAN | The premise already has foodies salivating: "anthropomorphic universe" of local and organic cuisine. Chef Stéphane Modat, whose fame on this side of the pond is largely due to his masterful time in the kitchen of the Fairmont Le Château Frontenac, surrounds himself with precious collaborators (the name of the restaurant, "the clan," is by no means a coincidence) and brings his characterful verve to boreal gastronomy. **Known for:** local organic cuisine; French savoir faire; C$189 tasting menu. ⑤ *Average main: C$40 ⊠ 44 rue des Jardins, Upper Town ☎ 418/692–0333 ⊕ restaurantleclan.com ⊘ No lunch Mon. and Tues.*

Le Continental

$$$$ | EUROPEAN | If Québec City had a dining hall of fame, Le Continental would be there among the best. Since 1956 this historic spot, steps from the Château Frontenac, has been serving solid, traditionally gourmet dishes, such as tableside-prepared orange duckling and filet mignon, which is flambéed in a cognac sauce and then luxuriously covered in a gravy seasoned with mustard and sage. **Known for:** classic gastronomy; tableside

"guéridon" service; old-school excellence. $ *Average main: C$60 ⊠ 26 rue St-Louis, Upper Town* ☎ *418/694–9995* ⊕ *restaurantlecontinental.com* ⊗ *No lunch.*

L'Entrecôte St-Jean

$$$ | FRENCH | Steak frites (steak with fries) is on menus everywhere in Québec City and in lots of other places throughout the world, but this popular and lively establishment has a 30-year reputation as the master of the dish—*l' entrecôte* is a particular sirloin cut, usually long and relatively thin. Diners choose between three steak sizes, and each comes smothered in the restaurant's signature peppery sauce with a heaping pile of crispy fries. **Known for:** steak frites and signature sauce; simple and well-executed menu; great patio. $ *Average main: C$27 ⊠ 1080 rue St-Jean, Upper Town* ☎ *418/694–0234* ⊕ *www.entrecotesaint-jean.com* ⊗ *No lunch Sun. and Mon.*

Le Parlementaire

$$$ | MODERN CANADIAN | Despite its magnificent Beaux-Arts interior and its reasonable prices, the National Assembly's restaurant remains one of the best-kept secrets in town. Chef Martin Gagné prepares contemporary cuisine with products from Québec's various regions, such as mini fondues made with Charlevoix cheese, ravioli made from lobster caught in the Gaspé, pork from the Beauce region, trout from the Magdalen Islands, or candied-duck salad. **Known for:** elegant, historic décor; tasty regional dishes; lunch only. $ *Average main: C$30 ⊠ Hôtel du Parlement, 1045 rue des Parlementaires, Upper Town* ☎ *418/643–6640* ⊕ *assnat.qc.ca/fr/visi-teurs/restaurants/index.html* ⊗ *Closed weekends. No dinner.*

Le St-Amour

$$$$ | FRENCH | At one of the city's most romantic and treasured restaurants, chef Jean-Luc Boulay entices diners with such creations as the Foie Gras Experience (with five variations of this French delicacy) and arctic char with buttermilk sauce and lemon vervain oil. For dessert, try the seasonal hazelnut chocolate crème brûlée. **Known for:** foie gras; curated wine list; art nouveau–inspired décor. $ *Average main: C$50 ⊠ 48 rue Ste-Ursule, Upper Town* ☎ *418/694–0667* ⊕ *saint-amour.com* ⊗ *Closed Sun.–Tues. No lunch.*

★ Sagamité

$$$$ | CANADIAN | Sagamité restaurant offers an authentic Indigenous dining experience. Explore the rich flavors of First Nations cuisine, featuring hearty dishes like elk terrine and smoked bison ravioli. $ *Average main: C$50 ⊠ 68 rue St-Louis, Upper Town* ☎ *581/491–6999* ⊕ *sagamite.com/en/succursales/sagamite-vieux-quebec.*

Sapristi

$$ | ITALIAN | FAMILY | The menu at this Italian-leaning restaurant with a laid-back, industrial-cool feel is satisfying, with a number of imaginative pizzas, pastas, salads, and such. Try the fried mozzarella or the chef's risotto, which changes daily. **Known for:** creative pizzas; great patio; gluten-free options. $ *Average main: C$18 ⊠ 1001 rue St-Jean, Upper Town* ☎ *418/692–2030* ⊕ *sapristi.ca.*

Hotels

Upper Town, inside the Old City's walls, is famous for its accommodations in historic buildings, decorated with antique furnishings and heavy fabrics. Few have restaurants, but there are lots of places to eat nearby.

Auberge Place d'Armes

$$$ | B&B/INN | Old Québec charm meets modern convenience at this property near the Château Frontenac, which attracts a mix of couples and business-people staying on expense accounts. **Pros:** central location; comfortable, well-equipped rooms; good restaurant, Chez Jules, on premises. **Cons:** no elevator means working off breakfast on the stairs; traditional furniture may not be for everyone; no on-site parking. $ *Rooms from: C$235* ✉ *24 rue Ste-Anne, Upper Town* ☎ *418/694–9485* ⊕ *auberge-placedarmes.com* ⇱ *33 rooms* ⦿ *Free Breakfast.*

★ Fairmont Le Château Frontenac

$$$$ | HOTEL | In this landmark building, perked up with some sleek and well-integrated modern touches, the public rooms—from the cozy and elegant Bar 1608 to the 700-seat ballroom reminiscent of the Hall of Mirrors at Versailles—are all opulent; guest rooms are just as elegantly furnished, like mini châteaux, with cream, gold, and green touches. **Pros:** top historic attraction; river views; Le Labo toiletries. **Cons:** busy lobby; rooms are small for the price; some guest rooms inferior to Deluxe category are not renovated. $ *Rooms from: C$259* ✉ *1 rue des Carrières, Upper Town* ☎ *418/692–3861* ⊕ *fairmont.com/frontenac-quebec* ⇱ *648 rooms* ⦿ *No Meals.*

Hilton Québec

$$ | HOTEL | Next to Parliament Hill, this hotel may be all business (as in, it caters primarily to a corporate clientele) but it has chic and contemporary rooms with views of Vieux-Québec or the Laurentian Mountains to the north. **Pros:** direct access to the convention center; amazing executive lounge; great city views. **Cons:** blocky exterior; can be businesslike; lacks Old Québec charm. $ *Rooms from: C$199* ✉ *1100 boul. René-Lévesque Est, Upper Town* ☎ *800/447–2411* ⊕ *hilton-quebec.com* ⇱ *571 rooms* ⦿ *No Meals.*

Hôtel Cap Diamant

$$ | B&B/INN | An eclectic collection of vintage furniture and ecclesiastical accents—stained glass from a church, a confessional door, an angel or two—complement the decorative marble fireplaces, stone walls, and hardwood floors at this hotel. **Pros:** Victorian style and charm; a four-season veranda; some rooms have private balconies. **Cons:** stairs to third-floor rooms are a bit steep;

poor soundproofing; outdated furniture. $ *Rooms from: C$190* ✉ *39 av. Ste-Geneviève, Upper Town* ☎ *888/694–0313* ⊕ *hotelcapdiamant.com* ⇱ *12 rooms* ⦿ *Free Breakfast.*

Hôtel Château Bellevue

$$ | HOTEL | Behind the Château Frontenac, facing a pleasant park, this 1898 hotel occupies four heritage houses with the same green roofing and offers modern rooms with standard hotel furnishings in a good location, often with views of the St. Lawrence River. **Pros:** distinctive package deals; river views; good continental breakfast. **Cons:** décor can be eclectic; no pool or spa; poor soundproofing. $ *Rooms from: C$199* ✉ *16 rue de la Porte, Upper Town* ☎ *800/463–2617* ⊕ *hoteloldquebec.com* ⇱ *49 rooms* ⦿ *Free Breakfast.*

Hôtel Clarendon

$$ | HOTEL | This is the oldest operating hotel in Québec City; half of its rooms have excellent views over Old Québec, and the others overlook a courtyard. **Pros:** the piano in the lounge attracts merrymakers; valet service; some rooms have Old Québec views. **Cons:** décor can feel a bit bare; some rooms feel dark and small; rooms on the lower floors can be noisy. $ *Rooms from: C$164* ✉ *57 rue Ste-Anne, Upper Town* ☎ *888/554–6001* ⊕ *hotelclarendon.com* ⇱ *143 rooms* ⦿ *No Meals.*

Hôtel du Vieux-Québec

$$ | HOTEL | Nicely situated at the end of rue St-Jean, surrounded by stores and restaurants, this eco-friendly spot has rooms spread over three floors, including a suite with a king bed and huge flat-screen television, and a "superior room" with two queen beds and an exposed brick wall. **Pros:** amazing staff; lively location; carbon neutral. **Cons:** can be noisy; off-site parking; dim lighting. $ *Rooms from: C$180* ✉ *1190 rue St-Jean, Upper Town* ☎ *800/361–7787* ⊕ *hvq.com* ⇱ *45 rooms* ⦿ *No Meals.*

Hôtel Manoir Victoria

$$ | **HOTEL** | The recent renovations at this European-style hotel, with a discreet entrance on côte du Palais, include elegantly simple rooms with hardwood furnishings and white bedding. **Pros:** great location; indoor parking; heated bathroom floors. **Cons:** lobby can get busy with restaurant or convention crowds; lots of stairs at the entrance; not the best cleaning service. ⑤ *Rooms from: C$175* ⊠ *44 côte du Palais, Upper Town* ☎ *800/463–6283* ⊕ *manoir-victoria.com* ⮟ *156 rooms* �‹❍❚ *No Meals.*

Hôtel Marie Rollet

$ | **B&B/INN** | Located on a charming street corner at the heart of Vieux-Québec, this intimate inn built in 1876 by the Ursuline order has quaint décor and antiques and sometimes small but warm rooms, some with exposed brick. **Pros:** central location; rooftop terrace with garden view; free coffee in the morning. **Cons:** no elevator; steep stairs; very small bathrooms. ⑤ *Rooms from: C$129* ⊠ *81 rue Ste-Anne, Upper Town* ☎ *800/275–0338* ⊕ *hotelmarierollet.com* ⮟ *11 rooms* ❚❍❚ *No Meals.*

Hôtel Nomad

$ | **HOTEL** | At Hôtel Nomad, each of the six rooms has a story to tell and a personality all of its own. **Pros:** spa-and-meals packages available; charming, design-oriented rooms; great views of Old Québec landmarks. **Cons:** limited amenities in rooms; some rooms are tiny; no elevator. ⑤ *Rooms from: C$100* ⊠ *15 av. Ste-Geneviève, Upper Town* ☎ *418/694–1884* ⊕ *hotelnomad.ca* ⮟ *6 rooms* ❚❍❚ *No Meals.*

★ Le Capitole Hôtel

$$$$ | **HOTEL** | Freshly renovated, this turn-of-the-20th-century structure just outside the St-Jean Gate and the fortifications is a fancy hotel, dining destination, and 1920s cabaret-style dinner theater (the Théâtre Capitole) all rolled into one. **Pros:** luxurious bedding; rooftop garden with views; rain shower. **Cons:** theater-hotel complex not very peaceful; limited room service; some rooms are small. ⑤ *Rooms from: C$300* ⊠ *972 rue St-Jean, Upper Town* ☎ *800/363–4040* ⊕ *lecapitole.com* ⮟ *39 rooms, 1 suite* ❚❍❚ *No Meals.*

★ Le Monastère des Augustines

$ | **B&B/INN** | Stay in a 17th-century monastery—and the birthplace of the first hospital in North America—that's been transformed into a contemporary holistic retreat. **Pros:** historical building; modern, design-oriented rooms; free access to museum. **Cons:** mum's the word at this silent retreat; not the best staff; en suites in contemporary rooms only. ⑤ *Rooms from: C$95* ⊠ *77 rue des Remparts, Upper Town* ☎ *844/694–1639* ⊕ *monastere.ca* ⮟ *65 rooms* ❚❍❚ *Free Breakfast.*

Monsieur Jean

$$$$ | **HOTEL** | Quirky and whimsical, close to all the historical and culinary attractions of Old Québec, Monsieur Jean's suites will appeal to travelers who love Louis XIV luxury in its most contemporary expression. **Pros:** central location; impeccably appointed rooms; excellent views from rooms. **Cons:** front desk not always open; parking is expensive; street can get busy. ⑤ *Rooms from: C$300* ⊠ *2 rue Pierre-Olivier-Chauveau, Upper Town* ☎ *418/977–7777* ⊕ *monsieurjean.ca* ⮟ *49 rooms* ❚❍❚ *No Meals.*

Québec City Marriott Downtown

$$ | **HOTEL** | This former bank building exudes a quiet elegance, with modern guest rooms with wood furniture and stained-glass windows, two fireplaces, and a tiny wood-lined corner bar in the lobby. **Pros:** 24/7 fitness center; helpful staff; central location. **Cons:** lacks Old Québec charm; rooms are not sound-proofed; street can be busy. ⑤ *Rooms from: C$199* ⊠ *850 pl. d'Youville, Upper Town* ☎ *866/694–4004* ⊕ *marriott.com* ⮟ *111 rooms* ❚❍❚ *No Meals.*

Nightlife

BARS AND LOUNGES

★ Bar 1608

COCKTAIL BARS | One of the city's most romantic spots is the Fairmont Le Château Frontenac's bar, which boasts the most interesting cocktail menu in town. You can also have some wine or a bit of charcuterie and cheese, and relax while looking at the St. Lawrence River or the two fireplaces. ⊠ *Fairmont Le Château Frontenac, 1 rue des Carrières, Upper Town* ☎ *418/266–3906* ⊕ *fairmont.com/frontenac-quebec.*

BREWPUBS

Le Pub St-Alexandre

BREWPUBS | This popular English-style pub offers dozens of single-malt Scotch options and more than 200 kinds of beer, 30 of which are on tap, and many of which are exclusive imports. There is also live music on most nights. ⊠ *1087 rue St-Jean, Upper Town* ☎ *418/694–0015* ⊕ *pubstalexandre.com.*

Performing Arts

Art is everywhere in Québec City—from theater and chic galleries to accordion-playing street performers and statue mimes in the parks. From September through May, a steady stream of concerts, plays, and performances is presented in theaters and halls. In summer, many indoor theaters close, and outdoor shows of all kinds appear, most of them free.

Le Diamant

PERFORMANCE VENUES | Le Diamant is a multidisciplinary space that welcomes the world's most prestigious contemporary creations to its strikingly modern stage in the heart of Old Québec. It is also the home of EX MACHINA, the production company of Robert Lepage, director and author known worldwide for his large-scale projects (including the *Image Mill*, the largest architectural projection ever created). At Le Diamant, dance, theater, and opera productions are enhanced by new technologies, continuously pushing the limits of the imagination. ⊠ *966 rue St-Jean, Upper Town* ☎ *418/692–5353* ⊕ *lediamant.ca.*

★ Orchestre Symphonique de Québec

(*Québec Symphony Orchestra*)
MUSIC | Canada's oldest symphony orchestra, directed by the dynamic German conductor Clemens Schuldt, performs mainly at Louis-Fréchette Hall in the Grand Théâtre de Québec. Expect some of the most acclaimed classical works, but also fun surprises like hip-hop renditions and movie scores. ⊠ *269 boul. René-Lévesque Est, St-Jean-Baptiste* ☎ *418/643–8486* ⊕ *osq.org* 🎫 *From C$45.*

Théâtre Capitole

MUSIC | This cabaret-style theater schedules pop music and musical comedy shows by the most famous French-speaking artists in Québec. ⊠ *972 rue St-Jean, Upper Town* ☎ *418/694–4444* ⊕ *lecapitole.com.*

WINTER CARNIVAL

For two weekends in February, Québec City throws one of the biggest winter parties in the world. Each year, an Ice Palace is built as the center of the festivities, which include dog sled races, two parades, and events on several city streets. Ice bars are plentiful on the Grande Allée, and the streets fill with families and visitors singing songs and blowing into trumpets.

★ Carnaval de Québec

FESTIVALS | FAMILY | A flurry of activity, mainly on the Plains of Abraham but also on several of the city's main drags, surrounds Carnaval de Québec, which occurs over two weekends every February. Snow- and ice-sculpture contests, dog sled relays, and canoe races on the icy St. Lawrence River chase away winter doldrums. Visitors brave the cold to get a glimpse of Bonhomme, the friendly

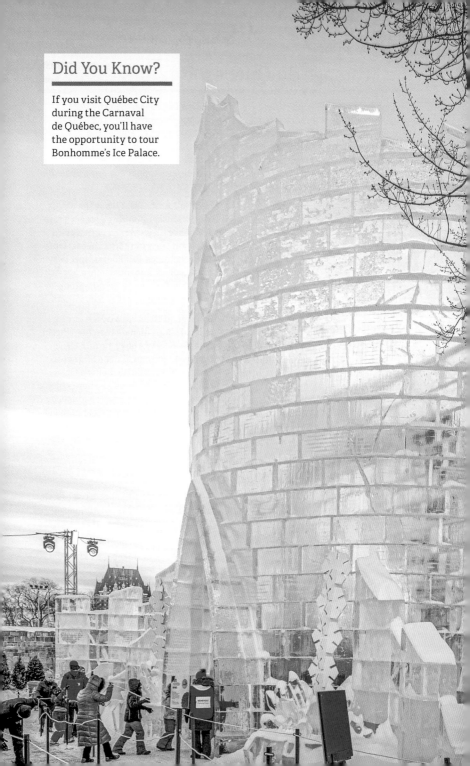

Did You Know?

If you visit Québec City during the Carnaval de Québec, you'll have the opportunity to tour Bonhomme's Ice Palace.

Le Fromage du Québec

It used to be that all good cheese in Québec City was imported from France—not anymore. During the last several decades there's been an impressive and still-growing cheese movement in La Belle Province. Regional cheese makers long produced award-winning aged cheddar, but that's been joined by a wealth of specialty cheeses, including *lait cru* (unpasteurized) cheeses that you'll want to sample before going home. There are more than 400 original varieties made here.

Luckily, there are enough cheese shops to keep you cheese-shop-hopping all afternoon. Smile, and say "fromage"!

Aux Petits Délices. In the market at Les Halles du Petit Quartier, Aux Petits Délices has a large selection of specialty cheeses, along with crackers, charcuterie, and condiments for a picnic on the Plains. ⊠ *1191 av. Cartier, Montcalm* ☎ *418/522–5154.*

Épicerie Européenne. Stop by the Épicerie Européenne in the St-Jean-Baptiste quarter, and let the knowledgeable consultants help you choose from their excellent selection of cheeses. ⊠ *560 rue St-Jean, St-Jean-Baptiste* ☎ *418/529–4847.*

Épicerie J.A. Moisan. This is the oldest continuously operating grocery store in Québec City, stocked with a great selection of charcuterie, cheese, fruit and vegetables, local beers, specialty sodas, spices, and much more. ⊠ *699 rue St-Jean, St-Jean-Baptiste* ☎ *418/522–0685.*

Some good cheeses to watch out for at local shops include Bleu Bénédictin from St-Benoît Abbey, Île aux-Grues four-year-old cheddar, Le Migneron de Charlevoix, and Le Louis d'Or, made in Central Québec. There's also a *chèvre noire*, a raw, goat "cheddar" by Fromagerie Tournevent—wrapped in black wax—that's not to be missed. If Gouda is your thing, try a piece from Fromagerie Bergeron.

carnival master, and tour his Ice Palace, which is rebuilt each year. Caribou, a strong mixture of red wine, hard liquor, and maple syrup, is a popular libation during the festivities. ⊠ *Québec City* ⊕ *carnaval.qc.ca.*

🛍 Shopping

ART GALLERIES

★ Galerie Art Inuit Brousseau

ART GALLERY | Inuit art is the specialty of this large, well-known gallery. The gallery director, Jean-Francois Brousseau, selects works by artists represented by the North Canadian Inuit cooperatives, and the gallery receives much praise for improving life in the Canadian

Arctic. ⊠ *35 rue St-Louis, Upper Town* ☎ *418/694–1828* ⊕ *artinuitbrousseau.ca.*

CLOTHING

Ça Va de Soi

CLOTHING | "Montréal-based knitwear"— the raison d'être alone evokes a feeling of respect for the material and the kind of luxury that's usually reserved for products crafted with great care. Founded in 1991 by Odile and Antoine Nasri with the desire to democratize access to slow fashion and responsibly produced clothing, Ça Va de Soi is a ready-to-wear boutique focused on natural fibers. Sweaters, scarves, socks, and all the essentials of snow fashion are there. ⊠ *1154 rue*

St-Jean, Upper Town ☎ 418/692–0077 ⊕ cavadesoi.com ⊗ Closed weekends.

GIFTS AND SOUVENIRS

★ Artisans Canada

SOUVENIRS | The Racine family has been operating a family boutique on this site since 1946, formerly of handmade furniture, now of objects by more than 200 nearby artisans. The current owners, Sara and Thomas, handpick their collaborators with great care and sell clothing, jewelry, leather goods, skin care products, and home décor in a historic building in Old Québec. ☒ 30 côte de la Fabrique, Upper Town ☎ 418/692–2109 ⊕ artisanscanada. com.

DEPARTMENT STORES

La Maison Simons

DEPARTMENT STORE | This growing Canadian chain store started here in Québec City in the 19th century and is still owned by its founding family. The store carries affordable women's and men's wear, designer brands, linens, and other household items. ☒ 20 côte de la Fabrique, Upper Town ☎ 418/692–3630 ⊕ simons.ca.

 Activities

ICE-SKATING

Ice-skating in Québec City is a popular pastime for locals and visitors alike.

★ Place d'Youville

ICE-SKATING | FAMILY | This well-known outdoor rink, just outside St-Jean Gate, is open daily November through the end of March, from noon to 10. ☒ Upper Town 🛒 Skate rental for 2 hours is C$9 per person or C$26 for a family (2 adults, 2 kids).

Plains of Abraham

ICE-SKATING | FAMILY | The sports field at the western end of Battlefields Park features a large, 350-meter-long skating rink open from December to March, complete with music and fire pits. ☒ Terrain des Sports, 255 Grande Allée Ouest,

Montcalm 🛒 Skate rental for 2 hours is C$9 per person or C$26 for a family (2 adults, 2 kids).

SKIING

Plains of Abraham

SKIING & SNOWBOARDING | FAMILY | This park is a must for winter sports. In addition to its ice-skating facilities, it also has 10 km (6 miles) of marked and groomed cross-country ski trails for beginner, intermediate, and expert skiers. There are also trails for snowshoeing. Moreover, skis and snowshoes can be rented at the Plains of Abraham Museum, on the northeast side of the park. ☒ Montcalm.

SNOW SLIDES

★ Glissade de la Terrasse

SNOW SPORTS | FAMILY | This snow slide on Dufferin Terrace is easily one of the most exciting winter activities in Québec City. A wooden toboggan takes you down a 270-foot-high snow slide that's adjacent to the Château Frontenac at 43 miles per hour. The slide is open every day, December to March. ☒ Terrasse Dufferin, Upper Town ☎ 418/528-1884 ⊕ au1884.ca/en 🛒 Four rides C$12.

Lower Town

Seeing all the bustle and upscale commerce here, it's hard to imagine that 40 years ago, this area was run-down and looking for a new lease on life. Today, after exploring Place Royale and its cobblestoned streets, you can walk along the edge of the St. Lawrence River and watch the sailboats and ships go by, shop at the market, or kick back on a terrasse (patio) with a local craft beer. Rue du Petit-Champlain also has charming places to stop and listen to street musicians, and the scene near the Old Port starts buzzing as soon as the sun goes down.

If there's a cradle of French civilization in North America, you're standing in it when you visit Lower Town. In 1608, Champlain

Lower Town

TO SAINT-ROCH

TO VIA RAIL
CANADA STATION

Marché du
Vieux-Port

Bassin
Louise

UPPER TOWN

Parc de
l'Artillerie

Place de
l'Hôtel-de-Ville

Couvent des
Ursulines

Séminaire
du Québec

Antiques
District

Notre-Dame
de Québec
Basilica-Cathedral

Parc
Montmorency

Escalier
Frontenac

Fairmont
Le Château
Frontenac

Funicular

Musée de la
Civilisation

VIEUX PORT

Musée Naval
de Québec

Lock

Agora
Port de
Québec

Le Terminal-
Port of Québec

Place des
Canotiers

LOWER TOWN

Promenade de la Pointe-à-Carcy

Terrasse Dufferin

QUARTIER
PETIT-
CHAMPLAIN

St. Lawrence River

TO LÉVIS

0   1/8 mile
0   200 meters

KEY

🔴	Sights
🔴	Restaurants
🔴	Hotels
⛴	Ferry
⊢⊢⊢	Rail Line
—	Ramparts
🛈	Tourist Information

Sights ▼

1 Église Notre-Dame-
   des-Victoires **C6**
2 L'Escalier Casse-Cou ... **B6**
3 Maison Chevalier **B6**
4 Musée de la
   Civilisation **D5**
5 Place des Canotiers **D6**
6 Place Royale **C6**
7 Rue du Petit-
   Champlain **A6**

Restaurants ▼

1 Bistro L'Orygine **C6**
2 Buffet de L'Antiquaire .. **C4**
3 Café La Maison Smith ... **C5**
4 Café Le Packwood **C3**
5 Chez Muffy **C5**
6 Chez Rioux &
   Pettigrew **C3**
7 La Tanière **C6**
8 Laurie Raphaël **D4**
9 Le Café du Monde **E5**
10 Le Cochon Dingue **B6**
11 L'Échaudé **D4**
12 Légende **B2**

Hotels ▼

1 Auberge St-Antoine **C5**
2 Hôtel des Coutellier **B2**
3 Hôtel Le Germain
   Québec **D4**
4 Hôtel Le Priori **C5**
5 Hôtel Le St-Paul **C2**
6 Hôtel 71 .... **C5**
7 Lofts Vieux-Québec **D5**

chose this narrow, U-shaped spit of land sandwiched between the frigid waters of the St. Lawrence River and the craggy heights of Cap Diamant as the site for his settlement. Champlain later abandoned the fortified *habitation* (residence) at the foot of Cap Diamant and relocated to the more easily defendable Upper Town.

Nevertheless, the area continued to flourish as a bustling port and trading center for French merchants, fur traders, and *coureurs des bois* (woodsmen) and France's Native American allies. It was also the base from which dozens of military campaigns and fact-finding missions were launched into the heart of the continent. A bust of France's Sun King, Louis XIV, was erected in the main square, Place du Marché, which was renamed Place Royale in 1686. Destroyed by British cannons that were set up on the opposite shore during the siege of 1759, the port and buildings were rebuilt by the British, and the area quickly regained its role as Canada's leading commercial and business center.

Lower Town went into an economic tailspin in the late 1800s, becoming a slum whose narrow streets were lined with pawnshops, rough-and-tumble taverns, and smoky brothels that catered to sailors and lumberjacks. This lasted until the 1960s, when it received a multimillion-dollar face-lift that remade it into a sanitized version of its 1700s self. Today, once-dilapidated houses and warehouses contain busy boutique hotels, stylish shops, art galleries, and popular restaurants and bars. Lower Town, home to approximately 850 people, is bounded by the Dufferin-Montmorency Highway to the west, the St. Charles River to the north, the St. Lawrence River to the east, and Petit Champlain shopping area to the south.

GETTING HERE AND AROUND
Because Lower Town is the oldest part of the city, many prefer to see it first to get a sense of how the city developed

chronologically. If coming from Upper Town, head down L'Escalier Casse-Cou, a stairway steep enough to earn that name, which means "Breakneck Stairs." Have your camera ready; you'll get that quintessential Petit Champlain photo at the top of the staircase.

TIMING
You'll need one full day to see the area surrounding two of the city's most famous squares, Place Royale and Place de Paris. Pause for lunch before touring the Musée de la Civilisation and the antiques district.

 # Sights

★ **Église Notre-Dame-des-Victoires** (*Our Lady of Victory Church*)
CHURCH | Welcome to the oldest stone church in North America. The fortress shape of the altar is no accident; this small but beautiful stone church on Place Royale is linked to a bellicose past. Grateful French colonists named it in honor of the Virgin Mary, whom they credited with helping French forces defeat two British invasions: one in 1690 by Admiral William Phipps and the other by Sir Hovendon Walker in 1711. The church itself was built in 1688, making it the city's oldest—it has been restored twice since then. Several interesting paintings decorate the walls, and a model of *Le Brezé,* the boat that transported French soldiers to New France in 1664, hangs from the ceiling. The side chapel is dedicated to Ste-Geneviève, the patron saint of Paris. ✉ *32 rue Sous-le-Fort, Lower Town* ☎ *418/692–1650* ⊕ *notre-dame-de-que-bec.org* 🎫 *Guided tours C$5* 🕙 *Closed Mon.–Sat.*

★ **L'Escalier Casse-Cou**
VIEWPOINT | This is often regarded as one of the most iconic attractions in the Old City due to its location and stunning views of the neighborhood. But the steepness of the city's first iron stairway, an ambitious 1893 design

by city architect and engineer Charles Baillairgé, is ample evidence of how it got its name: Breakneck Steps. No serious injuries have been reported on the stairs, despite their ominous name. Still, those 59 steps were quite an improvement on the original wooden stairway, built in the 17th century, that linked the Upper Town and Lower Town. ⊠ *Lower Town.*

Maison Chevalier

NOTABLE BUILDING | This graded stone house (which is actually three houses brought together) was built in 1752 for the shipowner Jean-Baptiste Chevalier. This location near the docks was popular with import-export merchants and, later, with innkeepers. The architecture is quintessential New France, with its mansards and scarlet roof. Although the building is not open to visitors, it's well worth a look from the outside. ⊠ *50 rue du Marché-Champlain, Lower Town.*

★ Musée de la Civilisation (*Museum of Civilization*)

HISTORY MUSEUM | **FAMILY** | Wedged between narrow streets at the foot of the cliff, this spacious museum with a striking limestone-and-glass façade was designed by architect Moshe Safdie to blend into the landscape. Its bell tower echoes the shape of the city's church steeples. A new exhibition, which will be on until 2030, plays witness to the narratives of 95,000 First Nations and Inuit women and men of Québec, as they reflect on history, embrace the present, and envision a hopeful future. The temporary exhibits here are also always worth a visit. ⊠ *85 rue Dalhousie, Lower Town* ☎ *866/710–8031* ⊕ *mcq.org* ☑ *C$19* ⊘ *Closed Mon.*

Place des Canotiers

CITY PARK | What used to be a vast parking lot across from the Musée de la Civilisation has been replaced by an elegant and modern park that provides great views of Upper Town and improves access to the river for locals who now linger and stroll here and also for the cruise ships that

A View from the Water

Crossing the St. Lawrence River on the Québec–Lévis Ferry will reward you with a striking view of the Québec City skyline, with the Château Frontenac in plain view, which is even more impressive at night. Ferries generally run every 20 or 30 minutes from 6 am until 6 pm, and then every hour until 2:20 am; there are additional ferries from April through November. ⊠ *10 rue des Traversiers, 1 block south of pl. de Paris* ⊕ *traversiers.com* ☑ *C$3.95 each way (pedestrians, cyclists, car passengers).*

often moor here. Even the new multistory parking garage has been dressed up in an elegant wooden façade that gives the area extra character. ⊠ *Lower Town.*

★ Place Royale

PLAZA/SQUARE | Place Royale is where Samuel de Champlain founded the City of Québec in 1608; more than 400 years and several iterations later, this cobblestone square is still considered to be the cradle of French-speaking North America. Flanked on one side by the oldest stone church in North America, Église Notre-Dame-des-Victoires, and on the other by houses with steep Normandy-style roofs, dormer windows, and chimneys, once the homes of wealthy merchants, Place Royale is the epicenter of Old Québec. Until 1686 the area was called Place du Marché, but its name changed when a bust of Louis XIV was placed at its center. During the late 1600s and early 1700s, when Place Royale was continually under threat of British attack, the colonists moved progressively higher to safer quarters atop the cliff in Upper Town. After the French colony fell to British rule in 1759, Place Royale flourished again

One of Lower Town's top sights is the Place Royale, also one of the oldest public squares in the country.

with shipbuilding, logging, fishing, and fur trading. The *Fresque des Québécois,* a 4,665-square-foot trompe-l'oeil mural depicting 400 years of Québec's history, is to the east of the square, at the corner of rue Notre-Dame and côte de la Montagne. ⊠ *Lower Town.*

★ Rue du Petit-Champlain

NEIGHBORHOOD | Rue du Petit-Champlain, the oldest street in the city, was once the main thoroughfare of a harbor village, with trading posts and the homes of rich merchants. Today it has pleasant boutiques, art galleries, and cafés, and on summer days the street is packed with tourists. Natural-fiber weaving, Inuit carvings, hand-painted silks, local designers, and enameled copper crafts are among local specialties for sale here. If you're coming from Upper Town, take the Escalier Casse-Cou (Breakneck Steps) down, and the funicular back up (or round-trip): both deliver you to the start of this busy, unique street. ⊠ *Lower Town* ⊕ *quartier-petitchamplain.com.*

🍽 Restaurants

Lower Town has its fair share of renowned eateries, and you'll find some of the best terraces in town. Dine after the sun goes down under twinkling lights at L'Échaudé, discover the best of Québécois savoir faire with Laurie Raphaël's tasting menu, or for impeccable wines, go to L'Orygine.

Bistro L'Orygine

$$$ | MODERN CANADIAN | One hundred percent organic—that is the promise of L'Orygine, a brand-new bistro in the heart of the Lower Town. With an emphasis on freshness and local flavors, the chef prepares seasonal and shareable plates that are (almost) guilt-free, such as lobster cavatelli and a creative mix of duck and eggplant. **Known for:** vegetarian menu; vast patio; small plates to share. ⑤ *Average main: C$25* ⊠ *36 1/2 rue St-Pierre, Lower Town* ☎ *418/872–4386* ⊕ *lorygine.com* ⊘ *Closed Mon. No lunch. No dinner Sun.*

Did You Know?

You'll find some of the best buys on Inuit carvings, hand-painted silks, and enameled copper crafts on touristy rue du Petit-Champlain.

Buffet de L'Antiquaire

$$ | CANADIAN | Hearty home cooking, generous portions, and rock-bottom prices have made this no-frills, diner-style eatery in the heart of the antiques district a Lower Town institution. It's a good place to sample traditional Québécois dishes such as pea soup and *cipaille* (a deep-dish layered pie using poultry, meat, or seafood) and the homemade and delicious sugar pie, crepes, and other desserts. **Known for:** traditional dishes; gluten-free options; Québec City institution. ⑤ *Average main: C$15* ⊠ *95 rue St-Paul, Lower Town* ☎ *418/692–2661* ⊕ *lebuffetdelantiquaire.com.*

Café La Maison Smith

$ | CAFÉ | This casual and attractive café right on the corner of scenic Place Royale is a great place to stop for an afternoon pick-me-up, be it coffee or various indulgent sweets. For a light lunch, there are yummy sandwiches, quiches, and soups. **Known for:** outdoor seating; great sandwiches; coffee roasted on-site. ⑤ *Average main: C$9* ⊠ *23 rue Notre-Dame, Lower Town* ☎ *581/742–6777* ⊕ *smithcafe.com.*

Café Le Packwood

$ | CAFÉ | The Packwood is a charming, intimate café-boutique that hosts over 50 handpicked artisans from various regions of Québec. Set in a former general store, the café offers homemade sandwiches and salads at very affordable prices as well as excellent third-wave coffee. **Known for:** barista-grade espressos; cheerful, welcoming owner; atmospheric space filled with antiques. ⑤ *Average main: C$10* ⊠ *152 rue St-Paul, Lower Town* ☎ *418/694–3066* ⊕ *lepackwoodcafeetboutique.com* ☾ *Closed Mon. and Tues.*

Chez Muffy

$$$$ | MODERN CANADIAN | At this restaurant, inside the museum-like Auberge St-Antoine, dishes change with the seasons with fresh, locally sourced ingredients at the core of the exclusively prix-fixe menu set at C$32 for breakfast (two courses) and C$132 for dinner (four courses). The space has stone walls, attractive wooden floors, and exposed beams from the building's warehouse days in the early 1800s. **Known for:** historic setting; prix-fixe menu. ⑤ *Average main: C$120* ⊠ *10 rue St-Antoine, Lower Town* ☎ *418/692–1022* ⊕ *saint-antoine.com/chez-muffy* ☾ *No lunch.*

Chez Rioux & Pettigrew

$$$ | MODERN CANADIAN | This is the place to go for the freshest flavors of Canadian cuisine (think seafood, terroir vegetables, game meat) without the white-tablecloth fuss. Chez Rioux & Pettigrew is a casual dining experience in a convivial, inviting venue with exposed brick. **Known for:** local, seasonal ingredients; C$79 tasting menu; Sunday brunch. ⑤ *Average main: C$25* ⊠ *160 rue St-Paul, Lower Town* ☎ *418/694–4448* ⊕ *chezriouxetpettigrew.com* ☾ *No lunch. No dinner Sun.*

★ Laurie Raphaël

$$$$ | MODERN CANADIAN | Local and regional products are emphasized here, and the food is among the best gastronomical offerings in Québec. Among local celebrity chef Daniel Vézina's creations are crystallized foie gras with truffle snow, and venison tartare. **Known for:** high-end gastronomy; elegant setting; tasting menus. ⑤ *Average main: C$145* ⊠ *117 rue Dalhousie, Lower Town* ☎ *418/692–4555* ⊕ *laurieraphael.com* ☾ *Closed Sun. and Mon. No lunch.*

La Tanière

$$$ | MODERN CANADIAN | This superb "hidden" restaurant is located in the Old Port and opened in 1977. La Tanière is divided into three historic stone vaults, guaranteeing a cozy and intimate atmosphere. **Known for:** vaulted stone ceilings from the 1700s; mandatory tasting menu; chef's table experience. ⑤ *Average main: C$30* ⊠ *36 ½ rue St-Pierre, Lower Town* ☎ *418/872–4386* ⊕ *taniere3.com* ☾ *Closed Mon.–Wed. No lunch.*

Did You Know?

Many of the chairs found at cafés along the rue du Petit-Champlain are styled after those of famous cafés found in Paris.

Le Café du Monde

$$$ | BISTRO | Next to the cruise terminal in the Old Port, this massive, Parisian-bistro-style restaurant with etched-glass dividers and palm trees has a spectacular view. The outdoor terrace in front overlooks the St. Lawrence River, while the side *verrière* (glass atrium) looks onto l'Agora amphitheater and the old stone Customs House. **Known for:** lively scene; great views; delicious seafood. $ *Average main: C$30 ⊠ 84 rue Dalhousie, Suite 140, Lower Town* ☎ *418/692–4455* ⊕ *lecafedumonde.com* ⊗ *Closed Mon. and Tues. No dinner Sun.*

Le Cochon Dingue

$$ | CAFÉ | FAMILY | The café dishes at this cheerful chain, whose name translates into the Crazy Pig, include delicious tartares, steak with fries, hearty soups, a selection of international dishes like satays and "Général Dingue" chicken, as well as substantial desserts like sugar pie with vanilla cream. Sidewalk tables and indoor dining rooms artfully blend the chic and the antique; black-and-white checkerboard floors contrast with ancient stone walls. **Known for:** long lines; affordable bistro; good people-watching. $ *Average main: C$16 ⊠ 46 boul. Champlain, Lower Town* ☎ *418/692–2013* ⊕ *cochondingue.com* ⊗ *No dinner Tues. and Wed.*

★ L'Échaudé

$$$ | FRENCH | A mix of businesspeople and tourists having been frequenting L'Échaudé for the past 30 years because of its location between the nearby business and antiques districts. For lunch, the flank steak with shallots is a classic, and every day there's excellent fish, tartares, and pasta on the menu. **Known for:** French-inspired dishes; cheese plate; three-course brunch. $ *Average main: C$30 ⊠ 73 rue Sault-au-Matelot, Lower Town* ☎ *418/692–1299* ⊕ *echaude.com* ⊗ *No lunch Sat.*

Légende

$$$$ | MODERN CANADIAN | Set on the ground floor of the Hôtel des Coutellier in the Old Port area, Légende is set in a large wood-and-stone room with plush banquettes and an elegant bar. There are a lot of sharing plates—the smartly prepared fish and seafood board (including things like salmon rillettes and whelk salad) is particularly delightful. **Known for:** local ingredients, served creatively; vast patio in summer; vegetarian menu available. $ *Average main: C$32 ⊠ 255 rue St-Paul, Lower Town* ☎ *418/614–2555* ⊕ *restaurantlegende.com* ⊗ *No lunch.*

🛏 Hotels

Many visitors insist on staying near the water, among the quays, warehouses, and cobblestoned squares—as well as many boutique hotels, inspired eateries, and impressive entertainment venues.

★ Auberge St-Antoine Relais and Châteaux

$$$$ | HOTEL | This elegant hotel incorporates the historic stone walls of a 19th-century warehouse along with artifacts dating to the 1600s, many of which were found during an expansion and are now in glass displays in the public areas and guest rooms. **Pros:** unique architectural accents and exhibits; some rooms have fireplaces and terraces; excellent restaurant. **Cons:** low vacancy means guests must plan well in advance; the eclectic décor doesn't always match the price; not all terraces have nice views. $ *Rooms from: C$349 ⊠ 8 rue St-Antoine, Lower Town* ☎ *888/692–2211* ⊕ *saint-antoine.com* ⇌ *95 rooms* ⦿ *No Meals.*

Hôtel des Coutellier

$$$ | HOTEL | Charming details like buttery croissants delivered to the room each morning, exposed brick walls, and lush linens make this boutique hotel a popular base for demanding travelers. **Pros:** an elevator (a rarity in this part of town); breakfast delivered each morning;

old-world charm. **Cons:** small and open-plan bathrooms; in-room temperature controls aren't intuitive; a bit of a climb to Upper Town attractions. ⑤ *Rooms from: C$205* ⊠ *253 rue St-Paul, Lower Town* ☎ *888/523–9696* ⊕ *hoteldescoutellier.com* ⤶ *24 rooms* ⑩ *Free Breakfast.*

★ Hôtel Le Germain Québec

$$$$ | HOTEL | Sophistication and attention to every detail prevails in the modern rooms of this chic boutique hotel—from the custom-designed swing-out night tables to the white goose-down duvets and custom umbrellas. **Pros:** deluxe continental breakfast; higher floors have views of the St. Lawrence River or the Old City; pets welcome. **Cons:** minimal interior is not for everyone; lacks Old Québec spirit; not all rooms have separate bath and shower. ⑤ *Rooms from: C$295* ⊠ *126 rue St-Pierre, Lower Town* ☎ *888/833–5253* ⊕ *germainhotels.com/en/le-germain-hotel/quebec* ⤶ *60 rooms* ⑩ *No Meals.*

Hôtel Le Priori

$$ | HOTEL | Housed in a 300-year-old building with stone and brick walls, this boutique hotel has a rigorously modern décor, with custom leather beds, stainless steel sinks, slate floors, and three-head shower jets. **Pros:** outdoor terrace; unbeatable Old Québec location; breakfast box delivered to the room. **Cons:** high-occupancy rates mean that you'll need to reserve some time ahead; some rooms are small; suites are in a separate building. ⑤ *Rooms from: C$199* ⊠ *15 rue Sault-au-Matelot, Lower Town* ☎ *800/351–3992* ⊕ *hotellepriori.com* ⤶ *28 rooms* ⑩ *Free Breakfast.*

Hôtel Le St-Paul

$$$ | HOTEL | Perched at the edge of the antiques district, this four-story hotel inside what was once a 19th-century office building, is near art galleries, trendy restaurants, and the train station. **Pros:** charming vintage details; modern bathrooms; convenient location. **Cons:** mostly no-frills; not all rooms

are renovated; ambient street noise. ⑤ *Rooms from: C$209* ⊠ *229 rue St-Paul, Lower Town* ☎ *888/794–4414* ⊕ *lesaintpaul.qc.ca* ⤶ *26 rooms* ⑩ *No Meals.*

★ Hôtel 71

$$$ | HOTEL | Guest rooms at this luxury hotel, inside the city's first National Bank of Canada office, have 12-foot-high ceilings, excellent amenities, and stunning views of Old Québec. **Pros:** decadent and modern; luxurious packages; boxed breakfast delivered to the room. **Cons:** chic interiors not kid friendly; valet service is steep; poor soundproofing. ⑤ *Rooms from: C$209* ⊠ *71 rue St-Pierre, Lower Town* ☎ *888/692–1171* ⊕ *hotel71.ca* ⤶ *69 rooms* ⑩ *No Meals.*

★ Lofts Vieux-Québec

$$ | APARTMENT | This collection of lofts, located in some of the Lower Town's most historic buildings (although not all), offers travelers the chance to live like locals, at their own pace. **Pros:** feels like a home, not a hotel; tons of character; full kitchens. **Cons:** some are 21+; some apartments lack sunlight; not all are in historic buildings. ⑤ *Rooms from: C$195* ⊠ *Various locations, Lower Town* ☎ *418/431–9905* ⊕ *loftsvieuxquebec.com* ⤶ *13 properties* ⑩ *No Meals.*

ⓨ Nightlife

Archibald Microbrasserie

BREWPUBS | This microbrewery is one of the biggest trade names in the province. Both the décor and the service are quintessentially Canadian, with lots of wood and plaid and lots of smiles and conviviality. This is a great place to grab a local pint and a burger in a no-fuss, laid-back environment; on a sunny day, try to snag a table on the massive outdoor patio. There is also a location at the Montréal airport. ⊠ *40 rue du Marché-Champlain, Lower Town* ☎ *418/694–9144* ⊕ *archibaldmicrobrasserie.ca.*

Québec Summer Festival

Festival d'Été de Québec *(Québec City Summer Festival).* An annual highlight in the first half of July is the exuberant Summer Festival, with over seven days of rock, folk, hip-hop, and world music. The main concerts take place each evening on three outdoor stages in or near the Old City, including one holding up to 80,000 people on the Plains of Abraham. A pass (⬛ *C$115*) grants admission to all events throughout the festival. Some concerts at indoor theaters cost extra, but free music and activities, such as family concerts and street performers during the day, are also plentiful. At night rue St-Jean near the city gate turns into a free street theater, with drummers, dancers, and skits. Book accommodation several months in advance if you plan to attend. ✉ *Québec City* ☎ *888/992–5200* ⊕ *feq.ca.*

Justine

COCKTAIL BARS | Just across the Gare du Palais, Justine is a classic speakeasy that's just mysterious enough, with a décor that takes us back to the days of Prohibition, with thick black velvet curtains and no visible sign outside. A hushed atmosphere and emblematic cocktails from the 1920s are on the menu, alongside nice platters of gourmet charcuterie and cheeses. ✉ *303 rue St-Paul, Lower Town* ☎ *418/914–5637* 🕓 *Closed Mon.–Wed.*

Terroir – Vins et Compagnie

WINE BAR | At this charming wine bar in the Petit Champlain district overlooking the St. Lawrence River, you'll feel like you've crossed the pond to Europe for the evening. You'll find an exceptional selection of unique wines from hand-picked producers, whether you prefer white, red, rosé, bubbly, or skin-contact. The board of charcuterie and cheeses from Québec is a must. ✉ *72 boul. Champlain, Lower Town* ☎ *418/914-9040* ⊕ *facebook.com/terroirpetitchamplain.*

🎭 Performing Arts

Théâtre Petit-Champlain

CONCERTS | The charming and intimate Théâtre Petit-Champlain is a fine spot to hear contemporary francophone music and comedy acts during the year and take in a play in summer. ✉ *68 rue du Petit-Champlain, Lower Town* ☎ *418/692–2631* ⊕ *theatrepetitchamplain.com.*

🛍 Shopping

ANTIQUES

French Canadian, Victorian, and art deco furniture, clocks, silverware, and porcelain are some of the rare collectibles found here, mainly on quaint and historic rue St-Paul street. Be aware, however, that authentic Québec pine furniture, characterized by simple forms and lines, is rare—and pricey.

Antiquités Bolduc

ANTIQUES & COLLECTIBLES | The largest antiques store on rue St-Paul sells furniture, household items, old paintings, and knickknacks from the 19th and 20th centuries. ✉ *89 rue St-Paul, Lower Town* ☎ *418/694–9558* ⊕ *lesantiquitesbolduc. com* 🕓 *Closed Sun.*

G & M Bourguet Antiquaires

ANTIQUES & COLLECTIBLES | You're not likely to find any bargains here, but this shop has a very good selection of authentic 18th- and 19th-century Québec pine furniture. ✉ *97 rue St-Paul, Lower Town* ☎ *418/694–0896* ⊕ *gmbourguet.com.*

La Nouvelle-France Antiquités

This is probably the best place in the antiques district to find good Québécois furniture, clocks, oil lamps, porcelain, and ceramics. It also specializes in old-timey sports paraphernalia such as Québec Nordiques and Montréal Canadiens. It's a very welcoming store as well. ⊠ *225 rue St-Paul, Lower Town* ☎ *418/694–1807.*

CLOTHING

★ Charlevoix Pure Laine

CLOTHING | Discover the beautiful Charlevoix sheep wool at this lovely boutique. Passionate craftspeople work tirelessly to upcycle and recycle this regional wool, transforming it into stockings, toques, throws, and soles. ⊠ *61 rue du Petit-Champlain, Lower Town* ☎ *418/692–7272* ⊕ *charlevoixpurelaine.ca.*

les ptits mosüs

CHILDREN'S CLOTHING | FAMILY | The name says it all: *les ptits mosüs* means "the naughty kids" in Québécois, so it's only logical that this lovely boutique is dedicated to the little ones. Expect a highly curated selection of local designers with items ranging from clothing to toys and from books to tableware. ⊠ *88 1/2 rue du Petit Champlain, Lower Town* ☎ *418/914–5838* ⊕ *lesptitsmosus.com.*

CRAFTS

Boutique des Métiers d'Art du Québec

CRAFTS | This boutique, run by the Conseil des Métiers d'Art, a coordinating body that oversees all kinds of arts and crafts disciplines and organizes annual fairs, features the best from Québec in glass art, porcelain, jewelry, woodworking, and much more, most with a stylish, contemporary feel. ⊠ *29 rue Notre-Dame, Lower Town* ☎ *418/694–0267* ⊕ *boutiquesmetiersdart.ca.*

FOOD

La Petite Cabane à Sucre de Québec

FOOD | The best place in Québec City to buy maple-flavored goods in a typical sugar shack atmosphere (think lots of wood and plenty of plaid). You'll find

syrup of course, but also butters, candies, teas, vinaigrettes, chocolates, and other indulgent Québec-made gourmet goods. ⊠ *94 rue du Petit-Champlain, Lower Town* ☎ *418/692–5875.*

 Activities

SPAS

★ Strøm Spa Nordique

SPA | Designed by a local star-architect firm, this Nordic-oriented spa—a branch of the Montréal-based upscale spa company—has a panoramic view of the St. Lawrence River. Enjoy outdoor whirlpools, thermal and Nordic baths, a Finnish sauna, a eucalyptus steam bath, and thermal and Nordic waterfalls. ⊠ *515 boul. Champlain, Lower Town* ☎ *418/425–2772* ⊕ *stromspa.com* ☞ *Reservations essential.*

Outside the Old City

Venture outside the walls for a glimpse of the real Québec City. Grande Allée and avenue Cartier, in the Montcalm neighborhood, buzz with clubs and bars inside Queen Anne–style mansions. Cafés, galleries, and good restaurants are popping up regularly in St-Roch, the city's urban core. If you do have a car, it's a beautiful drive on boulevard Champlain, which runs from Lower Town all around the southern edge of Québec City, following the St. Lawrence River: you might want to take a stroll along the Promenade Samuel-de-Champlain, a stunning, modern linear park created in 2008 for the city's 400th anniversary. Above are the cliffs that lead to the Plains of Abraham, and farther on are the Sillery Coves. Any one of the steep hills will take you back toward the main roads that run east–west or the highways that cross north–south: Duplessis, the farthest west; Henri IV; Robert-Bourassa; and Dufferin-Montmorency.

GETTING HERE AND AROUND

It's a breezy and lovely 15-minute walk from the Old City to avenue Cartier in the Montcalm neighborhood, but the bus system is excellent here and easy to use. There are many bus stops throughout Upper Town, and a number of lines run up and down boulevard René-Lévesque and Grande Allée from place d'Youville. If you do choose to walk, take a detour to avenue Laurier or avenue Georges VI for a tour through leafy green streets with gorgeous homes.

St-Roch, on the other hand, is just down the hill from place d'Youville if you're in Upper Town; it can also easily be reached by bus from the Lower Town and Petit Champlain.

When in doubt, just catch a cab, which aren't hard to find, to take you there and back. But with increasing attractiveness and atmosphere of both neighborhoods, it's a no-brainer.

TIMING

There's no need to dedicate more than half a day to see the area around Grande Allée or the St-Roch neighborhood. Both are great destinations for lunch, an afternoon browsing in the shops, or an evening out at a restaurant or bar.

Sights

Aquarium du Québec

AQUARIUM | FAMILY | Have breakfast with the walruses, lunch (carefully) with the polar bears, and spend the afternoon watching the seals do their tricks at this cliff-top aquarium overlooking the St. Lawrence and Québec City's two main bridges. When you tire of the mammals, check out the thousands of species of fresh and saltwater fish in the aquarium's massive, three-level aquatic gallery, or have some hands-on experiences with mollusks, starfish, and stingrays. Don't miss the jellyfish ballet or seahorse tanks. This is the only aquarium in North America with examples of all five species of cold-water seals. Experience the Arctic with the brand-new immersive projections of polar bear, narwhal, whale, polar fox, and more in their natural habitat. For an even more immersive experience, there is a re-creation of the feeling of cold, even in summer. Chill factor guaranteed! ⊠ *1675 av. des Hôtels, Outside the Old City* ☎ *418/659-5264* ⊕ *sepaq.com/ct/paq* ⊠ *C$22.50.*

★ Avenue Cartier

STREET | The mix of reasonably priced restaurants and bars, groceries and specialty food shops, and boutiques makes avenue Cartier a favorite lunchtime and after-work stop for many local residents. After business hours the street hums with locals running errands or soaking up the sun on patios. When darkness falls, the avenue's patrons get noticeably younger. The attraction? A half-dozen nightclubs and pubs that offer everything from wine and quiet conversation to Latin music and earsplitting dance tunes. ⊠ *Montcalm.*

Grande-Allée

STREET | One of the city's oldest streets, the Grande Allée was the route people took from outlying areas to come sell their furs in town. In the 19th century, the wealthy built neo-Gothic and Queen Anne–style mansions here, which now house trendy cafés, clubs, and restaurants. The street actually has four names: inside the city walls it's rue St-Louis; outside the walls, Grande Allée Est; farther west, Grande Allée Ouest; then finally, boulevard Laurier. ⊠ *Grande-Allée, Montcalm.*

★ Musée National des Beaux-Arts du Québec

ART MUSEUM | Situated on the city's liveliest avenue, the Grand Allée, this neoclassical museum in the park with a slick and modern wing is a remarkable steel-and-glass setting for its collection of 22,000 traditional and contemporary pieces of Québec art. Designed by starchitects Rem Koolhaas and Shohei Shigematsu,

Sights ▼

1 Aquarium du Québec.............. **H9**
2 Avenue Cartier..................... **A9**
3 Grande-Allée........................ **E8**
4 Musée National des
   Beaux-Arts du Québec........... **B9**
5 Observatoire de la Capitale........ **E6**
6 Parc Linéaire de la Rivière
   St-Charles **A2**
7 Promenade
   Samuel-de-Champlain **H9**
8 St. Matthew's Cemetery **E5**
9 St-Roch **B2**

Restaurants ▼

1 Albacore............................. **E4**
2 ARVI.................................. **C1**
3 Battuto **A5**
4 Bistro B **B9**
5 Buvette Scott....................... **C6**
6 Ciel! **E8**
7 Ficelle Sandwicherie.............. **D5**
8 Izakaya Honō....................... **C2**
9 jjacques.............................. **B3**
10 Le Billig **C6**
11 Le Clocher Penché **A3**
12 Nina Pizza Napolitaine........... **A3**
13 Patente et Machin................. **A3**
14 Pied Bleu **A3**
15 Sardines **A7**
16 Tora-Ya Ramen.................... **A3**

Quick Bites ▼

1 Café Cantook...................... **D5**
2 Café Saint-Henri **E2**
3 La Boîte à Pain.................... **A3**
4 Nektar Caféologue **A3**
5 Pâtisserie Chouquette **E4**

Hotels ▼

1 Hôtel Château Laurier............. **F7**
2 Hôtel de Glace **F1**
3 Hôtel Delta par Marriott
   Québec.............................. **E5**
4 Hôtel Le Bonne Entente........... **A7**
5 Hôtel Le Concorde Québec........ **E8**
6 Hotel PUR.......................... **B3**
7 Hôtel-Musée
   Premières Nations................. **A2**
8 J.A. Moisan Auberge.............. **D5**
9 Le C3 Hôtel **B9**
10 Les Lofts de L'Adresse **D8**

the Lassonde Pavilion, added in 2016, features three stacked, cascading galleries; a grand stairwell that spirals dramatically from the top floor to the basement, where a rising almost-mile-long tunnel connects to the museum's three other wings. MNBAQ houses works by local legends Jean-Paul Riopelle, Jean-Paul Lemieux, Alfred Pellan, Fernand Leduc, and Horatio Walker that are particularly notable, as well as temporary exhibits by international artists such as Turner, Miró, and Giacometti. The original museum building in Parc des Champs-de-Bataille is part of an abandoned prison dating from 1867; a hallway of cells, with the iron bars and courtyard, has been preserved as part of a permanent exhibition on the prison's history. ✉ *179 Grande Allée Ouest, Upper Town* ☎ *418/643–2150* ⊕ *mnbaq.org* 🎫 *C$25* 🕙 *Closed Mon.*

★ Observatoire de la Capitale

VIEWPOINT | Located atop the Édifice Marie-Guyart, the city's tallest building, Observatoire de la Capitale offers a spectacular panorama of Québec City from 31 stories up. The site features an overview of the city's history with 3-D imagery, audiovisual displays in both French and English, and a time-travel theme with a 1960s twist. ✉ *1037 rue de la Chevrotière, St-Jean-Baptiste* ☎ *418/644–9841* ⊕ *observatoire-capitale.com* 🎫 *C$14.75* ⚠ *Reservations mandatory.*

Parc Linéaire de la Rivière St-Charles (*St. Charles River Linear Park*)

CITY PARK | This 32-km (20-mile) stretch of trails and walkways follows the St. Charles River from its source at Lake St. Charles, to the northwest (which supplies a large part of Québec City's drinking water), all the way to the Bassin Louise Marina, in Vieux-Port. Many sections are in quiet stretches of forests, or run along wetlands and meadows. The trails immediately west of the harbor offer a green oasis at the heart of the city. The recently-reimagined Cartier-Brébeuf National Historic Site in Limoilou is particularly lovely and explains the various ways Jacques Cartier helped shape the city as we see it today. It's also possible to rent kayaks and paddle over 11 km (6.5 miles) of the northernmost part of the river. ✉ *Maison Dorion-Coulombe, Outside the Old City* ☎ *418/691–4710* ⊕ *societerivierestcharles.qc.ca.*

★ Promenade Samuel-de-Champlain

PROMENADE | FAMILY | This 6.8 km (4.2-mile) promenade along the St. Lawrence River is a beloved local hotspot, offering stunning vistas of the river and the two bridges spanning it to the west. The park boasts creative and contemporary landscape design, attracting a lively crowd of pedestrians, cyclists, and inline skaters on sunny summer days. Children can be seen playing by the fountains and on the lawns. Toward the western end, you'll discover a café and an observation tower. During the high season, special buses conveniently transport visitors from Lower Town to this scenic promenade. Summer 2023 saw the inauguration of a spectacular addition—a sandy beach area complete with chairs and umbrellas, alongside an infinity pool giving the impression of bathing in the river and featuring cascading water fountains. ✉ *boul. Champlain, Outside the Old City* ☎ *418/528–0773* ⊕ *capitale.gouv. qc.ca/sites-de-la-capitale/parcs/promenade-samuel-de-champlain* 🎫 *Free.*

St. Matthew's Cemetery

CEMETERY | The burial place of many of the earliest English settlers in Canada was established in 1771 and is the oldest cemetery remaining in Québec City. Also buried here is Robert Wood, the disavowed half brother of Queen Victoria. Closed in 1860, the cemetery has been turned into a park. Next door is St. Matthew's Anglican Church, now a recently renovated public library. It has a book listing most of the original tombstone inscriptions, including those on tombstones removed to make way for the city's modern convention center. ⊠ *755 rue St-Jean, St-Jean-Baptiste.*

★ St-Roch

NEIGHBORHOOD | Once an industrial area and now a technology hub, St-Roch is dotted with hip bars and trendy shops. Because there are so few locals living in the old part of the city, St-Roch is a great place to mingle with the locals. And if Old Québec is a magnet for European gastronomy and fine dining, St-Roch is where the younger chefs are having the most fun; as a result, new spots are popping up all the time.

Rue St-Joseph is the neighborhood's main street. It's a mix of office buildings, modern lunch spots, and after-work hangouts. You'll quickly find the neighborhood's main thoroughfare by looking for the Église St-Roch, a massive stone church. Curated shops, third-wave cafés, trendy bistros, crowded microbreweries, and oyster bars are plentiful, creating a thriving, vibrant atmosphere. For good people-watching, head to the Jardin Jean-Paul-L'Allier, a large leafy square.

Art also abounds in the neighborhood, from the famous street-art-covered viaduct (just off rue St-Paul) and modern sculptures to outdoor theater and circus acts.

St-Roch is a long but downhill jaunt from the Old City, though easily walkable if you have the time. If you're not in the mood for exercise, the best way to get there is by taxi. Plan on spending about C$9 each way. There are usually plenty of cabs available for the return trip. Taking the bus (800 or 801) is also an option. ⊠ *St-Roch* ⊕ *quebec-cite.com/en/ neighbourhoods-quebec-city/saint-roch.*

🍴 Restaurants

There are many cute cafés and fine eateries within the walls of the Old City, but don't miss the thriving culinary scene beyond them. Le Clocher Penché

is arguably the bistro with the friendliest service, and it gives you an excuse to visit trendy St-Roch. Or if you're looking for a little more luxury, head to Le Parlementaire for lunch to sample trendy dishes while playing "spot the politico."

Work up a good appetite by wandering through the streets—and climbing those steep stairs. For something to nibble on for a picnic in the park, pop into one of the city's little out-of-the-way pâtisseries for buttery croissants and heavenly brioches.

★ Albacore

$$$ | **SEAFOOD** | Seafood lovers, rejoice: Québec City now has its very own ocean-based restaurant, and a great one at that. Helmed by a team of seasoned chefs, this gourmet restaurant provides diners with flavorful, flawless, and generously sized dishes of anything from scallops to clams and marlin *tatakis*, all nicely complemented by delicate side dishes such as lentils, sorbet (yes, ice cream for dinner), and edible flowers. **Known for:** mandatory reservations; imaginative seafood; beautiful décor. ⑤ *Average main: C$25* ⊠ *819 côte d'Abraham, St-Jean-Baptiste* ☎ *418/914–6441* ⊕ *albacore.business.site* ⊙ *Closed Mon. and Tues. No lunch.*

ARVI

$$$ | **MODERN CANADIAN** | The trek to Limoilou is worth it, if it's to dine at ARVI. Local critics have deemed ARVI an unforgettable gourmet experience, and it was recently selected as one of Canada's 35 top restaurants by Air Canada's in-flight magazine. **Known for:** vegetarian menu; wine pairings; delicate, creative plates. ⑤ *Average main: C$30* ⊠ *519 3e av., Limoilou* ☎ *581/742–4202* ⊕ *restaurantarvi.ca* ⊙ *Closed Sun. and Mon. No lunch.*

★ Battuto

$$$ | **MODERN ITALIAN** | Chef Guillaume Saint-Pierre's love for authentic Italian cuisine led him to open this popular 25-seat restaurant, located off the main St-Roch thoroughfares, where he can fully concentrate on that passion with gusto and skill. Italian tradition (there's arancini and *vitello tonatto*) blends with local flair (there's *cacio e pepe* with Swiss chard, and scallop crudo). **Known for:** perfect fresh pasta; a blend of local flair and Italian know-how; tiramisu for two. ⑤ *Average main: C$24* ⊠ *527 boul. Langelier, St-Roch* ☎ *418/614–4414* ⊕ *battuto.ca* ⊘ *Closed Sun.–Tues. No lunch.*

Bistro B

$$$$ | **BISTRO** | The culinary genius behind the success of city hotspot Chez Muffy, Chef François Blais decided on a more casual approach, including having a simple interior, when he opened his own restaurant on avenue Cartier. The "market cuisine" is straight to the point and well executed, and the whole menu fits on a blackboard, with a handful of appetizers, main courses, and desserts that change daily. **Known for:** open kitchen; upbeat atmosphere; popularity with locals. ⑤ *Average main: C$35* ⊠ *1144 av. Cartier, Montcalm* ☎ *418/614–5444* ⊕ *bistrob.ca* ⊘ *Closed Sun.–Tues. No lunch Sat.*

Buvette Scott

$$ | **MODERN CANADIAN** | Buvette Scott is at an unpretentious address that pleasantly surprises with its attractive menu and impeccable service. Located in the heart of St-Jean-Baptiste, it's quickly been adopted by locals who have made this place their favorite neighborhood hangout. **Known for:** affordable plates to share; vast selection of local microbrews; unfussy, convivial atmosphere. ⑤ *Average main: C$18* ⊠ *821 rue Scott, St-Jean-Baptiste* ☎ *581/741–4464* ⊕ *buvettescott.com* ⊘ *Closed Sun. and Mon. No lunch.*

Ciel!

$$$ | **MODERN CANADIAN** | Spectacular views of the whole city are not the only reason to climb up to this rotating restaurant with unobstructed, panoramic views. The service here is friendly and well managed, and the food is creative, and delicious—try the roasted arctic char with lemon gnocchi and shiitakes or something from the solid brunch menu. **Known for:** 360-degree view of the city; weekend brunch; tasty farm-to-table dishes. ⑤ *Average main: C$30* ⊠ *Hôtel Le Concorde Québec, 1225 cours du Général-de-Montcalm, St-Jean-Baptiste* ☎ *418/640–5802* ⊕ *cielbistrobar.com.*

Ficelle Sandwicherie

$$ | **BAKERY** | Everything is homemade in this new neighborhood sandwich shop. Located in the heart of rue St-Jean, Ficelle prepares freshly made dishes of the day, such as sandwiches (baguette or focaccia) with a variety of fillings and soups. **Known for:** superior vegan options; home cooking;. ⑤ *Average main: C$13* ⊠ *599 rue St-Jean, Montcalm* ☎ *418/647–3707* ⊕ *ficellesandwicherie. com.*

Izakaya Honō

$$ | **JAPANESE** | Small dishes are served in the purest tradition of *izakayas* (Japanese taverns) in a venue that's flooded with light and minimally decorated with birch and green plants. On the menu are just classics: *yakitori* (mini skewers), sashimi, *okonomiyaki* (savory pancakes), and dumplings, as well as a tataki that changes daily. **Known for:** popularity with locals; excellent, classic Japanese small plates; creative cocktails. ⑤ *Average main: C$15* ⊠ *670 rue St-Joseph Est, St-Roch* ☎ *418/524–2888* ⊕ *honoizakaya. com* ⊘ *Closed Tues. No lunch.*

jjacques

$$$ | **SEAFOOD** | Halfway between a discreet speakeasy and an oyster bar, this is an unlikely pearl in the heart of the St-Roch district. Cross the threshold of the hidden entrance and you'll find yourself in a stunning interior. **Known for:** natural wines; seafood platters; romantic atmosphere. ⑤ *Average main: C$25* ⊠ *341 rue Notre-Dame-des-Anges, St-Roch* ☎ *581/491–3286* ⊕ *jjacques.ca.*

Le Billig

$$ | **CANADIAN** | **FAMILY** | At this lovely crepe shop, buckwheat-flour crepes are filled with simple ham and cheese or fancier combos like duck confit with onion marmalade, while a wheat crepe with salted caramel and sweet Chantilly cream makes a good dessert. The large shop also has bistro items like cod beignets, charcuterie plates, and cassoulet, and there's a nice selection of ciders and beers. **Known for:** great crepes, often original; ciders; gluten-free items. ⑤ *Average main: C$16* ⊠ *481 rue St-Jean, St-Jean-Baptiste* ☎ *418/524–8341.*

★ Le Clocher Penché

$$$ | **MODERN CANADIAN** | The high ceilings and imposing vault door give away the fact that this was once a bank, but an amiable staff and inventive bistro cuisine (without pretentious fluff) make this establishment a favorite among locals, who munch on well-prepared seasonal, creative, flavorful shareable plates like smoked aubergine with *romesco* sauce or veal tartare with lemon and fiddleheads. ■**TIP➔ Wine lovers, this restaurant recently hired the best sommelier in Québec City. Known for:** changing menu using fresh, regional ingredients; on-site sommelier; beautiful, inviting décor. ⑤ *Average main: C$27* ⊠ *203 rue St-Joseph Est, St-Roch* ☎ *418/640–0597* ⊕ *clocherpenche.ca* ⊘ *Closed Sun. and Mon. No lunch.*

★ Nina Pizza Napolitaine

$$ | **ITALIAN** | Specializing in Neapolitan-style pizza and antipasti, this stylish pizzeria has been on everyone's lips ever since it opened (thanks to crowdfunding). Its beast of an oven weighs 2.5 tons and was imported straight from Italy—and it's worth it: the thin-crust pizzas are cooked in just 90 seconds at 900 degrees. **Known for:** wood-fired pizzas; charcuterie plates; Aperol spritz. ⑤ *Average main: C$16* ⊠ *410 rue St-Anselme, St-Roch* ☎ *581/742–2012* ⊕ *ninapizzanapolitaine. ca* ⊘ *Closed Mon.–Wed.*

Patente et Machin

$$$ | **ECLECTIC** | This fun and friendly place has a menu with terrific meats, grilled cheese, and whimsical ideas, like the use of guinea fowl wings in lieu of chicken wings. The food here has personality, humor, and … lots of butter. **Known for:** playful dishes; pleasantly chaotic service; great wine selection. ⑤ *Average main: C$25* ⊠ *82 rue St-Joseph Ouest, St-Roch* ☎ *581/981–3999* ⊘ *Closed Sun.–Tues.*

★ Pied Bleu

$$$$ | **BISTRO** | It's worth heading to the outskirts of the St-Roch downtown district for this unique dining experience, inspired by French *bouchons* (as bistros are called in the city of Lyon). "In the pig, everything is good": so goes the French adage that advocates responsible, farm-to-table gastronomy. This is precisely what drives Pied Bleu: every week, the chefs receive a whole pig and come up with proven, creative ways to serve it (the charcuterie plate is a must). **Known for:** prix-fixe tasting menu; charcuterie plate; Lyon-style restaurant. ⑤ *Average main: C$35* ⊠ *181 rue St-Vallier Ouest, St-Roch* ☎ *418/914–3554* ⊕ *piedbleu.com* ⊘ *Closed Mon. No lunch Tues.–Fri. No dinner weekends.*

Sardines

$$ | **MODERN CANADIAN** | A living metaphor for a can of sardines, with its small, cozy space (only about 20 seats) and its explosion of flavors, Sardines is a must-stop for foodie travelers. Upon entering, the display case features the chef's bakery creations, including his famous baguette. **Known for:** creative small plates; good beer selection; heartfelt service. ⑤ *Average main: C$18* ⊠ *1 rue St-Jean, Montcalm* ☎ *581/300–9449* ⊕ *spoursardines. ca* ⊘ *Closed Sun. and Mon. No lunch.*

Tora-Ya Ramen

$$ | **JAPANESE** | Tora Ya Ramen offers a delightful journey to Japan through chef Miyano Sakai's generational expertise. Each ramen comes with a choice of four broths (soy, miso, Korean-style miso, or veggie miso) that are sure to satisfy both small and gargantuan appetites on cold winter days. **Known for:** variety of ramen broth options; friendly service; Japanese authenticity. $ *Average main: C$20* ✉ *72 rue St-Joseph est, St-Roch* ☎ *418/780–1903* ⊕ *torayaramen.com* ⊗ *Closed Sun.*

Coffee and Quick Bites

Café Cantook

$ | **CAFÉ** | One of the newer additions to the St-Jean-Baptiste neighborhood, Cantook is a microroaster that is more traditional than trendy, but no less excellent. Visit for a cappuccino, a good conversation with the owner, or maybe even both. **Known for:** friendly staff; popular with locals; fuss-free atmosphere. $ *Average main: C$5* ✉ *575 rue St-Jean, St-Jean-Baptiste* ☎ *418/529–4769* ⊕ *cantookcafe.com.*

Café Saint-Henri

$ | **CAFÉ** | Expect the usual crowd of students, freelancers, and others toting laptops at this third-wave café that has thoughtfully selected beans roasted on-site. Even so, the contemporary, all-white café is a welcome respite from the cold in wintertime—and the doughnuts alone are worth a visit. **Known for:** delicious artisan doughnuts; architectural highlight; beans roasted on the premises. $ *Average main: C$5* ✉ *849 rue St-Joseph Est, Outside the Old City* ☎ *581/300–7211* ⊕ *sainthenri.ca.*

★ La Boîte à Pain

$ | **BAKERY** | La Boîte à Pain makes it a point of honor to serve fresh products prepared on site every day. In a convivial atmosphere, this European-inspired bakery has been making gourmet and artisanal products for more than 20 years. **Known for:** intricate, affordable pastries; large coffee selection; on-site daily baking. $ *Average main: C$10* ✉ *289 rue St-Joseph Est, St-Roch* ☎ *418/647–3666* ⊕ *boiteapain.com.*

Nektar Caféologue

$ | **CAFÉ** | This is another five-star coffee shop to visit in St-Roch, either for a roasting lesson or a warm macchiato respite from the Québec winter. Known for its ecological and humanist approach, Nektar works closely with its fair trade producers in Brazil to produce the Para Ela blend, which means "for her" and is harvested by hand and processed exclusively by women who are paid 50% more than the regional average. **Known for:** fair trade coffee; several flavors to choose from; vegan milk. $ *Average main: C$5* ✉ *235 rue St-Joseph Est, St-Roch* ☎ *418/977–9236* ⊕ *nektar.ca.*

Pâtisserie Chouquette

$ | **BAKERY** | Some of Québec City's finest pastries are made at this gourmet newcomer on rue St-Jean. The weekly rotation of four flavorful *chouquettes,* puffy, bite-sized treats that are so good, no amount of guilt can stop you from indulging. **Known for:** vegan selection; cozy interior; bite-size delicacies. $ *Average main: C$10* ✉ *778 rue St-Jean, Outside the Old City* ☎ *418/614–3500* ⊕ *patisseriechouquette.myshopify.com.*

🛏 Hotels

Booking a room outside the walled city puts you in a mixed area of student housing, convention hotels, and chains, although there are still a few inns and B&Bs to choose from. Many of the options are within easy proximity to the Plains of Abraham, the restaurants of avenue Cartier, and museums such as the Musée des Beaux-Arts du Québec.

Hôtel Château Laurier

$$$$ | **HOTEL** | Brown leather sofas and wrought-iron chandeliers fill the spacious lobby of this former private house. **Pros:** professional and helpful staff; some rooms for budget travelers; convenient to Grande Allée. **Cons:** some ambient noise; hotel a bit of a maze; not all rooms are renovated. $ *Rooms from: C$280*

Hôtel de Glace—North America's first ice hotel, rebuilt each winter—is only 15 minutes from Québec City by car, and worth a tour even if you don't spend the night.

✉ *1220 pl. George V Ouest, Upper Town* ☎ *888/522–8108* ⊕ *hotelchateaulaurier.com* ↝ *289 rooms* ⓘ◉⃒ *No Meals.*

★ Hôtel de Glace

$$$$ | HOTEL | The first of its kind in North America, this hotel, open from the first week in January to the end of March at Village Vacances Valcartier, is built entirely from ice and snow each year. **Pros:** unique experience; spectacular engineering feat and design; festive atmosphere. **Cons:** 30-minute drive from downtown Québec City; can get cold; limited availability. ⑤ *Rooms from: C$399* ✉ *Village Vacances Valcartier, 1860 boul. Valcartier, Outside the Old City* ☎ *888/384-5524* ⊕ *valcartier.com/en/lodging/hotel-de-glace-ice-hotel* ↝ *24 rooms* ⓘ◉⃒ *No Meals.*

Hôtel Delta par Marriott Québec

$$$$ | HOTEL | This recently renovated hotel with large, functional rooms is an excellent and stylish option for business and budget-minded travelers. **Pros:** kid-friendly environment; some rooms are adapted for people with limited mobility; four-season outdoor pool. **Cons:**
building is uninspiring; attracts convention groups; not all rooms are renovated. ⑤ *Rooms from: C$400* ✉ *690 boul. René-Lévesque Est, St-Jean-Baptiste* ☎ *888/884–7777* ⊕ *marriott.com/en-us/hotels/yqbdr-delta-hotels-quebec* ↝ *377 rooms* ⓘ◉⃒ *No Meals.*

Hôtel Le Bonne Entente

$$ | HOTEL | Twenty minutes from downtown, the 11-acre Château Bonne Entente offers tasteful simplicity at its finest, with classic rooms featuring white duvets, marble bathrooms (toiletries by the White Company), and refinished wood furniture. **Pros:** country-club feel; chic, relaxing atmosphere; free shuttle to Old Québec and downtown. **Cons:** golf is 20 minutes away; not the best room service; shuttle not available fall through spring. ⑤ *Rooms from: C$199* ✉ *3400 chemin Ste-Foy, Outside the Old City* ☎ *800/463–4390* ⊕ *lebonneentente.com* ↝ *165 rooms* ⓘ◉⃒ *No Meals.*

Hôtel Le Concorde Québec

$$$$ | HOTEL | Built in 1974, this 29-story concrete high-rise with an excellent location on Grande Allée offers larger-than-average rooms with Keurig coffeemakers, huge windows, and good views of Battlefields Park and the St. Lawrence River. **Pros:** central location; revolving rooftop restaurant; heated pool. **Cons:** high-traffic hotel; pool is open only in summer; décor is dated in some rooms. ⑤ *Rooms from: C$280* ✉ *1225 cours du Général-de-Montcalm, Upper Town* ☎ *800/463–5256* ⊕ *hotellecordequebec.com* ⤴ *406 rooms* ❍*❙ No Meals.*

★ Hôtel-Musée Premières Nations

$$$ | **HOTEL** | **FAMILY** | Welcome to one of Canada's premier Indigenous tourism destinations, where visitors can experience warm Huron-Wendat hospitality. **Pros:** Indigenous cultural experience; spa features Nordic pools, heated sidewalks, a fire pit, and a yurt; excellent restaurant. **Cons:** rustic style might not appeal to animal lovers; pet fee; 20-minute drive from the Old City. ⑤ *Rooms from: C$250* ✉ *5 pl. de la Rencontre, Outside the Old City* ☎ *418/847–2222* ⊕ *hotelpremieresnations.ca* ⤴ *55 rooms* ❍*❙ No Meals.*

★ Hotel PUR

$$$ | **HOTEL** | Travelers with a preference for minimal and modern design will appreciate this slick boutique hotel (part of Tribute Portfolio/Marriott alliance) with its light-filled rooms, great views, and location in an interesting neighborhood. **Pros:** clean, modern design; great dining room doubles as a bar late evenings; in bustling St-Roch district. **Cons:** minimal design doesn't work for everyone; customer service can vary in quality; a bit of a trek from Old Québec on foot. ⑤ *Rooms from: C$240* ✉ *395 rue de la Couronne, St-Roch* ☎ *888/627–8397* ⊕ *marriott.com/en-us/hotels/yqbpu-hotel-pur-quebec-a-tribute-portfolio-hotel* ⤴ *242 rooms* ❍*❙ No Meals.*

J.A. Moisan Auberge

$$$ | **B&B/INN** | This exceptional B&B is in one of Québec City's most iconic buildings: right above the famous renowned J.A. Moisan fine grocery store, which was founded in 1871. **Pros:** like stepping back in time; within walking distance of the Old City; excellent breakfast. **Cons:** some may not like staying above a grocery store; Victorian style isn't for everyone; rooms are very small. ⑤ *Rooms from: C$250* ✉ *695 rue St-Jean, St-Jean-Baptiste* ☎ *418/914–3777* ⊕ *jamoisan.com* ⤴ *4 rooms* ❍*❙ Free Breakfast.*

Le C3 Hôtel

$$ | **HOTEL** | Located right across the street from Musée National des Beaux-Arts du Québec and within minutes from some of the best bars and restaurants in the city, Le C3 Hôtel is all history on the outside, being set in a stunning 19th-century building, but all modern fun on the inside, with its colorful rooms, iPod docks, and crisp white linens. **Pros:** easy access to Montcalm and St-Jean-Baptiste nightlife; modern furniture and linens; beautiful building. **Cons:** rooms in the Creative category are in the basement; limited parking; 10-minute walk from the Old City. ⑤ *Rooms from: C$200* ✉ *170 Grande Allée Ouest, Montcalm* ☎ *418/525–9726* ⊕ *lec3hotel.com* ⤴ *24 rooms* ❍*❙ No Meals.*

Les Lofts de L'Adresse

$$ | **APARTMENT** | Built in 1899 at the request of an affluent bourgeois family, this historic redbrick residence exudes refinement, authenticity, and commands attention. **Pros:** historic stay, minus the dated amenities; private parking; kitchenettes. **Cons:** some lofts can feel small; no lobby; décor can feel impersonal, almost bare. ⑤ *Rooms from: C$175* ✉ *401 Grande Allée Est, Upper Town* ☎ *877/515–2730* ⊕ *ladresse.ca* ⤴ *14 lofts* ❍*❙ No Meals.*

ⓨ Nightlife

BARS AND LOUNGES

Korrigane Brasserie Artisanale

BREWPUBS | A popular after-work spot with the locals, this brewery crafts high-quality beer and tapas-inspired pub fare. A friendly vibe and ample seating make Korrigane the ideal spot for a *cinq à sept* or a low-key night out. In addition to the house brews, there's a good selection of other local options. ⊠ *380 rue Dorchester, St-Roch* 🕾 *418/614–0932* ⊕ *korrigane.ca*.

Le Projet

BREWPUBS | With 30 beer and cider lines (a great way to discover Québec's brewery scene), Le Projet is a 65-seat bistro-pub specializing in Québec micro-brewery beers and ciders in a beautiful 112-year-old building—a former bank—where the architecture is reminiscent of the quintessential English pub. The cozy façade and the imposing ceiling moldings contribute to the welcoming atmosphere that makes the food (and beer) even tastier. ⊠ *399 rue St-Jean, St-Jean-Baptiste* 🕾 *418/914–5322* ⊕ *publeprojet.com*.

★ Noctem Artisans Brasseurs

BREWPUBS | A great selection of beers, brewed on-premises or coming from some of the best microbreweries in Québec, attract diners here, along with the smart menu of reinvented pub fare (fish and waffle, blood sausage pie, or braised pork belly with chimichurri sauce and parsley root chips, for example). The décor, with raw plywood and exposed structures, is modern and trendy. ⊠ *438 rue du Parvis, St-Roch* 🕾 *581/742–7979* ⊕ *noctem.ca* ⊗ *No lunch Mon*.

ⓧ Performing Arts

Carrefour International de Théâtre de Québec

THEATER | This international theatrical festival takes over several spaces in late May and early June: the Salle Albert-Rousseau, the Grand Théâtre de Québec, the Théâtre Périscope (near avenue Cartier), and Complexe Méduse. There are usually at least one or two productions in English or with English subtitles, and an outdoor show that takes over different parts of the downtown area. ⊠ *Québec City* 🕾 *888/529–1996* ⊕ *carrefourtheatre.qc.ca*.

Centre Vidéotron

MUSIC | This state-of-the-art arena opened in the fall of 2015, with the hope of attracting a National Hockey League franchise. For now, the hockey is from a junior league, but there are world-class concerts and popular acts playing here regularly. ⊠ *Parc de l'Expocité, 250 boul. Wilfrid-Hamel, Outside the Old City* 🕾 *855/790–1245* ⊕ *lecentrevideotron.ca*.

Coopérative Méduse

THEATER | This multidisciplinary arts center, built in a row of historic houses mixed with new structures, is a hub for local artists and presents edgy installations and live shows, including a modern dance series. ⊠ *650 côte d'Abraham, St-Roch* 🕾 *418/640–9218* ⊕ *meduse.org*.

École de Cirque

CIRCUSES | For two weeks every June, students of this circus school and others take to the trapeze to promote their art form through the Circus Days festival. Throughout the year, students and teachers put on various shows, training camps, and workshops, including a Christmas Cabaret, in the former church that now houses their school. ⊠ *750 2e av., Outside the Old City* 🕾 *418/525–0101* ⊕ *ecoledecirque.com*.

Grand Théâtre de Québec

PERFORMANCE VENUES | Québec City's main theater has two stages for symphonic concerts, opera, plays, and touring companies of all sorts. The Grand Théâtre also presents a dance series with Canadian and international companies. Inside, a three-wall mural by the Québec sculptor Jordi Bonet depicts death, life, and liberty. Bonet wrote "La Liberté" on one wall to bring attention to the Québécois struggle for freedom and cultural distinction. ✉ *269 boul. René-Lévesque Est, St-Jean-Baptiste* ☎ *418/643–8131* ⊕ *grandtheatre.qc.ca.*

★ **Orchestre Symphonique de Québec**
(*Québec Symphony Orchestra*)
MUSIC | Canada's oldest symphony orchestra, directed by the dynamic German conductor Clemens Schuldt, performs mainly at Louis-Fréchette Hall in the Grand Théâtre de Québec. Expect some of the most acclaimed classical works, but also fun surprises like hip-hop renditions and movie scores. ✉ *269 boul. René-Lévesque Est, St-Jean-Baptiste* ☎ *418/643–8486* ⊕ *osq.org* 🎟 *From C$45.*

Salle Albert-Rousseau
THEATER | A diverse repertoire, from classical music to comedy, is staged here. ✉ *2410 chemin Ste-Foy, Ste-Foy* ☎ *418/659–6710* ⊕ *sallealbertrousseau. com.*

Théâtre Périscope
THEATER | This multipurpose theater hosts about a dozen different productions a year, staged by several different theater companies. New creations and experimental productions are always a strong part of the mix. ✉ *2 rue Crémazie Est, St-Jean-Baptiste* ☎ *418/529–2183* ⊕ *theatreperiscope.qc.ca.*

 Shopping

CLOTHING
Ivy
CLOTHING | The mother-daughter duo at the helm of this charming boutique selects the trendiest clothing pieces from both local and international brands, in addition to second-hand accessories, jewelry from local artisans, delicate undergarments, leather bags, and even candles. ✉ *3B boul. René-Lévesque Est, Montcalm* ☎ *418/353–2371* ⊕ *ivyboutique.ca.*

Stop and Shop

Les Halles Cartier is a small but busy food mall on avenue Cartier. It has restaurants and shops that sell fish, flowers, pastries, breads, vegetables, fresh coffee, candies, and some excellent local cheeses, as well as a few Italian and other European specialties. There's no fast food here, but if you're looking for picnic snacks for a day-trip to the Plains of Abraham, plan to fill your basket here before you head to the park. ⊕ *hallescartier.ca.*

★ **Jupon Pressé**
CLOTHING | Lovers of fashion with a penchant for retro, the two friendly owners of this boho-chic boutique, Sylvie and Josiane, curate each season a selection of women's outfits from more than 60 trendy brands. You can also find all kinds of accessories, jewelry, bags, and even vegan body products. ✉ *790 rue St-Jean, Montcalm* ☎ *418/704–7114* ⊕ *jupon-presse.com* ⊗ *Closed Sun.*

Latulippe
SPORTING GOODS | Latulippe is an outdoor equipment and clothing store, a true institution in Québec City operated by the same family since 1940. Visitors will find quality winter coats, boots, and various accessories from the most trusted brands (including a few local ones), just in case they've seriously underpacked and came underprepared for the harsh, sometimes unpredictable Québec climate. The store is slightly outside the core downtown area; hailing a cab is the best way to get there and back. ✉ *637 rue St-Vallier Ouest, Outside the Old City* ☎ *877/529–0024* ⊕ *latulippe.com.*

FOOD

Apikol

WINE/SPIRITS | Apikol combines a honey house, mead house, distillery, and tasting room all under one roof. This innovative microenterprise is equipped to reduce its environmental footprint by practicing zero waste and sustainable beekeeping, respecting the colonies' way of life, conserving resources, and protecting biodiversity. On-site, you'll find gin, mead, and even vodka; you can even participate in a personalized gin-making workshop and tour of the facilities (in English). ⊠ 627 boul. Charest Est, Québec City ☎ 418/522–7000 ⊕ apikol.ca ⊘ Closed Mon. and Tues.

Camellia Sinensis Maison de Thé

FOOD | This modern and elegant space stocks 150 different teas from China, Japan, Africa, and beyond, most of them imported by the owners themselves. You can sign up for a number of tea-tasting sessions and workshops, or just sip some tea on the premises. ⊠ 624 rue St-Joseph Est, St-Roch ☎ 418/525–0247 ⊕ camellia-sinensis.com.

★ Épicerie J.A. Moisan

FOOD | Founded in 1871 by Jean-Alfred Moisan, this place claims the title of the oldest continuously operating grocery store in North America. The original display cases, woodwork, and tin ceilings preserve the old-time feel. The store sells hard-to-find products from various regions of Québec, including cheeses, charcuterie, and some outstanding local ales. The original owner's upstairs home has now been turned into a classic B&B with all the trimmings. ⊠ 699 rue St-Jean, St-Jean-Baptiste ☎ 418/522–0685 ⊕ jamoisan.com.

Le Grand Marché

FOOD | Québec City's answer to Paris's Le Bon Marché, this shop is a must for gourmet-loving travelers. Expect tons of artisan-made goods, such as upscale jams, honeys, ciders, cheeses, chocolate, beers, and maple—all locally made. It's a bit farther out in the suburbs of Québec City, but there is easy and regular bus service on Route 801. ⊠ 250-M boul. Wilfrid-Hamel, Outside the Old City ☎ 418/692–2517 ⊕ www.legrand-marchedequebec.com.

GIFTS

Zone

HOUSEWARES | Design-oriented, whimsical yet practical objects abound in this popular store, which features tons of modern décor, tableware, and accessories for the home and office. From the latest cooking implement to lovely decorative objects and fancy clocks, there's something for just about everyone. ⊠ 999 av. Cartier, Montcalm ☎ 418/522–7373 ⊕ zonemaison.com.

PERFUME/COSMETICS

Aliksir

HEALTH & BEAUTY | This small boutique is packed with essential oils and natural beauty products of all kinds, from skin care to dental care products, mostly organic and largely produced just outside of Québec City. ⊠ 89 rue St-Joseph Est, St-Roch ☎ 418/977–3715 ⊕ aliksir.com ⊘ Closed Mon. and Tues.

SHOPPING MALLS

Galeries de la Capitale

MALL | FAMILY | Thirty-five restaurants, some 280 shops, an IMAX theater, and an adjacent indoor amusement park make this recently and extensively renovated mall ideal for a whole day of family retail therapy. ⊠ 5401 boul. des Galeries, Lebourgneuf, Outside the Old City ☎ 418/627–5800 ⊕ galeriesdelacapitale.com.

Laurier Québec

MALL | There are more than 300 stores in Québec City's busiest mall, with everything from fashion and electronics to children's toys and books. Easily accessible by bus or (from some downtown hotels) shuttle, it's next door to Place de la Cité and Place Ste-Foy. Together, the three malls form the largest stretch of shopping in the city. ✉ *2700 boul. Laurier, Ste-Foy* ☎ *418/651–5000* ⊕ *laurierquebec.com.*

TOYS/GAMES
Benjo
TOYS | FAMILY | Whimsy runs wild at Benjo. This store features games and toys, kids' clothes, a large café with thrones for little princes and princesses, an ample bookstore filled with French storybooks (and some English), and even an electric train you can ride around the store. ✉ *550 boul. Charest Est, St-Roch* ☎ *418/640–0001* ⊕ *benjo.ca.*

Activities

Scenic rivers and nearby mountains (no more than 30 minutes away by car) make Québec City a great place for exploring the outdoors.

Québec City Tourist Center
VISITOR INFORMATION | Contact the tourist board for information about sports and fitness activities around the city. ✉ *12 rue Ste-Anne, Upper Town* ☎ *877/266–5687* ⊕ *quebec-cite.com.*

BIKING
There are more than 100 km (60 miles) of fairly flat, well-maintained bike paths on Québec City's side of the St. Lawrence River and a similar amount on the south shore. Detailed route maps are available through tourism offices. The two best and most scenic of the bike paths are the one that follows the old railway bed in Lévis, accessible near the Québec-Lévis Ferry terminal, and the one that follows the St. Lawrence River on the north shore, all the way to Montmorency Falls. Many parts of the regional network are now part of the province-wide Route Verte, a government-funded, 5,000-km-long (3,100-mile-long) circuit of long-distance bicycle paths and road routes.

Corridor des Cheminots
BIKING | Ambitious cyclists can embark on the 22-km-long (14-mile-long) trail that runs from Québec City near Old Québec to the town of Shannon. It's a slow uphill on the way out—with the reward of an easier ride back. ✉ *Outside the Old City.*

Côte-de-Beaupré
BIKING | Paths along the beginning of the Beaupré coast, at the confluence of the St. Charles and St. Lawrence Rivers, are especially scenic. Ride along bucolic panoramas and scenic views of the river through New France villages along one of the oldest roads in Canada, avenue Royale, on the new Marie-Hélène-Prémont cycling route. The 55-km (3-mile) path starts at Montmorency Falls and finishes at Mont-Ste-Anne. ✉ *Outside the Old City.*

Mont-Ste-Anne
BIKING | The site of the 1998 world mountain-biking championship and races for the annual World Cup has around 150 km (93 miles) of mountain-bike trails and an extreme-mountain-biking park. ✉ *Outside the Old City* ☎ *800/463–1568* ⊕ *mont-sainte-anne.com* 🎫 *C$52 for unlimited access to ski lift and trails.*

BOATING AND FISHING
Permits are needed for fishing in Québec. Most sporting-goods stores and all Walmart and Canadian Tire stores sell permits. A one-day fishing permit for a nonresident is C$20, a three-day permit is C$35, and a seven-day permit is C$53 (and includes all sport fish except Atlantic salmon).

Parc Nautique de Cap-Rouge
KAYAKING | This park, at the western tip of Québec City on the St. Lawrence River, has canoes and pedal boats to rent. ✉ *4155 chemin de la Plage-Jacques-Cartier, Outside the Old City* ☎ *418/641–6148* ⊕ *quebec-cite.com/fr/entreprises/parc-nautique-de-cap-rouge.*

Réserve Faunique des Laurentides

FISHING | This wildlife reserve has good lakes for fishing. It's approximately 48 km (30 miles) north of Québec City via Route 73. Reserve a boat 48 hours in advance by phone. ✉ *Camp Mercier, Outside the Old City* ☎ *800/665–6527* ⊕ *sepaq.com/rf/lau.*

DOG SLEDDING

For centuries, dog sledding has been a part of the Canadian winter experience. Outfitters around Québec City generally offer excursions from January through March.

Au Chalet en Bois Rond

LOCAL SPORTS | FAMILY | This long-established outfitter will teach you how to mush in the forest in the Portneuf area. A half-day expedition, which includes a crash course, dog sledding, a guided tour of kennels, and a snack, costs C$92 per person. The site is a kid's idea of paradise, with winter activites such as snowmobiling, visiting a sugar shack, fatibiking, ice-skating, snowshoeing and more. In the warmer months, swimming at the lake, kayaking, fishing, mountain biking, and more also offered. There are cozy, Canadiana-core cabins to rent on-site year-round. ✉ *325 rang St-Jacques, Ste-Christine-d'Auvergne, Outside the Old City* ☎ *877/629–1233* ⊕ *auchaletenboisrond.com/en.*

★ Secrets Nordiques

LOCAL SPORTS | FAMILY | Experience dog sledding in one of Québec's most beautiful forest villages. A half-day expedition, which includes a crash course, riding your own sled, touring the kennels, and a snack, costs C$130 per person. Snowshoeing, Nordic thermal baths, and a scenic gondola ride atop Mont-Ste-Anne are also available on-site. Visitors can even experience the real workday of a dogsledding musher by spending eight hours feeding, nurturing, harnessing, and taking care of the 65 huskies. In summer, this location offers fishing, mountain biking,

and kennel tours. ✉ *300 rang St-Julien, St-Ferréol-les-Neiges, Outside the Old City* ☎ *418/827–2227* ⊕ *secretsnordiques.com.*

GOLF

The Québec City region has 18 golf courses, and most are open to the public. Reservations are essential in summer.

Club de Golf Cap-Rouge

GOLF | Established in 1959, this is one of the closest courses to the city center, just 25 minutes by car from Vieux-Québec in a pleasant suburban area. Its 18-hole course is set up with variations for women, men, and advanced players. You're close to the St. Lawrence River, so be careful not to let the wind play tricks on you. ✉ *4600 rue St-Félix, Cap-Rouge* ☎ *418/653–9381* ⊕ *golfcap-rouge.qc.ca* ☞ *From C$35* ⛳ *18 holes, 6756 yards, par 72.*

Club de Golf de Mont Tourbillon

GOLF | The cooler air of the Laurentian Mountains is quite welcome on a hot summer day, as you play golf and enjoy views of the rolling hillside and Lac Beauport. Mont Tourbillon features three courses, and the brand-new, modern clubhouse offers a bistro with a pleasant terrace. It's 25 minutes from the city by car via Route 73 North (take the Lac Beauport exit). In winter, golfing yields the way to long, fun slides. ✉ *55 montée du Golf, Lac-Beauport* ☎ *418/849–4418* ⊕ *monttourbillon.com* ☞ *From C$40 weekends, from C$35 weekdays* ⛳ *Blue Course: 18 holes, 6090 yards, par 70; White Course: 18 holes, 5590 yards, par 70; Red Course: 18 holes, 4625 yards, par 70.*

Club de Golf Le St-Ferréol

GOLF | Located within sight of the Mont-Ste-Anne ski slopes, this club has one of the best and best-priced courses in the region—it's been fine-tuned by pro Denis Gagné. The course is a half-hour drive northeast of Québec City, and features a large driving range for practice. ✉ *1700 boul. les Neiges, St-Ferréol-les-Neiges*

☎ 418/827–3778 ⊕ golfstferreol.com ✉ From C$41 ⚑ 18 holes, 6445 yards, par 72.

HIKING AND JOGGING

Runners and foot soldiers have a choice of routes in areas like Battlefields Park, Cartier-Brébeuf, and along the waterfront in the city itself.

Bois-de-Coulonge Park

RUNNING | Along with Battlefields Park, Bois-de-Coulonge is one of the most popular places for jogging, with forest trails and river views. ✉ 1215 Grande Allée Ouest, Outside the Old City ☎ 418/528–0773.

ICE-SKATING

In addition to rinks in town, Village Vacances Valcartier (⇨ see the Snow Slides section), just outside Québec City, offers skating trails with lighting and sound systems.

RAFTING

Just outside the city, the Jacques-Cartier River (to the west) and Malbaie River (to the east) both make for an easy white-water rafting day-trip. Village Vacances Valcartier (⇨ see the Snow Slides section) also runs three-hour rafting excursions on the river from May through September.

Excursions Jacques-Cartier

WHITE-WATER RAFTING | This outfitter runs rafting trips on the Jacques-Cartier River, about 48 km (30 miles) northwest of Québec City, from May through October. Tours originate from Tewkesbury, a half-hour drive from Québec City. A half-day trip ranges from C$129 per person, wet suits included. ✉ 860 av. Jacques-Cartier Nord, Stoneham-et-Tewkesbury ☎ 418/848–7238 ⊕ excursionsj-cartier.com.

Expéditions Nouvelle-Vague

RAFTING | FAMILY | Navigate the exhilarating rapids of the Jacques-Cartier River while enjoying the breathtaking natural beauty just a 35 minute drive from Québec City. Passionate and expert guides ensure a safe and thrilling journey for all adventure seekers of all ages. A three-hour ride costs around C$119. ✉ 1472 5e av., St-Gabriel-de-Valcartier, Québec City ☎ 418/520–7238 ⊕ expeditionsnouvellevague.com.

SKIING

Skiing is very popular here, whether it's downhill on one of the mountains surrounding the city or cross-country in an urban park. A dynamic landscape, top-notch ski resorts, and lots of fresh powder have helped make this a major training area for some of Canada's top athletes.

⇨ For more cross-country and downhill skiing options near Québec City, see the Side Trips from Québec City chapter.

CROSS-COUNTRY

Regroupement des Stations de Ski de Fond

SKIING & SNOWBOARDING | Thirty-seven cross-country ski centers in the Québec area have 2,000 km (1,240 miles) of groomed trails and heated shelters between them; contact this group for more information. Many also offer snowshoeing trails. ✉ Québec City ⊕ skidefondraquette.com.

DOWNHILL

Multiple downhill ski resorts are nearby, and some are barely 30 minutes away from downtown Québec City. Most have night skiing. ⇨ For information on Le Massif and Mont-Ste-Anne, see the Côte-de-Beaupré section in Side Trips from Québec City.

Le Relais

SKIING & SNOWBOARDING | There are 28 trails and a vertical drop of 734 feet at this relatively small, family-friendly ski center, where you can buy lift tickets by the hour. Le Relais is about 20 minutes from downtown Québec City. ✉ 1084 boul. du Lac, Lac-Beauport ☎ 418/849–1851 ⊕ skirelais.com ✉ C$57.

Station Touristique Stoneham

SKIING & SNOWBOARDING | Stoneham is 20 minutes north of Old Québec. The hill has a vertical drop of 1,380 feet, with a number of long, easy slopes and some more challenging runs. It has 42 downhill runs and seven lifts, plus three terrain parks and one super-half-pipe. ✉ *600 chemin du Hibou, Stoneham-et-Tewkesbury* ☎ *800/463–6888* ⊕ *ski-stoneham. com* 🎟 *C$89.*

SKI CENTERS

Les Sentiers du Moulin

SKIING & SNOWBOARDING | This center is 19 km (12 miles) north of the city and has more than 20 marked trails covering 48 km (28 miles), overall, with 28 km (17 miles) multitrack. There's even fatbiking and snowshoeing. ✉ *99 chemin du Moulin, Lac-Beauport* ☎ *418/849–9652* ⊕ *sentiersdumoulin.com* 🎟 *C$22.*

Station Touristique Duchesnay

SKIING & SNOWBOARDING | Located west of Québec City, this center has 150 km (93 miles) of marked trails, which can be used for snowshoeing and cross-country skiing in the winter. There's a wonderful lakeside inn on-site. ✉ *140 montée de l'Auberge, Ste-Catherine-de-la-Jacques-Cartier* ☎ *866/683–2711* ⊕ *sepaq.com/ct/ duc* 🎟 *C$45.*

SNOWMOBILING

Québec is the birthplace of the snowmobile, and with 32,000 km (19,840 miles) of trails, it's one of the best places in the world for the sport. Two major trails, the 2,000-km (1,250-mile) Trans-Québec Snowmobile Trail and the 1,300-km (806-mile) Fur Traders Tour, run just north of Québec City. Trail maps are available at tourist offices. Several of the dog-sledding operators (⇨ *see the Dog Sledding section*) also run snowmobiling excursions and expeditions.

Nord Expe

SNOW SPORTS | Full-day and half-day introductory snowmobile packages are available 30 minutes from Québec City, with professional certified snowmobile guides. Access to snowmobile circuits and routes is provided in a safe and natural setting, in the middle of the mountains and the Jacques-Cartier Valley. Depending on the duration of the expedition, rates vary from C$200 to C$600. ✉ *354 rue Auclair, Outside the Old City* ☎ *418/825–1772* ⊕ *nordexpe.com.*

SNOW SLIDES

Village Vacances Valcartier

SNOW SPORTS | FAMILY | Hop on an inner tube or carpet and shoot down one of more than 35 snow slides here. Or join six to 12 others for a snow-raft ride on one of three groomed trails. You can also take a dizzying ride on the Tornado, a giant inner tube that seats eight and spins down the slopes. Rafting and sliding cost C$45 per day for those taller than 52 inches, C$38 for those between 39 and 52 inches, and are free for those under 39 inches. Trails open daily at 10 am; closing times vary. ✉ *1860 boul. Valcartier, St-Gabriel-de-Valcartier* ☎ *888/384–5524* ⊕ *valcartier.com.*

SPAS

Nordique Spa Stoneham

SPA | Located on the banks of the majestic Jacques-Cartier River, Nordique offers a Scandinavian-style relaxation concept based on alternating heat and cold. Finnish sauna, Turkish steam bath, outdoor whirlpool, and massage therapy are available. The site also offers the rental of mini-cabins, also Nordic, for two people; access to the spa is included in the price of the night. ✉ *747 rue Jacques-Cartier Nord, Stoneham-et-Tewkesbury* ☎ *418/848–7727* ⊕ *lenordique.com* 🎟 *C$64.*

Sibéria Spa

SPA | A 20-minute drive from Vieux-Québec, Siberia Spa offers thermal and cold baths, a eucalyptus steam room, a relaxing yurt, an elegant café set inside a former chapel, and a quiet pavilion where you can sit by a fire and look out to the Jacques-Cartier River. Massages and packages run from C$100 to C$300. It's normally adults only, but families are welcome on Sunday morning (between 9 and noon) and in regular hours during holidays and spring break. ✉ *339 rue de Genève, Lac-Beauport* ☎ *855/841–1325* ⊕ *siberiaspa.com* ⌂ *C$55, C$44 evenings.*

WATER PARKS

Village Vacances Valcartier

WATER SPORTS | FAMILY | The largest water park in Canada has a wave pool, a 1-km (½-mile) tropical-river adventure called the Amazon, more than 35 water slides, and a 100-foot accelerating slide on which bathers reach a speed of up to 80 kph (50 mph). The interior Bora Parc, featuring 14 slides, a river, and a wave pool, is open year-round. ✉ *1860 boul. Valcartier, St-Gabriel-de-Valcartier* ☎ *888/384–5524* ⊕ *valcartier.com* ⌂ *C$50.*

Chapter 6

SIDE TRIPS FROM QUÉBEC CITY

Updated by
Chris Barry

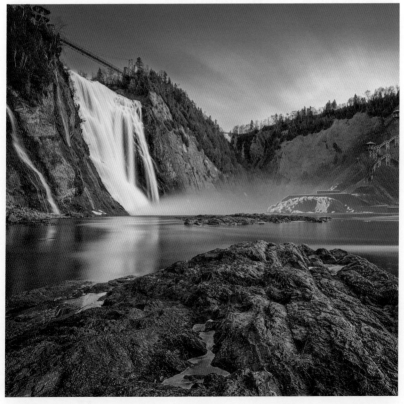

👁 Sights   🍴 Restaurants   🛏 Hotels   🛍 Shopping   🍸 Nightlife

★★★★★   ★★★★★   ★★★★★   ★★★★★   ★★★★★

WELCOME TO
SIDE TRIPS FROM QUÉBEC CITY

TOP REASONS TO GO

★ **Ski at Le Massif:** This three-peak ski resort has the largest vertical drop in eastern Canada, at more than 2,500 feet.

★ **Whale-watch in Tadoussac:** About 220 km (137 miles) east of Québec City, you can see small white beluga whales—an endangered species—year-round in the Saguenay River.

★ **Farm-hop on Île d'Orléans:** The "Garden of Québec" is covered with farmland and bed-and-breakfasts, and makes for the perfect day or overnight trip from Québec City.

★ **Take the footbridge across Montmorency Falls:** These waterfalls on the Côte-de-Beaupré are double the height of Niagara Falls. The bridge and stairs, which go over and around them, make for a spectacular stroll.

★ **See Basilique Ste-Anne-de-Beaupré:** More than a million people a year make pilgrimages to this church, named after the patron saint of Québec.

1 **Ste-Pétronille.** Enjoy splendid views of Montmorency Falls and Cap Diamant.

2 **St-Laurent de l'Île d'Orléans.** Farm stands and strawberry fields.

3 **St-Jean.** Find preserved row houses from the 1800s and strawberry farms.

4 **St-François.** A rustic village with an observation tower.

5 **Ste-Famille.** The island's oldest parish.

6 **St-Pierre.** Shop for local specialties at the most populated part of the island.

7 **Côte-de-Beaupré.** Rich landscapes alongside the St. Lawrence River.

8 **Baie-St-Paul.** The cultural capital of the Charlevoix region.

9 **St-Joseph-de-la-Rive.** Board the ferry to the majestic L'Île-aux-Coudres.

10 **La Malbaie.** Rich in history and natural beauty.

11 **Tadoussac.** One of the best whale-watching centers in Québec.

12 **Port Saguenay.** Famous for Lac St-Jean.

13 **Trois-Rivières.** The second-oldest city in Québec.

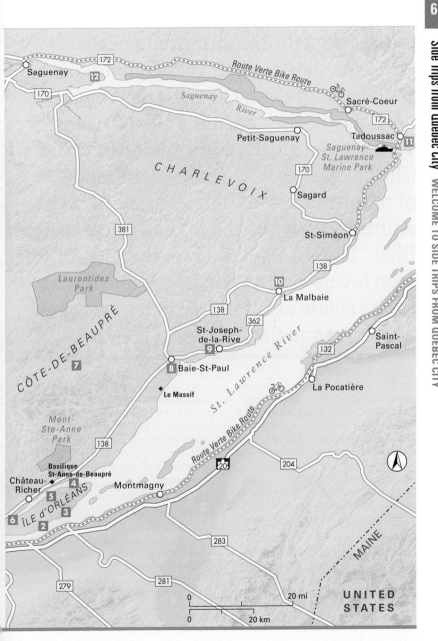

Experience a deeper understanding of this region's history and culture by venturing outside the city. In addition to the beauty of Montmorency Falls and Côte-de-Beaupré, get acquainted with rural life and the region's French heritage on the charming Île d'Orléans. There's also much to see and do in the Charlevoix area—a diverse landscape of mountains and rolling valleys with stunning views of the St. Lawrence River. Baie-St-Paul is a hub for art and food lovers, and Tadoussac is known for its rustic excursions, such as whale-watching and fjord tours.

Montmorency Falls is an excellent first stop on any adventure outside the city. From there, you can cruise up Québec's Côte-de-Beaupré and eventually make your way to Ste-Anne-de-Beaupré, where there's an immense neo-Roman basilica. Or take the bridge to Île d'Orléans, where you can pick fresh berries, sample ice cider fermented from frozen apples, and shop for antiques. A leisurely drive around the island can be done in a day.

Charlevoix, a couple of hours from Québec City, takes more planning and probably an overnight stay, but is well worth the drive. There are plenty of gorgeous villages and picnic spots along the way. Artists of all disciplines draw inspiration from this region, which is steeped in natural beauty and Algonquin history. Approaching Tadoussac, at the eastern edge of Charlevoix, the St. Lawrence River begins to seem like the open sea—it's more than 20 km (12 miles) wide at this point. Slicing into the land is the dramatic Saguenay Fjord, one of the largest fjords in the world.

MAJOR REGIONS

Île d'Orléans. The Algonquins called it Minigo, the "Bewitched Place," and over the years the island's tranquil rural beauty has inspired poets and painters. Île d'Orléans is only 15 minutes by car from downtown Québec City, but a visit here is one of the best ways to get a feel for traditional life in rural Québec. Centuries-old homes and some of the oldest churches in the region dot the road that rings the island. About 8 km (5 miles) wide and 35 km (22 miles) long, Île d'Orléans is made up of six small villages that have sought over the years to retain their identities: Ste-Pétronille, St-Laurent de l'Île d'Orléans, St-Jean, St-François, Ste-Famille, and St-Pierre. The bridge to the mainland was built in 1935, and in 1970 the island was declared a historic area to protect it from most sorts of development.

To get to Île d'Orléans, take Route 440 (Autoroute Dufferin–Montmorency) northeast. After a drive of about 10 km (6 miles), take the bridge (Pont de l'Île d'Orléans) to the island. The main road, chemin Royal (Route 368), circles the island, extending 67 km (42 miles) through the island's six villages; the route turns into chemin du Bout de l'Île as it loops around the western tip of the island.

Côte-de-Beaupré. Driving along this coast offers views of Île d'Orléans, as well as Montmorency Falls and the famous pilgrimage site, Ste-Anne-de-Beaupré.

To get to Côte-de-Beaupré, take Route 440 (Autoroute Dufferin–Montmorency) northeast from Québec City. It's approximately 9.5 km (6 miles) to the exit for the Chutes Montmorency and about 35 km (21 miles) to Ste-Anne-de-Beaupré.

Charlevoix. People refer to Charlevoix as the "Switzerland of Québec" due to its terrain of mountains, valleys, streams, and waterfalls. A couple of hours from Québec City, it takes more planning and probably an overnight stay but is well worth the drive. Charlevoix's charming villages line the shore of the St. Lawrence River for about 200 km (125 miles). Artists of all disciplines draw inspiration from this region, which is steeped in natural beauty and Algonquin history. Approaching Tadoussac, at the eastern edge of Charlevoix, the St. Lawrence River begins to seem like the open sea—it's

more than 20 km (12 miles) wide at this point. Winter activities include downhill and cross-country skiing, snowmobiling, ice fishing, dog sledding, and snowshoeing. Charlevoix's many great local food products and restaurants are also a big draw for tourists. Slicing into the land is the dramatic Saguenay Fjord, one of the largest fjords in the world.

To get to Charlevoix from Québec City, take Route 440 (Autoroute Dufferin–Montmorency) northeast and then continue on Route 138 past Côte-de-Beaupré. From there you'll be able to branch out for destinations such as Petite-Rivière-St-François or Baie-St-Paul.

Planning

When to Go

Côte-de-Beaupré, Île d'Orléans, and Charlevoix are spectacular in the fall, when you can leaf-peep and go apple picking. Summer means roadside stands featuring fresh-from-the-farm produce on Île d'Orléans or Côte-de-Beaupré. Artists and art lovers flock to Baie-St-Paul in Charlevoix for festivals and gallery openings. It's also the perfect time to see beluga whales in Tadoussac. In winter, in all regions, there are plenty of cold-weather activities, including cross-country skiing, snowshoeing, and ice fishing. The area's best downhill skiing can be found in Charlevoix, but if you don't want to tackle driving on mountain roads, consider taking a shuttle. Spring has its own magic, when the snow melts and the maple syrup starts to flow.

Getting Here and Around

The best, and in some cases the only way to explore these regions is by car, and this makes it easy to spend as much or as little time as desired in any given area. Start by heading northeast out of Québec City on Route 440 (Autoroute Dufferin–Montmorency) and then Route 138 (boulevard Ste-Anne).

Another way to explore the exceptional beauty of the region is to hop aboard Le Train du Massif Charlevoix, a train that runs mid-June through mid-October along the shoreline from Parc de la Chute-Montmorency station to Baie-St-Paul or La Malbaie, with several excursion options. ⇨ *For further details, see the Baie-St-Paul and La Malbaie sections of this chapter.*

TRAIN CONTACT Train de Charlevoix.
☎ *418/240–4124, 844/737–3282* ⊕ *www. traindecharlevoix.com.*

Québec continues to expand its Route Verte (Green Route), a 5,000-km (3,100-mile) network of bike trails in the southern part of the province.

⇨ *For more information on getting here and around, refer to the Travel Smart chapter.*

Hotels

Reservations at hotels are highly recommended, although off-season it's possible to book a room the same day. B&Bs are the most common lodging options on Île d'Orléans, although there is a handful of inns and one motel. Côte-de-Beaupré, on the other hand, has not only plenty of inns and B&Bs but several hotels and motels as well.

Given its status as one of Québec's premier summer vacation destinations, the Charlevoix region has lots to offer travelers on almost any budget. Nevertheless, it's wise to book ahead in high season, especially if you're looking for one of the less expensive rooms here, which tend to fill up pretty quickly during the summer months.

⇨ *Hotel and restaurant reviews have been shortened. For full information, visit Fodors.com. Hotel prices are the lowest cost of a standard double room in high season. Restaurant prices are the average cost of a main course at dinner or, if dinner is not served, at lunch.*

WHAT IT COSTS in Canadian Dollars

	$	$$	$$$	$$$$
HOTELS				
	under C$160	C$160–C$200	C$201–C$250	over C$250
RESTAURANTS				
	under C$12	C$12–C$20	C$21–C$30	over C$30

Restaurants

Some of the restaurants on the Côte-de-Beaupré and Île d'Orléans are open only during high season, May to October, so check ahead. But visitors who do arrive in season won't be disappointed. Fast-food or chain outlets are essentially absent from the island, and your best—and most widely available—option is to sample some of the regional cuisine on offer. And while fine dining is the order of the day on Île d'Orléans, those traveling on a budget won't go hungry, as there are some good pubs and family-style restaurants with fairly reasonable prices.

In Charlevoix, the same rules apply—call ahead if you're visiting from June to September or during the Christmas holidays. During summer, Charlevoix is a food lover's haven, with fresh berries and cheeses sold roadside and plenty of bistros in the towns. Pick up a map (available at most hotels and restaurants) of La Route des Saveurs, a route through the region dotted with restaurants and farms, and taste your way to Tadoussac.

Visitor Information

CONTACTS Association Touristique Régionale de Charlevoix. ✉ *495 boul. de Comporté, La Malbaie* ☎ *418/665–4454, 800/667–2276* ⊕ *www.tourisme-charlevoix.com.* **Bureau touristique de l'île d'Orléans.** (*Tourist Information Center Île d'Orléans*) ✉ *490 côte du Pont, St-Pierre-de-l'Île-d'Orléans* ☎ *418/828–9411, 866/941–9411* ⊕ *tourisme.iledorleans.com.* **Centre d'Interpretation de la Côte-de-Beaupré.** (*Beaupré Coast Interpretation Center*) ✉ *7976 av. Royale, C.P. 40, Château-Richer* ☎ *418/824–3677, 877/824–3677.*

Ste-Pétronille

17 km (10½ miles) northeast of Québec City.

The lovely village of Ste-Pétronille, the first to be settled on Île d'Orléans, is west of the bridge to the island. Founded in 1648, the community was chosen in 1759 by British general James Wolfe for his headquarters. With 40,000 soldiers and 100 ships, the English bombarded French-occupied Québec City and the surrounding shorelines.

In the late 19th century, the English population of Québec developed Ste-Pétronille into a resort village. This area is considered to be the island's most beautiful, not only because of its spectacular views of Montmorency Falls and Québec City but also for its Regency-style English villas and exquisitely tended gardens.

GETTING HERE AND AROUND
Once across the bridge from the mainland, côte du Pont leads to Route 368. Turn right on chemin Royal and drive 4 km (2½ miles) to Ste-Pétronille.

◉ Sights

Maison Gourdeau de Beaulieu
HISTORIC HOME | The island's first home was built in 1648 for Jacques Gourdeau de Beaulieu, who was the first seigneur (a landholder who distributed lots to tenant farmers) of Ste-Pétronille. Remodeled over the years, this white house with blue shutters now incorporates both French and Québec styles. Its thick walls and dormer windows are characteristic of Breton architecture, but its sloping, bell-shaped roof, designed to protect buildings from large amounts of snow, is typical Québec style. The house is not open to the public. ✉ *137 chemin du Bout de l'Île, Ste-Pétronille.*

Plante Family Farm
FARM/RANCH | Pick apples and strawberries (in season) or buy fresh fruits, vegetables, and apple cider at this family farm. In March/April, enjoy maple-sugar treats from the roadside shack. ✉ *8684 chemin Royal, Ste-Pétronille* ☎ *418/828–9603, 418/828–0028* ⊕ *www.polyculture-plante.com.*

Rue Horatio-Walker
STREET | Art fans might want to explore this tiny street off chemin Royal, named after the early-19th-century painter known for his landscapes of the island. Horatio Walker lived on this street from 1904 until his death in 1938. At nos. 11 and 13 rue Horatio-Walker are his home and workshop, but neither are open to the public. ✉ *Ste-Pétronille.*

Vignoble de Ste-Pétronille
WINERY | Since they bought it in 2003, Louis Denault and Nathalie Lane have turned this vineyard into one of the best wine producers in Québec. Most of the wine is produced from a hybrid variety called vandal-cliche, which was bred by a Laval University biologist to thrive in the area's climate, along with a growing proportion of vidal. The results are a range of fresh, crisp white wines (still and bubbly), as well as ice wine. The

winery has also started producing small amounts of Riesling, and does some tasty reds. In summer, Panache Mobile, a food cart managed by Panache, one of Québec City's best restaurants, serves delicious lunches on a terrace with a stunning view of the St. Lawrence River and Montmorency Falls. ✉ *8705 chemin Royal, Ste-Pétronille* ☎ *418/828–9554* ⊕ *www.vs-p.ca* ✉ *Wed.–Sat. 1-hour VIP tasting tour C$25.*

Hotels

Auberge La Goéliche

$$$$ | **B&B/INN** | This English-style country manor (rebuilt in 1996–97 following a fire) is steps away from the St. Lawrence River, and the small but elegant rooms, decorated with antiques, all have river views. **Pros:** spectacular location; great base for exploring the island; beautiful views of the river. **Cons:** riverfront but no access to the water; some rooms are quite small; restaurant has a limited menu. $ *Rooms from: C$325* ✉ *22 rue du Quai, Ste-Pétronille* ☎ *418/828–2248, 888/511–2248* ⊕ *www.goeliche.ca* ⌑ *16 rooms, 3 suites* ۞ *Free Breakfast.*

🛍 Shopping

FOOD

Chocolaterie de l'Île d'Orléans

CHOCOLATE | Belgian chocolate is combined with local ingredients to produce the handmade confections here: with a maple butter filling, for example, or *framboisette,* made from raspberries. In summer, try the 24 different kinds of ice creams and sherbets, or bring home some chocolate-infused jams. There's a smaller counter in the presbytery of St-François, at the other end of the island. ✉ *8830 chemin Royal, Ste-Pétronille* ☎ *418/828–2252* ⊕ *www.chocolaterieorleans.com.*

What's in a Name?

l'île d'Orléans was discovered in 1935, around the same time as the future site of Québec City. Explorer Jacques Cartier noticed an abundance of vines and called it the Island of Bacchus, after the Greek god of wine. (A couple of vineyards are working hard to earn back that moniker.) In 1536, Cartier renamed the island in honor of the duke of Orléans, son of the French king François I. Its fertile soil and abundant fishing made it so attractive to settlers that in the 17th century there were more people living here than in Québec City.

St-Laurent de l'Île d'Orléans

9 km (5½ miles) east of Ste-Pétronille.

Founded in 1679, St-Laurent is one of the island's maritime villages. Until as late as 1935, residents used boats as their main means of transportation. St-Laurent has a rich history in farming and fishing. Work is under way to help bring back to the island some of the species of fish that were once abundant here.

GETTING HERE AND AROUND

Continue along chemin Royal from Ste-Pétronille, looping around the western end of the island and driving east along the southern shore.

Sights

Église St-Laurent

CHURCH | The tall, inspiring church that stands next to the village marina on chemin Royal was built in 1860 on the site of an 18th-century church that had to be torn down. One of the church's procession chapels is a miniature stone reproduction of the original. ⊠ *1532 chemin Royal, St-Laurent* ☎ *418/828–2551* ✉ *Free.*

La Forge à Pique-Assaut

STORE/MALL | This working forge belongs to the talented local artisan Guy Bel, who has done ironwork restoration for Québec City. He was born in Lyon, France, and studied there at the École des Beaux-Arts. You can watch him and his team at work; his stylish candlesticks, chandeliers, fireplace tools, and other ironwork are for sale. ⊠ *2200 chemin Royal, St-Laurent* ☎ *418/828–9300* ⊕ *www.forge-pique-assaut.com.*

Parc Maritime de St-Laurent

CITY PARK | This former boatyard includes the Chalouperie Godbout (Godbout Longboat), which holds a collection of tools used by specialist craftsmen during the golden era of boat-building. You can picnic here and watch fishermen at work, trapping eels in tall nets at low tide. ⊠ *120 chemin de la Chalouperie, St-Laurent* ☎ *418/828–9673* ⊕ *www.parcmaritime.ca* ✉ *C$8.*

Restaurants

Moulin de St-Laurent

$$$ | **CAFÉ** | You can dine inside amid old stone walls or outside on the patios at the foot of a tiny, peaceful waterfall at this restaurant, which was converted from an early-18th-century stone mill. Scrumptious snacks, such as quiche and salads, are available on the terrace, and evening dishes include local pork tenderloin and venison stew. **Known for:** cozy atmosphere; hearty dishes; pleasant patio. ⑤ *Average main: C$25* ⊠ *6436 chemin Royal, St-Laurent* ☎ *418/829–3888, 888/629–3888* ⊕ *www.moulin-stlaurent.qc.ca* ⊗ *No dinner Mon. and Fri. No lunch weekends. Schedule may vary May, June, Sept., and Oct.*

St-Jean

12 km (7 miles) northeast of St-Laurent.

The village of St-Jean used to be occupied by river pilots and navigators. At sea most of the time, the sailors didn't need the large homes and plots of land that the farmers did. Often richer than farmers, they displayed their affluence by building their houses with bricks brought back from Scotland as ballast. Most of St-Jean's small, homogeneous row houses were built between 1840 and 1860.

GETTING HERE AND AROUND

From St-Laurent, continue northeast along chemin Royal.

◉ Sights

Église St-Jean

CHURCH | At the eastern end of the village sits a massive granite structure built in 1749, with large red doors and a towering steeple. The church resembles a ship; it's big, round, and appears to be sitting right on the river. Paintings of the patron saints of seamen line the interior walls. The church's cemetery is also intriguing, especially if you can read French. Back in the 1700s, piloting the St. Lawrence was a dangerous profession; the cemetery tombstones recall the many lives lost in these harsh waters. ⊠ *2001 chemin Royal, St-Jean* ☎ *418/828–2551* ⊕ *www.ecdq.org/eglise-saint-jean* ✉ *Free.*

Manoir Mauvide-Genest

HISTORIC HOME | St-Jean's beautiful Normandy-style manor was built in 1734 for Jean Mauvide, the surgeon to Louis XV, and his wife, Marie-Anne Genest. The most notable thing about this house, which still has its original thick walls, ceiling beams, and fireplaces, is the degree to which it has held up over the years. The house serves as an interpretation center of New France's seigneurial regime, with 18th-century furniture, a historic vegetable garden,

Tucked away on the far southeastern side of Île d'Orléans, St-Jean is perhaps the most picturesque of all the small villages that pepper the island.

a multimedia presentation, and tours with guides dressed in 18th-century costumes. ⊠ 4818 chemin Royal, St-Jean ☎ 418/829–2630 ⊕ www.manoirmauvidegenest.com ✉ Prices vary depending on exhibitions.

🍴 Restaurants

La Midinette Boulangerie de Fancy and Restaurant

$$ | BAKERY | This excellent, friendly bakery is located in the village of St-Jean's historic rectory, across the street from the church and a promenade along the river. In addition to delicious fresh croissants, pastries, and breads, La Midinette also offers pizzas and other light lunches that you can enjoy on the large covered porch in the summer. **Known for:** great pastries; light lunches; covered patio. ⑤ Average main: C$14 ⊠ 4624 chemin Royal, St-Jean ☎ 418/829–3162 ⊙ No dinner.

St-François

12 km (7 miles) northeast of St-Jean.

Sprawling open fields separate 17th-century farmhouses in St-François, the island's least-toured and most rustic village. At the eastern tip of the island, this community was settled mainly by farmers. St-François is the perfect place to visit one of the island's *cabanes à sucre* (maple-sugaring shacks), found along chemin Royal. Stop at a hut for a tasting tour; sap is gathered from the maple groves and boiled until it's reduced to syrup (it takes 40 gallons of sap to produce one gallon of syrup). Boiled a little more and poured over snow, it becomes a delicious toffee. Maple-syrup season is from mid-March through April.

GETTING HERE AND AROUND

From St-Jean, continue northeast along chemin Royal.

◉ Sights

Église St-François

CHURCH | Built in 1734, St-François is one of eight extant churches in Québec dating from the French regime. At the time the English seized Québec City in 1759, General James Wolfe knew St-François to be a strategic point along the St. Lawrence. Consequently, he stationed British troops here and used the church as a military hospital. In 1988, a car crash set the church on fire, and most of the interior treasures were lost. A separate children's cemetery stands as a silent witness to the difficult life of early residents. ⊠ *3497 chemin Royal, St-François* ☎ *418/828–2551* 🖘 *Free.*

Observation Tower

VIEWPOINT | This 60-foot-high wooden tower within a picnic area is well sited for viewing the majestic St. Lawrence and the many small islands in the estuary. In spring and fall, wild Canada geese can be seen here. The area is about 2 km (1 mile) north of Église St-François on chemin Royal. ⊠ *3465 chemin Royal, St-François* ☎ *418/829–3100.*

Ste-Famille

14 km (9 miles) west of St-François.

The village of Ste-Famille, founded in 1661, has exquisite scenery, including abundant apple orchards and strawberry fields with views of Côte-de-Beaupré and Mont-Ste-Anne in the distance. But it also has historic charm, with the area's highest concentration of stone houses dating from the French regime.

GETTING HERE AND AROUND

From St-François, chemin Royal cuts north across the eastern tip of the island and continues west along the northern shore.

◉ Sights

Église Ste-Famille

CHURCH | This impressive church, constructed in 1749, is the only one in Québec to have three bell towers at its front. The ceiling was redone in the mid-19th century with elaborate designs in wood and gold. The church also holds a famous painting, *L'Enfant Jésus Voyant la Croix (Baby Jesus Looking at the Cross)*; it was done in 1670 by Frère Luc (Brother Luc), who had been sent from France to decorate churches in the area. ⊠ *2483 chemin Royal, Ste-Famille* ☎ *418/828–2656* 🖘 *Free.*

◉ Restaurants

Microbrasserie de l'île d'Orléans

$$ | CANADIAN | This is one of the most interesting microbreweries in the Québec City region, producing a colorful range of beers named after historical characters from Île d'Orléans. You can taste them all at the adjoining Pub Le Mitan, along with standard pub fare including burgers, pizzas, and fries. **Known for:** great beer; pub fare; river view. ⑤ *Average main: C$23* ⊠ *2471 chemin Royal, Ste-Famille* ☎ *418/203–0588 microbrewery, 418/829–0408 Pub Le Matin* ⊕ *www.microorleans.com* ⊙ *Kitchen closes at 8.*

St-Pierre

14 km (9 miles) southwest of Ste-Famille.

Established in 1679, this town is set on a plateau that has the island's most fertile land and has long been the center of traditional farming industries. The best products grown here are potatoes, asparagus, and corn. The Espace Félix-Leclerc—an exhibit by day and a *boîte à chansons* (combination coffeehouse and bar with live performances) by night—works to honor the late singer and songwriter, who made St-Pierre his home. The bridge back to the mainland and Route 440 is just west on chemin Royal.

GETTING HERE AND AROUND
From Ste-Famille, continue southwest along chemin Royal. After visiting St-Pierre, the same road will take you back to the bridge to return to the mainland.

Sights

Cassis Monna et Filles
STORE/MALL | This family farm has won international awards for its crème de cassis, a liqueur made from black currants. In its vast and attractive tasting room and shop, you can taste free samples of the strong, sweet cassis or black currant wines; the tour explains how they are made. In summer, you can sample foods made with cassis at La Monnaguette, the house bistro featuring a terrace overlooking the river. ⊠ *1225 chemin Royal, St-Pierre-de-l'Île-d'Orléans* ☎ *418/828–2525* ⊕ *www.cassismonna.com/en* 🍴 *Free* ⊙ *Dairy Bar and La Monnaguette restaurant closed late Oct.–Apr.* ☞ *Check website for hours.*

Église St-Pierre
CHURCH | The oldest church on the island dates from 1717. It's no longer used for worship, but it was restored during the 1960s and is open to visitors. Many original components are still intact, such as benches with compartments below where hot bricks and stones were placed to keep people warm in winter. Félix Leclerc, the first Québécois singer-songwriter to make a mark in Europe, is buried in the cemetery nearby. ⊠ *1445 chemin Royal, St-Pierre-de-l'Île-d'Orléans* ☎ *418/828–9824* 🍴 *Free.*

Restaurants

Les Ancêtres Auberge Restaurant
$$$$ | **CANADIAN** | If you're in the market for traditional French Canadian food, Les Ancêtres Auberge is highly unlikely to disappoint. With all dishes created from local ingredients, you can dine on classic Québécois fare like meatballs and pork hock ragout with root vegetables and pickled beets, or try another house specialty, the "famous" Ancêtres pea-and-ham soup. **Known for:** excellent views; Ancêtres pea-and-ham soup; local ingredients. $ *Average main: C$35* ⊠ *1101 chemin Royal, St-Pierre-de-l'Île-d'Orléans* ☎ *418/828-2718, 855/828-1362* ⊕ *www.lesancetres.ca/en* ⊙ *Closed Sun. and Mon. No lunch.*

Côte-de-Beaupré

25 km (15 miles) east of Québec City.

As legend has it, when explorer Jacques Cartier first caught sight of the north shore of the St. Lawrence River in 1535, he exclaimed, "*Quel beau pré!*" ("What a lovely meadow!"), because the area was the first inviting piece of land he had spotted since leaving France. Today the Côte-de-Beaupré (Beaupré Coast), first settled by French farmers, stretches 40 km (25 miles) east from Québec City to the famous pilgrimage site of Ste-Anne-de-Beaupré. Historic Route 360, or avenue Royale, winds its way from Beauport to St-Joachim, east of Ste-Anne-de-Beaupré. The impressive Chute Montmorency (Montmorency Falls) lie between Québec City and Ste-Anne-de-Beaupré.

GETTING HERE AND AROUND
Route 440 (Autoroute Dufferin–Montmorency) heads northeast from Québec City along the Côte-de-Beaupré. It's approximately 9.5 km (6 miles) to the exit for the Chutes Montmorency and about 35 km (21 miles) to Ste-Anne-de-Beaupré.

Côte-de-Beaupré
and Île d'Orléans

Did You Know?

The Basilique Ste-Anne-de-Beaupré draws more than a million pilgrims each year.

⊙ Sights

Atelier Paré *(Economuseum of Wood Sculpture)*

SPECIALTY MUSEUM | Québec legends are the theme for the wood sculptures showcased at this "economuseum," a workshop, gallery, garden, and boutique. Visitors may watch and interact with artisans at work and spend anywhere from a few hours to a full day enjoying the unique experience provided here. The grounds are ideal for strolling, picnicking, and discovering the fascinating characters of Québec's history and culture that have inspired the artists at this charming atelier, off the beaten path but well worth the quick trip from Québec City. ⊠ *9269 av. Royale, Ste-Anne-de-Beaupré* 🕾 *418/827–3992* ⊕ *www.atelierpare.com* 🖃 *C$5.*

★ Basilique Ste-Anne-de-Beaupré

RELIGIOUS BUILDING | Named for Québec's patron saint (the mother of the Virgin Mary), the small town of Ste-Anne-de-Beaupré is on Route 138, east of Québec City. It attracts more than a million pilgrims each year who come to visit the region's most famous religious site.

The French brought their devotion to St. Anne (also the patron saint of shipwrecked sailors) when they sailed across the Atlantic to New France. According to local legend, St. Anne was responsible for saving voyagers from shipwrecks in the harsh waters of the St. Lawrence. In 1650, Breton sailors caught in a storm vowed to erect a chapel in honor of this patron saint at the exact spot where they landed.

The present neo-Roman basilica, constructed in 1923, is the fifth to be built on the site where the sailors first touched ground. The original 17th-century wood chapel was built too close to the St. Lawrence and was swept away by river flooding.

The gigantic structure is in the shape of a Latin cross and has two imposing granite steeples. The interior has 22 chapels and 18 altars, as well as rounded arches and numerous ornaments in the Romanesque style. The 214 stained-glass windows, completed in 1949, are by Frenchmen Auguste Labouret and Pierre Chaudière.

Tributes to St. Anne can be seen in the shrine's mosaics, murals, altars, and ceilings. A bas-relief at the entrance depicts St. Anne welcoming her pilgrims, and ceiling mosaics represent her life. Numerous crutches and braces posted on the back pillars have been left by those who have felt the saint's healing powers. ⊠ *10018 av. Royale, Ste-Anne-de-Beaupré* 🕾 *418/827–3781* ⊕ *www.ssadb.qc.ca* 🖃 *Free* ☞ *Shuttle service (round trip C$15) is available June–Oct. and is located near the Québec-Lévis Ferry. Check site for mass schedule.*

Chapelle Commémorative *(Memorial Chapel)*

RELIGIOUS BUILDING | Across from Basilique Ste-Anne-de-Beaupré, this chapel was designed by Claude Bailiff and built in 1878. It was constructed on the transept of a church built in 1676, and Bailiff made use of the old stones and foundation. Among the remnants is a white-and-gold-trimmed pulpit designed by François Baillargé in 1807 and adorned with a sculpture depicting Moses and the 10 Commandments.

Scala Santa, a smaller chapel next to this one, resembles a wedding cake. On bended knees, pilgrims climb its replica of the Holy Stairs, representing the steps Jesus climbed to meet Pontius Pilate. ⊠ *10018 av. Royale, Ste-Anne-de-Beaupré* 🕾 *418/827–3781* ⊕ *www.sanctuaire-sainteanne.org* 🖃 *Free.*

Chute Montmorency *(Montmorency Falls)*

NATURE SIGHT | The river cascading over a cliff into the St. Lawrence River is one of the most beautiful sights in the province—and at 27 stories high, the falls are

Montmorency Falls along the Côte-de-Beaupré might not be as wide, but it's nearly twice as tall as Niagara Falls.

almost double the height of Niagara's. The Montmorency River was named for Charles de Montmorency, viceroy of New France in the 1620s and explorer Samuel de Champlain's immediate commander. A cable car runs to the top of the falls in Parc de la Chute-Montmorency (Montmorency Falls Park) from late April to late October. During very cold weather the falls' heavy spray freezes and forms a giant loaf-shaped ice cone known to the Québécois as the Pain du Sucre (Sugarloaf); this phenomenon attracts sledders and sliders from Québec City. Summer activities include three *via ferrata* trails built onto the cliff, as well as a zip line that shoots across the canyon in front of the falls.

The park also has a history. The British general James Wolfe, on his way to conquer New France, camped here in 1759. In 1780, Sir Frederick Haldimand, then the governor of Canada, built a summer home atop the cliff. The structure burned down in 1993, however, and what stands today, Manoir Montmorency, is

a re-creation. Offering a stunning view of the falls and river below, it's open year-round, with a restaurant and terrace open in summertime. ⊠ *2490 av. Royale, Beauport* ☎ *418/663–3330* ⊕ *www.sepaq.com/destinations/parc-chute-montmorency* ⊠ *Park C$5.74–C$7.57, parking C$5.22, cable car C$14.95.*

La Halte Miel
STORE/MALL | FAMILY | Things are buzzing at this workshop and store devoted to bees and honey. An exhibit explains every aspect of honey production, and you can taste honey and honey ice creams, chocolates, and snacks made by bees that have fed on different kinds of flowers, including clover and blueberry. It's a 10-minute drive east of Montmorency Falls. ⊠ *8862 boul. Ste-Anne, Château-Richer* ☎ *418/824–4411* ⊕ *www.naturoney.com/en* ⊠ *Free.*

Réserve Faunique des Laurentides
NATIONAL PARK | The Réserve Faunique des Laurentides wildlife reserve, which incorporates the Parc National de la Jacques-Cartier and hundreds of lakes,

is approximately 60 km (37 miles) north of Québec City via Highway 73, which leads to the Saguenay region. It has great hiking trails and camping spots, and good lakes for canoeing and fishing (but you should phone 48 hours in advance to reserve a fishing time). From July to September, you can join bilingual guides to observe black bears in their natural environment from the safety of the park's observation towers. In winter, the park is a popular venue for sledding, snowshoeing, and cross-country skiing. ⊠ *Route QC-175 Km 94* ☎ *418/528–6868, 418/890–6527 reservations* ⊕ *www. sepaq.com/rf/lau.*

★ **Réserve Faunique du Cap Tourmente**
(*Cap Tourmente Wildlife Reserve*)
NATURE PRESERVE | FAMILY | Recognized as a Wetland of International Significance, this nature reserve protects a vital habitat for migrating greater snow geese and sees more than a million fly through every October and May, with tens of thousands of birds present every day. The park harbors hundreds of other kinds of birds and mammals, and more than 700 plant species. This enclave also has 18 km (11 miles) of hiking trails; naturalists give guided tours. It's on the north shore of the St. Lawrence River, about 8 km (5 miles) east of Ste-Anne-de-Beaupré. ⊠ *570 chemin du Cap Tourmente, St-Joachim* ☎ *418/827–4591* ⊕ *www.canada.ca/ en/environment-climate-change/services/ national-wildlife-areas/locations/cap-tourmente.html* 🎟 *C$4–C$6.*

🍴 Restaurants

★ **Auberge Baker**
$$$$ | CANADIAN | The best of old and new blend at this restaurant in an 1840 French Canadian farmhouse, built by the owners' ancestors, which lies east of Château-Richer toward Ste-Anne-de-Beaupré. Antiques and old-fashioned woodstoves decorate the dining rooms, where you can sample traditional Québec dishes, from *tourtière* (meat pie) and pork hocks

to maple-sugar pie. **Known for:** French Canadian pea soup; tourtière; sugar pies. ⑤ *Average main: C$38* ⊠ *8790 av. Royale, Château-Richer* ☎ *418/824–4478, 866/824–4478* ⊕ *www.aubergebaker. com* ⊘ *No lunch Mon.–Sat.*

🏃 Activities

SPAS
Spa des Neiges
SPA | An *inukshuk* (Inuit stone marker) greets you at the entrance to this spa, set in elegant wood buildings right by the St. Lawrence River. Just the view, looking toward Île d'Orléans, is enough to relax anyone, but you can also enjoy the thermal baths (C$42–C$55) or get one of many treatments, including massages, body wraps, mani-pedi, exfoliation, and light therapy. ⊠ *9480 boul. Ste-Anne, Ste-Anne-de-Beaupré* ☎ *418/702–0631, 855/963-4437* ⊕ *www.spadesneiges.ca* ☞ *There is a bistro on-site with light fare options and alcoholic beverages.*

SKIING
Le Massif
SKIING & SNOWBOARDING | This three-peak ski resort has Canada's longest vertical drop east of the Rockies—2,526 feet. Owned by Daniel Gauthier, a cofounder of Cirque du Soleil, the resort has two multiservice chalets at the top and bottom. Six lifts and one gondola service the 53 trails, which are divided into runs for different levels; the longest run is 4.8 km (3 miles). There's also a section of expert glades. Non-skiers can go snowshoeing at the top of the mountain, and there is also an exciting, 7½-km (4¾-mile) sled trail. Equipment can be rented on-site, and the resort offers day care for younger children and shuttles from Québec City, Beaupré, Baie-St-Paul, and the Montréal area. ⊠ *1350 rue Principale, Petite-Rivière-St-François* ☎ *418/632–5876, 877/536–2774* ⊕ *www.lemassif.com* ☞ *Check website for up-to-date rates.*

Charlevoix

172

170 Jonquière
← TO ZOO SAUVAGE DE
SAINT-FELICIEN
AND VILLAGE HISTORIQUE
DE VAL-JALBERT

Saguenay 172

Port Saguenay

La Baie

Saguenay River

175

Lac Kénogami

Parc National du
Fjord-du-Saguenay 170

Saguenay Fjord 172

175

381

Tadoussac

Baie-Ste-
Catherine 170

Parc Marin
du Saguenay–
St-Laurent

138

Parc national des
Hautes-Gorges-
de-la-Rivière-Malbaie

Port-au-Persil

Mont-Grand
Fonds

381

La Malbaie

Lac
Malbaie

138

362 Casino de Charlevoix

20

289

175

Lac des
Neiges

Route 362

Ste-Irenée

St-Joseph-de-la-Rive

Baie-St-Paul

Île-aux-
Coudres

St. Lawrence River

La Pocatière

287

Le Massif
138

La-Petite-
Rivière

132

Mont-Ste-Anne

Beaupré

362

Ste-Anne-de-Beaupré

*Ile
d'Orléans* 132

Montmagny

QUÉBEC
MAINE

Beauport

QUÉBEC
CITY 20

283

Trois-Rivières

281

73

277

216

283

0   20 mi

0   20 km

Mont-Ste-Anne

SKIING & SNOWBOARDING | Part of the World Cup downhill circuit, Mont-Ste-Anne is one of the largest resorts in eastern Canada, with a vertical drop of 2,050 feet, 71 downhill trails, two half-pipes for snowboarders, a terrain park, and 13 lifts, including a gondola. The mountain stays active even after the sun goes down, with 19 lighted downhill trails. Cross-country skiing is also a draw here, with 21 trails totaling 224 km (139 miles). When the weather warms, mountain biking becomes the sport of choice. Enthusiasts can choose from 150 km (93 miles) of mountain-bike trails and 14 downhill runs (and a gondola up to the top). Three bike runs are designated "extreme zones." ⊠ *2000 boul. du Beau-Pré, Beaupré* ☎ *418/827–4561, 888/827–4579* ⊕ *www.mont-sainte-anne. com* ☞ *Downhill skiing C$79–C$109.*

Baie-St-Paul

120 km (72 miles) northeast of Québec City.

Baie-St-Paul, one of the oldest towns in the province, is popular with craftspeople, artists, and foodies. With its centuries-old mansard-roof houses, the village is on the banks of a winding river, on a wide plain encircled by high hills—the crater of a large meteor that crashed to earth 350 million years ago. Boutiques and a handful of commercial galleries line the historic narrow streets in the town center; most have original artwork and crafts for sale. In addition, each August more than a dozen artists from across Canada take part in the Symposium of Modern Art.

GETTING HERE AND AROUND

By road, Baie-St-Paul is approximately 95 km (59 miles) northeast of Québec City via Route 440 and Route 138. Le Massif de Charlevoix train runs day-trips from the Chute-Montmorency station mid-June through early July Thursday through Sunday, then Wednesday through Sunday until mid-October. Departing at 9:10 am and including breakfast en route, it arrives in Baie-St-Paul at 11:45 am; the return journey, including dinner, leaves at 3 pm and arrives back at Chute-Montmorency station at 4:45. The fare is C$229 round-trip, plus C$60 for a guaranteed riverside seat.

Sights

Maison d'Affinage Maurice Dufour

FARM/RANCH | **FAMILY** | The Dufour family produces some of the best cheese in the region, made from the milk of the herds of sheep and cows that can be seen grazing around the property in the summer. A modern and elegant tasting room allows visitors to discover the various cheeses and find out more about production, and taste the fresh and fun wines that they make from local vines. They've even started distilling vodka and spirits from whey, a fun way to produce something delicious from cheese-making by-products. A restaurant called Les Faux Bergers, featuring lots of wood-fired dishes, is also on the premises. ⊠ *1339 boul. Monseigneur-de Laval, Baie-St-Paul* ☎ *418/435–5692* ⊕ *www.famillemign-eron.com.*

Maison René Richard

ART GALLERY | Many of Québec's greatest landscape artists, including Jean-Paul Lemieux and Clarence Gagnon, have depicted the area, and a selection of these works is on show here (some are also for sale). The gallery was Gagnon's former studio and also the home of painter René Richard for the last 43 years of his life. Guided tours of the studio are available for groups. ⊠ *58 rue St-Jean-Baptiste, Baie-St-Paul* ☎ *418/435–5571* ⊕ *www.grandquebec. com/charlevoix/maison-rene-richard* ☞ *Free; call for group tour rates.*

Baie-St-Paul is a charming small town popular with writers and artists. Each August it hosts a modern art show.

Musée d'Art Contemporain de Baie-St-Paul

ART GALLERY | This museum highlights modern and contemporary art created by Charlevoix artists from 1920 to 1970. It also has a robust collection from the province in general, with works from Georges D. Pepper, Kathleen Daly, René Richard, the Bolduc sisters, and others. For more than 30 years, the museum has been organizing a yearly modern art symposium, held in late July and early August. ⊠ *23 rue Ambroise-Fafard, Baie-St-Paul* ☎ *418/435–3681* ⊕ *www. macbsp.com* ⚏ *C$12.*

 Hotels

Auberge à l'Ancrage

$$ | B&B/INN | A restored 1920s redbrick home with antiques, a maritime theme, a wraparound porch, and a back garden that sits at the edge of the Gouffre River, Auberge à l'Ancrage is run by a charming couple who offer delicious, multicourse breakfasts and eagerly share information about activities and attractions in the area. **Pros:** quiet and privacy; only a few minutes' walk from downtown; riverside yard. **Cons:** rooms are on the smaller side; inconsistent customer service; pricey. ⑤ *Rooms from: C$199* ⊠ *29 rue Ste-Anne, Baie-St-Paul* ☎ *418/240–3264, 866/344–3264* ⊕ *www.aubergeancrage. com* ⤳ *4 rooms* |◯| *Free Breakfast.*

★ Le Germain Charlevoix Hotel & Spa

$$$$ | HOTEL | This stylish and modern hotel, owned by one of the best boutique hotel groups in Canada, consists of five distinct pavilions housing three eateries and rooms in various styles, including lofts and dormitories, all with contemporary finishes and elegant design. **Pros:** convenient location on public square with train station; farm-to-table cuisine in three on-site eateries; contemporary design. **Cons:** layout with multiple pavilions is a bit complicated; some rooms are small; inconsistent service. ⑤ *Rooms from: C$315* ⊠ *50 rue de la Ferme, Baie-St-Paul* ☎ *418/240–4100, 844/240–4700* ⊕ *www.legermainhotels.com/en/charlevoix* ⤳ *145 rooms* |◯| *No Meals.*

St-Joseph-de-la-Rive

20 km (12½ miles) northeast of Baie-St-Paul.

A secondary road descends sharply into St-Joseph-de-la-Rive, with its line of old houses hugging the mountain base on a narrow shore route. Enjoyed for its warm microclimate, the town features peaceful inns and inviting restaurants. Drive through and see the traces of early town life and the beginning of local industry: an old firehouse and a hydroelectric building that houses a generator dating back to 1928.

GETTING HERE AND AROUND
From Baie-St-Paul, drive northeast on rue Leclerc (Route 362).

Sights

Île-aux-Coudres

ISLAND | A free, government-run ferry from the wharf in St-Joseph-de-la-Rive takes you on the 15-minute trip to the island where Jacques Cartier's men gathered *coudres* (hazelnuts) in 1535. Since then, the island has produced many a *goélette* (a type of sailing ship), and the families of former captains now run several small inns. You can bike around the island and see windmills and water mills, or stop at the stores selling paintings and crafts, such as traditional handwoven household linens. ⊠ *St-Joseph-de-la-Rive* ☎ *877/787–7483 Ferry schedule* ⊕ *www. traversiers.com/en/our-ferries/lisle-aux-coudres-saint-joseph-de-la-rive-ferry/contact-information* ⊒ *Free.*

Musée Maritime de Charlevoix *(Maritime Museum)*

SPECIALTY MUSEUM | This museum, housed in an old shipyard, commemorates the days of the St. Lawrence goélettes, the feisty little wooden freighters that were the chief means of transporting goods along the north shore of the St. Lawrence River well into the 1960s. Very large families lived in cramped conditions aboard the boats, some of which are part of the exhibits. To modern eyes, it doesn't look like a comfortable existence, but the folklore of the goélettes, celebrated in poetry, paintings, and song, is part of the region's strong cultural identity. ⊠ *305 rue de l'Église, St-Joseph-de-la-Rive* ☎ *418/635–1131 ext. 1* ⊕ *www. museemaritime.com* ⊒ *C$14.*

Hotels

Hôtel Cap-aux-Pierres

$ | **HOTEL** | New ownership invested in a substantial renovation of the Cap-aux-Pierres, and the rooms now have a modern and stylish décor and many have river views. **Pros:** indoor and outdoor pools; beautiful environment; good food. **Cons:** no air-conditioning; rooms are somewhat outdated; restaurant is a little pricey. ⑤ *Rooms from: C$159* ⊠ *444 chemin de la Baleine, Île-aux-Coudres, St-Joseph-de-la-Rive* ☎ *888/554–6003, 418/438–2711* ⊕ *www.hotelcapauxpierres.com* ⊘ *Closed Nov.–Apr.* ⌁ *98 rooms* ⦿ *Free Breakfast.*

The Scenic Route

From Baie-St-Paul, instead of the faster Route 138 to La Malbaie, drivers can choose the open, scenic coastal drive on Route 362. This section of road has memorable views of charming villages and rolling hills—green, white, or ablaze with fiery hues, depending on the season—meeting the broad expanse of the "sea," as the locals like to call the St. Lawrence estuary.

Shopping

BOOKS

Papeterie Saint-Gilles

STATIONERY | This paper factory produces handcrafted stationery using a 17th-century process. There's also a small museum, which explains through photographs and demonstrations how paper is manufactured the old-fashioned way. Slivers of wood and flower petals are pressed into the paper sheets, which are as thick as the covers of a paperback book. The finished products—made into writing paper, greeting cards, and one-page poems or quotations—make beautiful, if pricey, gifts. Visitors can wander through the museum for free, and guided tours can be arranged for groups. ⊠ *304 rue Félix-Antoine Savard, St-Joseph-de-la-Rive* ☎ *418/635–2430, 866/635–2430* ⊕ *www.papeteriesaintgilles.com* ☞ *Guided tours C$8.*

La Malbaie

35 km (22 miles) northeast of St-Joseph-de-la-Rive.

La Malbaie, one of the province's most elegant and historically interesting resort towns, was known as Murray Bay when wealthy anglophones summered here. The area became popular with American and Canadian politicians in the late 1800s, when Ottawa Liberals and Washington Republicans partied decorously all summer with members of the Québec bourgeoisie. William Howard Taft built the "summer White House," the first of three summer residences, in 1894, when he was the American civil governor of the Philippines. He became the 27th president of the United States in 1908.

Many Taft-era homes now serve as handsome inns, offering old-fashioned coddling with such extras as breakfast in bed, whirlpool baths, and free shuttles to the ski areas in winter. Many serve lunch and dinner to nonresidents, so you can tour the area going from one great French or Québécois meal to the next.

GETTING HERE AND AROUND

Even if you don't want to visit St-Joseph-de-la-Rive, Route 362 between Baie-St-Paul and La Malbaie is much more scenic and well worth the extra half hour it adds to the trip from Québec City. From mid-June to early November, Le Train de Charlevoix offers round trips from Québec's Chute-Montmorency station to La Malbaie and Baie-St-Paul starting at C$99. The trip passes through seven coastal towns and villages along the St. Lawrence River, and passengers can disembark at any one of these stations if they prefer. Le Train de Charlevoix has several different packages along this tremendously scenic route, many with meals and accommodation included from C$416 (⊕ *traindecharlevoix.com/en* ☎ *844/737-3282*).

Take a day-trip to La Malbaie Thursday through Sunday from mid-June to early July and Wednesday through Sunday until mid-October. The train departs Chute-Montmorency station at 9:10 am, with a stop en route at Baie-St-Paul; the round trip takes 11 hours including time to get off and explore, and the fare, including breakfast and a four-course dinner, is C$369 (plus C$60 for a guaranteed riverside seat).

Sights

Casino de Charlevoix

CASINO | The casino is one of four gaming halls in Québec (the others are in Montréal, Gatineau, and Mont-Tremblant) owned and operated by Loto-Québec. Charlevoix's, the smallest of the lot, still draws around 800,000 visitors a year—some of whom stay at the Fairmont Le Manoir Richelieu, which is connected to the casino by a tunnel. Largely renovated in 2016, it offers 21 gaming tables and more than 800 slot machines. The

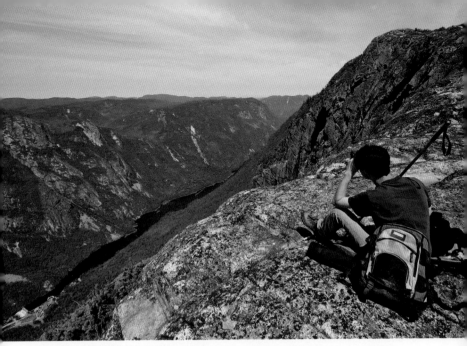

A hiker takes in the view of an ancient glacial valley in Parc national des Hautes-Gorges-de-la-Rivière-Malbaie.

minimum gambling age is 18, and a photo ID is required to enter the casino. ⊠ 183 rue Richelieu, Pointe-au-Pic ☎ 418/665–5300, 800/665–2274 ⊕ casinos.lotoquebec.com/fr/charlevoix/accueil.

Musée de Charlevoix

HISTORY MUSEUM | The museum traces the region's history through a major permanent exhibit. Folk art, paintings, and artifacts help reveal the past, starting with the French, then the Scottish settlers, and the area's evolution into a vacation spot and artists' haven. Temporary exhibits change every season. ⊠ 10 chemin du Havre, La Malbaie ☎ 418/665–4411 ⊕ www.museedecharlevoix.qc.ca ➔ C$11.

Parc National des Hautes-Gorges-de-la-Rivière-Malbaie

NATIONAL PARK | FAMILY | A 40-minute drive from La Malbaie will bring you to a stunning stretch of the Malbaie River, surrounded by impressive steep slopes and rocky peaks. There are plenty of beautiful views to take in—whether it's from a kayak on the river or while hiking a network of trails—and lots of fresh air, in this central part of the Charlevoix Biosphere Preserve. ⊠ 25 boul. Notre-Dame, Clermont, La Malbaie ☎ 418/439–1227 ⊕ www.sepaq.com/pq/hgo ➔ C$9.55, camping from C$27.

☕ Coffee and Quick Bites

Pains d'Exclamation

$$ | BAKERY | FAMILY | This lively café and bakery offers a wide variety of classic and unique pastries and breads (hello, preserved-lemon bread!), sandwiches, and quick breakfast and lunch options. It's a favorite with locals, who either eat in or take out after a quick chat with the friendly staff. **Known for:** great pastries; patio dining; quick, delicious lunches. ⑤ Average main: C$12 ⊠ 398 rue St-Étienne, Pointe-au-Pic ☎ 418/665–4000 ⊕ www.painsdexclamation.com ☽ No dinner.

Hotels

Auberge des Peupliers

$ | B&B/INN | About half the guest rooms at this hilltop inn overlook the St. Lawrence River, and the country-style accommodations are spread among three buildings, including a farmhouse more than two centuries old. **Pros:** lounge with fireplace and bar perfect for relaxing; excellent service; scenic location. **Cons:** need to drive to downtown La Malbaie; some rooms may not have air conditioning; complaints of average food at a high price in the restaurant. ⑤ *Rooms from: C$132* ⌧ *381 rue St-Raphaël, La Malbaie* ☎ *418/665–4423, 888/282–3743* ⊕ *www. aubergedespeupliers.com* ⇨ *22 rooms* ⑩ *Free Breakfast.*

Chez Truchon Bistro Auberge

$ | B&B/INN | Located in a quiet neighborhood within easy walking distance to the heart of La Malbaie, the Chez Truchon Auberge is a distinctively elegant inn that was originally constructed in 1902. **Pros:** above an excellent bistro; beautiful historic building; friendly, professional service. **Cons:** some rooms don't have river views; some guests on the lower floors have complained about noise from the restaurant below; the rooms along the second-floor veranda are less private. ⑤ *Rooms from: C$125* ⌧ *1065 rue Richelieu, La Malbaie* ☎ *888/662– 4622, 418/665–4622 bistro* ⊕ *www. aubergecheztruchon.com* ⇨ *9 rooms* ⑩ *No Meals.*

Fairmont Le Manoir Richelieu

$$$$ | RESORT | FAMILY | Linked to the Casino de Charlevoix by tunnel, this castle-like building and its sweeping grounds come with stunning views and some great sports and leisure facilities. **Pros:** good for families, with kids' club, kids' menu, and babysitting; scenic location; variety of dining options on-site. **Cons:** some rooms could use updating; not the best room service; complaints of inadequate amount of and attitude of staff. ⑤ *Rooms from: C$335* ⌧ *181 rue Richelieu, Pointe-au-Pic* ☎ *418/665–3703, 866/540-4464* ⊕ *www.fairmont.com/ richelieu-charlevoix* ⇨ *405 rooms* ⑩ *Free Breakfast.*

Performing Arts

Domaine Forget

MUSIC | This music and dance academy has a 604-seat hall in Ste-Irénée, 15 km (9 miles) south of La Malbaie. Musicians from around the world, many of whom teach or study at the school, perform during its International Festival. The festival, which runs from mid-June to late August, includes Sunday brunches with music, a buffet, and a view of the St. Lawrence. Some weekend concerts are also held in the fall and spring. ⌧ *5 rang St-Antoine, St-Irénée* ☎ *418/452–3535, 888/336– 7438* ⊕ *www.domaineforget.com.*

Activities

GOLF

★ Club de Golf Fairmont Le Manoir Richelieu

GOLF | Be warned: if you play this course, you'll have to work hard to focus on the game and not the gorgeous scenery overlooking the St. Lawrence River. Originally established in 1925 and recently restored and expanded, this is a links-style course with three nine-hole courses that offers quite a bit of challenge, thanks to the design (the fairways are relatively wide but feature a number of strategically placed bunkers, trees, and mounds) and to the course's hilltop undulations. ⌧ *Fairmont Le Manoir Richelieu, 181 rue Richelieu, Pointe-au-Pic* ☎ *418/665–2526* ⊕ *www.fairmont.com/richelieu-charlevoix/golf/club-de-golf-fairmont-le-manoir-richelieu* ⚐ *From C$70* ⛳ *St-Laurent Course: 9 holes, 3178 yards, par 36; Richelieu Course: 9 holes, 3148 yards, par 36; Tadoussac Course: 9 holes, 2918 yards, par 35.*

In Tadoussac from May to October, you can see whales living in the Saguenay River.

SKIING
Mont-Grand Fonds

SKIING & SNOWBOARDING | This winter-sports center 12 km (7 miles) north of La Malbaie has 20 downhill slopes (including four recently opened glades in an area called The Lynx), a 1,105-foot vertical drop, and three lifts. It also has 184 km (113 miles) of cross-country trails. Two trails meet International Ski Federation standards, and the ski center occasionally hosts major competitions. You can also go dog sledding, sleigh riding, ice-skating, and tobogganing here. ⊠ *1000 chemin des Loisirs, La Malbaie* ☎ *418/665–0095, 877/665–0095* ⊕ *www.montgrandfonds. com* ⊡ *Full day C$60.*

Tadoussac

71 km (44 miles) north of La Malbaie.

Most people come to Tadoussac for the whale-watching excursions and cruises along the magnificent Saguenay Fjord. Beluga whales, highly recognizable because of their all-white color, small size, and high-pitched call, live here year-round and breed in the lower portion of the Saguenay in summer. The many marine species that live at the confluence of the fjord and the seaway attract other whales, too, such as pilots, finbacks, and humpbacks.

Sadly, the beluga is endangered; the whales, together with 35 other species of mammals and birds and 21 species of fish, are threatened by pollution in the St. Lawrence River. This has spurred a C$100 million project (funded by the federal and provincial governments) aimed at removing or capping sediment in the most polluted areas, stopping industrial and residential emissions into the river, and restoring natural habitat. There's still much work to be done, but greater attention is being given to this unique ecosystem, now a National Marine Conservation Area.

The short drive here from La Malbaie leads past lovely villages and views along the St. Lawrence. Jacques Cartier made a stop at this point in 1535, and from 1600 to the mid-19th century it was an important meeting site for fur traders. As the Saguenay River flows south from Lac St-Jean, it has a dual character: between Alma and Chicoutimi, the once rapidly flowing river has been harnessed for hydroelectric power; in its lower section, it becomes wider and deeper and flows by steep mountains and cliffs en route to the St. Lawrence.

GETTING HERE AND AROUND
From La Malbaie, drive northeast on Route 138. You must take a free 10-minute ferry ride from Baie-Ste-Catherine to get to Tadoussac. The ferries leave every 20 minutes, from 4 am to midnight, then every half hour until 4 am. For more information on ferry schedules, call ☎ *418/643–2019.*

VISITOR INFORMATION
CONTACT Tourist Information Center Tadoussac. ✉ *197 rue des Pionniers, Tadoussac* ☎ *418/235–4744, 866/235–4744* ⊕ *www.tadoussac.com.*

◉ Sights

Centre d'Interprétation des Mammifères Marins
VISITOR CENTER | You can learn more about the whales and their habitat at this interpretation center run by a locally based research team. They're only too glad to answer questions. In addition, explanatory videos and exhibits (including a collection of whale skeletons) serve as a good introduction to the mighty but endangered cetaceans. ✉ *108 rue de la Cale-Sèche, Tadoussac* ☎ *418/235–4701* ⊕ *gremm.org/cimm-horaire-et-tarification* *C$15.*

Parc Marin du Saguenay–St-Laurent
NATURE PRESERVE | The 800-square-km (309-square-mile) marine park, at the confluence of the Saguenay and St. Lawrence Rivers, has been created to protect this marine area's three fragile ecosystems. ✉ *Park office, 182 rue de*

l'Église, Tadoussac ☎ *418/235–4703, 888/773–8888* ⊕ *parcmarin.qc.ca/home.*

Hotels

Hôtel Tadoussac
$$$ | HOTEL | FAMILY | A stunning natural environment and the 1942 Victorian-style building make this an equally great choice for an active or romantic stay. **Pros:** views over the bay; summer kids' club with day care; good spa. **Cons:** no air-conditioning in rooms; a little pricey for largely unrenovated rooms; walls very thin. ⑤ *Rooms from: C$240* ✉ *165 rue du Bord de l'Eau, Tadoussac* ☎ *418/235–4421* ⊕ *www.hoteltadoussac.com* ⊙ *Closed Nov.–mid-May* ➾ *149 rooms* ⦿| *Free Breakfast.*

Activities

WHALE-WATCHING
The best months for seeing whales are August and September, although some operators extend the season at either end if whales are around. Fjord tours are also available.

Croisières AML
WHALE-WATCHING | This outfitter offers two- and three-hour whale-watching cruises starting at C$99.99. The tours, in Zodiacs or larger boats, depart from Tadoussac pier. Tours of the Saguenay Fjord are available, and you can also take a daylong excursion on a chartered bus from Québec City, including a three-hour whale-watching cruise. ✉ *Tadoussac* ☎ *418/692–1159, 800/463–1292* ⊕ *www.croisieresaml.com.*

Port Saguenay

This seaport is appreciated more for its natural beauty than for its shipping industry. Although it's interesting to see the big vessels and the huge equipment used to load and unload them, the scenes simply can't compete with the surrounding wilderness of cliffs, fjords, and the bare rock faces of the Canadian shield, not to mention the whales that inhabit the waters seasonally.

Sights

★ Parc National du Fjord-du-Saguenay

NATURE SIGHT | Colossal rock cliffs and forest-covered mountains meet the still waters of the Saguenay Fjord, one of the longest in the world, and the namesake national park runs its entire 105-km (65-mile) length. Of the park's three regions, the Baie-Éternité, which hosts the visitor center, is about 60 km (37 miles) south of the city of Saguenay, where you can visit the Fjord Museum (Musée du Fjord). Outdoor enthusiasts have much to do here, including kayaking, fishing, hiking, camping, bird-watching, whale-watching, and mountain biking, and the park can supply equipment and guides. The spectacular Baie-Éternité escarpments provide thrilling climbs and a via ferrata. Or you can take it easy on sailboat and sightseeing boat cruises, or enjoy a thrilling whale-watching experience. ✉ *91 Rue Notre Dame* ☎ *418/272–1556 camping Baie-Éternité* ⊕ *www.sepaq.com/pq/sag/index.dot?language_id=1* ✇ *C$9.55.*

★ Village Historique de Val-Jalbert

MUSEUM VILLAGE | **FAMILY** | Powerful Ouiatchouan Falls, higher than Niagara Falls, overlook and long ago powered this once thriving mill town. Ultramodern in its day, the village had electricity and running water 25 years before the rest of Québec, but administrative and production pitfalls closed the mill and by 1927 all the residents had departed. Today, you can see the beautifully restored mill, post office, general store, and butcher shop, then hike to the top of the falls, where a glass platform puts you directly over the center of the cascade. Modern accommodations are available within the general store and some restored period houses, and campgrounds and rustic cottages to rent are other options.

✉ *95 rue St.-Georges, Chambord* ☎ *418/275–3132* ⊕ *valjalbert.com/en* ✇ *C$41.01.*

★ Zoo Sauvage de Saint-Felicien

ZOO | **FAMILY** | Cougars, polar bears, grizzly bears, Canadian lynx, American bison, and Japanese macaques are among the 75 species that roam open environments here. Between June and October, guides lead overnight tours in the Land of the Caribou, including hiking, a campfire meal, and canoeing on Lac Montagnais, where caribou may swim right by your boat. ✉ *2230 boul. du Jardin, St-Félicien* ☎ *800/667–5687, 418/679–0543* ⊕ *zoo-sauvage.org/en* ✇ *C$38.99.*

Restaurants

Le Restaurant La Cuisine

$$$ | **ECLECTIC** | World cuisines influence chefs who are well-versed in French techniques and fond of using local ingredients. Thai cuisine inspires five-spice chicken with cashew nuts, rice noodles, vegetables, and sweet chili sauce; a taste of Italy is clearly evident in the veal flank with mushrooms, truffle oil, and Parmesan risotto. **Known for:** local produce; chic décor; good selection of beer and wine. ⓢ *Average main: C$30* ✉ *387 rue Racine Est, Chicoutimi* ☎ *418/698–2822* ⊕ *www.restaurantlacuisine.ca* ⊘ *No lunch weekends.*

Rouge Burger Bar

$$ | **BURGER** | Towering gourmet burgers are made exactly to order with a choice of lamb, chicken, salmon, local beef, or a vegetarian patty. Dress it up with one of several cheeses (maybe fresh chevre), various garnishes (how about caramelized onions and smoked bacon?), and a range of sauces (a dab of citrus tarragon mayonnaise?). **Known for:** their own line of barbecue and other sauces; popularity, so reservations necessary; several TVs, making it perfect for sports fans. ⓢ *Average main: C$15* ✉ *460 rue Racine Est, Chicoutimi* ☎ *418/690–5029*

⊕ *www.rougeburgerbar.ca* ⊘ *Closed Mon. and Tues. No lunch.*

Coffee and Quick Bites

Boucherie Davis Ltee

$$ | CANADIAN | Come hungry—really hungry—to this foodie destination, where the full-service, family butcher shop dating back to 1943 also hosts a café and gourmet food market featuring locally made artisanal products. Tuck into a thick rib steak with a local *saison* beer, select from the hot and cold buffets, or go for the "menu of the day" and watch butchers in action as you dine. **Known for:** high-quality produce and products; warm, welcoming environment; wide variety of products available for purchase on-site. ⑤ *Average main: C$20* ✉ *1959 rue Davis, Jonquière* ☎ *418/548–5243* ⊕ *www.boucheriedavis.com* ▭ *No credit cards* ⊘ *Closed Sun.*

Hotels

Auberge de la Riviere Saguenay

$ | B&B/INN | Set on a slope overlooking the Saguenay Fjord, this lovely inn is a fine launching place for waterway or mountain adventures. **Pros:** most rooms have stunning fjord views; convenient base for exploring; beach access. **Cons:** no air-conditioning; décor is a little dated; breakfast is not included. ⑤ *Rooms from: C$125* ✉ *9122 chemin de la Batture, La Baie* ☎ *418/697–0222, 866/697–0222 toll-free number* ⊕ *www.aubergesaguenay.com* ▭ *No credit cards* ⇄ *15 rooms* ⦿ *No Meals.*

★ Gite Du Haut des Arbres

$ | B&B/INN | With nine tastefully decorated modern rooms in a spectacular setting overlooking the fjord, this family-owned and-operated *gite* is a nature lover's paradise located less than 10 minutes from the center of Chicoutimi. **Pros:** swimming pool; beautiful grounds; modern rooms. **Cons:** small parking spaces; can be noisy; no commercial establishments

within walking distance. ⑤ *Rooms from: C$124* ✉ *744 rue du Ruisseau-Lachance, Chicoutimi* ☎ *581/306–1963* ⊕ *www.giteduhautdesarbres.com* ⇄ *9 rooms* ⦿ *No Meals.*

Motel Panoramique

$ | MOTEL | Set back from the road and nestled along the banks of the Saguenay River just 4 km (2.5 miles) from downtown Chicoutimi, Motel Panoramique is a pleasant, unassuming motel that feels a world away from the hustle and bustle of the nearby city. **Pros:** great value; friendly service; excellent location. **Cons:** some rooms may feel outdated; rooms on ground floor may lack privacy; the rooms in the front of the establishment are off a busy road. ⑤ *Rooms from: C$139* ✉ *1303 boul. du Saguenay Ouest, Chicoutimi* ☎ *418/549–7102, 418/590–7455* ⊕ *www.motelpanoramique.ca* ⇄ *54 rooms* ⦿ *No Meals.*

Shopping

Bons Délices et Péchés

CHOCOLATE | Chocolatiers here make truffles, cream-filled chocolates, spirit-spiked bonbons, chocolate-dipped ice cream in chocolate-dipped cones, and dark, white, and milk chocolate. Fancy cookies and custom cakes are sold, too. ✉ *244 rue La Fontaine, Chicoutimi* ☎ *418/545–1660.*

Domaine de la Savonnière

SPECIALTY STORE | FAMILY | Herbs, flowers, fruit, spices, and essential oils are used to make soaps prepared on the premises. The soap maker is usually in and happy to explain the process and answer questions about the soaps' healthful properties. Soap-making workshops are available for adults and kids. ✉ *3289 boul. de la Grande-Baie Sud, La Baie* ☎ *418/544–8484.*

Trois-Rivières

Where the Rivière St-Maurice divides into three channels, the town that grew up around it came to be known as Trois-Rivières (Three Rivers). Today it's a busy industrial hub but still retains pleasant shady streets and historical sites; a bygone iron and steel mill are worth a look. The town is also a good base for exploring the waterfalls and rock faces of the Parc National de la Mauricie, just 64 km (40 miles) away.

Sights

Boréalis

FACTORY | FAMILY | Back when Trois-Rivières was a lumber, paper, and pulp industry leader, this plant's machinery whizzed and whirled. Built in the early 1920s, it pumped, filtered, and stored water for the paper mill. By the mid-1950s, the plant filtered more than 20 million gallons of water a day that was used to produce 1,000 tons of newsprint. Today, it is eerily quiet, especially the long-abandoned underground vaults, which are part of the original architecture and machinery that's on display. ⊠ *200 av. des Draveurs, Trois-Rivières* ☎ *819/372–4633* ⊕ *www.borealis3r.ca* 🖃 *C$14.*

Sanctuaire Notre-Dame-du-Cap

RELIGIOUS BUILDING | Built in 1955, on the site of earlier churches dating back to 1659, this is Canada's national shrine to Notre Dame (Our Blessed Mother) and an important pilgrimage site. As impressive as the great European cathedrals, this white granite, octagonal building hosts up to 1,660 people, and its lofty dome is topped by a pyramid and cross 258 feet above the ground. Reinforced concrete arches outline the building. Five bells ring A, Bb, D, F, and G notes, and the sanctuary's organ has 5,425 pipes. Inside, the altar is a single block of marble, and nary a pillar blocks views of magnificent architecture and stained-glass masterpieces. ⊠ *626 rue Notre-Dame Est, Trois-Rivières* ☎ *819/374–2441* ⊕ *www.sanctuaire-ndc.ca* 🖃 *Free.*

Vieille Prison de Trois-Rivières

JAIL/PRISON | Dating to the early 1800s, this was the oldest continuously operating prison in Canada prior to its closure in 1986. The stark, stone structure with thick bars on the windows makes it clear that nobody is getting out. Originally built to house 40 inmates, the facility at times hosted up to 100 convicted criminals. If only the old doors and cedar basement joists could talk, what tales of mayhem might they tell? Tour guides share a few. The prison is attached to the Musée Québécois de Culture Populaire. The museum's collection of more than 70,000 objects, plus traveling and changing exhibitions, showcase Québec's history and culture, including crime and prison life. ⊠ *200 rue Laviolette, Trois-Rivières* ☎ *819/372–0406* ⊕ *www.culturepop.qc.ca* 🖃 *Jail C$17, museum C$20, combined ticket C$28.*

🍴 Restaurants

Le Sacristain

$$ | ECLECTIC | What was once a Wesleyan church has become a sanctuary for salads and grilled sandwiches. Ingredients stretch beyond ham and cheese; choose capers, smoked salmon, grilled mango, and hearts of palm. **Known for:** great stop between Montréal and Québec City; English-speaking staff; unique location in a converted church. ⑤ *Average main: C$15* ⊠ *300 rue Bonaventure, Trois-Rivières* ☎ *819/694–1344* ⊕ *www.lesacristain.ca* ⊗ *Closed weekends. No dinner.*

Poivre Noir

$$$$ | FRENCH | Sleek and modern, this friendly restaurant hits all the right spots—it's devoted to local ingredients and its dining room and deck overlook the St. Lawrence River. While the menu items are constantly evolving, expect creative plates: bison tartare, pickled mushrooms, and salt foie gras; sablefish, lime mousseline, and clementine white butter; and savarin, elderberry, and white chocolate Chantilly as dessert. **Known for:** creative cocktails; outside bar and terrasse overlooking the St. Lawrence; accommodations to food allergies. ⑤ *Average main: C$70* ⊠ *1300 rue du Fleuve, Trois-Rivières* ☎ *819/378–5772* ⊕ *www.poivrenoir.com* ⊘ *Closed Sun.–Tues. No lunch.*

Restaurant le St-Antoine

$$$ | **BISTRO** | This family-owned restaurant is rooted in French classics but has a taste for pizza and pasta, too. Escargots, steak tartare, veal scallops with mushroom cream sauce, grilled steaks, and various steamed mussel presentations join numerous Italian-style linguine dishes including Alfredo, Bolognese, and carbonara. **Known for:** bring-your-own alcoholic beverage; seafood and pasta dishes; pleasant terrasse. ⑤ *Average main: C$28* ⊠ *151 rue St-Antoine, Trois-Rivières* ☎ *819/378–6420* ⊕ *www.lestantoine.ca* ▭ *No credit cards* ⊘ *No lunch.*

Hotels

Motel Canadien

$ | **HOTEL** | A nice cross between a hotel and an inn, the rooms are not fancy but well appointed and clean, and the innkeepers are friendly and helpful. **Pros:** free Wi-Fi; air-conditioning; electric fireplaces in rooms. **Cons:** 50 percent deposit required when booking; small rooms; interior design feels dated. ⑤ *Rooms from: C$105* ⊠ *1821 rue Notre-Dame Est, Trois-Rivières* ☎ *819/375–5542* ⊕ *www.motelcanadien.ca* ▭ *No credit cards* ⤶ *10 rooms* ⫯⃝ *Free Breakfast.*

Shopping

Cabane à Sucre Chez Dany

SPECIALTY STORE | **FAMILY** | Maple syrup, maple taffy, maple candy, maple everything—when it's "sugaring time" in Québec, this shack is busy. Visitors get to not only purchase the fruits of this labor, but they may also see how maple sap becomes syrup and how to make taffy in the snow. There's an all-you-can-eat restaurant with a maple-centric menu, and live music of the region. ⊠ *195 rue de la Sablière, Trois-Rivières* ☎ *819/370–4769* ⊕ *www.cabanechezdany.com.*

Les Jardins Dugré

FOOD | Just a few minutes from downtown, the Dugré family tends a large vegetable farm. Besides selling their own berries, asparagus, and sweet corn, among other produce, the farm market offers various other local choices, including baked goods, cheeses, jams, pickles, honey, vinaigrettes, fresh pasta, maple products, and more. Arrive in the right season and you may pick your own strawberries. ⊠ *3861 rang St-Charles, Trois-Rivières* ☎ *819/377–3108* ⊕ *www.fermegagnon.com/lesjardinsdugre.*

Index

Photo Credits

Front cover: Susanne Kremer/Huber/eStock Photo [Descr.: Bonsecours Market at the Old Port in Montreal, Province of Quebec, Canada].
Back cover, from left to right: Simon Eizner/Shutterstock. Songquan Deng/Shutterstock. Marc Bruxelle/Shutterstock. **Spine:** Pierre Leclerc/Shutterstock. **Interior, from left to right:** Pinkcandy/Shutterstock (1). iPIX Stock/Shutterstock (2-3). **Chapter 1: Experience Montréal and Québec City:** Pierre Leclerc/Shutterstock (6-7). Susanne Pommer/Shutterstock (8-9). Kristi Blokhin/Shutterstock (9). Carnaval de Québec (9). J. Schultes/Dreamstime (10). Rabbit75/Dreamstime (10). Kristi Blokhin/Shutterstock (10). Wickedgood/Dreamstime (10). Jiawangkun/Dreamstime (11). Rob Crandall/Shutterstock (11). Kristi Blokhin/Shutterstock (12). Rabbit75/Dreamstime (12). Dennizn/Dreamstime (12) Bill_comstock/Flickr (12). Benoit Daoust / Shutterstock (13). William Manning/Alamy Stock Photo (13). Stephane Audet (13). Rabbit75/Dreamstime (13). Mbruxelle/Dreamstime (14). Cybernesco/Dreamstime (14). Beaustock/Dreamstime (14). Bigjohn3650/Dreamstime (14). Jiawangkun/Dreamstime (15). Michael L Brown/Dreamstime (18). Georges Alexandar Hashtag Media/Juliette & Chocolat (Plateau) (18). Vsl/Shutterstock (18). Caroline Perron/MTL (19). Jen Lobo/iStockphoto (19). Eva Blue/Montreal Tourism (20). Charles Prot (21). Alexi Hobbs/MTL (22). Marie/Reine Mattera (22). Dylan Stewart Page/Sibéria Spa (22). Spa Bolton (22). Courtesy of Balnea Spa and Réserve Thermale (23). Grogl/Shutterstock (23). Bianca Des Jardins/Strøm Nordic Spa (23). Bianca Des Jardins/ Strøm spa nordique (23). Andriy Blokhin/Shutterstock (24). iPIX Stock/Shutterstock (24). Kristi Blokhin/Shutterstock (24). Maridav/Shutterstock (24). Mathieu Dupuis (25). **Chapter 3: Montréal:** Laweach/Shutterstock (61). Felix Lipov/Shutterstock (72). Studio du Ruisseau (77). Vlad2003/ Dreamstime (94). Louriv/Dreamstime (99). Benoit Aquin (100). Le Mount Stephen (107). Canadian Tourism Commission (117). Quartier des spectacles, Martine Doyon (132). Stéphan Poulin/Tourisme Montréal (152). C.I.I.O/iStockphoto (156). Hakat/Shutterstock (160). Jonasfriard/Dreamstime (164). Meunierd/Shutterstock (167). Ververidis Vasilis/Shutterstock (175). **Chapter 4: Side Trips from Montréal:** Vlad G/Shutterstock (177). Design Pics Inc/Alamy Stock Photo (185). Hadimor/iStockphoto (192-193). Benoit Aquin (198). Mustafa Quraish/Shutterstock (209). **Chapter 5: Québec City:** Edwin Tseng/Shutterstock (211). Mervas/Shutterstock (221). Meunierd/Shutterstock (225). Senturkserkan/Shutterstock (235). Emperorcosar/Shutterstock (241). Andriy Blokhin/Shutterstock (242). Chris Cheadle/Alamy Stock Photo (244). Anne Richard/Shutterstock (257). **Chapter 6: Side Trips from Québec City:** Magnus L/Shutterstock (267). Delpixel/Shutterstock (276). Melanie Marin (280). Kavram/Shutterstock (282). Sebastienlemyre/Shutterstock (286). Julien Robitaille/Alamy Stock Photo (289). Sylvie Bouchard/Shutterstock (291). **About Our Writers:** All photos are courtesy of the writers except for the following: Chris Barry, courtesy of Mark Bouchett (304).

Every effort has been made to trace the copyright holders, and we apologize in advance for any accidental errors. We would be happy to apply the corrections in the following edition of this publication.

Fodor's MONTRÉAL & QUÉBEC CITY

Publisher: Stephen Horowitz, *General Manager*

Editorial: Douglas Stallings, *Editorial Director;* Jill Fergus, Amanda Sadlowski, *Senior Editors;* Brian Eschrich, Alexis Kelly, *Editors;* Angelique Kennedy-Chavannes, *Assistant Editor;* Yoojin Shin, *Associate Editor*

Design: Tina Malaney, *Director of Design and Production;* Jessica Gonzalez, *Senior Designer;* Jaimee Shaye, *Graphic Design Associate*

Production: Jennifer DePrima, *Editorial Production Manager;* Elyse Rozelle, *Senior Production Editor;* Monica White, *Production Editor*

Maps: Rebecca Baer, *Map Director;* David Lindroth, Mark Stroud (Moon Street Cartography), *Cartographers*

Photography: Viviane Teles, *Director of Photography;* Namrata Aggarwal, Neha Gupta, Payal Gupta, Ashok Kumar, *Photo Editors;* Jade Rodgers, *Photo Production Intern*

Business and Operations: Chuck Hoover, *Chief Marketing Officer;* Robert Ames, *Group General Manager*

Public Relations and Marketing: Joe Ewaskiw, *Senior Director of Communications and Public Relations*

Fodors.com: Jeremy Tarr, *Editorial Director;* Rachael Levitt, *Managing Editor*

Technology: Jon Atkinson, *Executive Director of Technology;* Rudresh Teotia, *Associate Director of Technology;* Alison Lieu, *Project Manager*

Writers: Chris Barry, Marie-Ève Vallières, Elizabeth Warkentin, Barbara Woolsey

Editor: Angelique Kennedy-Chavannes

Production Editor: Monica White

32nd Edition

ISBN 978-1-6409-7686-3

ISSN 1525-5867

SPECIAL SALES
This book is available at special discounts for bulk purchases for sales promotions or premiums. For more information, e-mail SpecialMarkets@fodors.com.

PRINTED IN CHINA

10 9 8 7 6 5 4 3 2 1

About Our Writers

 Chris Barry is a native Montréaler and freelance journalist who has contributed to scores of publications over the years and has been writing for the *Fodor's Montréal and Québec City* guide since 2002. He's currently finishing a book documenting his years as a professional rock-and-roll musician in the 1970s, '80s, and '90s.

 Born and raised in Montréal, **Marie-Ève Vallières** knows the city like the back of her hand, despite that it is constantly evolving. Marie-Eve has written for *AFAR Magazine,* Expedia Canada, and Viator, and she has been interviewed regularly on CBC Radio One. Check out her blog, To Europe And Beyond, at www.toeuropeandbeyond.com.

 Elizabeth Warkentin is a freelance writer who was born and raised in Montréal and is enjoying getting reacquainted with her native city after a 20-year absence. She is an avid photographer and freelance journalist and has contributed to a variety of publications including BBC Travel, the *Boston Globe,* the *Toronto Star,* and the *Vancouver Sun.*

 Barbara Woolsey is a Canadian journalist who's trekked across the world by plane, train, and motorbike. She currently spends most of her time in Berlin, producing for Reuters TV and contributing to publications such as the *Guardian,* the *Telegraph,* and Thrillist. Barbara studied French at the Université de Montréal and has returned regularly to cover the city for different outlets.